Lecture Notes in Computer Science   9960

Commenced Publication in 1973
Founding and Former Series Editors:
Gerhard Goos, Juris Hartmanis, and Jan van Leeuwen

More information about this series at http://www.springer.com/series/15545

Bernhard Steffen (Ed.)

Transactions on Foundations for Mastering Change I

 Springer

Editor-in-Chief

Bernhard Steffen
TU Dortmund
Dortmund
Germany

ISSN 0302-9743   ISSN 1611-3349   (electronic)
Lecture Notes in Computer Science
ISBN 978-3-319-46507-4   ISBN 978-3-319-46508-1   (eBook)
DOI 10.1007/978-3-319-46508-1

Library of Congress Control Number: 2016951710

Printed on acid-free paper

This Springer imprint is published by Springer Nature
The registered company is Springer International Publishing AG
The registered company address is: Gewerbestrasse 11, 6330 Cham, Switzerland

Preface

The goal of the LNCS–Transactions on Foundations for Mastering Change (FoMaC) is to establish a community for developing theories, methods, and tools for dealing with the fact that change is not an exception, but the norm for today's systems. The initial issue of FoMaC comprises, in particular, contributions by the members of the editorial board, in order to indicate its envisioned style and range of papers, which cross-cuts various traditional research directions, but is characterized by its clear focus on change.

August 2016   Bernhard Steffen

Organization

Editor-in-Chief

Bernhard Steffen   TU Dortmund University, Germany

Editorial Board

Michael Felderer   University of Innsbruck, Austria
Klaus Havelund   Jet Propulsion Laboratory/NASA, USA
Mike Hinchey   Lero, Ireland
Reiner Hähnle   TU Darmstadt, Germany
Axel Legay   Inria, France
Tiziana Margaria   Lero, Ireland
Arend Rensink   University of Twente, The Netherlands
Bernhard Steffen   TU Dortmund University, Germany
Stavros Tripakis   Aalto University and University of California, Berkeley, USA
Martin Wirsing   LMU, Munich, Germany

LNCS Transaction on the Foundations for Mastering Change (FoMaC) Aims and Scope

Everything Moves: Change Is No Exception for Today's Systems — It Is the Norm

The LNCS *Transactions on Foundations for Mastering Change* (FoMaC) intend to establish a forum for foundational research that fosters a discipline for rigorously dealing with the phenomenon of change. In particular it addresses the very nature of today's agile system development, which is characterized by unclear premises, unforeseen change, and the need for fast reaction, in a context of hard-to-control frame conditions, such as third-party components, network problems, and attacks. We envision focused contributions that reflect and enhance the state of the art under the perspective of change. This may comprise new theoretical results, analysis technology, tool support, experience reports and case studies, as well as pragmatics for change, i.e., user-centric approaches that make inevitable changes controllable in practice. Papers may well focus on individual techniques, but must clearly position themselves in the FoMaC landscape.

Scope

FoMaC is concerned with the foundations for mastering *change and variation* during the whole systems lifecycle at various conceptual levels, in particular during

Meta-Modeling:
This can be regarded as a technology transfer issue, where methods are considered to systematically adapt solutions from one (application) domain for another domain. This comprises meta-modeling, generation of and transformations between domain-specific languages, as well as other issues of domain modeling and validation.

Modeling and Design:
This is the main level at which "classic" variability modeling operates. The methods considered here generalize classic modeling to specifically address variability issues, e.g., where and how to change things, and technology to maintain structural and semantical properties within the range of modeled variability. Here methods such as feature modeling, "150 % modeling," product-line management, model-to-model transformations, constraint-based (requirement) specification, synthesis-based model completion, model checking, and feature interaction detection are considered.

Implementation:
At this level, FoMaC addresses methods beyond classic parametric and modular programming approaches, such as aspect orientation, delta programming, program generation, generative programming, and program transformation, but

also static and dynamic validation techniques, e.g., program verification, symbolic execution, runtime verification, (model-based) testing, and test-based modeling,

Runtime:

This is the level of self-X technology, where methods are addressed that allow, steer, and control the autonomous evolution of systems during runtime. These methods comprise techniques to achieve fault tolerance, runtime planning and synthesis, higher-order exchange of functionality, hot deployment and fail-over, and they should go hand in hand with the aforementioned dynamic validation techniques, such as program verification, symbolic execution, runtime verification, (model-based) testing, test-based modeling, and monitoring.

Evolution/Migration:

This level is concerned with the long-term perspective of system evolution, i.e., the part where the bulk of costs is accumulated. Central issues here are the change of platform, the merging of systems of overlapping functionality, the maintenance of downward compatibility, and the support of a continuous (system) improvement process, as well as continuous quality assurance, comprising regression testing, monitoring, delta testing, and model-based diagnostic features.

FoMaC comprises regular papers and Special Sections. Both need to clearly focus on change. Special Sections, however, provide the unique opportunity to shed light on a wider thematic context while establishing appropriate (change-oriented) links between the subtopics.

Submission of Manuscripts

More detailed information, in particular concerning the submission process as well as a direct access to the editorial system, can be found under http://www.fomac.de/.

Contents

Introduction to the First Issue of FoMaC

Bernhard Steffen[✉]

Chair of Programming Systems, TU Dortmund University,
44227 Dortmund, Germany
steffen@cs.tu-dortmund.de

Abstract. We briefly introduce the envisioned style and scope of the LNCS Transactions on *Foundations for Mastering Change* (FoMaC) on the basis of the individual contributions of the initial issue, which mainly features invited papers co-authored by the founding members of the editorial board.

1 Motivation

Today's development of modern software-based systems is characterized by (1) vaguely defined problems (the result of some requirements engineering), (2) typically expressed in natural language or, in the best case, in a semi-formal notation, (3) implementation on top of large software libraries or other third-party code as an overall system of millions of lines of code that (4) run on highly complex enterprise environments, which may even critically involve services connected via wide area networks, i.e., the internet. It should, of course, also be (5) easily adaptable to changing requests.

Industrial practice answers these requests with quite some success with approaches like extreme programming and Scrum that essentially replace any kind of foundational method by close cooperation and communication within the team and with the customer, combined with early prototyping and testing. Main critique to such a formal methods-free approach is merely its lack of scalability, which is partly compensated by involving increasingly complex third-party components, while keeping the complexity of their orchestration at a Scrum-manageable level.

Does this state of the art reduce the role of the classical formal methods-based approaches in the sense of Hoare and Dijkstra to the niche of (extremely) safety-critical systems, simply because it is unclear

- what should be formally verified in cases where the problem is not stated precisely upfront? In fact, in many software projects, adapting the development to last-minute revealed changing needs is a dominating task.
- what does a fully verified program help, if it comes too late? In fact, in many projects the half-life period is far too short to economically accommodate any verification activities.

In fact, in some sense the opposite is true: the formal methods developed in the last decades are almost everywhere. E.g., type systems are omnipresent,

© Springer International Publishing AG 2016
B. Steffen (Ed.): Transactions on FoMaC I, LNCS 9960, pp. 1–6, 2016.
DOI: 10.1007/978-3-319-46508-1_1

but seamlessly working in the back of most integrated development environments (IDEs), which are typically supported by complex dataflow analyses and sophisticated code generation methods. In addition, (software) model checking has become popular to control application-specific properties. Even the originally very pragmatic software testing community gradually employs more and more model-based technologies.

However, admittedly, development and debugging as supported by complex IDEs like Eclipse and IntelliJ or by dedicated bug-tracking tools do not attempt to guarantee full functional correctness, the ultimate and very hard to achieve goal of Dijkstra and Hoare. Rather, they are characterized by their community-driven reactiveness:

- software is developed quickly by large communities,
- documentation is largely replaced by online forums,
- quality assurance is a community effort,
- success of a software depends on the vitality of its community.

This more lightweight approach to guarantee quality supports a much more agile system development where change is **not an exception but the norm**.

FoMaC is concerned with the foundations of mastering change and variability during the whole system's lifecycle at various conceptual levels, in particular during

- *Metamodeling* that provides methods for systematically adapting solutions from one (application) domain for another domain,
- *Modeling and Design*, where 'classical' variability modeling and product lining happens,
- *Implementation*, where modern paradigms like aspect orientation, delta programming, program generation, and generative programming complement classical static and dynamic validation techniques,
- *Runtime and Use*, where the, e.g., self-* technologies for autonomic systems apply, and
- *Maintenance/Evolution/Migration*, the longest and typically extremely expensive phase of the system lifecycle.

It is envisioned to e.g. comprise turning the latter into a continuous (system) improvement process, and thereby, in particular, overcome the typical legacy-degradation of systems along their lifecycle.

The following section summarizes the content of the initial issue. It dominantly presents contributions of the members of the editorial board in order to indicate the envisioned style and scope of papers, which cross-cuts various traditional research directions, but is characterized by its clear focus on change.

2   Individual Contributions

Knowledge Management for Inclusive System Evolution. [1] discusses the current practice of software design from the perspective of knowledge management and change enactment. It advocates a co-creation environment in the context of modern agile and lean IT development approaches. In particular, it emphasizes that true and functioning inclusion of non-IT stakeholders on equal terms hinges on adequate, i.e., accessible and understandable, representation and management of knowledge about the system under development along the entire tool chain of design, development, and maintenance. In particular in the context of change, consistent knowledge management, as aimed at in the One-Thing-Approach, is important to enable a continuous engineering approach involving all stakeholders.

Traceability Types for Mastering Change in Collaborative Software Quality Management. [2] proposes a novel approach to traceability as a cornerstone for successful impact analysis and change management in the context of collaborative software quality management. Software is constantly evolving. To successfully comprehend and manage this evolutionary change is a challenging task which requires traceability support. The paper categorizes software quality management services and identifies novel types of traceability on the basis of the model-based collaborative software quality management framework of Living Models as a basis for future research concerning the mastering of change.

Model Patterns: The Quest for the Right Level of Abstraction. [3] aims at establishing a modeling discipline with a built-in notion of refinement, so that domain concepts can be defined and understood on their appropriate level of abstraction, and change can be captured on that same level. Refinement serves to connect levels of abstraction within the same model, enabling a simultaneous understanding of that same model on different levels. Key to this approach is the introduction of an appropriate notion of model pattern in order to formalize, capture, and thereby master the essence of change at the meta level. The paper is accompanied by illustrative examples focusing on classical data modeling. This is a didactical choice of examples that does not limit the underlying approach.

Archimedean Points: The Essence for Mastering Change. [4] illustrates how explicit *Archimedean Point-driven* (software) system development, which aims at maintaining as much control as possible via the 'things' that do not change, may radically change the role of modeling and development tools. The idea is to incorporate as much knowledge as possible into the modeling/development tools themselves. This way tools do not only become domain-specific, but problem-specific, or even specific to a particular new requirement for a system already in operation.

The effectiveness of this approach is illustrated along the stepwise construction of a basic BPMN tool via a chain of increasingly expressive Petri net tools, which, by construction, has a conceptually very clean semantic foundation, which enables features like various consistency checks, type-controlled activity integration, and true full code generation.

Good Change and Bad Change: An Analysis Perspective on Software Evolution. [5] elaborates on the idea of regarding the evolution/change of a single piece of software with its numerous individual versions as special case of establishing a product line, and to exploit the corresponding technologies and tools.

This concerns, in particular, both the identification of architectural commonalities and differences among various releases in order to understand the impact and to manage the diversity of the entire change history, and a perspective-based presentation of the current status of the individual products. The paper describes and illustrates example-based two corresponding tools, where the status-related tool also detects and removes architectural violations that threaten the variability points and built-in flexibility.

Compositional Model-Based System Design and Other Foundations for Mastering Change. [6] investigates the design of dynamical systems, such as embedded or cyber-physical systems, under three perspectives – modeling, analysis, and implementation – and discusses fundamental research challenges in each category. This way it establishes compositionality as primary cross-cutting concern, and thereby as a key concept for mastering change in a scalable fashion. Other identified objectives when dealing with change are multi-view modeling in order to include the increasingly many stakeholders with different backgrounds into the development process and to distinguish the different environments in which the system should run, as well as synthesis for raising the level of abstraction, and learning for automatically revealing the impact of change.

Proof Repositories for Compositional Verification of Evolving Software Systems. [7] proposes a framework for proof reuse in the context of deductive software verification. The framework generalizes abstract contracts to incremental proof repositories in order to enable separation of concerns between called methods and their implementations. Combined with corresponding proof repositories for caching partial proofs that can be adapted to different method implementations this facilitates systematic proof reuse. This approach can be regarded as foundational for mastering change, because the presented framework provides flexible support for compositional verification in the context of, e.g., partly developed programs, evolution of programs and contracts, and product variability.

Verified Change. [8] presents the textual wide-spectrum modeling and programming language K, which has been designed for representing graphical SysML models, in order to provide semantics to SysML, and pave the way for the analysis of SysML models. K aims at supporting engineers in designing space missions, and in particular NASA's proposed mission to Jupiter's moon Europa to cope with the inevitable changes of their software systems over time. Key to the proposed K-based solution is to perceive change as a software verification problem, which can therefore be treated using more traditional software verification techniques. The current K environment aims at demonstrating that no harm has been done due to a change using the Z3 SMT theorem prover for proving the corresponding consistency constraints.

Statistical Model Checking with Change Detection. [9] presents an extension of statistical model checking (SMC) that enables to monitor changes in the probability distribution to satisfy a bounded-time property at runtime, as well as a programming interface of the SMC-tool PLASMA Lab that allows designers to easily apply SMC technology. Whereas the former is based on constantly monitoring the execution of the deployed system, and raising a flag when it observes that the probability has changed significantly, the latter works by exploiting simulation facilities of design tools. Thus the paper provides both a direct way for SMC – a verification technique not suffering from the state explosion problem – to deal with an important change-related property and a way to make the SMC technology widely applicable.

Collective Autonomic Systems: Towards Engineering Principles and their Foundations. [10] proposes and discusses eight engineering principles for mastering collective autonomic systems (CASs), which are characterized by being adaptive, open-ended, highly parallel, interactive and distributed software systems that consist of many collaborative entities for managing their own knowledge and processes. CASs present many change-related engineering challenges, such as awareness of the environmental situation, performing suitable and adequate adaptations in response to environmental changes, or preserving adaptations over system updates and modifications. The proposed engineering principles, which closely resemble the ensembles development lifecycle, aim at encouraging and structuring future work in order to establish a foundational framework for dealing with these change-related challenges.

Continuous Collaboration for Changing Environments. [11] presents a continuous collaboration (CC) development approach for capturing many of the principles proposed in the context of the ensembles development lifecycle for developing CASs. Conceptually, the CC development approach is based on the teacher/student architecture for locally coordinated distributed learning in order to aggregate agent success and planned behaviour during the runtime cycle. It is shown that in certain scenarios the performance of a swarm using teacher/student learning can be significantly better than that of agents learning individually, a contribution that can be regarded foundational for the practical realization of self-adapting systems.

Issues on Software Quality Models for Mastering Change. [12] discusses and exemplifies unresolved key issues on descriptive, generative and predictive software quality models with regard to the (1) creation and maintenance of models, (2) support for extra-functional aspects, (3) traceability between quality models and unstructured artifacts, (4) integration of software analytics and runtime information, (5) balance between quality and risk, (6) process integration, as well as (7) justification by empirical evidence. The goal of this analysis is to establish means for leveraging the high potential of software quality models in order to improve the effectiveness and efficiency of quality assurance to cope with software change, and by this increase the acceptance and spread in the software industry.

3 Conclusion

The summaries presented above, which range from position statements over more focused technical contributions to case studies, illustrate the broad scope of

FoMaC which cross-cuts various traditional research directions and communities. As change is of major concern almost everywhere, the presented selection is far from being exhaustive. Rather, we envisage that the increasing pace of today's developments will steadily enrich the potential FoMaC portfolio, which is only limited by its foundational character and its clear focus on change.

References

1. Margaria, T.: Knowledge management for inclusive system evolution. In: Steffen, B. (ed.) Transactions on FoMaC I. LNCS, vol. 9960, pp. 7–21. Springer, Heidelberg (2016)
2. Celebic, B., Breu, R., Felderer, M.: Traceability types for mastering change in collaborative software quality management. In: Steffen, B. (ed.) Transactions on FoMaC I. LNCS, vol. 9960, pp. 242–256. Springer, Heidelberg (2016)
3. Rensink, A.: Model patterns: the quest for the right level of abstraction. In: Steffen, B. (ed.) Transactions on FoMaC I. LNCS, vol. 9960, pp. 47–70. Springer, Heidelberg (2016)
4. Steffen, B., Naujokat, S.: Archimedean points: the essence for mastering change. In: Steffen, B. (ed.) Transactions on FoMaC I. LNCS, vol. 9960, pp. 22–46. Springer, Heidelberg (2016)
5. Hinchey, M.: Good change and bad change: an analysis perspective on software evolution. In: Steffen, B. (ed.) Transactions on FoMaC I. LNCS, vol. 9960, pp. 90–112. Springer, Heidelberg (2016)
6. Tripakis, S.: Compositional model-based system design and other foundations for mastering change. In: Steffen, B. (ed.) Transactions on FoMaC I. LNCS, vol. 9960, pp. 113–129. Springer, Heidelberg (2016)
7. Bubel, R., Damiani, F., Hähnle, R., Johnsen, E., Owe, O., Schaefer, I., Yu, I.: Proof repositories for compositional verification of evolving software systems. In: Steffen, B. (ed.) Transactions on FoMaC I. LNCS, vol. 9960, pp. 130–156. Springer, Heidelberg (2016)
8. Havelund, K., Kumar, R.: Verified change. In: Steffen, B. (ed.) Transactions on FoMaC I. LNCS, vol. 9960, pp. 71–89. Springer, Heidelberg (2016)
9. Legay, A., Traonouez, L.M.: Statistical model checking with change detection. In: Steffen, B. (ed.) Transactions on FoMaC I. LNCS, vol. 9960, pp. 157–179. Springer, Heidelberg (2016)
10. Wirsing, M., Hölzl, M., Koch, N., Belzner, L.: Collective autonomic systems: towards engineering principles and their foundations. In: Steffen, B. (ed.) Transactions on FoMaC I. LNCS, vol. 9960, pp. 180–200. Springer, Heidelberg (2016)
11. Hölzl, M., Gabor, T.: Continuous collaboration for changing environments. In: Steffen, B. (ed.) Transactions on FoMaC I. LNCS, vol. 9960, pp. 201–224. Springer, Heidelberg (2016)
12. Felderer, M.: Issues on software quality models for mastering change. In: Steffen, B. (ed.) Transactions on FoMaC I. LNCS, vol. 9960, pp. 225–241. Springer, Heidelberg (2016)

Knowledge Management for Inclusive System Evolution

Tiziana Margaria[(✉)]

Lero and Chair of Software Systems, University of Limerick, Limerick, Ireland
tiziana.margaria@lero.ie

Abstract. When systems evolve in today's complex, connected, and heterogeneous IT landscapes, waves of change ripple in every direction. Sometimes a change mandates other changes elsewhere, very often it is needed and opportune to check that a change indeed has no effects, or maybe only the announced effects, on other portions of the connected landscape, and impacts are often assessable only or also by expert professionals distinct from IT professionals. In this paper, we discuss the state of affairs with the current practice of software design, and examine it from the point of view of the adequacy of knowledge management and change enactment in a co-creation environment, as it is predicated and practiced by modern agile and lean IT development approaches, and in software ecosystems. True and functioning inclusion of non-IT stakeholders on equal terms, in our opinion, hinges on adequate, i.e., accessible and understandable, representation and management of knowledge about the system under development along the entire toolchain of design, development, and maintenance.

1 Change Is Not Always Just Change

As we have observed at the International Symposium On Leveraging Applications (ISoLA) conference over the course of its 12 years and seven occurrences, research and adoption of new technologies, design principles, and tools in the software design area at large happen, but at a different pace and with different enthusiasm in different domains.

While the internet-dominated branches have adopted apps, the cloud, and thinking in collaborative design and viral distribution models, counting among the enthusiasts those who make a business out of innovation, other markets have adopted novelties either forced by need, like the transportation-related sectors, or by law, like the US government mandated higher auditing standards related to Sarbanes-Oxley, and the financial sector.

Other areas have readily adopted hardware innovation but have tried to deny, resist, and otherwise oppose software-driven agility deriving from the internet economy. An illustrative example is the traditional telecommunication companies, cornered in several markets by the technology that came together with the social networks wave.

© Springer International Publishing AG 2016
B. Steffen (Ed.): Transactions on FoMaC I, LNCS 9960, pp. 7–21, 2016.
DOI: 10.1007/978-3-319-46508-1_2

Still others are undecided on what to do but for different reasons; mostly they are stuck into oligopolies such as in the ERP and business information system-related enterprise management software industry. These oligopolies set the pace of adoption: they try on one hand to slowdown change in order to protect their old products and on the other hand they try with little success to jump on the internet wagon but failing repeatedly. A prominent example is SAP with their "On demand" offers, whose development was recently stopped.

One other cause of current indecision, as prominently found in the healthcare industry, is an unhealthy combination of concurring factors which include:

– the *fragmentation* of the software and IT market where big players occupy significant cornerstones,
– the *cultural distance* between the care providers (doctors, nurses, therapists, chemists...) and care managers (hospital administrators, payers, and politicians) from the IT professionals and their way of thinking in general and the software design leading-edge reality in particular,
– and the *hyperregulation* in several undercorrelated layers of responsibility by laws as well as by professional organizations and other networks that represent and defend specific interests of niche actors.

2   Change at Large

In this very diverse context, we see that change in these different domains faces an amazing diversification of challenges. These challenges are never addressed in simple, rational decisions of adoption based on factual measurements of improvement of some metric such as cost, efficiency, or performance as in the ideal world every engineer fancies. Instead, they involve complex processes of a socio-technical character, where a wealth of organizational layers and both short and long term interests must be aligned in order to create a sufficiently scoped backing to some envisaged change management measure.

Once this is achieved (good luck with that!), there is the operationalization problem of facing the concrete individuals that need to be retrained, the concrete systems that need to be overhauled (or substituted), and the concrete ecosystem surrounding these islands of change: they need to support or at least tolerate the intrusion of novelty in a possibly graceful way.

Seen this way, it does not surprise anymore that the success rate of software projects stagnates in the low double digit quartile. It is also clear that the pure technical prowess of the staff and team, while a necessary condition for success, is by far not sufficient to achieve a successful end of a new IT-related project.

While we, within IT, are used to smirk at cartoons that depict traits of the inner software development teams facets[1], we are not used to look at ourselves from the "outside". For example from the point of view of those other professionals we de facto closely work with, and whose professional and societal life we

---

[1] For instance, in the famous "tree-swing-comic". Here [3] you find a commented version and also its derivation history, dating back to the '70s.

directly or indirectly influence - to the point of true domination[2]. There is hardly anything today that is not software-impacted, and as Arend Rensink writes [27], software is never finished.

I use to tell my students that to create a piece of software is like getting a baby. First of all, it takes a couple for it: IT and those who (also) wish this piece of software and provide their contribution. In both cases, although technically an initial seed is technically sufficient, the outcome is better if a heterogeneous team joins forces, collaborating all the time for the health and safety along the build process, and preparing a welcoming environment for the new system in its future home. While we in Software Development care a lot about the (9 months equivalent of the) creation time and what can go wrong during this relatively short building period spent in the lab, we hardly practice as much care and foresight as optimal parents do for the delivery itself and its acclimation in the operational environment. This phase is called installation or implementation, depending on whether you are a software engineer or an information system person, resp. In addition, we fail quite miserably short when considering the subsequent 18–21 years of nurturing, care, and responsibility. Concerning maintenance and product evolution, in fact, our practice is still trailing the care and dedication of good parents. The Manifesto of FoMaC [29] addresses in fact this phase, and what can be done before in order to face it in the most adequate and informed fashion.

As for parents, once the baby is born and brought home, one is not done and able to move to the next project, but the real fun begins. There is a long time of nurturing and care and responsibility, that in theory is 18–21 years long. Funnily, this is not so distant from the age of maturity of most large software systems, and it is usual to find installations that are even older than this, especially for core modules in business critical platforms. In reality, however, the bond of care never fades completely. If we were parents, with our current "best practices" in IT, we would be utterly careless, and in several nations we would have the youth protection offices on our door, determined to put our children in foster care.

So, what can we do?

3   Change and Simplicity

A first step would be to improve our awareness of the impact radius of our products (software, hardware, communication infrastructure, and the systems in which all the above is embedded or that use it as part of their operating environment), artefacts (models, code, test cases, reports, documentation, specifications, bits and pieces of knowledge formulated in text, diagrams, constraints, ontologies, and scribbled notes from innumerable meetings), and professional decisions. This cartoon brought me to think: As long as "the world" sees the IT professionals as extraterrestrial geeks who speak some incomprehensible lingo, there is a deep disconnect that is worse than the already abundantly demonized but still unsolved "business-to-IT" gap. We are not a cohort of Sheldons (from The Big Bang Theory), nor Morks (of the unforgettable Mork and Mindy),

---

[2] This is genuine bidirectional incomprehension: as aptly captured in [1].

nor wizards that dominate machines with some impenetrable arts and crafts as in Harry Potter's world. As engineers, we must become understandable to the world. In this direction, there are three actions to be taken: simplify, simplify, simplify.

- Dramatically simplify the **domain knowledge gathering** process: requirements and specification come from the field, far out there where no IT culture is present. We depend on "them" to produce what they need, and it is our responsibility to go all the way down to their homes and make their ways and languages understandable to us.
- Simplify **the way we design systems**. It can no longer be that we have n different kinds of memories, m layers of middleware between the firmware on one side and more layers of software on the other side. This is too much inherent diversity that leads to hardships in keeping coherence and faithfulness between the different representations, interpretations, and implementations in a world where every few weeks there is a patch, every few months a new version or a new release, and this for every component in the assembly of systems we face
- Simplify the way we take **decisions about the evolution** of systems. This decision making needs to be tight between the domain experts, who define the end product, its features, and express desires driven by the application's side needs, and the IT team that manages the technical artifacts that describe, implement, and document the current status, the next version, and a feasible design and migration path between the two. Repeat forever.

This is the central scope of FoMaC, and these different aspects are its itemized workprogramme, only recast in terms of simplicity as a core value.

4   Simplifying Knowledge Management

For a functioning handshake between business and IT, knowledge sharing and trading across cultural borders and barriers is a must. As a convinced formal methodist, I firmly believe in the power of materializing rules, regulations, preferences, best practices, how-to's, do's and don'ts in terms of properties, expressed as constraints. Such constraints are materialized in some logic in order to be able to reason about them, and the choice of which logic depends on the nature of the properties and on the technical means for working with those properties. Knowledge, like energy, can assume different forms, and become useful for different purposes. There is a cost of transformation that includes the IT needed to "manage" the transformation, in terms of data mediation across different formats, compilers across different representations (that for me include programming and process languages), or preparations for being more universally accessible, as in ontologies and Linked Open Data. Taking a constraints view at knowledge, facts ("things", concepts, and data are facts) are just constants, properties are unary predicates, and n-ary predicates formalise multiparty relations, including relations about constants and other relations.

The conceptualization and materialization of knowledge in formally well defined terms that can be analyzed by tools is an essential step towards knowledge exchange, use, and even growth. How can we know that something is new if we don't know what is known today? In different flavours, this question pops up in many application domains: what is evidence-based medicine, if we cannot describe and evaluate the fit of the available evidence to the case for which a doctor submits a query? The knowledge and evaluation of the plausibility, up-to-dateness, and overall fit of background evidence knowledge is of paramount importance for its applicability to the extrapolation to the single subject: evidence gathered in the past, in unclear experimental circumstances, from a different population basis, might not be applicable at all, and even lead to wrong diagnosis or treatment. For example, the fact that there are biases in the wealth of widely accessible medical experimental data is well known to pediatricians or gynecologists, who constantly need to treat children or (pregnant) women resorting to assessed evidence mostly collected from experience with adult male patients - experiments with "at risk" groups are extremely rare and very difficult to achieve ethical approval. Indeed, even the processes of paediatric first aid in Emergency Medicine are not defined, and we are working right now with the European Society of Emergency Medicine to model a variant of the adult processes. This model materializes the knowledge of the expert EM paediatricians, exposing their practices and beliefs for the first time to a methodological discussion that is amenable to further machine-based reasoning. Properties can be declarative, describing abstract traits of a domain or thing or process, or also be very concrete, if applied to single elements of the domain of choice. In terms of knowledge management, subject matter experts usually expect IT specialists to master the knowledge description and its corresponding manipulation, for several reasons:

- knowledge is usually expressed in difficult ways, not accessible to non-IT specialists, like logics formulas and constraint or programming languages. Also ontologies and their languages of expression, that in theory should make semantics and concept description easy for everyone, are still for initiated.
- manipulating knowledge concerns handling complex structures, and is mostly carried out at the programming level. Also query languages are not easy, especially in the semantic domain: description logics and W-SML or SPARQL are not easy to master.
- knowledge evolution and sharing by normal practitioners function today only in a non-formal context, mostly textual: they are able to update and manage Wikis for communities, access repositories of abstracts and papers, but it is not common for subject matter experts with little or no IT proficiency to go beyond this on their own. Few of the target people master spreadsheets (which are at best semistructured and primitively typed repositories), and far fewer are proficient in database use and management.

The key to enlarging the participation to knowledge definition and management lies therefore in a system design that fosters bridges into the IT world, instead of creating generation after generation of IT walls and canyons. Ideally, it should start with the high level requirements and continue coherently throughout the entire lifetime of the system and its components.

5 Simplifying System Design

In the IT industry, system design today still happens mostly at the code level, with some application domains adopting model driven design in UML, SysML or SimuLink style. Other application domains, mostly in the business sector, are gradually embracing an agile development paradigm that shortcuts the modelling phase and promotes instead code-based prototyping.

5.1 The Issues with Code

The tendency to directly code may have immediate advantages for the IT professionals that right now write the code, but it tends to hinder communication with everybody else. With or without agility, code first scores consistently low on the post-hoc comprehension scala pretty much independently of the programming language. Indeed, a widespread exercise for programming newcomers is to give them a more or less large pre-coded system and ask them to make sense of it. Reverse engineering is difficult when starting from models, but gruelling if starting from code. A technical and pretty cryptic (en)coding is not an adequate mean of communication to non-programmers and fails the purpose of simplifying domain knowledge management as discussed in the previous section. To compensate, according to best practice guidelines, it should be in theory accompanied by a variety of ancillary artefacts like documentation, assertions as in JML [17], contracts [26] as in Eiffel, diagrams as in the early days of SDL[3] and MSCs in the telecommunication domain, and test cases as the de facto most widespread handcrafted subsidiary to source code. In practice, these artefacts are rarely crafted, if ever crafted they are rarely consistent, and if they are consistent at some design point, they are rarely maintained along the long lifetime of a system. Even if they were maintained consistent, a complete system description would also require information about the usage context. For example, if a platform changes, an API is deprecated, a library in the entire technology stack above or below evolves, this may impact the correct functioning of the system under design or maintenance.

In theory, such changes and their effects need to be captured in a precise context model. It is pretty safe to assume that such a context model is nonexistent for any system of decent size and complexity. Most experts would feel comfortable in stating that such a model is impossible to create and maintain due to the high volatility of this IT landscape.

Current software engineering practice has no built-in cure, it tries instead to infuse virtuous behaviour to the software engineers it forms by preaching the

---

[3] The Specification and Description Language (SDL), including the Message Sequence Charts (MSC), was defined by ITU-T in Recommendations Z.100 to Z.106.

importance of documentation, coding standards, test cases, annotations, etc. with little success. Unfortunately, the curricularly formed software engineers are just a fraction of the programmers employed today in industry and consultancies [12]: the large majority of the extra- or non-curricular practitioners have never received a formal programming or software engineering education, and are prone to underestimate and neglect ancillary activities aimed at enhancing correctness or comprehension.

Even if these ancillary artefacts existed, they would be difficult to use as a source of knowledge. Test cases express wanted and unwanted behaviours, and have been extensively used as source of models "from the outside" of a system. Test based model inference was, in fact, used already over 15 years ago to reconstruct knowledge about a system from its test case suite [13,14]. Automated generation of test cases is also at the core of modern efficient model learning techniques, starting from [15,20,32] to [16]. The recovered models, however, describe the behaviour of the systems at a specific level of abstraction (from the outside). They are quite technical (usually some form of automata) and, thus, not adequate for non-IT experts. Additionally, they describe only the system as-is, but do not provide clues on the why, nor on whether some modifications would still be correct or acceptable or not.

Other ancillary artefacts are closer to the properties mentioned in the previous section as a good choice for formulating knowledge. Textual descriptions and diagrams basically just verbalize or illustrate the purpose, structure, or functioning of the system therefore seem "simple" and easy to produce at first sight. However, if are not linked to a formal semantics nor the code, they are not inherently coupled with analysis techniques not with the runtime behaviour, and suffer of a detachment (a form of semantic gap) that intrinsically undermines their reliability as a source of up-to-date knowledge.

APIs in the component based design and service interfaces for the service oriented world are used as a borderline description that couples and decouples the inside and the outside of subsystems. Like a Goldilocks model, APIs and service descriptions are expected to expose enough information on the functioning of a subsystem so that an external system can use it, but shield all the internal information that is not strictly necessary for that use. We have discussed elsewhere in detail [11,18] the mismatch of this information with what a user really needs to know. In short, APIs and services expose typically programming level datatypes (e,g. integer, string) that are too coarse to enforce an application specific correctness check. Age of a patient and a purchase quantity, both commonly represented as integers, would be perfectly compatible, as well as any name with a DNA subsequence. Thus, APIs need to have additional documentation explaining how to use them (e.g., first this call, with these parameters, then this other call, with these other parameters, etc.), and the domain semantic level (attacked, so far still with little spread, by Semantic approaches, e.g. to Web services). This documentation is mostly textual, i.e. not machine readable, i.e. not automatically discoverable nor checkable. The OWL-S standard [2] had with the "process model" a built-in provision for these usage models, essentially the protocol patterns of service consumption, but it was considered a cumbersome approach, and thus has gained limited spread in practice.

Even APIs may suddenly change. Famous in our group is the day the CeBIT 2009 opened in Hannover: we had a perfectly running stable demo of a mashup that combined geographic GIS information with advanced NGI telecommunication services, plus Wikipedia, Amazon and other services... that on site on that morning partout did not work. Having excluded all the hardware, network, and communication whims that typically collude to ruin a carefully prepared grand opening, only the impossible remained to be checked: the world must have changed overnight. Indeed, the Google maps service API had changed overnight in such a way that our simple, basic service call (the first thing the demo did) did not work anymore. In other words, any application worldwide using that very basic functionality had become broken, instantly and without any notice.

Artefacts like assertions and contracts are the closest to the knowledge assets mentioned above: indeed they express as properties the rules of the game, and in fact they are typically formulated at the type level, not for specific instances. On the one side they fulfil the need of expressing knowledge in a higher-level style. On the other side, however, they are typically situated in the code and concern implementation-level properties and issues that may be too detailed to really embody domain knowledge in the way a domain expert would formulate and manipulate.

In terms of communication with subject matter experts, therefore, none of these alternatives seems to be ideal.

5.2   The Issues with Models

Looking at system design models from the point of view of simplicity-driven system design, we see a large spread. UML, likely the most widespread modelling language today, unifies in one uniform notation a wide selection of previously successful modelling formalisms. In its almost 20 years of existence and over 10 years as an ISO standard, it has conquered a wide range of application domains, effectively spreading the adoption of those individual formalisms well beyond their initial reach and beyond the pure object oriented design community. Particularly due to customized, profiles it has been adapted to cover specialized concepts for different publics. For example SysML, a dialect of UML for systems engineering, removes a number of software-centric constructs and instead adds diagrams for requirements, for performance, and quantitative analysis. The central weakness of UML lies in the "unified" trait: its 16 diagram types cover different aspects, sharing a notation but without integrating their semantics. Like a cubist portrait, each diagram type depicts a distinct point of view - a facet in a multifaceted description of a complex system - and the UML tools do not support the consistency of the various viewpoints nor the translation to running code. In other words, given a collection of UML diagrams of a certain number of types, there is a gap between what they describe and the (executable) complete code of this system.

Other modelling languages have different issues: specialized languages for process modelling, like BPMN [36], ARIS [28], and YAWL [34], often lack a clean and consistent formal semantic. This makes it difficult to carry out verification and code generation, thus leaving gaps like in UML. Formalisms for distributed systems like Petri Nets and its derivatives have a clear and clean semantic, but the models become quickly large and unwieldy. Due to their closer proximity to the formal semantic model, they are less comprehensible and thus much less attractive to non-initiated.

Complex and articulated model scenarios that preserve properties and aim at code generation exist, as in [10]: they succeed in different ways to cover the modelling and expression needs of IT specialists, and to provide to the models sufficient structure and information that code generation is to a large extent possible or easily integratable. However, non-IT experts would be overwhelmed by the rich formalisms and the level of detail and precision addressed in these modelling environments.

5.3 Living Models for Communication Across the IT Gap

For the past 20 years we have tried, in many approximations and refinements, to achieve a modelling style and relative tool landscape that allows non-IT experts to sit at the table of system design and development, and co-create it. Called in different communities stakeholders, engaged professionals, subject area experts, subject matter experts, these are people with skills and interests different from the technical software development. In order to make a software or system design framework palatable to these adopters, three ingredients are essential:

- it should not look like IT,
- it should allow extensive automatic support for customization of look and feel,
- it should allow knowledge to be expressed in an intuitive fashion (intuitive for these people) and provide built-in correctness, analysis/verification, and code generation features.

Such a design environment should be perceived by these stakeholders as familiar, easy to use, easy to manipulate, and providing "immediate" feedback for queries and changes. In short, we need "living models", that grow and become increasingly rich and precise along the design lifecycle of a system. They need to remain accessible and understandable, morphing over time along the chain of changes brought by evolution.

The Look. *Living models* are first of all models, and not code. Especially with school pupils in Summer camps and users in professions distant from the abstract textuality of source code, the fact of dealing with models has proven a vital asset. Successful models are those that one can "face-lift" and customize in the look and feel to iconically depict the real thing, the person, the artefact of importance in a certain activity.

In our system design approach, the user-facing representation is highly customizable. This has happened over time and at two different levels:

- when we started, in 1994, the META-Frame Tool could be regarded as the first service-oriented environments where tool building blocks could be graphically composed into workflows [21,31,35]. already back then, META-Frame featured a customizable look and feel of the nodes of the graphs in its graphical modelling layer, where the usual look as single or double contoured circles (as in normal DFAs, for accepting and non-accepting states), could be painted over with what today would be called sprites. So we had models in which the icons had been changed to the likeness of Calvin and Hobbes, and the entire tool was multilingual in ... for example Swabian dialect. This pliability was essential to win an industrial project with Siemens Nixdorf in 1995/96, where the IN-METAFrame tool was applied to construct a service definition environment for value-added services subsequently sold to over 30 Telecoms world-wide [5,30]. Using their own icons was back then an essential feature, central to the decision for this product against all odds. This capability is still essential today when we talk to healthcare professionals [8,19].

– today, with CINCO [33] we can customize the look and feel of the native design tools, generate the code of such tools, and customize the semantics of the "things" they design. An example of a design tool generated as a Cinco-product is DIME [7,9] for web applications, but also the Business Model Developer tool (BMT) [6] for type-safe, semantically suported, and analyzable Business Model Canvas, that are a widespread design tool in business schools. Systems are specified via **model assembly**. Here we use **orchestration** in each model, **hierarchy** for behavioural refinement, and **configuration** as composition techniques.

Knowledge and Use. Living models are robust towards knowledge evolution. These models are not just intuitive and likable drawings, they are formal models and thus amenable to automated analysis, verification, and, under some circumstances, synthesis, as originally described in the Lightweight Process Coordination approach [22]. The LPC approach then matured into the eXtreme Model Driven Development [23,25] and the One Thing Approach [24]. Central to all them is the ease of annotation: because they are formal models their elements can be enriched by annotations that address layers of knowledge, or concerns.

Type information is one such knowledge layer, but semantic information, annotations coming from other analyses and from external sources like ontologies or rich semantic descriptions can be attached to the nodes and edges of the graphs, and to the graphs and subgraphs themselves. Resource consumption, timing information, or any kind of property that can be seen as atomic propositions in the logic of the behavioural constraints can overlay the concrete model (e.g., quantitative for performance, qualitative for Service Level Agreements). This way, property-specific knowledge layers can be easily added to the bare graph model and allow a true 360° description, essential for the One Thing Approach: one model, but many layers of information addressing the multiplicity of knowledge and concerns of all the stakeholders.

In this modelling paradigm, layers of information corresponding to different concerns enrich the basic behavioural (functional) description, and are accessible as interpreted or non-interpreted information to the plugins. Atomic propositions are useful to the model checker. Information like execution duration, costs, etc.

are accessible to the interpreter or to various simulation environments. Compatibility information is seen by the type checker in the design environment. In the PROPHETS automated synthesis tool, structural properties of the graphs are exploited by the code generator. Knowledge, mostly in form of facts and rules used by plugins, is the central collagen that expresses different intents, different capabilities, different concerns. Consequently, it is also useful to connect different tools, different purposes, different roles and stakeholders along the design and the evolution history of a system.

Knowledge and requirements are expressed by means of properties, via constraints that are formulated in an automatically verifiable fashion. Actually, some of the constraints happen to be domain-independent, and to be already taken care of at design time of the jABC or more recently the DIME design environment. Here, for instance, this covers both the functional correctness of each model element (Action), but also the patterns of usage inside processes and workflows, like for example behavioural constraints expressed in temporal logics (typically CTL) and verified by model checking.

The Knowledge in Use. As our models are immediately executable, first in animation mode that proposes a walk through the system, then with real code (for simulation or for implementation), these models are enactable from the very beginning, hence the "living models" name [24] that distinguishes them from the usual software design models, which are purely descriptive and illustrative, but not "live". In most cases, such living models get refined in this style until the atomic actions get implemented, in source code or reusing previous assets like a data base, components via an API, or services. In this case, there is no inherent design/implementation gap between the initial prototype and the final product: the finished running system is co-created incrementally along the design process, and grows from the model through prototypes into the fully implemented and running system.

The execution makes the models easy to understand because it lends them a dynamic aspect that makes it possible for users that are distant from the IT design culture to "get it". I like to call this the Haptic of the design: in German, to understand is called "begreifen" which comes from "greifen", meaning "to grab", understanding comes through touch. In living models, knowledge and models are connected. Taken together, they become understandable by IT experts and Subject Matter Experts alike, bridging the cultural gap.

6 Simplifying Evolution Management

Managing system evolution means managing change in any ingredient of a system's well being: the needs of the user (requirements), the components or subsystems used (architecture, interfaces), the technical context (external libraries, platforms, and services), the business/legal context (regulations, standards, but also changed market needs or opportunities). Whether largely manual or largely independent (as in autonomous systems and self-* systems), addressing evolution means having provisions in place for

1. intercepting and understanding which change this evolution step requires
2. having the means to design and express the change in a swift and correct way, validating its suitability in theory for this purpose
3. having the provisions to implement the change in the real system
4. ideally, having the possibility to backtrack and redo in case the adopted change was not fit for purpose.

The fourth condition occurs very seldom in reality, as many systems work in real time environments where there is no possibility to backtrack and undo. This makes then the second element - the validation before effecting the change - even more crucial. Indeed, formal verification methods have been pushed to success and widely adopted in the hardware circuit design industry, where design errors in the chip cannot be undone nor patched post-production.

Evolution can be seen as a transition from one condition of equilibrium (the "well functioning" steady state before the change) to another condition of equilibrium after the change. Equilibrium is seen here as the compatibility and well functioning of a hardware, software, and communication landscape that additionally properly serves the system's (business) purposes. The more the knowledge is available about the system, its purpose, and its environment, the easier it is to detect what is affected and to build transition strategies to a global configuration of equal stability and reliability.

We are convinced that it is here that the advantages of the One Thing Approach and XMDD express themselves most prominently. While at first design time they provide clarity and foster co-creation by continuous cooperation by the different knowledge and responsibility owners, in case of change it is of vital importance to be able to identify who and what is affected, what options exist within the regulatory, legal, and optimal/preferential exploration space, and then be able to execute with predictable coherence and known outcome quality.

Traditionally, change was a big deal. Architecture was the first decision, fixing the structure, often the technology, and surely the data model of the system. Essentially, architectures fixed the basic assets (hardware, software, and communications) in a very early binding fashion. This was from then on a given, an axiom too costly to overturn or amend. So it went that generations of large IT systems remained constrained and distorted by initial decisions that became obsolete and even counterproductive in the course of their life. The disruptive power of the cloud concerns firstly the dematerialization of the hardware, which is rendered pliable, and amenable to late binding, and decisions by need or as opportune. Hardware becomes a flexible part of the system design. The UI has also turned into a culturally demanded flexibility. Nowadays the digital natives wish to be mobile, on the phone, on the tablet, on the laptop. The commoditization of computing power that comes with the decline of residential computing for front-office tasks today demands GUIs that offer the same user experience on any platform, across operating systems, and possibly a smooth migration across all of them. So, after the architecture, also the user consumption paradigm cannot be anymore the defining anchor for a system design.

What remains as the core of a system or application, be it in the cloud, mobile, actually anywhere, and is the "thing" that needs to be well controlled and flexibly adapted, migrated, and evolved, is the **behaviour of the system**. The behaviour needs to be designed (and verified) once, and then brought as seamlessly as possible onto a growing variety of UIs and IT platforms, along the entire life span of usually one or more decades. Processes, workflows, and models that describe what the system does rise now in importance to the top position. In such an inherently evolving landscape, living models that are easy to design, incorporate diverse knowledge layers (also about technical issues and adaptability), are anytime executable, be it by animation, simulation, or once deployed, seem to be a very reasonable and efficient way to go.

7   Conclusions

The success of evolution hinges on the realization that we intrinsically depend upon the understanding and informed support and collaboration of a huge cloud of other non-IT professionals, without which no software system can be successful in the long term. As explained in this quite well known story [4], in any IT-related project, we need the right marketing, the right press releases, the right communication, the right bosses and the right customers to achieve what can only be a shared, co-owned success.

We really hope, in a few years from now, to be able to look back at this first collection of papers and see what advancements have occurred in the way we deal with change in IT, economy, and society.

References

1. The business-it gap illustrated. http://modeling-languages.com/how-users-and-programmers-see-each-other/
2. Owl-s: Semantic markup for web services. W3C Member Submission 22 November 2004. http://www.w3.org/Submission/OWL-S/
3. The tree-swing cartoon. http://www.businessballs.com/treeswing.htm
4. The tree-swing cartoon. http://www.businessballs.com/businessballs_treeswing_pictures.htm
5. Blum, N., Magedanz, T., Kleessen, J., Margaria, T.: Enabling eXtreme model driven design of parlay X-based communications services for end-to-end multi-platform service orchestrations. In: 2009 14th IEEE International Conference on Engineering of Complex Computer Systems, pp. 240–247, June 2009
6. Boßelmann, S., Margaria, T.: Guided business modeling and analysis for business professionals. In: Pfannstiel, M.A., Rasche, C. (eds.) Service Business Model Innovation in Healthcare and Hospital Management. Springer, November 2016. ISBN 978-3-319-46411-4
7. Boßelmann, S., Frohme, M., Kopetzki, D., Lybecait, M., Naujokat, S., Neubauer, J., Wirkner, D., Zweihoff, P., Bernhard Steffen, D.: A programming-less modeling environment for web applications. In: Proceedings of the 7th International Symposium on Leveraging Applications of Formal Methods, Verification and Validation (ISoLA 2016) (2016)

8. Boßelmann, S., Wickert, A., Lamprecht, A-L., Margaria, T.: Modeling directly executable processes for healthcare professionals with xmdd. In: Pfannstiel, M.A., Rasche, C. (eds). Service Business Model Innovation in Healthcare and Hospital Management. Springer Verlag, November 2016. ISBN 978-3-319-46411-4

9. Boßelmann, S., Neubauer, J., Naujokat, S., Steffen, B.: Model-driven design of secure high assurance systems: an introduction to the open platform from the user perspective. In: Margaria, T., Solo, A.M.G. (eds). The 2016 International Conference on Security and Management (SAM 2016), Special Track End-to-End Security and Cybersecurity: From the Hardware to Application, pp. 145–151. CREA Press (2016)

10. Celebic, B., Breu, R., Felderer, M.: Traceability types for mastering change in collaborative software quality management. In: Steffen, B. (ed.) Transactions on FoMaC I. LNCS, vol. 9960, pp. 242–256. Springer, Heidelberg (2016)

11. Doedt, M., Steffen, B.: An evaluation of service integration approaches of business process management systems. In: Proceedings of the 35th Annual IEEE Software Engineering Workshop (SEW 2012) (2012)

12. Fitzgerald, B.: Software crisis 2.0. In: Keynote at EASE 2016, 20th International Conference on Evaluation and Assessment in Software Engineering, Limerick (Irealnd), June 2016

13. Hagerer, A., Hungar, H., Niese, O., Steffen, B.: Model generation by moderated regular extrapolation. In: Kutsche, R.-D., Weber, H. (eds.) FASE 2002. LNCS, vol. 2306, pp. 80–95. Springer, Heidelberg (2002). doi:10.1007/3-540-45923-5_6

14. Hagerer, A., Margaria, T., Niese, O., Steffen, B., Brune, G., Ide, H.-D.: Efficient regression testing of CTI-systems: testing a complex call-center solution. Ann. Rev. Commun. Int. Eng. Consortium (IEC) **55**, 1033–1040 (2001)

15. Hungar, H., Margaria, T., Steffen, B.: Test-based model generation for legacy systems. In: Test Conference, Proceedings, ITC 2003, International, vol. 1, pp. 971–980, October 2003

16. Isberner, M., Howar, F., Steffen, B.: Learning register automata: from languages to program structures. Mach. Learn. **96**, 1–34 (2013)

17. Cok, D., Ernst, M., Kiniry, J., Leavens, G.T., Rustan, K., Leino, M., Burdy, L., Cheon, Y., Poll, E.: An overview of jml tools and applications. STTT **7**(3), 212–232 (2005)

18. Margaria, T., Boßelmann, S., Doedt, M., Floyd, B.D., Steffen, B.: Customer-oriented business process management: visions and obstacles. In: Hinchey, M., Coyle, L. (eds.) Conquering Complexity, pp. 407–429. Springer, London (2012)

19. Margaria, T., Floyd, B.D., Gonzalez Camargo, R., Lamprecht, A.-L., Neubauer, J., Seelaender, M.: Simple management of high assurance data in long-lived interdisciplinary healthcare research: a proposal. In: Margaria, T., Steffen, B. (eds.) ISoLA 2014. LNCS, vol. 8803, pp. 526–544. Springer, Heidelberg (2014). doi:10. 1007/978-3-662-45231-8_44

20. Margaria, T., Raffelt, H., Steffen, B.: Analyzing second-order effects between optimizations for system-level test-based model generation. In: Test Conference, Proceedings. ITC 2005, IEEE International. IEEE Computer Society, November 2005

21. Margaria, T., Steffen, B.: Backtracking-free design planning by automatic synthesis in METAFrame. In: Astesiano, E. (ed.) FASE 1998. LNCS, vol. 1382, pp. 188–204. Springer, Heidelberg (1998). doi:10.1007/BFb0053591

22. Margaria, T., Steffen, B.: Lightweight coarse-grained coordination: a scalable system-level approach. Softw. Tools Technol. Transf. **5**(2–3), 107–123 (2004)

23. Margaria, T., Steffen, B.: Agile IT: thinking in user-centric models. In: Margaria, T., Steffen, B. (eds.) ISoLA 2008. CCIS, vol. 17, pp. 490–502. Springer, Heidelberg (2008). doi:10.1007/978-3-540-88479-8_35

24. Margaria, T., Steffen, B.: Business process modelling in the jABC: the one-thing-approach. In: Cardoso, J., van der Aalst, W. (eds.) Handbook of Research on Business Process Modeling. IGI Global, Hershey (2009)

25. Margaria, T., Steffen, B.: Service-orientation: conquering complexity with XMDD. In: Hinchey, M., Coyle, L. (eds.) Conquering Complexity, pp. 217–236. Springer, London (2012)

26. Meyer, B.: Applying "design by contract". Computer **25**(10), 40–51 (1992)

27. Rensink, A.: Model patterns: the quest for the right level of abstraction. In: Steffen, B. (ed.) Transactions on FoMaC I. LNCS, vol. 9960, pp. 47–70. Springer, Heidelberg (2016)

28. Scheer, A.-W.: Architecture of integrated information systems (ARIS). In: DIISM, pp. 85–99 (1993)

29. Steffen, B.: LNCS transaction on the foundations for mastering change: preliminary manifesto. In: Steffen, B., Margaria, T. (eds.) ISoLA 2014. LNCS, vol. 8802, p. 514. Springer, Heidelberg (2014)

30. Steffen, B., Margaria, T.: METAFrame in practice: design of intelligent network services. In: Olderog, E.-R., Steffen, B. (eds.) Correct System Design. LNCS, vol. 1710, pp. 390–415. Springer, Heidelberg (1999). doi:10.1007/3-540-48092-7_17

31. Steffen, B., Margaria, T., Claßen, A., Braun, V.: The METAFrame'95 environment. In: Alur, R., Henzinger, T.A. (eds.) CAV 1996. LNCS, vol. 1102, pp. 450–453. Springer, Heidelberg (1996). doi:10.1007/3-540-61474-5_100

32. Steffen, B., Margaria, T., Raffelt, H., Niese, O.: Efficient test-based model generation of legacy systems. In: Proceedings of the 9th IEEE International Workshop on High Level Design Validation and Test (HLDVT 2004), pp. 95–100. IEEE Computer Society Press, Sonoma, November 2004

33. Steffen, B., Naujokat, S.: Archimedean points: the essence for mastering of change. In: Steffen, B. (ed.) Transactions on FoMaC I. LNCS, vol. 9960, pp. 24–46. Springer, Heidelberg (2016)

34. van der Aalst, W.M.P., ter Hofstede, A.H.M.: YAWL: yet another workflow language. Inform. Syst. **30**(4), 245–275 (2005)

35. Beeck, M., Braun, V., Claßen, A., Dannecker, A., Friedrich, C., Koschützki, D., Margaria, T., Schreiber, F., Steffen, B.: Graphs in METAFrame: the unifying power of polymorphism. In: Brinksma, E. (ed.) TACAS 1997. LNCS, vol. 1217, pp. 112–129. Springer, Heidelberg (1997). doi:10.1007/BFb0035384

36. White, S.A., Miers, D.: BPMN Modeling and Reference Guide. Future Strategies Inc., Lighthouse Point (2008)

Archimedean Points: The Essence for Mastering Change

Bernhard Steffen[(✉)] and Stefan Naujokat

Chair for Programming Systems, TU Dortmund University,
44227 Dortmund, Germany
{steffen,stefan.naujokat}@cs.tu-dortmund.de

Abstract. Explicit Archimedean Point-driven (software) system development aims at maintaining as much control as possible via 'things' that do not change, and may radically alter the role of modeling and development tools. The idea is to incorporate as much knowledge as possible into the tools themselves. This way they become domain-specific, problem-specific, or even specific to a particular new requirement for a system already in operation. Key to the practicality of this approach is a much increased ease of tool development: it must be economic to alter the modeling tool as part of specific development tasks. The CINCO framework aims at exactly this kind of ease: once the intended change is specified, generating a new tool is essential a push button activity. This philosophy and tool chain are illustrated along the stepwise construction of a BPMN tool via a chain of increasingly expressive Petri net tools. By construction, the resulting BPMN tool has a conceptually very clean semantic foundation, which enables tool features like various consistency checks, type-controlled activity integration, and true full code generation.

1 Motivation

Today's development of modern software-based systems is characterized by change at almost all levels along their lifecycle: requirements, frameworks, components, platform, etc. continuously evolve. Central for mastering these changes is the identification of things that do *not* change (often referred to as the corresponding Archimedean Point[1]): this way it is possible to maintain an understanding and to stay in control of the development. In practice, this quest for stability is typically reflected by splitting major changes into a sequence of small increments in order to be better able to observe and control their effect. Pragmatically, such a splitting is certainly advantageous, in particular when combined with systematic version control. It helps following the effects of the increments and revealing unwanted side effects stepwise. However, it does not provide a tangible notion of Archimedean Point, i.e. a clear description of the essence of what

---

[1] Archimedes' dictum "Give me a place to stand on, and I will move the earth" was part of his intuitive explanation of the lever principle. Today this quote is often transferred into other scenarios as a metaphor for the power of invariance.

© Springer International Publishing AG 2016
B. Steffen (Ed.): Transactions on FoMaC I, LNCS 9960, pp. 22–46, 2016.
DOI: 10.1007/978-3-319-46508-1_3

stays unchanged and therefore can be still relied on, and it is only of indirect help when it comes to guaranteeing the Archimedean Point in the long run.

A more rigid approach for Archimedean Point-based control is based on architectures specifically designed for ensuring a clear separation of concerns. E.g., the popular three tier architectures [1] aim at separating platform aspects, application logic, and (graphical) interface. This decoupling is intended to support changes at each of these levels, essentially without any impact on the other two. This layered pattern is very common and has a tradition also in specific domains, e.g. in compiler construction. Compilation frameworks typically comprise a common intermediate language into which all source languages can be translated and from which code for all target languages can be generated. The Archimedean Points that make these approaches successful are the stable APIs between the tiers of the considered multi-tier architecture, and the common intermediate language in the compilation example.

Indeed, the whole modular and compositional system/program development generates its power through decoupling via Archimedean Points in terms of APIs, and it is the lack of adequate Archimedean Points that makes parallel programming so intricate [2–5]. Inter-component communication and synchronization easily destroy syntactic modularity at the semantic level, a problem approaches like aspect-oriented programming [6] conceptually have to fight with. The point here is to tame the complexity of parallel and distributed computing in order to be able to maintain sufficient Archimedean Points, and to turn the syntactic modularity into a suitable semantic modularity. This is a matter of complexity reduction: aspect code must follow rigid rules to prohibit potential harm.

Also, domain-specific approaches [7,8] try to simplify software and system development by restriction. Domain-specific modeling environments provide complex domain-specific functionality from the shelf, but they typically constrain the modeling in a quite rigid way in order to maintain e.g. executability. In a sense, aspect-oriented programming can be regarded as a form of domain-specific development dedicated to resolve cross-cutting concerns without introducing unwanted interference. More generally, the charm of most generative programming [9,10] approaches (besides saving code writing) lies in the fact that the more prescriptive structure of the specification is preserved during the generation process, establishing yet another form of Archimedean Point.

Typical Archimedean Points that occur during software/system development concern the syntactic structure like code or architectural similarity, but also the static semantics, e.g. in terms of type correctness or statically checkable binding properties. More ambitious are assertion-based Archimedean Points as they can be expressed e.g. by OCL [11] or computational invariants typically expressed in first order logic [12]. Whereas the latter introduce undecidability into the language and therefore require manual proofs or a delay of the checking ability to the runtime [13–17], the former can be frequently automatically checked at design time.

However, there are many more potential candidates: enforced conventions, designated platforms, temporal properties, unquestioned requirements and their use cases, domain ontologies, designated test suites, deployed software libraries, and even sociological properties like preservation of the development team or of the considered user base may be considered Archimedean Points of the one or the other nature and scope.

In fact, mastering change can be regarded as a discipline of maintaining and adapting Archimedean Points along the whole lifecycle of a system. This requires not only to enforce vital Archimedean Points, but also their continuous adaption in order to take care of the changing needs. One of the major challenges is to establish adequate tool support for this enterprise, which gives rise to Archimedean Points at the meta level: domain-specific structures and functionalities, stable construction processes, tool landscapes, deployment scenarios, and quality assurance processes significantly add to the solidity of the developed artifacts. In particular, in tailored domain-specific scenarios these meta-level Archimedean Points may directly impose both model-level and application-level Archimedean Points.

In this paper we discuss the Archimedean Point-driven construction of domain-specific modeling tools. The point is to provide as much domain-specific or even application-specific support as possible to the users in order to lower the required expertise, entry hurdles, amount of modeling, and quality assurance effort. In other words, by exploiting as many Archimedean Points as possible we aim at maximizing model-level simplicity through powerful generation facilities, built-in property checkers, full code generation, and automated validation support.

Of course, much of the simplicity of the generated tools is due to the so-called Pareto or 80/20 principle, which is sometimes also described as the "easy for the many difficult for the few" paradigm [18]: The bulk of the work can be done extremely easily, however, if something more special is desired, this may require to involve IT experts. In this paper we illustrate that rather than coordinating the work of the various roles (application expert, domain expert, IT expert, security expert,...) at modeling time it may be advantageous to provide the application expert simply with a new tool specifically tailored to the changed requirements. In fact, we believe that the imposed new way of version and change management may significantly improve both time to market and quality to market.

Our discussion focusses on *graph-based, graphical modeling tools*. This focus simplifies the according metamodeling, allows dedicated user interfaces, structures the required code generators, and eases model-to-model transformations, at a comparably low price. In fact, in our (industrial) projects we never faced a situation where the restriction to graph models was critical.

Our holistic approach to the generation of domain/application-specific modeling tools exploits four layers of Archimedean Points which take specific roles during tool generation, modeling, code generation, validation, and evolution:

– **Rigid Archimedean Points** (RAPs) are directly enforced by by construction: it is simply impossible to construct violating models with the corresponding modeling tool. E.g., if a RAP requires that every edge is meant to connect two nodes, then the tool will not allow to draw dangling edges. The enforcement of RAPs should be immediate and intuitive in order to not trouble the modeler. In fact, there is little as annoying as something which does not work without any explanation.

- **Verifiable Archimedean Points** (VAPs) concern properties that can be automatically verified at the model level in order to provide the modeler with feedback. VAPs very much resemble the 'intelligence' of modern IDEs which give feedback about syntax and type violations, certain dataflow properties, and the like. In contrast to RAPs, VAPs do not prevent the construction of violating models, but leave the correction to the user of the modeling tool. This detection strategy is in particular advantageous for properties which cannot be established without any intermediate violation. Consider for example the connectivity of a graph in a context of the RAP example above: In order to guarantee that each edge has always a source and a target, one may need to place the nodes first, before one can introduce the connecting edge. But this requires an unconnected intermediate graph.

  Another reason to sometimes prefer VAPs to RAPs is simply performance. It is not a big problem if a hard to compute feedback only appears with some delay, as long as the flow of modeling is not blocked in the meantime.

- **Observable Archimedean Points** (OAPs) concern properties that cannot be automatically taken care of by the tool, e.g., because the underlying analysis problem is undecidable. Examples are computational invariants, termination, and many other OCL properties etc. [11]. Their treatment typically requires some involved user interaction, which would exceed the expertise of the envisioned modeler. However, they may by validated with simulation and testing methods, or by means of runtime verification by injecting the required checking code via some aspect-oriented code generation.

- **Descriptive Archimedean Points** (DAPs) refer to properties that are meant to be taken care of by the modeler/developer without tool support. In some sense they have the character of documentation or a hint, and their validity is not treated by the domain-specific modeling tools. Some service-level agreements may fall into this category, as well as any other form of annotation, textual guidance etc.

This classification is not absolute, but tool-specific. The same property may be a RAP in one tool and a VAP in another. In fact, it is even possible for some properties to move through all four level in the course of maturation: Initially a property may be just a DAP and successively become more tightly integrated, first by some according testing mechanisms to become an OAP, before it turns into a VAP after an according checking procedure has been realized, and finally becomes a RAP after it has been tightly bound to the tools metamodel.

This paper focusses on illustrating the pragmatics and effects of Archimedean Point-oriented tool generation along the example lifecycle of a product line of Petri net-based modeling tools. As sketched in Fig. 1, the discussion follows the evolution of an initial graphical modeling tool for place/transition nets into a tool for business process modeling by successively adding features covering a subset of the Business Process Model and Notation (BPMN 2.0) standard and adapting the graphical representation.

Already considering just place/transition nets is sufficient to explain the upwards movement of properties. Their characteristic bipartite structure may

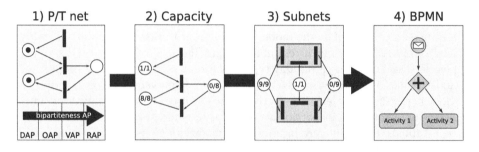

Fig. 1. Evolution of the modeling tool from place/transition nets to BPMN

| bipartiteness AP | | | |
Docu-mentation	Runtime Observation	Model Verification	Model En-forcement
DAP	OAP	VAP	RAP

Fig. 2. Evolution of the bipartiteness Archimedean Point from DAP to RAP

first be simply annotated to the model type as informal documentation. In the next version of the modeling tool there may be some model tracing mechanism which checks for individual runs whether in the modeled graphs places and transition always alternate, turning the DAP into an OAP. This validation may be subsequently enhanced using model checking, which makes the bipartite structure a VAP. In the last step two kinds of edges may be syntactically introduced, one for connecting edges with transitions and another for connecting transitions with edges. In a tool which only allows to draw 'type-correct' edges, bipartiteness has eventually become a RAP (cf. Fig. 2).

However, the strongest version of Archimedean Point is not necessarily the best. Rather, tool designers have the choice at which level they want certain properties to be treated, as every choice has its pros and cons. For example, enforcing properties at the RAP level provides the best guidance in particular for occasional and non-expert users, but may blow up the metamodel and requires the re-generation of the tool for every change. The looser VAP variant instead keeps the constraints separately, which can therefore be modified without changing the tool, but indicates constraint violations only afterwards, when explicitly invoked. This on demand flexibility is often preferred by 'power users'.

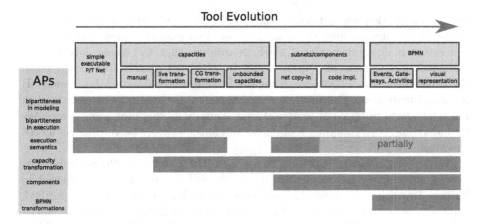

Fig. 3. Archimedean Points during the evolution of our tool from simple place/transition nets to a first version of a BPMN 2.0 modeling environment.

Of course, decidability and performance clearly limit the placement of properties in the hierarchy of Archimedean Points. However, it is quite surprising how many properties can be enforced already at the meta level in sufficiently constrained application scenarios. The rest of the paper can be regarded as an introduction to the according game of Archimedean Point construction, adaption, and placement. This perspective turns the mastering of variation, product-lining and general evolution into a tool generation discipline. Figure 3 sketches how the Archimedean Points evolve in the course of this paper.

In the following, Sect. 2 will first present Constraint-Oriented System Development and in particular our Continuous Model Driven Engineering (CMDE) approach, which is characterized by viewing system development essentially as a form of constraint refinement. The corresponding support framework, the Cinco Meta Tooling Suite, is introduced in Sect. 3. Subsequently, Sect. 4 illustrates how to play with Archimedean Points by successively refining a simple Petri net scenario to eventually arrive at a basic tool for BPMN 2.0. In particular, it will explain how Cinco helps to control change and evolution along a system's lifecycle. Finally, Sect. 5 will sketch related work before we conclude with Sect. 6.

2   Constraint-Oriented System Development

Continuous Model Driven Engineering (CMDE) [19] aims at managing change at the model/constraint level where the Archimedean Points are typically expressed either in the model structures themselves or in terms of complementing (temporal) logic invariants and rules. Formal verification techniques like model checking are used to monitor whether the Archimedean Points are indeed preserved and synthesis techniques serve for 'correctness by generation'. The success of CMDE hinges on the interplay of different roles with different expertise: programmers for implementing basic functionality in terms of building blocks, domain experts for providing adequate ontologies and constraints, and applications experts for modeling and maintaining the desired system in a guided fashion. The full code generation philosophy behind CMDE guarantees that the whole development and evolution process of a system can be observed at the application level. We distinguish this WHAT level from the HOW level, containing the (technical) details of realization. Essential user requirements can elegantly be expressed at the WHAT level in terms of temporal logic constraints, perhaps using some easy to understand corresponding templates, and automatically be verified via model checking.

In our original corresponding framework, the jABC [20–22], modeling has been done in terms of Service Logic Graphs (SLGs) which can be viewed as Kripke Transition Systems [23], and constraints have been formally specified, typically, in term of Semantic Linear Time Logic (SLTL) [24]. From a practical perspective, jABC's support of dynamic integration of (functional) building blocks for adding new, often domain-specific functionality is important. It allows one to maintain and control requirements at the WHAT level in a propositional fashion: associating (atomic) propositions with these building blocks provides control of their interplay and enforces the intended behavior. jABC has a successful history in imposing Archimedean Points directly at the application level using e.g. temporal logic constraints [25–28] and to follow the effect of changes e.g. in terms of feature interaction [29].

Metamodels impose constraints on the structure of conformant models, and therefore on the tolerance of the correspondingly generated graphical modeling tools. Thus metamodels can be ordered via implication: a metamodel is smaller than another if it imposes less constraints on the models' structure. It makes sense to keep this in mind during metamodel change/adaptation, as a metamodel that is implied by both the old and the new metamodel can be regarded as an Archimedean Point of the change/adaption itself, and therefore as an indication for reuse. In practice, it is not necessarily advisable to explicitly consider something like a 'supremum' metamodel, but rather to backtrack to a previously considered metamodel that subsumes both scenarios and to refine from there.

This technique nicely fits the constraint-driven approach underlying CMDE where

– system development is viewed as a process of (design) decision taking, or, in other words, of imposing constraints on potential solutions, and
– change as a process of relaxing some constraints in preparation of adding other constraints that are necessary for meeting new requirements.

A particularly convenient way to design special scenarios is via model templates, or as we also call them, loose or partially defined models [30,31]. The correspondingly generated modeling tool can then be regarded as a reliable guide for syntactically correct concretization, i.e., replacement of underspecified parts with concrete (sub-)models. This can be exploited to generate dedicated tools for feature model-based variability construction [32,33] as they are, e.g., common in product line engineering [34].

As discussed in the next section, the CINCO Meta Tooling Suite is more general than the jABC in that it allows one to construct domain-specific and even case-specific modeling languages using various forms of meta-level specification. This way vital constraints, like the bipartiteness of Petri net models, can often be directly built into the syntactical structure of the modeling language in order to establish a RAP. Other structural properties that may be turned into RAPs are tree models, which may be used for modeling syntax trees, Programmable Logical Controllers (PLCs) [35,36], and pools of typed triplets for modeling Event Conditions Action systems (ECAs) [37,38]. The other levels of Archimedean Points are then treated essentially in the same way as in the jABC [27].

3   The Cinco Meta Tooling Suite

CINCO is a framework for generating graphical modeling tools based on abstract meta-level tool specifications. It combines classical metamodeling techniques with specifications for the appearance of the graphical editor, some form of operational semantics for code generation, as well as domain constraints in terms of ontologies and temporal formulas for user guidance, in order to fully automatically generate a corresponding graphical modeling tool. CINCO is extended with so-called meta plug-ins that can be used for any CINCO-developed modeling tool. They contribute to CINCO's tool generation process itself to extend the tool's features or adapt its behavior.

The CINCO Meta Tooling Suite is built with the goal to provide as much stability as possible using (generalized) meta-level concepts. CINCO as such can be (re-)used during the change process in order to adequately adapt the graphical modeling tools for the new situation. Additionally, the embodied concept of meta plug-ins allows one to easily maintain features like model checking during the change process. This does not only make the preserved temporal constraints an Archimedean Point, but also their enforcement mechanism. Other meta-level Archimedean Points may concern layouting, view construction, code generation, and other forms of model transformation support.

We present here the corresponding ideas of CINCO. An in-depth presentation of its concepts and technical background can be found in [39]. Figure 4 shows the involved components when developing a modeling tool with CINCO. Based on the *specification*, the *product generator* automatically generates the fully functional *modeling tool*. The generated tool itself is based on many frameworks from the Eclipse ecosystem, which provide numerous facilities for metamodeling, graphical editors, rich client applications, and plug-in structures, but also various general technologies usually relevant for development tasks, e.g. integration of sourcecode management (Git, Subversion) or build management (Ant, Maven).

The tool specification can furthermore contain special elements for dedicated meta plug-ins. Such elements range from simple declarations like "use the meta plug-in for model checking", which characterizes a tool family for modeling tools that provide model checking, to more specific, parameterized configurations, which, e.g., constrain the model checking functionality to a certain

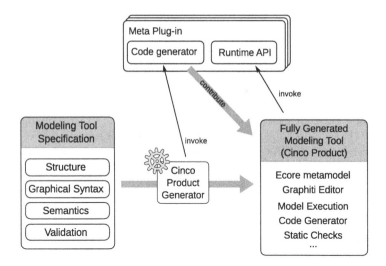

Fig. 4. CINCO architecture and meta plug-in concept

set of predefined temporal properties. This way it is possible to generate tools without visible model checking functionality that use embedded model checking to enforce *built-in* properties (Archimedean Points) like

- the end node is still reachable,
- each variable use has a defined value or
- termination is only possible after a certain resource has been released again.

Such configurations essentially establish a sub-family of the family of model checking supported tools that is adequate for users without knowledge about model checking.

When the CINCO product generator encounters such meta plug-in specifications during generation it invokes the code generator of the corresponding meta plug-in to contribute to the modeling tool. This is usually done in the form of special additions to the tool's codebase and its metamodel, so that at runtime some API provided by the meta plug-in or stand-alone code realizing some intended addition can be used by the modeling tool.

It is the declared goal of CINCO to make the construction of tailored modeling tools so easy that it even may pay off for single instance projects, e.g. realizing a new structural requirement for a system already in operation. This way it is possible to capture and support change in terms of variation and evolution directly at the level of the modeling tool: New frame conditions, rules and regulations are meant to be incorporated into the tool essentially like type disciplines in IDEs, to guide the modeler and prevent certain errors once and for all. Using, e.g., a model checking and/or constraint solving meta plug-in, this can happen at two levels:

- At the metamodeling level itself: In this case the considered properties typically form RAPs. They are rigidly built into the modeling tool which therefore only admits property-conform modeling. This can be seen as a form of partial evaluation as has been proposed in the *dataflow analysis as model checking* paradigm [40,41], where temporal formulae are transformed into concrete dataflow analysis code for a given compiler framework.
- As additional constraints: In this case these properties form VAPs. They are evaluated during the modeling phase on demand, usually utilizing the functionality of a generic meta plug-in for model checking or constraint solving. Thus modelers may freely proceed unconstrained and only check their models from time to time. In addition they may easily add or discard properties depending on the given situation.

In addition, runtime verification of the so-called OAPs can be supported using monitoring or (life-long) learning-based testing technology [42,43].

Often, the tool designer can choose at which level they want certain properties to be treated. E.g., in our Petri net example, the fact that Petri nets are bipartite graphs can be built into the tool's metamodel, which will then no longer admit any edge from one node type (place or transition) to a node of the same type, or it could be formulated as a simple temporal formula and only be checked on demand. Both ways have pros and cons: the built-in variant requires to provide within the metamodel two node types, places and transitions, and to specify that they need to alternate on each path. Such definitions may blow up the metamodel, and the imposed prevention of place-to-place or transition-to-transition connections would provide a very strong guidance (which in our experience is not always appreciated). The looser constraint variant keeps the constraints separately, which can therefore be exchanged without changing the tool, but indicates constraint violations only afterwards, when explicitly invoked (cf. Sect. 4.2).

The upcoming Sect. 4 will illustrate the Archimedean Point-driven evolution of a product line of graphical modeling tools: an initial tool for place/transition nets will be successively refined by adding more and more complex features to eventually provide a tool that captures the core features of a business process modeling tool for BPMN 2.0 [44]. We will see that each of these refinement steps is very easy, and that the generated tools conveniently preserve some vital structural Archimedean Points.

In order for this refinement to be convincing, also the GUI specification and the code generator have to be adapted. This happens, however, at a level independent of the actual modeling, and we will see that also major parts of the code generator can be preserved. In particular, one could say that changing the graphical representation has the syntactic structure and the behavioral semantics as Archimedean Points. This is the basis for a clear separation of concerns.

By following the development of a graphical modeling tool for place/transition nets and its successive refinement we will see how CINCO-based tool generation allows one to tailor and later on adapt the whole development environment to a domain or even to certain tasks in a fashion that accelerates the process and helps preserving vital properties with significant saving in terms of total cost of ownership.

4   Application Scenario: From Petri Nets to BPMN

In this section we sketch the development of a product line of modeling tools for Petri net-based structures and indicate how their incremental evolution can lead to a modeling tool for BPMN 2.0. The point of this development is to illustrate the 'play' with different Archimedean Points on multiple (meta) levels in order to better control the evolution.

As already depicted in Fig. 1, the development starts with a stepwise refinement for just treating the bi-partiteness of place/transition nets. Capacities are then introduced to simplify the modeling of structures that can hold more than one token. Subsequently, a subnet feature is added to derive a tool for a Petri net version able to handle and reuse even more complex model structures in a hierarchical fashion. The introduction of a 'service-oriented' generalization to deal with arbitrary component libraries is then used to realize BPMN's gateways, events, and activities. Our illustrative development ends with adapting the visual specification of the modeling tool to obtain the standard BPMN look and feel.

This entire evolution profits from the fact that the code generator and simulation interpreter remain unchanged throughout the development. Much of the simplicity of the following discussion, however, is owed to the fact that they are by far not the only arising Archimedean Points.

4.1   Tool Basics

We start with developing a tool for the modeling and execution of simple place/transition nets, the most basic form of Petri nets. Valid models are bipartite graph structures of *place* and *transition* nodes, meaning that all nodes connected via incoming or outgoing edges (called *arcs*) to a transition are places and vice versa. Furthermore, a place may (or may not) contain a *token*.

Execution of Petri nets (via direct simulation as well as after code generation) proceeds by subsequently *firing* enabled transitions in a random fashion. A transition is *enabled* if all predecessor places contain a token and all successor places are empty.[2] Firing then removes the token from all predecessor places and adds a token to all successor places. It is repeated until either no transition is enabled anymore (called deadlock or termination) or the execution is paused/ended.

Figure 5 shows the modeling tool generated with CINCO. As all CINCO products are based on the Eclipse environment, some elements might look familiar, e.g. menu structures and the Project Explorer on the left. CINCO adds some specific parts[3]: in addition to the main editor for the models in the center, which

---

[2] In order to deal with cyclic transitions, the emptiness requirement of successor places is dropped for places that are predecessor as well as successor of a transition.

[3] The term "part" is used in Eclipse applications for the sub-windows that can be arranged as tabs within the main window.

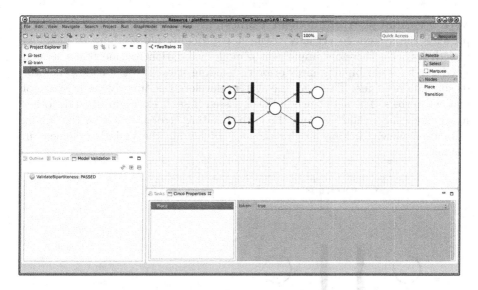

Fig. 5. Place/transition modeling tool generated with CINCO.

currently displays a Petri net for the commonly used 'shared track' example where two trains (on the left) cannot enter the shared track segment (in the middle) at the same time, CINCO provides

- a properties view at the bottom showing the editable attributes of the currently selected element (a place in this case),
- a tool palette on the right containing all model elements, as well as
- a validation view showing the results of all checks for the currently open model.

4.2 Bipartiteness as Archimedean Point

We use the requirement "a valid net must be bipartite" as a first simple example to illustrate the upwards movement of a property through our four levels of Archimedean Points (from weakest to strongest):

DAP (Descriptive Archimedean Points). In a DAP-style handling of the requirement, it is documented (e.g. somewhere in the tool's manual) that valid models need to be bipartite and the implementation just assumes that every user/modeler will obey that rule. In case of violation, the execution will produce a runtime exception, e.g. trying to class cast a transition to the place type.

OAP (Observable Archimedean Points). To make the execution more robust against crashes, the tool can be enhanced to check the correct type of a transition's predecessors and successors before determining whether it is enabled. When a violation is detected, the transition is marked as not enabled and an error message is shown or logged somewhere in the system.

VAP (Verifiable Archimedean Points). While the OAP implementation prevents the system to actually crash, it is probably not working as intended nonetheless. We therefore implement a model validation routine that checks a Petri net for valid bipartiteness prior to handing it over to the code generator or simulation engine. This way the system developer is directly made aware of modeling errors. The net shown in Fig. 5 passed that check. Figure 6 on the other hand shows an invalid net and the corresponding error message in the Model Validation view. Clicking on this message highlights the violating element in the net.

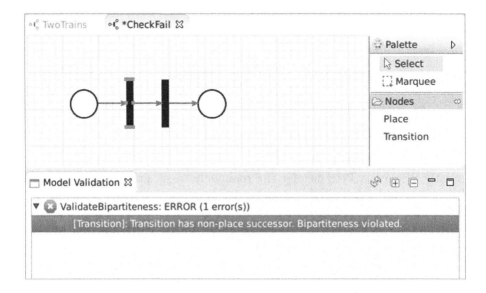

Fig. 6. Validation view detects the invalid net with bipartiteness violated.

RAP (Rigid Archimedean Points). For an even more direct guide of the modeler we may decide to enforce the bipartite structure on the syntactic level, so that it is simply not possible to connect a place to a place or a transition to a transition. We do this by replacing the arc by two specialized variants: a PlaceTransitionArc can only connect a place to a transition while a Transition-PlaceArc can only connect a transition to a place.

Defining this in the metamodel within CINCO (as part of the tool's structural specification, cf. Sect. 3) automatically enables the modeling tool to select the correct arc type when starting an edge from one of the node types. This way it simply will not be possible anymore to violate the bipartiteness. Figure 7 shows an attempt to directly connect two transitions: this is prevented by the tool and also indicated by the small *disabled* icon next to the mouse pointer.

It is not always possible to enforce complex constraints purely on the metamodel/syntactic level. For instance, deadlock-freedom can typically only be checked on the VAP level, or validated quite conveniently at run-time.

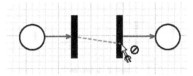

Fig. 7. Syntactically enforced bipartiteness does not allow to produce invalid models.

However, RAPs are not restricted to capture only typical syntactic errors. As already indicated by the bipartiteness discussion, it is possible to cover some simple form of semantics also syntactically, and it would also be possible to introduce, e.g., model checking control at the RAP level. This must, however, be done with care as e.g. enforcing 'continuous' deadlock freedom during modeling would be disastrous, as every introduction of a place or transition which causes an intermediate deadlock would be prohibited. This is perhaps the major reason why most IDE restrict their support to the VAP level.

4.3 Place Capacities

It is not uncommon for Petri nets to allow places that can hold multiple tokens (actually, our restriction with only one token is a less commonly used variant). As we aim at maintaining the code generator and simulation interpreter as Archimedean Points, we cannot simply introduce a new type of place where the modeler can define a capacity (in terms of an integer parameter), because this would require to adapt the firing rule to "transitions are enabled if all predecessor places contain *at least one token* while all successor places contain *at most capacity −1 tokens*" and actually firing a transition subtracts/adds tokens accordingly.

However, places with capacity can be *derived* from the previously introduced place/transition semantics in terms of appropriate substructures. This way it is even possible to control the input/output order of tokens, which might be relevant if individual tokens can be identified[4]. Figure 8 shows three variants of such a structure: queue, stack, and random access[5]. Assuming that transitions within this substructure are invisible (i.e. do not affect the global black box view of actions on the whole net), the observable behavior is identical to having places with a given capacity.

While the structures are semantically equivalent to places allowing to specify a capacity, they are very cumbersome for the modeler to realize. We therefore propose two possibilities for improvement while at the same time leaving the Archimedean Points for execution unchanged:

---

[4] In Petri nets this is usually done by *coloring* of tokens [45].

[5] Note that the random access structure could be realized to contain only a single input transition and a single output transition by introducing dedicated gate places, but the resulting overall structure would be more complex.

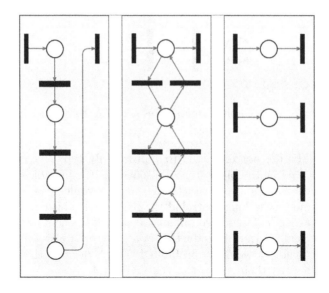

Fig. 8. Variants of substructures simulating a place with capacity=4: queue, stack and random access

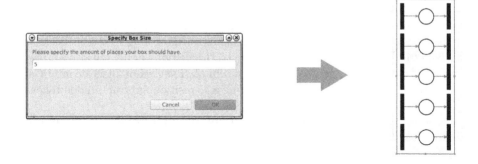

Fig. 9. 'live' model transformation after querying the user for a box size

- A special action on the model inserts the appropriate structure after querying the user for the amount of places (and maybe type of I/O behavior). A 'live' model transformation (i.e. model modification) of the net during editing then inserts the appropriate structure (see Fig. 9).
- We introduce a special node type with capacity into the metamodel, define the according visual syntax showing x/y with x being the current token count and y being the capacity, and apply the required model-to-model transformation simply as a preprocess to the code generation or simulation (see Fig. 10).

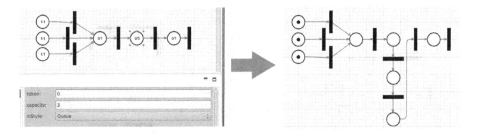

Fig. 10. To retain the code generation Archimedean Point, a Petri net containing places with capacity is transformed into one with binary tokens.

In fact, the required model transformation can again be regarded as an Archimedean Point during tool evolution: An initial version might just include the first variant until one realizes that creating a net is indeed simplified, but the results are rather incomprehensible. Postponing the model-to-model transformation as done in the second variant enables the modeler to just think in terms of places with capacity without being bothered by any technical detail.

With these approaches places with *bounded* capacity can be realized. If places with *unbounded* capacity are desired, the code generator and interpreter need to be adapted, which would invalidate their respective Archimedean Points.

4.4   Subnets as Components

As a next step in the evolution of our Petri net modeling tool we introduce a *subnet feature*, i.e. a given Petri net model can be used in another Petri net as a single component. Each place and transition of the subnet defines whether it should be visible on the higher level. This is the equivalent of an API, as Petri nets do not provide a classic notion of a *signature* like functions in a programming language.

Obviously, the Archimedean Points for execution are maintained, as the required transformation is a straightforward generalization of the transformation presented in the previous section that copies the subnet into the parent net as a preprocessing step.

The subnet feature primarily provides 'reuse' and 'separation of concerns' for the modeling environment. Modelers with a 'lower level'/technical field of expertise can prepare basic components, and application experts can simply use those in their applications. Figure 11 shows on the left the definition of a component realizing a place with capacity = 5 that can be enabled and disabled via dedicated API transitions, and on the right its according inclusion into a higher-level net. Note that the submodel is used more than once in the net. This means that each *instance* needs to have its own *state*, which our 'copy-in' preprocessing naturally provides. Of course, recursive structures are not possible with this approach as they typically require the execution to dynamically maintain some form of call stack.

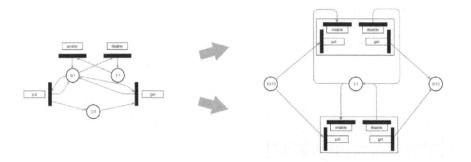

Fig. 11. Using a Petri net as component in other net.

Subnets open a whole new level of Archimedean Points: It becomes possible to design specialized tools only containing components from a given library so that they possess a predefined set of Archimedean Points. In fact, these Archimedean Points even 'survive' changes of the respective component implementations as long as the component behavior is maintained. This is also true for arbitrary code-level implementations (instead of just submodels). Of course, this costs the Archimedean Points of execution. On the other hand, it provides a truly service-oriented [46,47] extension of the modeling language, easily capturing the access to local devices like printers or to external REST/Web services called through the internet.

4.5   Realization of BPMN Features

As a final step in the evolution of our Petri net modeling tool we enhance it to cover basic functionality of the Business Process Model and Notation (BPMN 2.0) standard. All considered node types in BPMN can be mapped to special transition types in Petri nets. Places do not exist in BPMN processes. Consequently, there are no requirements for any bipartiteness at the modeling level. This Petri net-characteristic structure is (re-)introduced safely in the required model-to-model transformation which (re-)inserts the places implicitly lying on every edge, so that the code generator and simulation interpreter remain Achimedean Points.

Building on the features and enhancements we introduced before, we realize the following three aspects of BPMN:

Activities are single-in/single-out nodes stating that some (potentially complex or manual) task is performed and waited to be finished. The subnet feature we introduced before is most fitting for their realization. We require (by definition) activity subnets to have dedicated start and end transitions. The start transition is, as usual, enabled if the (implicit) predecessor place contains a token, but might also additionally involve some internal state.

The end transition is enabled internally once the activity is finished. Some activities might be realized using real subnets, but for most realistic scenarios the variant supporting arbitrary implementations will be required.

Events facilitate an indirect control flow. They can be emitted ('thrown') in one part of the system–potentially triggered by some external influence–and consumed ('caught') in a different one. Therefore, similar to cross-cutting concerns in the context of aspect orientation, they cannot be realized in a compositional way as a single inserted component. Instead, corresponding emitters and consumers for one event need to be connected through a dedicated place. This is realized via an appropriate model-to-model transformation prior to code generation.

Gateways require an individual consideration. The **Parallel Gateway** is very simple, as it realizes fork/join exactly matching the Petri net transition semantics. Thus, it can just be replaced by a single transition. It gets more complicated with the others, though. As there is no concept of *condition* in Petri nets, the **Exclusive Gateway** (only a single outgoing path is taken) and **Inclusive Gateway** (one or more outgoing paths are taken) can only be modeled as *non-deterministic decisions*, realized with according model-to-model transformations. However, for specific known conditions the subnet feature could be utilized. The subnet required for such conditions simply possesses one input transition and multiple output transitions, one for each outgoing edge. This approach also covers **Complex Gateways**, which are used in BPMN whenever the standard gateways are insufficient to express the desired condition. Finally, the **Event-Based Gateway** requires to combine the transformation realizing the non-deterministic decisions with the global graph transformation that connects event emitters with the gateway (the event consumer).

BPMN is strongly connected to a specific visual notation that does not have much in common with the Petri net representation we developed so far. Therefore, a last step is required: the editor needs to be adapted to actually look like BPMN. This is particularly simple with CINCO, as the visual representation and the structural metamodel are separately defined parts of the tool specification (cf. Sect. 3). While the visual representation needs to be changed for this step, the structural metamodel can remain the same, again making the previously defined components and transformations Archimedean Points.

Figure 12 shows an example BPMN process with this newly defined visual syntax as well as its transformation into the corresponding Petri net with implemented components for each activity. Indeed, the evolved tool conceptually improves over the state of the art BPMN tools concerning its well-defined semantics, which e.g., supports typing, its flexible component library concept, and its well-founded integration mechanism, which are all 'inherited' as Archimedean Points from the CINCO framework. Currently, we are extending the BPMN-coverage in a way that preserves all these properties.

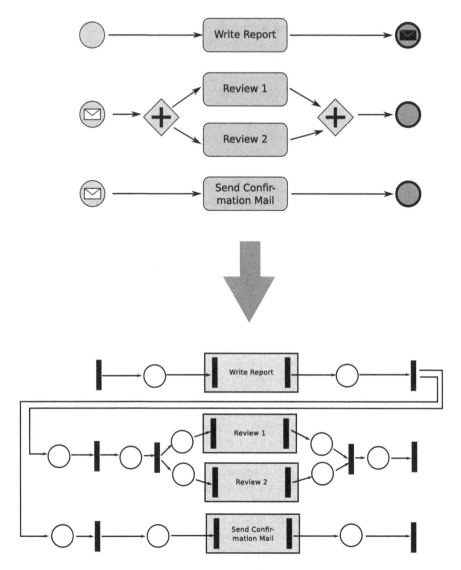

Fig. 12. Model transformation from BPMN process to its Petri net representation retains previously realized semantics of code generator and simulation interpreter.

5   Related Work

The concept of maintaining aspects that remain stable is commonly accepted as an essential ingredient for large software projects. This can come in various forms, such as stable APIs, modularity, separation of concerns [48], multi-tier architectures [1], portability through intermediate/bytecode languages, etc. What is largely neglected is a more rigorous support for *easily* maintaining such

Archimedean Points across the meta levels of the *tooling* for (model-based) software development. Metamodeling is a widespread approach and numerous basic frameworks, like JetBrains MPS [49] or from the Eclipse Modeling context [50–52] exist, but developing a sophisticated specialized modeling tool with those is usually considered too complex. This explains why many more specialized solutions emerged, some of which are based, like CINCO, on the Eclipse ecosystem:

Epsilon [53–56] is a (primarily) Eclipse-based framework that comprises several model specification, query, and transformation languages. Part of this framework is EuGENia, which generates a GMF editor based on an Ecore metamodel enchriched with specific annotations.

Spray [57] also focuses on the generation of graphical modeling tools for existing Eclipse EMF metamodels. It provides a dedicated DSL to specify graphical editors that are then generated for the Graphiti API.

Sirius [58] was released with Eclipse Luna (4.4.1) as a part of the Eclipse Modeling Project. For a given metamodel a tool developer can specify so-called modeling workbenches utilizing Sirius' declarative specification languages, providing graphical, table, or tree visualizations and editors for EMF models.

Marama [59,60] takes a more holistic approach towards the generation of Domain-Specific Visual Languages (DSVLs). It realizes a complete set of visual declarative specification languages to define all aspects of the generated DSVL tool and, unlike its predecessor Pounamu [61], is based on Eclipse.

MetaEdit+ [62,63] is a complete framework not based on the Eclipse ecosystem (or any other common framework providing metamodeling). It is a complex and mature stand-alone toolsuite functioning as the reference implementation of Domain-Specific Modeling [64].

DEViL [65,66], another framework not building on Eclipse, relies on several different specification and compiler frameworks and essentially provides a set of command-line tools that generate a wide range of visual structural editors from declarative specifications consisting of various textual formats.

All these tools and frameworks can be regarded as providing Archimedean Points to achieve some form of domain-specific stability. However, in contrast to CINCO with its strong focus on simplicity they are typically still too complex [39] and hardly pay off, in particular when utilized on a per-project basis.

6   Conclusion

We have illustrated Archimedean Point-driven evolutionary software development by stepwise deriving a basic BPMN tool from increasingly expressive Petri net tools. In particular, we have seen how Archimedean Points may evolve during such domain-specific model language refinements (cf. also Fig. 3). Of course, the concept of Archimedean Points is by no means restricted to this meta-level evolution. Rather, the meta-level evolution is a means to easily enhance the structural support provided by Archimedean Points during the domain-specific modeling phase.

That this can be done by also profiting from Archimedean Points during the modeling tool construction may be seen as an additional benefit, which results from bootstrapping: We model the modeling tools, which themselves may support also the construction of further modeling tools. Concretely, we are currently considering to generate CINCO itself using CINCO [67]. This has a lot of benefits, as our future CINCO products automatically run in the web. Thus the sketched self-application would directly generate a Web fronted for CINCO.

The impact of our approach is also evident when considering the future development of our BPMN product line. One important problem there is the adequate treatment of resources, which may be done in various ways. The answer of the Petri net community would typically be to move to colored Petri nets, where colored tokens impressively illustrate the flow of resources. Alternatively, from a classical programming language perspective, one may regard the tokens simply as generalized program counters and add an orthogonal concept of data model. Both views certainly have their benefits, and the adequate choice clearly depends on the given concrete context(domain of applications). In fact, it may often be ideal to go for a hybrid solution, where some resources are treated via the token structure and others via an orthogonal data model. CINCO is designed to flexibly react to such demands, and to easily generate an adequate modeling tool in a (modeling) building block fashion. This approach guarantees numerous Archimedean Points by construction both during the tool modeling phase and later during the use of the generated modeling tool. In particular, it allows one to fine-tune the modeling environment in a user-centric way, by choosing adequate levels of Archimedean Points in the four-level hierarchy described above.

One of the major challenges for the future is to design an adequate notion of 'inheritance' which allows one to easily migrate modeled applications between different domain-specific modeling environments. This is particularly important in scenarios where the modeling tool 'grows' with the developed applications during their lifecycle in tandem. In these cases, being able to easily build on the existing models is essential. We envisage here a wizard-based approach that aims at a maximal migration support.

References

1. Schuldt, H.: Multi-tier architecture. In: Liu, L., Özsu, M.T. (eds.) Encyclopedia of Database Systems, pp. 1862–1865. Springer, New York (2009)
2. Clarke, E.M., Grumberg, O.: Avoiding the state explosion problem in temporal logic model checking. In: Proceedings of the 6th Annual ACM Symposium on Principles of Distributed Computing (PODC 1987), pp. 294–303. ACM, New York (1987)
3. Clarke, E., Grumberg, O., Jha, S., Lu, Y., Veith, H.: Progress on the state explosion problem in model checking. In: Wilhelm, R. (ed.) Informatics. LNCS, vol. 2000, pp. 176–194. Springer, Heidelberg (2001). doi:10.1007/3-540-44577-3_12
4. Grumberg, O., Long, D.E.: Model checking and modular verification. ACM Trans. Program. Lang. Syst. (TOPLAS) 16(3), 843–871 (1994)

5. Zwiers, J.: Compositionality, Concurrency and Partial Correctness. Proof Theories for Networks of Processes, and Their Relationship. LNCS, vol. 321. Springer, Heidelberg (1989). doi:10.1007/BFb0020836
6. Kiczales, G., Lamping, J., Mendhekar, A., Maeda, C., Lopes, C., Loingtier, J.-M., Irwin, J.: Aspect-oriented programming. In: Akşit, M., Matsuoka, S. (eds.) ECOOP 1997. LNCS, vol. 1241, pp. 220–242. Springer, Heidelberg (1997). doi:10.1007/BFb0053381
7. Fowler, M., Parsons, R.: Domain-Specific Languages. Addison-Wesley/ACM Press, New York (2011)
8. Mernik, M., Heering, J., Sloane, A.M.: When and How to develop domain-specific languages. ACM Comput. Surv. **37**(4), 316–344 (2005)
9. Czarnecki, K., Eisenecker, U.W.: Generative Programming: Methods, Tools, and Applications. ACM Press/Addison-Wesley Publishing Co., New York (2000)
10. Herrington, J.: Code Generation in Action. Manning Publications Co., Greenwich (2003)
11. Object Management Group (OMG): Documents associated with Object Constraint Language (OCL), Version 2.4 (2014). http://www.omg.org/spec/OCL/2.4/
12. Barwise, J.: An introduction to first-order logic. In: Barwise, J. (ed.) Handbook of Mathematical Logic. Elsevier Science Publishers B.V, Amsterdam (1977)
13. Giannakopoulou, D., Havelund, K.: Automata-based verification of temporal properties on running programs. In: Proceedings of 16th IEEE International Conference on Automated Software Engineering (ASE 2001), pp. 412–416 (2001)
14. Barringer, H., Goldberg, A., Havelund, K., Sen, K.: Rule-based runtime verification. In: Steffen, B., Levi, G. (eds.) VMCAI 2004. LNCS, vol. 2937, pp. 44–57. Springer, Heidelberg (2004). doi:10.1007/978-3-540-24622-0_5
15. Leucker, M., Schallhart, C.: A brief account of runtime verification. J. Log. Algebr. Program. **78**(5), 293–303 (2009). The 1st Workshop on Formal Languages and Analysis of Contract-Oriented Software (FLACOS'07)
16. Bauer, A., Leucker, M., Schallhart, C.: Runtime verification for LTL and TLTL. ACM Trans. Softw. Eng. Methodol. **20**(4), 1–64 (2011)
17. Sokolsky, O., Havelund, K., Lee, I.: Introduction to the special section on runtime verification. Int. J. Softw. Tools Technol. Transf. **14**(3), 243–247 (2011)
18. Margaria, T., Steffen, B.: Simplicity as a driver for agile innovation. Computer **43**(6), 90–92 (2010)
19. Margaria, T., Steffen, B.: Continuous model-driven engineering. IEEE Comput. **42**(10), 106–109 (2009)
20. Steffen, B., Margaria, T., Nagel, R., Jörges, S., Kubczak, C.: Model-driven development with the jABC. In: Bin, E., Ziv, A., Ur, S. (eds.) HVC 2006. LNCS, vol. 4383, pp. 92–108. Springer, Heidelberg (2007). doi:10.1007/978-3-540-70889-6_7
21. Neubauer, J., Steffen, B.: Plug-and-play higher-order process integration. IEEE Comput. **46**(11), 56–62 (2013)
22. Neubauer, J., Steffen, B., Margaria, T.: Higher-order process modeling: productlining, variability modeling and beyond. Electr. Proc. Theor. Comput. Sci. **129**, 259–283 (2013)
23. Müller-Olm, M., Schmidt, D., Steffen, B.: Model-checking: a tutorial introduction. In: Cortesi, A., Filé, G. (eds.) SAS 1999. LNCS, vol. 1694, pp. 330–354. Springer, Heidelberg (1999). doi:10.1007/3-540-48294-6_22
24. Steffen, B., Margaria, T., Freitag, B.: Module configuration by minimal model construction. Technical report, Fakultät für Mathematik und Informatik, Universität Passau (1993)

25. Steffen, B., Margaria, T., Braun, V., Kalt, N.: Hierarchical service definition. Ann. Rev. Commun. ACM **51**, 847–856 (1997)
26. Olderog, E.-R., Steffen, B. (eds.): Correct System Design. LNCS, vol. 1710. Springer, Heidelberg (1999)
27. Steffen, B., Margaria, T., Claßen, A., Braun, V.: Incremental formalization. In: Wirsing, M., Nivat, M. (eds.) AMAST 1996. LNCS, vol. 1101, pp. 608–611. Springer, Heidelberg (1996). doi:10.1007/BFb0014354
28. Neubauer, J., Margaria, T., Steffen, B.: Design for verifiability: the OCS case study. In: Formal Methods for Industrial Critical Systems: A Survey of Applications, pp. 153–178. Wiley-IEEE Computer Society Press, March 2013
29. Jonsson, B., Margaria, T., Naeser, G., Nyström, J., Steffen, B.: Incremental requirement specification for evolving systems. Nordic J. Comput. **8**, 65–87 (2001)
30. Lamprecht, A.L., Naujokat, S., Margaria, T., Steffen, B.: Synthesis-based loose programming. In: Proceedings of the 7th International Conference on the Quality of Information and Communications Technology (QUATIC 2010), Porto, Portugal, pp. 262–267. IEEE, September 2010
31. Naujokat, S., Lamprecht, A.-L., Steffen, B.: Loose programming with PROPHETS. In: Lara, J., Zisman, A. (eds.) FASE 2012. LNCS, vol. 7212, pp. 94–98. Springer, Heidelberg (2012). doi:10.1007/978-3-642-28872-2_7
32. Jörges, S., Lamprecht, A.L., Margaria, T., Schaefer, I., Steffen, B.: A constraint-based variability modeling framework. Int. J. Softw. Tools Technol. Transf. (STTT) **14**(5), 511–530 (2012)
33. Lamprecht, A.L., Naujokat, S., Schaefer, I.: Variability management beyond feature models. IEEE Comput. **46**(11), 48–54 (2013)
34. Schaefer, I., Rabiser, R., Clarke, D., Bettini, L., Benavides, D., Botterweck, G., Pathak, A., Trujilol, S., Villela, K.: Software diversity - state of the art and perspectives. Int. J. Softw. Tools Technol. Transf. (STTT) **14**(5), 477–495 (2012)
35. Parr, A.: Industrial Control Handbook, 3rd edn. Newnes, Oxford, Auckland, Boston, Johannesburg, Melbourne, New Delhi (1998)
36. Bolton, W.: Programmable Logic Controllers, 6th edn. Newnes/Elsevier, Amsterdam/Boston (2015)
37. Dittrich, K.R., Gatziu, S., Geppert, A.: The active database management system manifesto: a rulebase of ADBMS features. In: Sellis, T. (ed.) RIDS 1995. LNCS, vol. 985, pp. 1–17. Springer, Heidelberg (1995). doi:10.1007/3-540-60365-4_116
38. Almeida, E.E., Luntz, J.E., Tilbury, D.M.: Event-condition-action systems for reconfigurable logic control. IEEE T. Autom. Sci. Eng. **4**(2), 167–181 (2007)
39. Naujokat, S., Lybecait, M., Kopetzki, D., Steffen, B.: CINCO: A Simplicity-Driven Approach to Full Generation of Domain-Specific Graphical Modeling Tools (2016, to appear)
40. Steffen, B.: Data flow analysis as model checking. In: Ito, T., Meyer, A.R. (eds.) TACS 1991. LNCS, vol. 526, pp. 346–364. Springer, Heidelberg (1991). doi:10. 1007/3-540-54415-1_54
41. Steffen, B.: Generating data flow analysis algorithms from modal specifications. Sci. Comput. Program. **21**(2), 115–139 (1993)
42. Windmüller, S., Neubauer, J., Steffen, B., Howar, F., Bauer, O.: Active continuous quality control. In: 16th International ACM SIGSOFT Symposium on Component-Based Software Engineering, CBSE 2013, pp. 111–120. ACM SIGSOFT, New York (2013)
43. Isberner, M., Howar, F., Steffen, B.: The open-source LearnLib: a framework for active automata learning. In: CAV 2015 (2015)

44. Object Management Group (OMG): Documents Associated with BPMN Version 2.0.1 (2013). http://www.omg.org/spec/BPMN/2.0.1/. Accessed 09 September 2015
45. Jensen, K.: Coloured Petri Nets: Basic Concepts, Analysis Methods and Practical Use, vol. 1, 2nd edn. Springer, Heidelberg (1996)
46. Margaria, T., Steffen, B., Reitenspieß, M.: Service-oriented design: the roots. In: Benatallah, B., Casati, F., Traverso, P. (eds.) ICSOC 2005. LNCS, vol. 3826, pp. 450–464. Springer, Heidelberg (2005). doi:10.1007/11596141_34
47. Erl, T.: SOA: Principles of Service Design. Prentice Hall, Upper Saddle River (2007)
48. Hürsch, W.L., Lopes, C.V.: Separation of concerns. Technical Report NU-CCS-95-03, Northeastern University, Boston, MA, February 1995
49. JetBrains: Meta Programming System. https://www.jetbrains.com/mps/. Accessed 07 April 2016
50. Gronback, R.C.: Eclipse Modeling Project: A Domain-Specific Language (DSL) Toolkit. Addison-Wesley, Boston (2008)
51. Steinberg, D., Budinsky, F., Paternostro, M., Merks, E.: EMF: Eclipse Modeling Framework, 2nd edn. Addison-Wesley, Boston (2008)
52. Eclipse Modeing Framework. http://www.eclipse.org/modeling/emf/
53. Kolovos, D., Rose, L., García-Domínguez, A., Paige, R.: The Epsilon Book (2015). http://eclipse.org/epsilon/doc/book/. Accessed 4 February 2015
54. Epsilon. www.eclipse.org/epsilon/. Accessed 21 May 2014
55. Epsilon EuGENia. http://www.eclipse.org/epsilon/doc/eugenia/. Accessed 21 May 2014
56. Kolovos, D.S., Rose, L.M., Abid, S.B., Paige, R.F., Polack, F.A.C., Botterweck, G.: Taming EMF and GMF using model transformation. In: Petriu, D.C., Rouquette, N., Haugen, Ø. (eds.) MODELS 2010. LNCS, vol. 6394, pp. 211–225. Springer, Heidelberg (2010). doi:10.1007/978-3-642-16145-2_15
57. Spray - a quick way of creating Graphiti. http://code.google.com/a/eclipselabs.org/p/spray/. Accessed 23 April 20014
58. Eclipse Sirius. http://www.eclipse.org/sirius/. Accessed 07 November 2014
59. Grundy, J., Hosking, J., Li, K.N., Ali, N.M., Huh, J., Li, R.L.: Generating domain-specific visual language tools from abstract visual specifications. IEEE Trans. Softw. Eng. 39(4), 487–515 (2013)
60. Marama. https://wiki.auckland.ac.nz/display/csidst/Welcome. Accessed 23 April 2014
61. Zhu, N., Grundy, J., Hosking, J.: Pounamu: a meta-tool for multi-view visual language environment construction. In: 2004 IEEE Symposium on Visual Languages and Human Centric Computing (2004)
62. Kelly, S., Lyytinen, K., Rossi, M.: MetaEdit+ a fully configurable multi-user and multi-tool CASE and CAME environment. In: Constantopoulos, P., Mylopoulos, J., Vassiliou, Y. (eds.) CAiSE 1996. LNCS, vol. 1080, pp. 1–21. Springer, Heidelberg (1996). doi:10.1007/3-540-61292-0_1
63. MetaCase Website. http://www.metacase.com/. Accessed 08 July 2015
64. Kelly, S., Tolvanen, J.P.: Domain-Specific Modeling: Enabling Full Code Generation. Wiley-IEEE Computer Society Press, Hoboken (2008)
65. Kastens, U., Pfahler, P., Jung, M.: The Eli system. In: Koskimies, K. (ed.) CC 1998. LNCS, vol. 1383, pp. 294–297. Springer, Heidelberg (1998). doi:10.1007/BFb0026439

66. Schmidt, C., Cramer, B., Kastens, U.: Generating visual structure editors from high-level specifications. Technical report, University of Paderborn, Germany (2008)
67. Naujokat, S., Neubauer, J., Margaria, T., Steffen, B.: Meta-level reuse for mastering domain specialization. In: Proceedings of the 7th International Symposium on Leveraging Applications of Formal Methods, Verification and Validation (ISoLA 2016) (2016)

Model Patterns

The Quest for the Right Level of Abstraction

Arend Rensink[(✉)]

University of Twente, Enschede, The Netherlands
arend.rensink@utwente.nl

Abstract. We know by now that evolution in software is inevitable. Given that is so, we should not just *allow* for but *accommodate* for change throughout the software lifecycle. The claim of this paper is that, in order to accommodate for change effectively, we need a modelling discipline with a built-in notion of refinement, so that domain concepts can be defined and understood on their appropriate level of abstraction, and change can be captured on that same level. Refinement serves to connect levels of abstraction within the same model, enabling a simultaneous understanding of that same model on different levels. We propose the term *model pattern* for the central concept in such a modelling discipline.

1 Introduction

Though computer science students start with the idea that when they create a new piece of software, then that software will be completed one day, running happily ever after and never to be looked at again, by the time they graduate we hope to have disabused them of that notion. For all sorts of reasons, software is *always* subject to change; the more successful and widely used, the more urgent the need to maintain it, adapt it, extend it, port it. Rather than always promising ourselves that "we will get it right next time" or thinking "we could do so much better if only we could start from scratch", we should accept and embrace that change is an intrinsic facet of software, and accommodate for it from the start.

This paper takes the position that accommodating for change involves finding the right conceptual level at which the change can be understood. This is, of course, the same level as that at which the architecture of the software can itself be understood. It is typically more abstract than the level of the executable code; instead, in this paper we look at (static, structural) models as the right medium to understand the software as well as the changes therein.

The Poverty of Metamodels. We argue that the current modelling formalisms — primarily UML and ECORE — lack machinery to capture the concepts that really make up the software architecture, and we present an idea for improving upon this. The building blocks of the established modelling formalisms are essentially *classifiers* and *associations*. Though we agree that in the end, a model must be refined to that level in order to bridge the gap to executable code, in our

© Springer International Publishing AG 2016
B. Steffen (Ed.): Transactions on FoMaC I, LNCS 9960, pp. 47–70, 2016.
DOI: 10.1007/978-3-319-46508-1_4

opinion there is a need to first express specific, complex structures from the problem domain directly into a model, before completely descending to the level of classifiers and associations. This is where *model patterns* come in.

Model patterns, as defined in the paper, come in several flavours: formal and informal, abstract and concrete. Being formal means to have a mathematically well-defined specification of the intended structure, in addition to an optional implementation in terms of existing metamodel technology; an informal pattern only defines an implementation. Abstract patterns (which are always formal) *only* embody the mathematially defined structure; concrete ones (which can be formal or informal) define an implementation. A concrete pattern implements an abstract one if its conforming (partial) models provide a one-to-one representation of the abstractly defined structure; if the concrete pattern is itself formal, this can be proved once and for all and relied upon when actually applying the pattern.

Model patterns allow one to take a declarative point of view while designing a domain-specific metamodel: rather than immediately choosing a concrete representation, one can first pencil in the abstract pattern and then choose a concrete pattern to implement it. The level on which the abstract patterns are chosen but not yet concretised is then the "right level of abstraction" of the subtitle of this paper, and change can often be understood as replacing one chosen concrete pattern for another that implements the same abstract pattern.

It should be noted that, in the debate of ECORE vs. UML, our models are inspired by the simpler setting of ECORE. In particular, the notion of an association in UML is quite a bit more complex than the corresponding notion in ECORE. The concepts that UML offers natively can, in fact, be captured by model patterns.

Meta versus Math. Though the primary purpose of introducing patterns is to help accommodating change by finding the right level of abstraction, there is a secondary purpose as well: to bridge the gap between "math" and "meta". By the former we refer to the kind of research, sometimes called "formal methods", where new ideas are presented mainly by using mathematical terminology to define structures, transformations and semantics; by the latter we mean the research in model-driven engineering. Though both fields make use of the same terminology (in particular, the word "model" is central in both), we feel that there is a barrier between them through which it is hard to transfer results. In particular, if one wants to turn conceptual results from the "math" sphere into practical implementations using "meta" technology, one of the recurring tasks at hand is to choose appropriate representations, in terms of metamodels, of common mathematical structures such as sequences, functions, powersets and tuples. Model patterns, as presented in this paper, can provide a systematic library of representation choices to support this process.

Because of the position of this paper in the small intersection between math and meta, we have chosen a certain style of presentation which we feel it may be necessary to say something about. This is a conceptual paper, rather than one that presents a concrete implementation. The ideas proposed here can be implemented on top of UML or ECORE by adapting the notions used here to those respective ecosystems. For instance, here we rely directly on first order logic to express constraints over models, whereas in a practical implementation one would probably want to use OCL instead. By staying away from that level of pragmatism, we avoid some issues (involving the semantics of OCL, among other things) that do not have to do with the ideas we propose, and would indeed threaten to hide those ideas.

The target reader of this article is a modelling expert not necessarily familiar with mathematical definitions, but with a precise enough turn of mind to understand and appreciate them. To serve this target group, we have kept the use of mathematical notation (e.g., the feared Greek alphabet) to a minimum (while making sure that there is an unambiguous formalisation backing everything up) and resisted the temptation to keep all names short. Also, we have refrained from formalising all of the concepts we introduce in the paper.

Roadmap. The remainder of the paper is structured as follows: Sect. 2 presents (our take on) the notions of models, constraints and metamodels on which our contribution is based. Section 3 then introduces model patterns, gives a small catalogue of simple patterns, and shows how they can be instantiated and applied in a metamodel. Section 4 discusses metamodel refinement, pattern discovery, and metamodel evolution using patterns. Finally, Sect. 5 evaluates the contributions of this paper, discusses future directions, and revise some related work.

2   Definitions

Throughout this paper, we assume the existence of a well-defined set of identifiers ID. For the sake of simplicity, we do not impose structure on the identifiers; in a more realistic setting, one can think of name spaces to hierarchically group identifiers. As we will see, identifiers are used to stand for a great number of things.

2.1   Models

The reason why metamodels exist at all is that they give rise to a structured set of models (which *conform* to them, in the terminology proposed in [3]), and so characterise the domain of discourse. In mathematical terms, the relation between a metamodel and its conforming models is exactly the relation between a language and its sentences.

Given that, in our view, the set of conforming models of a metamodel is its supremely important aspect, we concentrate first on properly defining the concept of a model. We take a very liberal view of models: they are essentially nothing but graphs, i.e., (labelled) nodes connected by (labelled) edges. As nodes we allow data values as well as more complex, user-defined entities; this means that attributes (edges to data values) are treated in much the same fashion as associations (edges to other user-defined nodes).

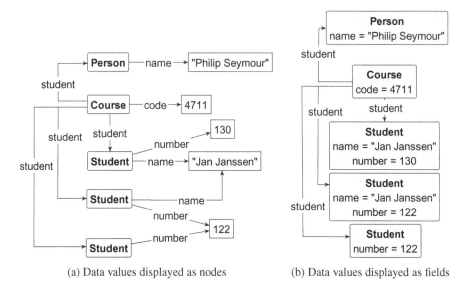

(a) Data values displayed as nodes (b) Data values displayed as fields

Fig. 1. Example model, in two distinct versions of concrete syntax

Definition 1 (model). *A model consists of*

- Node: *A finite set of nodes. We will use n (with sub- and superscripts) as a meta-variable to stand for elements of* Node.
- type: *A labelling function from* Node *to* ID, *associating a node type* type(n) *with every node n.*
- Edge: *A set of triples* $\langle n_1, lab, n_2 \rangle$ *consisting of source node* n_1, *edge label lab (an identifier from* ID*) and target node* n_2.

An example model is displayed in Fig. 1. Node-inscribed labels are node types.

Note that we put no restriction whatsoever on the nature of the elements of Node. As stated above and seen in the example, in particular data values may serve as model nodes; the type-function then yields the corresponding data type. In Fig. 1a we have left out the type inscription of nodes corresponding to data values and instead depicted the values themselves as node labels; however, in Definition 1 such nodes do not have any special status. In any case, one very important aspect of a node is its *identity*, as distinct from its *content*.

The identity of a node is that which distinguishes it from other nodes. For data value nodes, the identity *is* the value (there are no two distinct strings "Jan Janssen", for instance) whereas other nodes may have an external identity assigned at the time of their creation, whose precise value or representation is irrelevant except insofar it keeps nodes apart (there may very well be two *persons* called "Jan Janssen": that value is not their identity). For instance, at run-time the memory address of an object plays the role of node identity, yet the precise value of that address is irrelevant and may very well change as a result of compaction.

The content of a node consists of the information we can access and use. For data value nodes, this coincides with their identity, but for other nodes the content consists of the set of nodes that it has a relation to, in the form of outgoing edges. For instance, in the model of Fig. 1, the content of the **Course**-node consists of its code and the three associated students; the content of the **Person**-nodes consists of their respective names.

It is precisely the fact that, for data nodes, the identity coincides with the content which allows us to use the traditional alternative concrete syntax in Fig. 1b in which edges to data values are inscribed in the nodes.

It should be noted that, though liberal, models as defined in Definition 1 do not offer a lot of structure. Edges are just labelled pairs of nodes, which can easily be understood as records (by combining all outgoing edges of a node) and offer a straightforward encoding of pointers (essentially, edges are nothing but), but there is no notion of collections, lists, maps or other structures that are commonplace in programming languages. Instead, as we will see in the sequel, such structures are typically *encoded*.

2.2   Constraints

In any given concrete application, the models that make sense are typically subject to a lot of constraints imposed by the domain. Such constraints can be formulated in logic. In this paper we choose to use a variant very close to predicate logic, with notations adapted somewhat to make them more reader-friendly, for those not versed in logic. However, we would like to stress that the choice of logic or notation is coincidental to the main idea proposed in this paper; if preferred, one could substitute OCL without any conceptual changes.

Our constraints are first of all built upon expressions, which stand for sets of nodes. Expressions take one of the following forms:

- T, for any identifier T used as node type: The set of all nodes whose type is T or a subtype of T (the notion of subtype will be explained later).
- x, for any node variable x: The singleton set consisting only of the node x.
- E.*lab*, where E is a sub-expression and *lab* an identifier used as edge label: The set of all nodes reachable through a *lab*-labelled edge from a node in E.

Given such expressions, our constraint logic offers the following predicates and combinators:

- E_1 subsetof E_2: The nodes in the set E_1 are all also in the set E_2.
- isempty(E): The set E contains no elements.
- forall x in E : $C(x)$: All elements in the set E satisfy the constraint C (in which the variable x refers to the E-element in question).
- exists x in E : $C(x)$: There is at least one element in the set E that satisfies the constraint C (in which the variable x refers to the E-element in question).
- unique x in E : $C(x)$: There is precisely one element in the set E that satisfies the constraint C (in which the variable x refers to the E-element in question).

Furthermore, constraints can be combined using the usual logical connectives or, and, implies, not and iff (for "if and only if").

For instance, in the setting of Fig. 1 one may formulate the following constraints:

1. forall x in **Course** : x.student subsetof **Student**, expressing that every target of a student-edge from a **Course**-node is a **Student**-node.
2. forall x in **Student** : not isempty(x.name), expressing that every **Student**-node has a name-attribute.
3. forall x, y in **Student** : x.number $=$ y.number implies $x = y$, expressing that no two distinct **Student**s may have the same set of numbers. (In fact, we also expect that every student has exactly one number; however, that is not expressed by this constraint.)
4. forall x in **Student** : exists y in **Course** : x subsetof y.student, expressing that every **Student** is a student of at least one **Course**.

The essential point about a constraint is that it divides the universe of models into those that *satisfy* it and those that do not. There is a straightforward formal definition of satisfaction, but here we will assume that the concepts we have defined are familiar or straightforward enough so that we can skip that definition.

For instance, the model of Fig. 1 does not satisfy the first three example constraints above (there is a student-edge from a **Course** to a **Person**; there is a nameless **Student**; and there are two **Student**s with number 122) but it does satisfy the last.

In (meta)modelling, certain families of constraints are very common; so much so that (in graphically depicted metamodels) many of them have their own shorthand notation, as we will see. Some well-known examples of such families of constraints are:

$$\text{OutMult}^1[lab] \equiv \text{forall } x : \text{unique } y : y \text{ subsetof } x.lab$$

$$\text{InMult}^{0..1}[lab] \equiv \text{forall } y : (\text{not exists } x : y \text{ subsetof } x.lab)$$
$$\text{or } (\text{unique } x : y \text{ subsetof } x.lab)$$

$$\text{Opposite}[lab_1, lab_2] \equiv \text{forall } x, y : (y \text{ subsetof } x.lab_1 \text{ iff } x \text{ subsetof } y.lab_2)$$

$$\text{Singleton}[T] \equiv \text{unique } x : x \text{ subsetof } T$$

$$\text{Key}[lab_1, lab_2, \ldots] \equiv \forall x, y : (x.lab_1 = y.lab_2 \text{ and } x.lab_2 = y.lab_2 \text{ and } \ldots)$$
$$\text{implies } x = y$$

$\text{OutMult}^1[lab]$ expresses that lab-labelled edges have an outgoing multiplicity of 1. Likewise, $\text{InMult}^{0..1}[lab]$ restricts the incoming multiplicity of lab-labelled edges to either 0 or 1. This list is not complete: there are, several more very common multiplicity constraints, and all of them can be applied to incoming as well as outgoing edges. For instance, Constraint 2 above corresponds to $\text{OutMult}^{1..*}[name]$ and Constraint 4 to $\text{InMult}^{1..*}[student]$.

$\text{Opposite}[lab_1, lab_2]$ states that, whenever there is an edge (n_1, lab_1, n_2) in a graph, there must be an edge (n_2, lab_2, n_1) in the opposite direction, and vice versa. $\text{Singleton}[T]$ states that there is precisely one T-labelled node in the graph.

Finally, Key[lab_1, lab_2, ...] (the notation is meant to suggest that the Key-predicate can be used with an arbitrary positive number of parameters) states that the combined targets of the outgoing lab_i-edges ($i = 1, 2, ...$) together determine the identity of a node. This relates back to the earlier discussion about identity versus content: a Key-predicate can be used to specify that the identity of a node is entirely determined by a specific part of its content.

2.3 Metamodels

We insist on making a sharp distinction between the definition of metamodels and their (graphical) representation. An important place where this distinction shows up is that our metamodels include a set of constraints, of the form discussed above, some of which have a native graphical syntax whereas others do not; nevertheless, formally we treat all of them in the same way. When depicting metamodels graphically, though, we will make use of the well-known graphical conventions.

For the purpose of the following definition, we let Data stand for the set of primitive data types. In the context of this paper, we fix Data to consist only of **Boolean, Integer** and **String**. As a reminder, we add the stereotype «datatype» whenever we depict these types graphically.

Definition 2 (metamodel). *A metamodel consists of the following components:*

- Type: *A finite set of user-defined node types, which is a subset of* ID *disjoint from* Data. *We will use T as a meta-variable to stand for elements of* Type *or* Data.
- sub: *a subtype relation over types, consisting of pairs of elements of* Type *that impose an irreflexive partial order over* Type. *The latter means that subtyping is transitive (if T_1 sub T_2 and T_2 sub T_3 then T_1 sub T_3) and irreflexive (there is no type T such that T sub T).*
- assoc : *A function that assigns to every type T a partial map* assoc$_T$ *from association names (which are* IDs*) to target types (elements of* Type *or* Data*). If T_1 sub T_2, then* assoc$_{T_1}$(lab) = assoc$_{T_2}$(lab) *for all lab in the domain of* assoc$_{T_2}$.
- Constr: *a set of constraints, in which all occurring node type identifiers are elements of* Type *or* Data.

Note that the definition above speaks of *subtypes*. This is subtly different from the usual notion of *inheritance* (or *extension*) in that the latter stands for *direct* subtyping. We will sometimes use sub$^=$ to denote the reflexive closure of sub.

There is a limitation in Definition 2 in that subtypes may not redefine associations with a label already occurring in any of their supertypes: instead, they inherit all associations from their supertypes. For practical purposes this does not actually impose a restriction, since one may always prepend association names with their source types, and so disambiguate them.

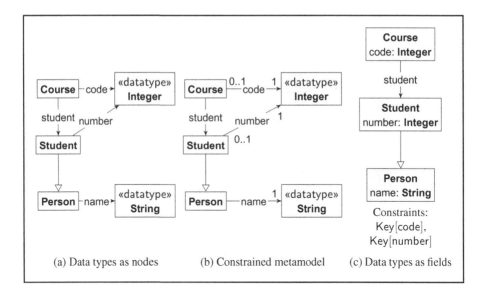

(a) Data types as nodes   (b) Constrained metamodel   (c) Data types as fields

Fig. 2. Example metamodels, in two distinct versions of concrete syntax

An example metamodel, without constraints, is given in Fig. 2a. We have adopted the well-known graphical convention of using open triangular arrows to represent extension, and labelled open-arrowed edges to represent associations. The set of types is given by **Course**, **Student** and **Person**, with subtype relation **Student** sub **Person**. The associations are given by:

$$\text{assoc }_{\textbf{Course}} = (\text{code} \mapsto \textbf{Integer}, \text{student} \mapsto \textbf{Student})$$
$$\text{assoc }_{\textbf{Person}} = (\text{name} \mapsto \textbf{String})$$
$$\text{assoc }_{\textbf{Student}} = (\text{name} \mapsto \textbf{String}, \text{number} \mapsto \textbf{Integer})$$

A reasonable (though incomplete) set of constraints is given by 2–4 in Sect. 2.2 above. We will see below that Constraint 1 is actually superfluous, since it is already enforced by the association definition of assoc $_{\textbf{Course}}$.

We started this section by stating that the *raison d'etre* of metamodels is that they define a set of conforming models as their extension. We are now in a position to formally define that notion of conformance.

Definition 3 (conformance). *A model is said to* conform *to a metamodel if all of the following hold:*

1. type(n) *is an element of* Type *or* Data *for all nodes n (meaning that nodes are labelled with metamodel types or data types)*
2. assoc $_{\text{type}(n_1)}(lab)$ sub$^=$ type(n_2) *for all edges (n_1, lab, n_2) (meaning that model edges must always correspond to an association defined in the metamodel, and the target node type must be a subtype of the type declared in the metamodel).*

3. The model satisfies all constraints in Constr.

For instance, the model of Fig. 1 does *not* conform to the metamodel of Fig. 2 augmented with the Constraints 2–4 of Sect. 2.2, for the following reasons:

– The condition in Definition 3.2 does not hold: there is a student-edge from a **Course**-node to a **Person**-node which really should go to a **Student**-node.
– The condition in Definition 3.3 does not hold: Constraints 2 and 3 are not satisfied (as remarked before).

A variation of this metamodel, with the same node and edge types but a more complete set of constraints, is given in Fig. 2b. Figure 2c also depicts this adapted metamodel, using a more conventional graphical syntax for data type-valued associations, which here are shown as fields inscribed in their source type nodes. This notation carries some implicit constraints: for every field *lab* : *T* appearing in such a metamodel, OutMult^1[*lab*] is implied. On the the hand, since these associations are no longer depicted as edges, we cannot directly represent the multiplicity constraints InMult$^{0..1}$[number] and InMult$^{0..1}$[student] in this notation; they are therefore given explicitly in the form of (equivalent) Key-constraints.[1]

3 Patterns

We now come to the core new concept of this paper, that of a model pattern. A pattern can be instantiated (invoked) any number of times in a metamodel. We propose to develop a library of pattern types with known refinement relations between them, so that metamodel evolution can be captured in terms of the replacement of one pattern type by another that is known to refine it, or at least (if pure refinement is not possible) to stand in a well-understood relation to it.

Definition 4 (pattern). *A pattern consists of*

– *A pattern signature, which is a combination of a pattern name (an element of* ID*) and a non-empty sequence* sort *of unique formal parameter names (elements of* ID*), the elements of which stand for types.*
– *An optional specification, being a mathematical description of the structure represented by the pattern, in terms of elements of the types in* sort. *This specification may make use of all the commonly understood machinery of mathematics, including functions, relations, powerset constructions, auxiliary types, and logical constraints.*
– *An optional implementation, being a metamodel such that each of the elements of* sort *are members of* Type, *and one of the elements of* sort *is a designated handle.*
– *If both specification and implementation are given, a proof of correctness. This proof should show that (a) all models conforming to the implementation satisfy the specification, and (b) all structures satisfying the specification can be unambiguously represented as models of the implementation.*

---

[1] In UML, one may denote this constraint by adding a suffix "{id}" behind the field declaration, as in "code: **Integer** {id}".

If a specification is given, we call the pattern *formal*, otherwise it is *informal*; if an implementation is given, we call the pattern *concrete*, otherwise it is *abstract*. Either the specification or the implementation must be given: abstract informal patterns are not allowed.

The *handle* will come into play when we discuss pattern instantiation: see Sect. 3.2 below. When depicting concrete patterns, we distinguish the handle by shading it gray.

3.1 Example Patterns

We will give a small set of sample patterns for frequently occurring situations, to illustrate the concept and give some intuition about where and how it can be used.

Designated Elements. It may happen that we want to globally mark a single element in a model as being special; for instance, the root of a tree. Mathematically, such a designated element is sometimes called a *point*. We can define this in the form of a pattern as follows:

– Pattern signature: *Point*⟨**T**⟩
– Pattern specification: **T** (i.e., the set **T** itself)

There is a number of ways to implement this: for instance, the designated element can have a boolean attribute set to true (there must then also be a constraint that only one **T**-element may have the value true for that attribute), or the designated element can be pointed to from a singleton type. These two implementations are depicted in Fig. 3.

Subsets. A subset is needed whenever we want to distinguish or select some of the elements of a given existing type. For instance, in our running example, we might want to distinguish the MSc-students from the others. First we give the formal abstract pattern for subsets:

– Pattern signature: *Set*⟨**T**⟩
– Pattern specification: $2^{\mathbf{T}}$ (the powerset of **T**)

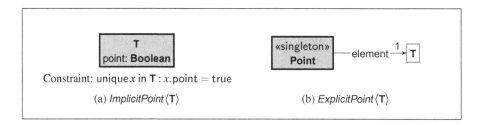

Fig. 3. Concrete patterns for designated elements (abstract pattern *Point*)

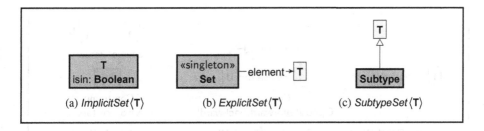

Fig. 4. Concrete patterns for subsets

Sets can be implemented in at least three obvious ways: by adding a boolean attribute to the sort **T**, by creating a singleton class with a set-valued association to **T**, or by introducing a subtype of **T**. These implementations are captured by distinct concrete patterns: *ImplicitSet*, *ExplicitSet* and *SubtypeSet*. Each of these has the same specification as *Set*, but a different implementation, depicted in Fig. 4.

As proofs of correctness for these three implementations, we offer the following.

– For *ImplicitSet*, the set elements are given by All x in **T** : x.isin = true. Clearly, any subset of **T** can be unambiguously represented in this way. (Essentially, *ImplicitSet* is a representation of the so-called characteristic function of a subset.)
– For *ExplicitSet*, the set elements are given by x.element, where x is the unique element of **Set**. The constraint Singleton[**Set**] guarantees that there is indeed such a unique element. Clearly, any subset of **T** can be unambiguously represented in this way.
– For *SubtypeSet*, the set elements are given by **Subtype**; by Definition 3, this is a subset of **T**. Clearly, any subset of **T** can be unambiguously represented in this way.

It should be noted that this pattern models a single, global set, and *not* a set associated with some other object. If, instead, one wants to model a set of **B**-objects associated with every **A**-object (such as, for instance, the set of **Student**s associated with every **Course** in our running example) this requires a set-valued function or relation, rather than a global set; see below.

Relations. Relations are more complicated than sets, in that they involve two types (source and target) rather than just one. From a mathematical standpoint, they are straightforward: the formal abstract pattern is given by

– Pattern signature: *Rel*⟨**T**, **U**⟩ (where **T** is the source type and **U** the target type).
– Pattern specification: $2^{T \times U}$ (the powerset of the cartesian product of **T** and **U**)

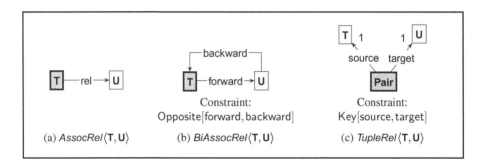

Fig. 5. Concrete patterns for relations

In this case, there are two bases for concrete implementing patterns: an ordinary association, or a relation class essentially consisting of a set of tuples. Those are shown in Fig. 5, together with a variation upon the first of the two involding an opposite edge, in case one would want to find the set of related **T**-elements from a given **U**-element.

The proof of correctness of *AssocRel* is straightforward, since the set of edge instances of rel precisely encodes a relation.

- For *TupleRel*, the relation is given by the set of $\langle n_1, n_2 \rangle$ for which there is an x in **Pair** such that $\langle x, \text{source}, n_1 \rangle$ and $\langle x, \text{target}, n_2 \rangle$ are edges. Vice versa, given a relation, for every $\langle n_1, n_2 \rangle$ contained in it, one can construct a **Pair**-labelled node with outgoing source- and target-edges to n_1 and n_2. The Key-constraint guarantees that this encoding is unambiguous (up to the choice of identity of the **Pair**-nodes, which however is completely determined by the source- and target-edges).

Predicates. Mathematically, tuples are nothing but sequences of values from a fixed number of sets. Thus, we can speak of n-tuples for any natural number n. Special cases are:

- $n = 0$, in which case there is just one value, the empty 0-tuple; this does not correspond to a very useful pattern.
- $n = 1$, in which case the tuples are just single elements of the single set over which the tuples are formed; hence the abstract tuple pattern over a type **T** corresponds to the pattern *Set*$\langle \textbf{T} \rangle$ discussed above.
- $n = 2$, in which case the tuples are pairs, i.e., elements of a binary relation between the two sets over which the tuples are formed; hence the abstract tuple pattern over types **T** and **U** corresponds precisely to the pattern *Rel*$\langle \textbf{T}, \textbf{U} \rangle$ discussed above.

Extending to higher values of n, we can express higher-arity relationships or *predicates* — which is a term borrowed from logic, where a n-ary predicate can be equated with the set of n-tuples that satisfy it. For predicates there is again a range of possible implementations. In any case, we need a special tuple type

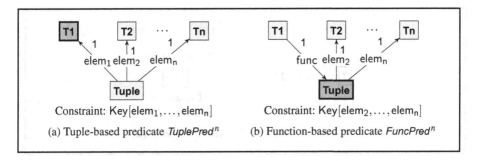

Fig. 6. Formal concrete patterns for $Pred^n$

with outgoing edges to its constituent sets. One may choose to include any of the opposite edges as well, or turn the predicate into a function from its first element.

– Pattern signature: $Pred^n\langle \mathbf{T}_1, \ldots, \mathbf{T}_n\rangle$ (with $n > 2$)
– Pattern specification: $2^{\mathbf{T}_1 \times \mathbf{T}_2 \times \cdots \times \mathbf{T}_n}$ (which is equivalent to $\mathbf{T}_1 \rightarrow 2^{\mathbf{T}_2 \times \cdots \times \mathbf{T}_n}$)
– Pattern implementations: See Fig. 6

Functions. Functions are essentially a restriction of relations, where every element in of the source type is related to precisely one elements in the target type. Mathematically, this makes them even simpler than relations.

– Pattern signature: $Func\langle \mathbf{T}, \mathbf{U}\rangle$
– Pattern specification: $\mathbf{T} \rightarrow \mathbf{U}$ (the function space from $\mathbf{T}$ to $\mathbf{U}$)

The concrete implementing patterns are also closely related to those for relations: either one may use a single-valued association (i.e., with outgoing multiplicity 1), or a map class essentially consisting of a set of tuples, where with respect to *TupleRel* one has to constrain the source arrows to be unique, i.e., to have incoming multiplicity 1.

The correctness proof obligations are a minor variation on those for relations and omitted here.

There are a number of relevant variations on the concept of a function, which we will not treat here in detail but which can be modelled in very similar ways:

– *Injective* functions *InjFunc*, which have the property that for any element of the target type, there is at most one element of the source type that maps to it. This can be captured in the implementation by adding an $\mathsf{InMult}^{0..1}$-constraint to func (Fig. 7a) or target (Fig. 7b).
– *Partial* functions *PartFunc*, which have the property that not every element of the source type has an associated element of the target type. This can be captured in the implementation by relaxing the $\mathsf{OutMult}^1$-constraint of func to $\mathsf{OutMult}^{0..1}$ (Fig. 7a) or doing the same for source (Fig. 7b).

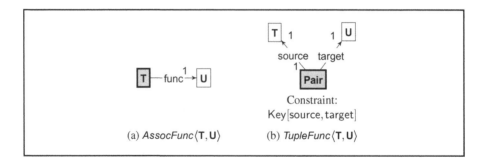

Fig. 7. Concrete patterns for functions

Sequence-Valued Functions. The last category of patterns we discuss here are those that involve (in common metamodel terminology) an *ordered* association from one type to another. Here we pay the price of the structural simplicity (one might say poverty) of our models, which have no in-built notion of ordering.

The formal abstract pattern is straightfoward:

– Pattern signature: *SeqFunc*⟨**T**, **U**⟩
– Pattern specification: **T** → **U*** (the function space from **T** to sequences of **U**)

When choosing an implementation, we are facing well-known issues: (a) Should we use special linking edges or indices to encode the ordering? (b) Should we introduce special nodes to carry the ordering information or integrate it into the existing (target) nodes? (c) Should we mark the start and finish of a list? To demonstrate the range of possibilities, in Figs. 8 and 9 we show four implementing patterns.

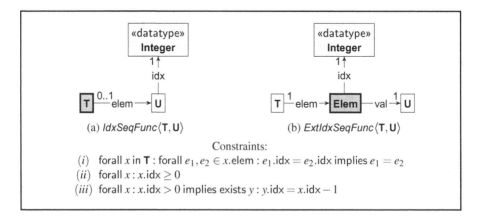

Fig. 8. Index-based concrete patterns for sequence-valued functions

Figure 8 shows two concrete indexed-based patterns, one in which the ordering structure (i.e., the index) is added to the target type and one in which it is put on a separate intermediate node type especially introduced for this purpose. The first solution is appropriate if no **U**-node can be in more than one list of this kind (as indicated by the incoming multiplicity of the elem-edge).

There are a number of non-trivial constraints associated with both of these patterns:

(i) This expresses that the identity of a list node is determined by its containing **T**-node in combination with its index. The effect is that no two nodes in the same list can have the same index.

(ii) This expresses that list indices are non-negative numbers.

(iii) This expresses that list indices form a consecutive sequence. In combination with Constraint (ii), it completely fixes the indices used for a list of n elements to $0, \ldots, n-1$. This is necessary to ensure the unambiguous encoding of a sequence in these concrete patterns.

Figure 9 shows two concrete link-based patterns; the difference is again that in one case the next-links are part of the target type **U**, making this solution suitable only if an **U**-node may appear in no more than one list of this kind, whereas the other, heavier-weight solution uses a dedicated intermediate node type. There are again some constraints involved:

(i) Each list should have a unique first element.

(ii) A list element is first if and only if there is no other list element with a next-pointer to it.

Multi-Parameter Functions. We cannot be comprehensive in this paper. A final important pattern, which we just briefly discuss here, is that of a function with two or more parameters — which can equivalently be seen as a function (of the first parameter) yielding a function (of the second parameter). The abstract pattern is:

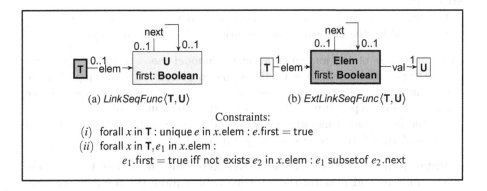

Fig. 9. Link-based concrete patterns for sequence-valued functions

– Pattern signature: $BinFunc\langle \mathbf{T}, \mathbf{U}, \mathbf{V} \rangle$
– Pattern specification: $(\mathbf{T} \times \mathbf{U}) \to \mathbf{V}$; or equivalently $\mathbf{T} \to (\mathbf{U} \to \mathbf{V})$

The equivalent formulations of the specification already suggest distinct directions of implementation. An intermediate type is almost unavoidable in this case. In fact, pattern *ExtIdxSeqFunc* in Fig. 8b can alternatively be seen as an implementation of $BinFunc\langle \mathbf{T}, \mathbf{Integer}, \mathbf{U} \rangle$. Qualified associations in UML are essentially also a way to implement the multi-parameter function pattern.

3.2 Pattern Instantiation

Patterns may be *instantiated* on top of a given metamodel.

Definition 5 (pattern instance). *Given a metamodel, a* pattern instance *consists of*

– *A pattern instance name (an element of* ID*)*
– *The name of the instantiated pattern together with an argument list, being a sequence of type and pattern instance names from the metamodel, of length equal to the* sort *of the pattern.*
– *If the instantiated pattern is concrete, an optional substitution of the identifiers used in the pattern implementation by identifiers to be used in the pattern instance.*

The substitution specified in the last item is necessary to ensure unambiguous naming: the names in the pattern implementation may overlap with the names already in the model, and so the former must be renamed to be able to merge the pattern implementation with the metamodel.

A *patterned metamodel* is a metamodel with (abstract or concrete) pattern instances. A pattern instance can be visualised in a given metamodel by (essentially) a labelled hyperedge connecting the arguments of the pattern instance, and labelled by the pattern name. Such a hyperedge can alternatively be thought of as a special node. For instance, consider Fig. 10: here the oval nodes are instantiated patterns.

A concrete pattern instance i occurring in a metamodel mm can be *applied* by replacing it by the pattern implementation, in the following way:

1. Create a copy of the implementation metamodel mm_i, replacing the parameter types in the definition by the actual arguments of i and applying the optional substitution of i. If an actual argument of i is a pattern instance (rather than a type), use the handle of that pattern instance.
2. Add the instantiated metamodel to mm. During this step, by the nature of metamodels, different copies of any given type are merged.

For instance, if we thus substitute the concrete patterns in Fig. 10b by their implementations and perform the intended substitution, the result is precisely the metamodel in Fig. 2 that we started with.

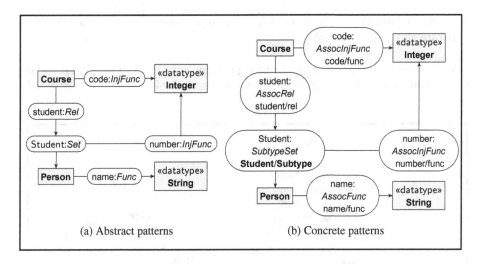

Fig. 10. Patterned metamodel

4   Usage Scenarios

Our claim is that one can benefit from the use of model patterns both when developing new metamodels and when updating existing ones to accommodate changes; and that the latter also applies if the metamodel was not initially pattern-based.

4.1   Refinement

With refinement we mean fleshing out and extending a metamodel, while keeping to the constraints that were imposed before. In other words, when a metamodel mm_1 is refined to a metamodel mm_2, every model of mm_2, when restricted to the node types and edge labels already occurring in mm_1, is a model of mm_1.

Model patterns can help in refinement because choices can be deferred: rather than selecting an concrete implementation from the start, one may first go with

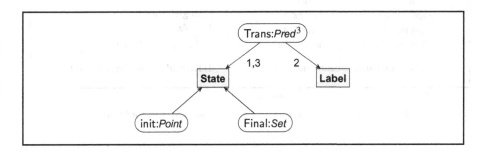

Fig. 11. Abstract patterned metamodel of an automaton

an abstract pattern and later on select an appropriate concrete one. We will illustrate this on an example.

Modelling an Automaton. The example problem is to model the concept of an automaton. Let us assume that we have a mathematical interpretation at hand.

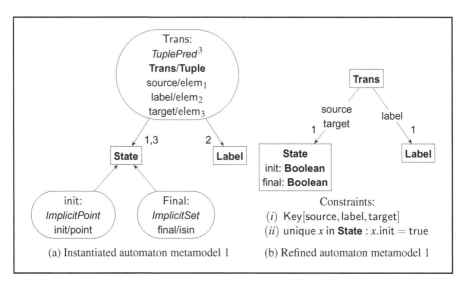

(a) Instantiated automaton metamodel 1   (b) Refined automaton metamodel 1

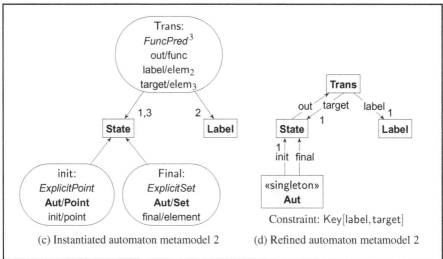

(c) Instantiated automaton metamodel 2   (d) Refined automaton metamodel 2

Fig. 12. Concrete instantiations of the automaton metamodel

Definition 6 (automaton). *An automaton consists of*

- State: *a set of states;*
- Label: *a set of labels;*
- Trans: *a set of transitions, being triples* $\langle q_0, lab, q_1 \rangle$ *consisting of a source state* q_0 *(from* State*), label lab (from* Label*) and target state* q_1 *(from* State*);*
- init: *an initial state (an element of* State*);*
- Final: *a set of final states (a subset of* State*).*

Using the abstract patterns presented in Sect. 3, we can immediately give a corresponding (patterned) metamodel: see Fig. 11.

Refinement is now a matter of choosing concrete implementations of these patterns. Two examples are shown in Fig. 12.

4.2   Discovery

With "discovery" we mean the process of identifying patterns in an existing, unpatterned metamodel. The process of instantiation discussed in the previous section is a *forward* application of a pattern. However, the instantiation rule may as well be inverted. That is, given an unpatterned metamodel *mm* and a library of concrete patterns, one can *pattern match* (in another use of the word pattern) the implementations of the concrete patterns in *mm*, to find places where the structure of the metamodel suggests a pattern.

For instance, in the example metamodel in Fig. 2b we can recognise instances of *ExplicitSet*, *AssocInjFunc* (twice)[2] and *AssocFunc*. By replacing the corresponding fragments of the metamodel with instances of those concrete patterns, one can (semi-)automatically derive the concrete patterned metamodel of Fig. 10b.

Essentially, therefore, pattern discovery is the process of reconstructing the semantics of a metamodel from its low-level structure. Obviously, this process cannot be fully automatic: any existing metamodel will have many potential instances of patterns. A domain expert will have to be involved to reconstruct the originally intended semantics, by selecting the most appropriate of those potential patterns. Proper tool support is needed to make this a viable, useful step.

We see pattern discovery as a great tool especially to refactor existing, legacy (meta)models.

4.3   Evolution and Migration

The motivation for this paper was *accommodating for change*. In the context of model-driven engineering, change means evolution of metamodels, in most cases accompanied by migration of existing models.

It is here that model patterns yield their greatest benefits. Given a sufficiently large library of (abstract and concrete) patterns, it is possible to *a priori* establish (and prove!) allowed substitutions of one pattern by another. Moreover, the required migration is also implied.

---

[2] The absract and concrete patterns for injective functions were omitted from Sect. 3.1.

In our modest current setting, such allowed substitutions are already present in the form of alternative implementations of the same abstract pattern. As an example, consider the following scenario pertaining to the metamodel of Fig. 2b:

Evolving the Student Metamodel. Suppose that we realise that it was not a good idea to distinguish the subset of students by turning them into a subtype of **Person**: for now it becomes hard for anyone to change his status from **Person** to **Student** and back. Instead, we want to encode the set of students through a boolean flag in the class **Person**.

In terms of the patterned metamodel in Fig. 10 (which could either be present already if the metamodel was developed through refinement, as advocated in Sect. 4.1, or could alternatively be discovered, as discussed in Sect. 4.2), this change is a matter of choosing another implementation for the Student-pattern. For instance, instead of *SubtypeSet* we could choose *ImplicitSet*, with substitution isStudent/isin. The resulting metamodel is shown in Fig. 13, together with an (automatically) migrated model conforming to the original metamodel to a model conforming to the evolved one.

Note that the handle of the new Student : *ImplicitSet* pattern is the argument type **Person**, meaning that also the number-attribute automatically migrates

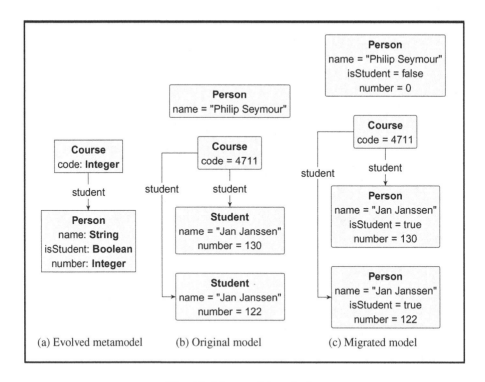

Fig. 13. Metamodel evolution

to **Person**. Thus, in the resulting metamodel, shown in Fig. 13, *all* persons have a number, but it is meaningful only for those for which the isStudent-flag is true.

5   Conclusion

5.1   Evaluation

This paper represents an initial attempt to formalise the notion of patterns. For that reason, rather than trying to be comprehensive and all-encompassing, we have simplified our setting sufficiently to expose the underlying ideas of patterns in a self-contained manner. Those simplifications show up in the stripped-down notions of models, constraints and metamodels, which we have chosen rather than going straight for ECORE or UML.

To summarise, the main benefits expected from patterns are:

- Commonly occurring implementation structures can be catalogued as patterns, while simultaneously capturing their intended semantics.
- Implementation relations can be defined between patterns and (if the patterns are formal) proved formally, enabling correctness by construction.
- Metamodel development, especially when occurring on the basis of existing mathematical definitions, can be eased by deferring the choice of concrete pattern implementations.
- Metamodel evolution can be understood as replacing one concrete pattern instance by another, typically implementing the same abstact pattern. Such replacement steps can be composed, and the corresponding correct model migration is automatically implied.
- Existing metamodels can be subjected to pattern discovery, bringing the benefits of pattern-based evolution also to legacy models.

Using two running examples, we have built a case for the potential of model patterns to eventually reap those benefits, but there is no denying that there is much work to be done before that potential is realised.

Behavioural Models. As remarked in the introduction, in this paper we have restricted ourselves to structural models only. This is, perhaps, misleading as it could strengthen the impression that model-driven engineering is mostly about (data) structures. That is very far from the truth: behavioural models are very widely used in business process modelling [1], and are also reaching the stage where they are as successful in specifying language semantics as structural models are in specifying their syntax: see [13] for an example.

5.2   Future Work

Pattern Library. The example patterns in this paper are actually still quite rudimentary, involving a few types at the most. One of the upcoming challenges will be to create a larger catalogue of more involved, but nevertheless generic patterns.

In Definition 4, we have defined patterns such that their specification is only optional, but in this paper we have actually only discussed patterns that indeed do have a specification; i.e., formal patterns. We believe that informal patterns are nevertheless a useful mechanism to encapsulate commonly occurring meta-model structures, without imposing the requirement to capture that structure in mathematical terms.

Dynamics of Models. We have here entirely ignored the *manipulation* of models — or in other words, the operations typically defined in a metamodel and (the specification of) their intended effect on the models.

Actually, the setup lends itself quite well to an extension with operations. They, too, can be specified formally, on the same level as the current pattern specification, and implemented concretely, for instance through model transformation definitions that work on the pattern implementation. The benefit of *a priori* proving that one pattern implements another can then easily be extended to operations as well.

As a small example, consider adding an element to a set. This is a well-defined operation in the specification of *Set*; in *ImplicitSet* it is a matter of setting the isin-field of the added **T**-element to true; in *ExplicitSet* one should create a new element of **Subset** with an element-edge to the added **T**-element; and in *SubtypeSet* addition is not well possible as this would require changing the runtime type of an object. (This is, in essence, the reason brought forward in Sect. 4.3 against using the *SubtypeSet*-pattern for modelling **Student**s.)

Validation. As the saying goes, the proof of the pudding is in the eating. At the moment of writing, this falls into the category of "future work." In the case of model patterns, validation should consist of

- Developing metamodels from scratch on the basis of patterns (as proposed in Sect. 4.1), or discovering patterns in existing metamodels (as proposed in Sect. 4.2).
- Breaking down existing examples of metamodel evolution in terms of pattern substitutions, as proposed in Sect. 4.3.

5.3   Related Work

This work has its roots in an attempt to formalise the semantics of UML class diagrams, started in [8]. However, we are neither the first nor the foremost to have worked on this: other approaches, with varying degree of comprehensiveness and formality, can be found in [2, 4, 14, 16, 17]. Is is, moreover, clear that no such approach can be complete without including first-order logic, mostly (and in the context of model-driven engineering naturally) on the basis of OCL, for which formal foundations have been studied in [5, 6, 9].

Obviously, a major source of inspiration has been the successful concept of *design pattern* promoted in [7] and a long chain of follow-up work. In contrast to our model patterns, however, design patterns are primarily behavioural (even the category called structural design patterns); together with our focus on model-driven engineering, this gives the current paper quite distinct aims and scope.

When it comes to model *transformation*, the idea of introducing patterns has been studied in [11] (pertaining to patterns in the model transformations themselves) and [10] (lifting this to model transformation *definitions*). Especially the first of these has a connection to our notion of model patterns and their potential use in transformation: if we can a priori prove semantic relationships between patterns, then repeatedly replacing an instance of one pattern by an instance of another is a way to synthesise correct-by-construction model transformations.

[12] introduces the notion of the *intent* of a model transformation, and derives properties as well as transformation themselves on this basis. It also proposes to establish a catalogue of such intents. However, there is no formalisation of intents along the lines of our pattern formalisation.

Finally, the idea of introducing patterns into model-driven engineering has recently inspired a workshop [15], which has, however, unfortunately not resulted in a written proceedings.

References

1. Aguilar-Saven, R.S.: Business process modelling: review and framework. Int. J. Prod. Econ. **90**(2), 129–149 (2004)
2. Atkinson, C., Kühne, T.: Model-driven development: a metamodeling foundation. IEEE Softw. **20**(5), 36–41 (2003)
3. Bézivin, J.: On the unification power of models. Softw. Syst. Model. **4**(2), 171–188 (2005)
4. Bézivin, J., Gerbé, O.: Towards a precise definition of the OMG/MDA framework. In: 16th IEEE International Conference on Automated Software Engineering (ASE 2001), 26–29 November 2001, Coronado Island, San Diego, CA, USA, pp. 273–280. IEEE Computer Society (2001)
5. Brucker, A.D., Tuong, F., Wolff, B.: Featherweight OCL: A proposal for a machine-checked formal semantics for OCL 2.5. Archive of Formal Proofs 2014 (2014)
6. Brucker, A.D., Wolff, B.: A Proposal for a formal OCL semantics in Isabelle/HOL. In: Carreño, V.A., Muñoz, C.A., Tahar, S. (eds.) TPHOLs 2002. LNCS, vol. 2410, pp. 99–114. Springer, Heidelberg (2002). doi:10.1007/3-540-45685-6_8
7. Gamma, E., Helm, R., Johnson, R., Vlissides, J.: Design Patterns: Elements of Reusable Object-Oriented Software. Addison-Wesley Longman Publishing Co., Inc., Boston (1995)
8. Kleppe, A.G., Rensink, A.: On a graph-based semantics for UML class and object diagrams. In: Ermel, C., De Lara, J., Heckel, R. (eds.) Graph Transformation and Visual Modelling Techniques. Electronic Communications of the EASST, Budapest, Hungary, vol. 10. EASST (2008)
9. Kyas, M., Fecher, H., de Boer, F.S., Jacob, J., Hooman, J., van der Zwaag, M., Arons, T., Kugler, H.: Formalizing UML models and OCL constraints in PVS. Electr. Notes Theoret. Comput. Sci. **115**, 39–47 (2005)
10. Lano, K., Rahimi, S.K.: Model-transformation design patterns. IEEE Trans. Softw. Eng. **40**(12), 1224–1259 (2014)
11. Lano, K., Rahimi, S.K., Poernomo, I., Terrell, J., Zschaler, S.: Correct-by-construction synthesis of model transformations using transformation patterns. Softw. Syst. Model. **13**(2), 873–907 (2014)

12. Lúcio, L., Amrani, M., Dingel, J., Lambers, L., Salay, R., Selim, G.M.K., Syriani, E., Wimmer, M.: Model transformation intents and their properties. Softw. Syst. Model. **15**(3), 647–684 (2016)
13. Naujokat, S., Lybecait, M., Kopetzki, D., Steffen, B.: CINCO: a simplicity-driven approach to full generation of domain-specific graphical modeling tools (2016, to appear)
14. Seidewitz, E.: What models mean. IEEE Softw. **20**(5), 26–32 (2003)
15. Syriani, E., Paige, R., Zschaler, S., Ergin, H.: First International Workshop on Patterns in Model Engineering (2015). http://www-ens.iro.umontreal.ca/~syriani/pame2015
16. Varró, D., Pataricza, A.: Metamodeling mathematics: a precise and visual framework for describing semantics domains of UML models. In: Jézéquel, J.-M., Hussmann, H., Cook, S. (eds.) UML 2002. LNCS, vol. 2460, pp. 18–33. Springer, Heidelberg (2002). doi:10.1007/3-540-45800-X_3
17. Varró, D., Pataricza, A.: VPM: a visual, precise and multilevel metamodeling framework for describing mathematical domains and UML (the mathematics of metamodeling is metamodeling mathematics). Softw. Syst. Model. **2**(3), 187–210 (2003)

Verified Change

Klaus Havelund$^{(\boxtimes)}$ and Rahul Kumar

Jet Propulsion Laboratory, California Institute of Technology, Pasadena, CA, USA
klaus.havelund@jpl.nasa.gov, rahulskumar@gmail.com

Abstract. We present the textual wide-spectrum modeling and pro-
graming language K, which has been designed for representing graphical
SysML models, in order to provide semantics to SysML, and pave the
way for analysis of SysML models. The current version is supported by
the Z3 SMT theorem prover, which allows to prove consistency of constraints. The language is intended to be used by engineers for designing
space missions, and in particular NASA's proposed mission to Jupiter's
moon Europa. One of the challenges facing software development teams
is the notion of change: the fact that code changes over time, and the
subsequent problem of demonstrating that no harm has been done due
to a change. K is in this paper being applied to demonstrate how change
can be perceived as a software verification problem, and hence verified
using more traditional software verification techniques.

Keywords: Modeling · Programming · Constraints · Refinement ·
Verification · Change

1 Introduction

The core topic of this paper is the concept of *change*, and how it relates to
the way we *model* as well as *program* our systems, and how we can ensure correctness of change using modern verification technology. We shall specifically
discuss this topic by introducing the wide-spectrum modeling and programming
language K, under development at NASA's Jet Propulsion Laboratory (JPL),
and demonstrate change scenarios and their verification in K.

The first call for opinion statements on the topic of change, with this journal
in mind, was published in [48], in which it is characterized as "*a discipline for
rigorously dealing with the nature of today's agile system development, which is
characterized by unclear premises, unforeseen change, and the need for fast reaction, in a context of hard to control frame conditions, like third party components,
network-problem, and attacks*". Our view is that change fundamentally can be
considered as a software verification problem, where the question is the following: given a program P_1, and a new program P_2, does P_2 implement/refine P_1?

The work described in this publication was carried out at Jet Propulsion Laboratory,
California Institute of Technology, under a contract with the National Aeronautics
and Space Administration.

B. Steffen (Ed.): Transactions on FoMaC I, LNCS 9960, pp. 71–89, 2016.
DOI: 10.1007/978-3-319-46508-1_5

As such, in the extreme, the topic of correctness under change can potentially be considered as the well known topic of correctness.

As is well known, analysis of correctness can be performed dynamically by analyzing execution traces. Dynamic methods include such topics as testing, runtime verification, and specification mining, where learned models of previous behavior are compared to models of current behavior (after change). Dynamic methods are known to scale well, which is their attraction, but are also known to yield false negatives: not to report errors that exist, and in some cases (i.e. in dynamic analysis of data races and deadlocks) to yield false positives (to report errors that do not exist). Our focus in this paper is on static analysis of code: where proofs are carried out on the basis of the structure of the code.

The K language is being developed at NASA's Jet Propulsion Laboratory (JPL), as part of a larger effort at JPL to develop an in-house systems modeling language and associated tool set, referred to as EMS (Engineering Modeling System). EMS is based on the graphical SysML formalism [49], which is a variant of UML [50], both designed by the OMG (Object Management Group) technology standards consortium. SysML is meant for systems development more broadly considered, including physical systems as well as software systems, in contrast to UML, which is mainly meant for software development. EMS is being developed (and already in use) to support the design of NASA's proposed mission to Jupiter's moon Europa, referred to as the *Europa Clipper mission* [13], planned to launch around 2022 at the moment of writing.

The K language design was initially triggered by a desire from within the EMS project to create a textual version of SysML. Although the graphical nature of SysML can be attractive from a readability point of view, it suffers from a number of issues, including lack of clear semantics, lack of analysis capabilities, requiring heavy mouse-movement and clicking, and generally demanding much more visual space than a textual formalism. The K language is in addition inspired by the idea of combining modeling and programming into one language. This idea has been, and is being, pursued by others in various forms, including past works on wide-spectrum specification languages. See the related work section (Sect. 4) for a more detailed discussion. It is interesting to observe, that modern programming languages to an increasing degree look and feel like specification languages from the past.

A constantly returning discussion point in the design of K has been whether to actually design a new language or adopt an existing specification or programming language. The decision to design a new language was in part influenced by the felt need (perhaps unwarranted) to control the syntax and the tool development stack, including parsers, compilers, etc. Whether this decision was/is correct, an important factor that makes K interesting is that it is being designed to meet the needs of a real space mission. As such it can be considered as a confirmation of already existing work in the area of specification as well as programming languages.

The contents of the paper is as follows. Section 2 introduces the K language, focusing on a small analyzable subset, which is currently being tested during the initial design phase of the Europa Clipper mission. Section 3 discusses various aspects of change by formalizing them in K. Section 4 outlines related work, and Sect. 5 concludes the paper. Appendix A contains the grammar for K in ANTLR [3] format.

2 The K Language

K is a textual language with various constructs for modeling and programming. The UML and SysML communities use the term *modeling*, whereas the formal methods community normally uses the term *specification*. We consider these terms for equivalent in this context, and shall use them interchangeably. A model (specification) is an abstract representation of a system (be it physical, conceptual, software, etc.), which has a concrete implementation, which in the software context is the program. It can be a physical object, however. The primary intended use for K is to easily create models and in the software context: implementations, and then be able to perform analysis on them. We primarily see K being used by system modelers who are used to expressing their models in SysML/UML. In this section, we briefly provide an overview of the K language. The presentation is centered around the example K model of geometric shapes, shown in Fig. 1.

Classes: Similar to classes in other object-oriented languages, the class in K is the construct for performing abstraction. It is K's module concept. Classes can be arranged in packages, as in Java. A class can contain properties (corresponding to fields in Java), functions, and constraints, as discussed below. For example, class *Triangle* contains three properties, which are of type *TAngle*.

Inheritance: K provides the `extends` keyword for specifying an inheritance relation. In Fig. 1, the *TAngle* class extends the *Angle* class. As a result, *TAngle*, not only inherits the properties and functions of *Angle*, but also the constraints. K also allows for multiple inheritance. Property and function names must be uniquely specified.

Primitive Types: K provides the following primitive types: `Int`, `Real`, `Bool`, `String`, `Char`, `Unit`.

Collections: K provides `Set`, `Seq`, and `Bag` as the three basic collections. K also provides support for tuples. The shapes model does not contain collections.

Properties: In K, properties can be present within classes or at the outermost level. Each property must have a name and a type. Our use of the term *property* is due to the use of this term in the model-based engineering (UML/SysML) community for name-type pairs, which in programming language and formal methods terminology normally are called constant/variable/field declarations. In the model shown in Fig. 1, class *Shape* contains a single property named *sides* of type `Int`.

Modifiers: Each property can also have one or more *modifiers* specified for it, for example **val**/**var** to make the property read only or writable (the default being read only). The shapes model does not contain modifiers.

Constraints: K provides syntax for specifying constraints in a class. This is done using the **req** keyword (we use the term *requirements* for constraints) followed by a name (optional), and an expression that specifies the constraint on the class. Constraints are class invariants. However, since side effects are not supported with analysis in the current version of K, constraints simply become axioms on names defined in the signature of a class. For example, in class *Angle*, the *value* of any angle should always be between 0 and 360°. Multiple constraints can also be specified. Their effect is the same as if all expressions were conjoined into a single constraint. For example, each instance of the *Triangle* class should have exactly three sides and the sum of the angles should be exactly 180°. Constraints are expressed in predicate logic, including universal and existential quantification.

Functions: A function provides the ability to perform computation. In K, functions can take arguments and return the result of the computation of the function. The *eq* function in class *Angle* compares a given argument angle's value to the class local angle value, returning a **Bool**.

Function Specifications: Each function in K can also have a *specification* associated with it. The specification can be a **pre**-condition and/or a **post**-condition. The shapes example does not contain function specifications. They are discussed in more detail along with an example in Sect. 3.

Expression Language: Similar to other high-level specification languages, K provides a rich expression language for specifying functions and requirements. K generally provides predicate logic with multiple operators, such as arithmetic operators, Boolean operators, if-then-else, blocks (a form of let-expressions inspired by Scala), set and sequence constructors and operators, and universal and existential quantification.

Annotations K provides the ability to create new annotations by specifying a name and a type for the annotation. The annotations can then be applied by writing an @ sign followed by the annotation name, and possible parameters, immediately before the element that is desired to be annotated. There is no limit on how many annotations can be applied to any entity.

Comments: Single line comments can be specified with the prefix −− and multi-line comments are specified with === as both the start and end of the multi-line comment.

In addition to the language constructs described here, K also has syntactic support for programming with *side effects* (assignment, sequential composition, and looping constructs, although these concepts are not yet supported by theorem proving or execution), *type abbreviations*, as well as SysML/UML specific concepts such as *associations* and *multiplicities* (which can be used for specifying the allowed size of a property). To conserve space, these constructs are not discussed in further detail. Appendix A shows part of the K ANTLR grammar, omitting grammar rules dealing with parsing of values of primitive types, such as digits, strings, etc.

Currently, the K infrastructure comes with a parser, that has been generated using ANTLR version 4. Using the parser, an abstract syntax tree is created that

```
class Shape { sides : Int }

class Angle {
  value : Int

  fun eq(other: Angle) : Bool { value = other.value }

  req value >= 0 && value <= 360
}

class TAngle extends Angle {
  req value < 180
}

class Triangle extends Shape {
  a : TAngle
  b : TAngle
  c : TAngle

  req sides = 3
  req Angles: a.value + b.value + c.value = 180
}

class Equilateral extends Triangle {
  req a.eq(b) && b.eq(c)
}

class Obtuse extends Triangle {
  req a.value > 90 || b.value > 90 || c.value > 90
}
```

Fig. 1. A simple model of geometrical shapes in K

is used for performing type checking. In addition, we have also developed a translator from K to SMT2, which currently is processed by the Z3 theorem prover [11]. This is used as a means to perform various checks such as function specification satisfiability, class consistency checking, and model generation. More generally, K works (similarly to Z3) by finding an assignment to all properties that satisfies the requirements (constraints). In case there are more than one assignment satisfying the requirements, an arbitrary is returned (although the result is deterministic). In case no assignment is possible, an identification of which requirements are inconsistent is returned. In the worst case scenario, the solver cannot determine the result in reasonable time, and it times out after a user-definable time period. The entire K infrastructure is implemented using Scala. It is planned to make a subset of the language executable. The source code along with binary releases along with a fully functional online solver and K editor can be found at [33]. It is used by engineers and developers at JPL for expressing requirements and verifying their consistency. The use is, however still in evaluation mode.

3   Change

3.1   Behavior

K at JPL so far, has mostly been used for specifying static structure, similar to what can be represented by UML/SysML class diagrams, with requirements typically constraining integer and real variables that represent properties of physical nature, such as for example weights and distances. The shapes model in Fig. 1 is an example of a model of structure, namely the shape of triangles. K can, however, also be used for specifying behavior, using the same concepts used for specifying structure, namely classes, properties, functions and requirements on these. The idea is in other words to use mathematical logic to represent behaviors. This is an illustration of the pursued objective during the design of K to keep the language as small as possible, relying as much as possible on the language of mathematics for expressing problems and solutions. This approach of course has algorithmic consequences when it comes to analyzing models. Our intention is to stay in mathematics as far as the tooling (existing theorem provers) allows us. In the following subsections we illustrate how one can encode two different behavior concepts in K, namely state machines and event scheduling.

State Machines. State machines are commonly used to specify the behavior of software as well as hardware systems. They are frequently used at JPL for specifying the behavior of embedded flight software modules controlling, for example, planetary rovers. A state machine is defined by a collection of states, a collection of events, and a labeled transition relation (labels are events) between states. This can of course be modeled in numerous ways. Here we shall assume deterministic state machines, and model the transition relation as a function. The K model in Fig. 2 represents an encoding of a state machine modeling a rocket engine, which can be in one of the states: *off*, *ready* or *firing*. Events include *turn_on*, *fire*, and *turn_off*. The types of states and events (*State* and *Event*) are modeled as body-less classes. The class *RocketEngine* models our state machine. It defines the three states as well as the three events as properties of the appropriate types. A requirement expresses that the states are all different (a similar requirement should in principle also be provided for events).

The function *move* represents the transition relation, and is declared to take two arguments: a state and event, and to return a state. It has no body, meaning that it is yet to be defined. The subsequent four requirements define the *move* function. For example the first requirement states that in the *off* state, on encountering a *turn_on* event, the engine moves to the *ready* state.

```
class State
class Event

class RocketEngine {

    off : State
    ready : State
    firing : State

    turn_on : Event
    fire : Event
    turn_off : Event

    req off != ready && off != firing && firing != ready

    fun move(s: State, e: Event) : State

    req move(off, turn on) = ready
    req move(ready, fire) = firing
    req move(firing, turn_off) = ready

    req move(ready, fire) = off -- added Monday morning
}
```

Fig. 2. State machine

The last requirement demanding the engine to move from the *ready* state to the *off* state on a *fire* event was added on a Monday morning by a tired modeler, and in our context represents a change to the model. This requirement, however, is inconsistent with a previous requirement that demands the resulting state to be *firing*. Since *move* is a function (the transition relation is deterministic), and cannot return two different values for the same argument, this is detected by the solver. Without this last requirement, the solver will declare the model satisfiable, and will synthesize the state machine function based on the provided requirements. Note, however, that not all transitions are modeled, hence the synthesized state machine may not be the desired one.

Event Scheduling. Event scheduling is a very common problem faced in a plethora of fields and domains. The typical scenario usually involves specifying multiple different allowed orderings of events and determining whether the specified ordering is satisfiable or not, and if satisfiable, generating a timeline for the specified events. Figure 3 shows one such example encoded using K.

The foundation of the scheduling problem is specified by the *Event* class, which represents a single event that has a start and end time (both of these specified using the `Int` type). The requirements on this class specify that the duration of any event has to be non-zero (**req** *nonZeroDuration*) and the start time of all events is greater than or equal to zero (**req** *afterBigBang*). Further, the three functions in the *Event* class encode Allen logic operators [2] using simple mathematical expressions on the start and end times of two events in question. The functions specify whether an event occurs *before* another event *e*, *meets* another event *e*, or *contains* another event *e*. We do not include the full set of Allen logic operators for sake of brevity.

Using this foundation, it is now easy to specify schedules and events. This is exactly what the *Schedule* class does. Five events are created as instances of the *Event* class. The actual schedule is specified as a requirement, which expresses

```
class Event {
  startTime  :  Int
  endTime  :  Int

  req afterBigBang  :  startTime >= 0
  req nonZeroDuration  :  endTime > startTime

  fun before (e  :  Event)  :  Bool { endTime < e.startTime }

  fun meets (e  :  Event)  :  Bool { endTime = e.startTime }

  fun contains (e  :  Event)  :  Bool {
    (startTime <= e.startTime && e.endTime < endTime) ||
    (startTime < e.startTime && e.endTime <= endTime)
  }
}

class Schedule {
  sciWin   :  Event
  digHole  :  Event
  takePic  :  Event
  commWin  :  Event
  config   :  Event
  comm     :  Event

  oneScienceActivity  :  Bool =
    (sciWin.contains(digHole) || sciWin.contains(takePic)) &&
    !(sciWin.contains(digHole) && sciWin.contains(takePic))

  req   sciWin.before(commWin) && oneScienceActivity &&
        commWin.contains(config) && commWin.contains(comm) &&
        config.meets(comm)
}
```

Fig. 3. Scheduling

the ordering of the events. In this particular example, the schedule specifies that the *sciWindow* (science window) must occur before the *commWindow* (communication window) and at least one science activity must have taken place. By translating the scheduling specification to SMT2 and applying the Z3 theorem prover, it can now be checked if the provided ordering on the events is satisfiable or not by checking if the *Schedule* class is satisfiable. A satisfying assignment to the class also provides us with a concrete time line of the events. It can be common for schedules and events to change as the project evolves and reaches maturity. Using such a mechanism for encoding the schedule of events provides great power and flexibility. Dealing with the changing schedule is easily done by either modifying existing requirements in the *Schedule* class, or by adding new events and requirements. Each change in the schedule is also verified using a theorem prover, which adds greater confidence in the change.

3.2   Refinement

Change can be considered as refinement. In the formal methods literature refinement usually refers to the situation where one model/program, the specification, and typically abstract of nature, is replaced by a lower level model/program, the implementation. Along with the refinement normally goes a proof, that the implementation refines the specification. The literature offers many solutions to how specifications, implementations and refinements are expressed as well as proved correct, see for example [6,7,16,17,31]. We shall not here enumerate all of these, but bring forward two examples, one illustrating function refinement, and one illustrating data refinement.

Function Refinement. Function refinement consists of making the body of a function more concrete, while the signature (name as well as argument and result types) of the function stays unchanged. More generally, data structures accessed by the function stay unchanged. One popular approach to this is design-by-contract, where a function is first specified using pre/post conditions, and then later implemented with a function body. This form of refinement is advocated for example in specification languages such as VDM [6,7,31] and RAISE [16,17], as well as in programming languages such as Eiffel [12] and Java in the form of the JML comment language [30].

  K supports design-by-contract using pre/post conditions. The example in Fig. 4 illustrates this with two class definitions. The left-most class *Util_Spec* represents the specification of a mathematics utility module containing two functions, *min* for computing the minimum of two values, and *abs* for returning the absolute value of an integer. Both functions are specified with a post condition stating what is expected to be true about the resulting value, denoted by *$result*. As an example, the post condition for the *min* function states that the result is equal to one of the arguments, and it is smallest such.

  The class *Util* to the right extends class *Util_Spec* and refines the functions with proper function bodies. The semantics of K is such that the refined function

Specification	Implementation
| ```
class Util_Spec {
  fun min(x:Int,y:Int): Int
    post
       ($result = x ||
        $result = y) &&
        $result <= x &&
        $result <= y

  fun abs(x:Int):Int
    post $result >= 0 &&
       ($result = x ||
        $result = -x)
}
``` | ```
class Util extends Util_Spec {
  fun min(x:Int,y:Int): Int {
    if x <= y then x else y
  }

  fun abs(x:Int):Int {
    if x < 0 then -x else x
  }
}
``` |

Fig. 4. Mathematical function refinement

bodies will have to satisfy the post conditions. The K solver proves this automatically in this case. The fact that the implementation class extends (inherits from) the specification class reflects that this form of refinement is a form of theory refinement, where the theory denoted by the implementation must imply that of the specification: the implementation signature contains that of the specification, and the requirements logically imply those of the specification:

$$Implementation \Rightarrow Specification$$

Data Refinement. Data refinement consists of changing the data structures used, which will cause functions to change as well. Data refinement has for example been advocated in the VDM method [6,7,31], which is the approach we shall illustrate here using K. The approach consists of defining a specification and an implementation as follows. The specification consists of a type Σ_a of abstract states, as well as abstract operations $opn_a : \Sigma_a \rightarrow \Sigma_a$ on this state. The implementation consists of a type Σ_c of concrete states, as well as concrete operations $opn_c : \Sigma_c \rightarrow \Sigma_c$ on this state. To perform a proof of correctness of the refinement, an abstraction function $abs : \Sigma_c \rightarrow \Sigma_a$ from the type of concrete implementation states to the type of abstract specification states must be provided, and the following property must (amongst others) be proved for each operation opn, where opn_a is the abstract version and opn_c is the concrete version, and $pre_a : \Sigma_a \rightarrow \mathbb{B}$ is the pre-condition of the abstraction operation opn_a:

$$\forall \sigma : \Sigma_c \cdot pre_a(abs(\sigma)) \Rightarrow opn_a(abs(\sigma)) = abs(opn_c(\sigma)) \tag{1}$$

Each concrete operation must in other words be proved to update the concrete state in a manner corresponding to the desired operation on the abstract state. We illustrate this approach with a rather simple K model of a light switch, which can be turned on and off. The specification is shown on the left of Fig. 5. A state is defined abstractly as an object of a class *State*. The two states *off* and *on* are defined as distinct states of that type. Two functions are defined, one for toggling the state (*toggle*), and one for testing whether the light switch is on (*isOn*). The *toggle* function is only declared by its signature, no function body is provided. The behavior is instead provided as a couple of requirements.

The implementation is shown on the right of Fig. 5. Here we have decided to model the state as an integer, being 1 when the light switch is on and 0 when it is off. Note that in this case the implementation does not extend (inherit from) the specification as was the case in the mathematical function refinement in Fig. 4. Instead, the proof corresponding to Eq. (1) above is provided in the separate class *RefinementProof* in Fig. 6. To express the refinement property to be proved, an instance *spec* of the specification and an instance *impl* of the implementation are created such that we can refer to their respective operations (functions). Then the abstraction function *abs* is defined from the concrete state of integers to the abstract state *State* of the specification. Finally, the requirement is the K formulation of Eq. (1) above, ignoring the pre-condition part since all pre-conditions in this example are true. The K solver proves the implementation

Specification	Implementation

```
class State

class LightSwitch_Spec {
  off : State
  on  : State                    class LightSwitch {
                                    fun toggle(cs: Int): Int {
  req off != on                       if cs = 1 then 0 else 1
                                    }
  fun toggle(s: State): State
                                    fun isOn(cs: Int): Bool {
  fun isOn(s: State): Bool {          cs = 1
    s = on                          }
  }                               }

  req toggle(off) = on
  req toggle(on) = off
}
```

Fig. 5. Lightswitch refinement

```
class RefinementProof {
  spec : LightSwitch_Spec
  impl : LightSwitch

  fun abs(cs:Int): State {
    if cs = 1 then spec.on else spec.off
  }

  req forall cs: Int :-
    spec.toggle(abs(cs)) = abs(impl.toggle(cs))

  req forall cs: Int :-
    spec.isOn(abs(cs)) = impl.isOn(cs)

}
```

Fig. 6. Lightswitch refinement proof

correct automatically. An incorrect modification of the implementation, such as for example to change the body of *isOn* in the implementation to $cs = 0$ will dually be caught by the solver.

4 Related Work

K is intended to represent a textual modeling language capable of representing SysML concepts, specifically class diagrams with constraints. However, as mentioned in the introduction, it also contains programming constructs, although these are not yet supported by theorem proving or execution. As such it can be perceived as a wide-spectrum modeling/programming language.

Wide-spectrum specification languages have been investigated to length in the formal methods community. One of the well-known examples is VDM [6,7,31,32]. VDM in its original form [6] provided a combination of procedural programming and functional programming, as well as specification using sets, lists and maps (with proper mathematical notation), and higher-order predicate logic. VDM^{++} [14] added object-orientation to VDM, which is now part of the VDM standard. The RAISE specification language (RSL) [16] is a wide-spectrum language taking inspiration from VDM as well as from other modeling languages such as Z [47], and algebraic equational specification languages. Here refinement is the simpler theory implication: the implementation shall imply the specification in a logic sense. AsmL [19] is a more recent wide-spectrum specification language, in many ways similar to VDM, but based on the idea that operations with side effects operate on algebras. Other fundamental works on refinement include (not a comprehensive list): [1,4,25,38,51,52].

Alloy [29] added new life to this community by being supported by an automated SAT solver. In many respects, K is close in spirit to Alloy, but differs by being supported by an automated SMT solver (in contrast to a SAT solver), resulting in a richer set of constructs, including arithmetic, being exposed to analysis. K also combines a type view as found in traditional specification and programming languages, as well as a relational view, whereas Alloy is purely relational. We are of the belief that the notion of a type is fundamental to programming as well as to modeling. In contrast to automated provers, interactive theorem provers such as PVS [41,43], Coq [10], and Isabelle [28], allow the user to steer the proofs. Although this allows to perform more complex proofs, it also requires more skills of the user, and time, which is often a limited resource in software development projects.

Several high-level programming languages have been developed over time, including the early SML (Standard ML) [37], its derivative Ocaml [39], and Haskell [21]. However, also Java can be considered high-level due to its libraries of collections (sets, lists, and maps), as well as the iterator concept. Python [44] is close to combining object-oriented and functional programming. Scala [45] does this to the full extent. The close relationship between Scala and VDM is discussed in [22]. Fortress [15] introduced built-in notation for sets, lists, and maps, very much resembling the notation in VDM.

Specification constructs have been introduced in programming languages, in the form of design-by-contract (pre/post conditions + class invariants). Examples are Eiffel [12] and Spec$^\#$ [46], where contracts are part of the language. Scala has library functions for writing pre/post conditions on functional programs [40]. Finally, The JML language [30] allows to write design-by-contract specifications for Java as comments. These are ignored by the standard Java compiler, and therefore must be processed with special tools. EML (Extended ML) [34] takes a slightly different approach to specification and formal development of SML programs. EML specifications look just like SML programs except that axioms are allowed in signatures and in place of code in structures and functors. Some EML specifications are executable, since SML function definitions are just axioms of a certain special form. This makes EML a wide-spectrum language.

Programming languages are now also being designed with verification in mind. Dafny [36] supports specifications that can be used to write correctness conditions for programs. It is supported by a verifier, which is implemented on top of the Boogie verification engine, which itself is built on top of Z3. Why3 [8] provides a rich language for specification and programming, called WhyML, and relies on external theorem provers, both automated and interactive, to discharge verification conditions. A user can write WhyML programs directly and get correct-by-construction Ocaml programs through an automated extraction mechanism. Model checking is another form of analysis that has been applied to programming languages. Java PathFinder [23,24] performs model checking of Java programs. SLAM [5] performs static analysis and counter-example guided abstraction refinement of device drivers, and has been applied in a large scale industry setting. Spin [27] performs model checking of models expressed in the

Promela language, but can also model check C code directly. The ABS [20] language and system provide various types of analysis such as resource analysis, deadlock analysis, as well as tools to perform test generation and formal verification. The notions of abstract contracts and abstract class invariants are introduced in [9], in order to reduce proof efforts when contracts change. In [26] is presented an approach to integrate a semiautomatic verification tool into a state-of-the-art integrated development environment (IDE), with the specific objective to keep implementation, specification and proofs in sync.

The great improvements in model checking, static analysis, theorem proving, and SMT solvers such as Z3 have all contributed to investigating and dealing with software change. To this effect, differential symbolic execution [42] has been investigated for establishing equivalence between two versions of a program. The work described in [35] uses verification conditions and SMT solvers for detecting semantic change between two closely related versions of a function (program), by discovering inputs to the function that cause the outputs to differ. The work described in [18] deals with regression verification and provides a technique for performing equivalence checking of C programs, by using the older version of the program as a specification for the new version of the program. A large part of the inspiration for such work comes from the theorem proving community.

An important use of K that we have observed so far, which differs in the way traditional verification tools are used, is that modelers tend to use K along with it's solving ability as a tool for *discovering* the right set of requirements for their class before introducing a change. For example, uncertainty about a particular variable and it's potential range of valid values can be quite common in modeling environments. Since K helps discover unsatisfiability, modelers use an iterative refinement technique to discover the appropriate range of a variable for their needs. K in this case is providing validation before a change is completely committed.

5   Conclusion

In this paper, we have addressed the topic of *change* in a software/modeling development environment. More generally, we have developed what we refer to as a *development language* for modeling as well as programming, also referred to as a wide-spectrum programming language, with verification support. This enables developers to easily study properties of their models and programs, and in particular, in this case, the effect of their change, thus helping to avoid making changes that could potentially lead to inconsistencies. We have studied various scenarios, and how *consistency* checking and *change* viewed as *refinement* can be applied to each of those. While the topic of change itself is extremely broad, we believe that a language oriented approach as presented in this paper provides concrete value and provides a good foundation for developing stronger techniques.

Acknowledgements. We would like to thank Chris Delp and Bradley Clement for the opportunities and insights they provided during the development of the K language.

A   K Grammar

```
model:
  packageDeclaration? importDeclaration*
  annotationDeclaration* topDeclaration* EOF;

packageDeclaration: 'package' qualifiedName ;

importDeclaration: 'import' qualifiedName ('.' '*')? ;

annotationDeclaration: 'annotation' Identifier ':' type ;

annotation: '@' Identifier '(' expression ')' ;

topDeclaration: annotation* entityDeclaration | annotation* memberDeclaration ;

entityDeclaration:
  ('class'|'assoc'|Identifier) Keyword? Identifier typeParameters? extending?
  ('{' block '}')? ;

Keyword: '<' Identifier '>' ;

typeParameters: '[' typeParameter (',' typeParameter)* ']' ;

typeParameter: Identifier (':' typeBound)? ;

typeBound: type ('+' type)* ;

extending: 'extends' type (',' type)* ;

block: blockDeclaration* ;

blockDeclaration: annotation* memberDeclaration  ;

memberDeclaration:
  typeDeclaration | propertyDeclaration | functionDeclaration |
  constraint | expression ;

typeDeclaration: 'type' Identifier (typeParameters? '=' type )? ;

propertyDeclaration:
  propertyModifier* Identifier ':' type multiplicity? (('='|':=') expression)? ;

propertyModifier:
  'part' | 'var' | 'val' | 'ordered' | 'unique' | 'source' | 'target';

functionDeclaration:
  'fun' Identifier typeParameters? ('(' paramList ')')? (':' type)?
  functionSpecification* ('{' block '}')? ;

paramList: param (',' param)* ;

param: Identifier ':' type ;

functionSpecification: 'pre' expression | 'post' expression ;

constraint: 'req' (Identifier ':')? expression ;

multiplicity: '[' expressionOrStar (',' expressionOrStar)? ']' ;

expressionOrStar: expression | '*' ;

type:
  primitiveType | classIdentifier typeArguments? | type ('*' type)+ |
  type '->' type | '(' type ')' | '{|' Identifier ':' type ':-' expression '|}' ;

primitiveType: 'Bool' | 'Char' | 'Int' | 'Real' | 'String' | 'Unit' ;
```

```
classIdentifier: qualifiedName | 'Class' | collectionKind ;

collectionKind: 'Set' | 'Bag' | 'Seq' ;

typeArguments: '[' type (',' type)* ']' ;

expression:
    '(' expression ')' | 'Tuple' '(' expression (',' expression)+ ')'
  | literal | Identifier | expression '.' Identifier
  | expression '(' argumentList? ')'
  | '!' expression | '{' block '}'
  | 'if' expression 'then' expression ('else' expression)?
  | 'match' expression 'with' match+
  | 'while' expression 'do' expression
  | 'for' pattern 'in' expression 'do' expression
  | collectionKind '{' expressionList? '}'
  | collectionKind '{' expression '..' expression '}'
  | collectionKind '{' expression '|' rngBindingList ':-' expression '}'
  | expression ('*'|'/'|'%'|'inter'|'\\'|'++'|'#'|'^') expression
  | expression ('+'|'-'|'union') expression
  | expression ('<='|'>='|'<'|'>'|'=') expression
  | expression ('!='|'isin'|'!isin'|'subset'|'psubset') expression
  | expression ('&&'|'||') expression
  | expression ('=>'|'<=>') expression
  | expression (':='|'is'|'as') expression
  | 'assert' '(' expression ')'
  | '-' expression
  | qualifiedName '~'
  | 'forall' rngBindingList ':-' expression
  | 'exists' rngBindingList ':-' expression
  | pattern '->' expression
  | 'continue' | 'break' | 'return' expression? | '$result' ;

match: 'case' pattern ('|' pattern)* '=>' expression ;

argumentList: positionalArgumentList | namedArgumentList ;

positionalArgumentList: expression (',' expression)* ;

namedArgumentList: namedArgument (',' namedArgument)* ;

namedArgument : Identifier '::' expression ;

collectionOrType: expression | type ;

rngBindingList: rngBinding (',' rngBinding)* ;

rngBinding: patternList ':' collectionOrType ;

patternList: pattern (',' pattern)* ;

pattern:
  literal | '_' | Identifier | '(' pattern (',' pattern)+ ')' | pattern ':' type ;

identifierList: Identifier (',' Identifier)* ;

expressionList: expression (',' expression)* ;

qualifiedName: Identifier ('.' Identifier)* ;

literal:
  IntegerLiteral | RealLiteral | CharacterLiteral | StringLiteral |
  BooleanLiteral | NullLiteral | ThisLiteral ;
```

References

1. Abrial, J.-R.: Modeling in Event-B. Cambridge University Press, New York (2010)
2. Allen, J.F.: Towards a general theory of action and time. Artif. Intell. **23**, 123–154 (1984)
3. ANTLR. http://www.antlr.org
4. Back, R.-J., von Wright, J.: Refinement Calculus: A Systematic Introduction. Texts in Computer Science. Springer, New York (1998)
5. Ball, T., Bounimova, E., Kumar, R., Levin, V.: SLAM2: static driver verification with under 4 % false alarms. In: Proceedings of the 2010 Conference on Formal Methods in Computer-Aided Design, pp. 35–42. FMCAD Inc. (2010)
6. Bjørner, D., Jones, C.B. (eds.): The Vienna Development Method: The Meta-Language. LNCS, vol. 61. Springer, Heidelberg (1978). doi:10.1007/3-540-08766-4
7. Bjørner, D., Jones, C.B.: Formal Specification and Software Development. Prentice Hall International, Englewood Cliffs (1982). ISBN: 0-13-880733-7
8. Bobot, F., Filliâtre, J.-C., Marché, C., Paskevich, A.: Why3: shepherd your herd of provers. In: Boogie 2011: First International Workshop on Intermediate Verification Languages, pp. 53–64, Wrocław, Poland, August 2011
9. Bubel, R., Hähnle, R., Pelevina, M.: Fully abstract operation contracts. In: Margaria, T., Steffen, B. (eds.) ISoLA 2014. LNCS, vol. 8803, pp. 120–134. Springer, Heidelberg (2014). doi:10.1007/978-3-662-45231-8_9
10. Coq. https://coq.inria.fr
11. De Moura, L., Bjørner, N.: Z3: an efficient SMT solver. In: Ramakrishnan, C.R., Rehof, J. (eds.) TACAS 2008. LNCS, vol. 4963, pp. 337–340. Springer, Heidelberg (2008). doi:10.1007/978-3-540-78800-3_24
12. Eiffel. http://www.eiffel.com
13. Europa Clipper Mission. http://www.jpl.nasa.gov/missions/europa-mission
14. Fitzgerald, J., Larsen, P.G., Mukherjee, P., Plat, N., Verhoef, M.: Validated Designs for Object-Oriented Systems. Springer, London (2005)
15. Fortress. http://java.net/projects/projectfortress
16. George, C., Haff, P., Havelund, K., Haxthausen, A., Milne, R., Nielsen, C.B., Prehn, S., Wagner, K.R.: The RAISE Specification Language. The BCS Practitioner Series. Prentice-Hall, Hemel Hampstead (1992)
17. George, C., Haxthausen, A.: The logic of the RAISE specification language. In: Bjørner, D., Henson, M. (eds.) Logics of Specification Languages. Monographs in Theoretical Computer Science, pp. 349–399. Springer, Heidelberg (2008)
18. Godlin, B., Strichman, O.: Regression verification. In: Proceedings of the 46th Annual Design Automation Conference, pp. 466–471. ACM (2009)
19. Gurevich, Y., Rossman, B., Schulte, W.: Semantic essence of AsmL. Theor. Comput. Sci. **343**(3), 370–412 (2005)
20. Hähnle, R.: The abstract behavioral specification language: a tutorial introduction. In: Giachino, E., Hähnle, R., Boer, F.S., Bonsangue, M.M. (eds.) FMCO 2012. LNCS, vol. 7866, pp. 1–37. Springer, Heidelberg (2013). doi:10.1007/978-3-642-40615-7_1
21. Haskell. http://www.haskell.org/haskellwiki/Haskell
22. Havelund, K.: Closing the gap between specification, programming: VDM^{++} and Scala. In: Korovina, M., Voronkov, A. (eds.) HOWARD-60: Higher-Order Workshop on Automated Runtime Verification and Debugging, EasyChair Proceedings, Manchester, vol. 1, December 2011

23. Havelund, K., Pressburger, T.: Model checking Java programs using Java PathFinder. Int. J. Softw. Tools Technol. Transf. STTT **2**(4), 366–381 (2000)
24. Havelund, K., Visser, W.: Program model checking as a new trend. STTT **4**(1), 8–20 (2002)
25. He, J., Hoare, C.A.R., Sanders, J.W.: Data refinement refined. In: Robinet, B., Wilhelm, R. (eds.) ESOP 1986. LNCS, vol. 213, pp. 187–196. Springer, Heidelberg (1986). doi:10.1007/3-540-16442-1_14
26. Hentschel, M., Käsdorf, S., Hähnle, R., Bubel, R.: An interactive verification tool meets an IDE. In: Albert, E., Sekerinski, E. (eds.) IFM 2014. LNCS, vol. 8739, pp. 55–70. Springer, Heidelberg (2014). doi:10.1007/978-3-319-10181-1_4
27. Holzmann, G.J.: The Spin Model Checker - Primer and Reference Manual. Addison-Wesley, Boston (2004)
28. Isabelle. https://isabelle.in.tum.de
29. Jackson, D., Abstractions, S.: Logic, Language, and Analysis. The MIT Press, Cambridge (2012)
30. JML. http://www.eecs.ucf.edu/leavens/JML
31. Jones, C.B.: Systematic Software Development using VDM. Prentice Hall, Upper Saddle River (1990). ISBN: 0-13-880733-7
32. Jones, C.B., Shaw, R.C. (eds.): Case Studies in Systematic Software Development. Prentice Hall International, Upper Saddle River (1990). ISBN: 0-13-880733-7
33. K. http://www.theklanguage.com
34. Kahrs, S., Sannella, D., Tarlecki, A.: The definition of Extended ML: a gentle introduction. Theor. Comput. Sci. **173**, 445–484 (1997)
35. Lahiri, S.K., Hawblitzel, C., Kawaguchi, M., Rebêlo, H.: SYMDIFF: a language-agnostic semantic diff tool for imperative programs. In: Madhusudan, P., Seshia, S.A. (eds.) CAV 2012. LNCS, vol. 7358, pp. 712–717. Springer, Heidelberg (2012). doi:10.1007/978-3-642-31424-7_54
36. Leino, K.R.M.: Dafny: an automatic program verifier for functional correctness. In: Clarke, E.M., Voronkov, A. (eds.) LPAR 2010. LNCS (LNAI), vol. 6355, pp. 348–370. Springer, Heidelberg (2010). doi:10.1007/978-3-642-17511-4_20
37. Milner, R., Tofte, M., Harper, R. (eds.): The Definition of Standard ML. MIT Press, Cambridge (1997). ISBN: 0-262-63181-4
38. Morgan, C.: Programming from Specifications, 2nd edn. Prentice Hall, New York (1994)
39. OCaml. http://caml.inria.fr/ocaml/index.en.html
40. Odersky, M.: Contracts for Scala. In: Barringer, H., Falcone, Y., Finkbeiner, B., Havelund, K., Lee, I., Pace, G., Roşu, G., Sokolsky, O., Tillmann, N. (eds.) RV 2010. LNCS, vol. 6418, pp. 51–57. Springer, Heidelberg (2010). doi:10.1007/978-3-642-16612-9_5
41. Owre, S., Rushby, J.M., Shankar, N.: PVS: a prototype verification system. In: Kapur, D. (ed.) CADE 1992. LNCS, vol. 607, pp. 748–752. Springer, Heidelberg (1992). doi:10.1007/3-540-55602-8_217
42. Person, S., Dwyer, M.B., Elbaum, S., Păsăreanu, C.S.: Differential symbolic execution. In: Proceedings of the 16th ACM SIGSOFT International Symposium on Foundations of Software Engineering, pp. 226–237. ACM (2008)
43. PVS. http://pvs.csl.sri.com
44. Python. http://www.python.org
45. Scala. http://www.scala-lang.org
46. Spec#. http://research.microsoft.com/en-us/projects/specsharp
47. Spivey, J.M.: Understanding Z: A Specification Language and Its Formal Semantics. Cambridge University Press, New York (1988)

48. Steffen, B.: LNCS transactions on foundations for mastering change: preliminary manifesto. In: Margaria, T., Steffen, B. (eds.) ISoLA 2014. LNCS. Theoretical Computer Science and General Issues, vol. 8803, pp. 514–517. Springer, Heidelberg (2014)
49. SysML. http://www.omgsysml.org
50. UML. http://www.uml.org
51. Wirth, N.: Program development by stepwise refinement. Commun. ACM (CACM) **14**, 221–227 (1971)
52. Woodcock, J., Davies, J.: Using Z. Specification, Refinement, and Proof. Prentice-Hall, New York (1996)

Good Change and Bad Change: An Analysis Perspective on Software Evolution

Mikael Lindvall[1], Martin Becker[2], Vasil Tenev[2],
Slawomir Duszynski[2], and Mike Hinchey[3(✉)]

[1] Fraunhofer Center for Experimental Software Engineering, College Park, MD, USA
[2] Fraunhofer Institute for Experimental Software Engineering, Kaiserslautern, Germany
[3] Lero – The Irish Software Research Centre, University of Limerick, Limerick, Ireland
mike.hinchey@lero.ie

Abstract. Software does change, and should change. Traditional industrial software systems often evolve over long periods of time with each new version forming a discreet milestone, while some new software systems involve constant adaptation to situations in the environment and therefore evolve continually. While necessary, software change can also be devastating, making the system difficult to change and maintain further. We believe that one promising way to manage and control change is to view an evolving system as a software product line where each version of the software is a product. Key to any successful software product line approach is a software architecture that supports variability management. Tools that can identify commonalities and differences among various releases are essential in collecting and managing the information on changed, added and deleted components. Equally important are tools that allow the architect to analyse the current status of the product line as well as its products from various perspectives, and to be able to detect and remove architectural violations that threaten the variability points and built-in flexibility. In this paper, we describe our current research on defining such a process and supporting tools for software evolution management based on product line concepts and apply it in a case study to a software testbed called TSAFE. We describe how we reverse engineer the actual architecture from the source code and how we develop new target architectures based on the reverse engineered one and the expected changes. We then described how we analyse the actual change across different implementations and visualize where the change actually occurred. We then describe how we determine if a particular implementation match the target architecture. The conclusion is that we have found that both these analysis techniques are particularly useful for analysing software evolution and complement each other.

1   Introduction

Software is *intended* to change. Lehman's first Law of Software Evolution holds that software must continually evolve or it will grow useless [1]. Changes to software may be the result of an organization evolving, of end-users discovering that the software system doesn't fully meet their needs, or indeed as a result of those needs (requirements) themselves changing.

© Springer International Publishing AG 2016
B. Steffen (Ed.): Transactions on FoMaC I, LNCS 9960, pp. 90–112, 2016.
DOI: 10.1007/978-3-319-46508-1_6

Software changes as the result of the discovery of errors, or bugs that must be fixed (so-called *corrective maintenance*). It may be changed or updated to exploit new technologies, to improve performance and to achieve greater efficiency (so-called *perfective maintenance*). Often however it simply has to adapt to reflect its changing environment (so-called *adaptive maintenance*), particularly if the software is long-lived. Increasingly, *preventative maintenance* is required to avoid problems in the future.

The point is that software does change, and *should* change. If we developed software that never changed, then we would be better off implementing everything as hardware, which traditionally we have been able to develop more reliably and efficiently than software. The motivation for using software is that changes can be made more easily and in many cases in situations where hardware components simply could not be accessed to switch components (e.g., in implanted medical devices or in spacecraft far from Earth).[1]

Some software evolves over long periods and versions, e.g., the releases of the Primary Avionics Shuttle Software, or PASS, over a 20+ year period [2]. Another example is NASA's Space Network (SN) which was established in the early 1980s[2]. Most of the original SN software is still in use but has been continuously changed over time. New classes of software systems involve constant adaptation to situations in the environment, in order to self-protect, self-heal and self-(re-)configure, self-organize, etc., resulting in an entirely new research area known by various groups as Autonomic Computing, Self-Organizing Systems, Self-Adaptive Systems, Organic Computing, and Selfware, amongst others [3]; for simplicity, we will refer to such systems as "adaptive systems".

We can view an evolving system as a software product line [4], where each version of the software is a product in the product line. Each product is in turn a specialization of a core (initial) implementation ("platform" in the parlance of the Software Product Lines community). This view is valid whether we are concerned with software systems that evolve over long periods such as the PASS, but also, and perhaps less obviously so, when we are dealing with the category of software systems described above that are constantly adapting. Such systems change to deal with unexpected events in their environment, exhibit varying degrees of contextual and situational awareness and involve reconfiguration and binding at runtime and can be viewed as a *dynamic software product line* [10].

Key to the successful application of any software product line approach is a good software architecture which can be used for *variability management*—identifying common components, components common to many but not all products, and products that have their own specific requirements. Analogous to this, in the context of an evolving system we must consider the components that are unchanged, those that are changed from one version of the software to another, or from one point in time to another, and finally those completely new software components that must be written or generated from scratch. Some systems were designed up-front as product lines and therefore have

---

[1] There have been times where the use of software was motivated by size and space limitations, but with advances in hardware this advantage has all but disappeared.

[2] http://www.nasa.gov/directorates/heo/scan/services/networks/txt_sn.html.

built in variability points while other systems were not designed as product lines but emerged as product lines after having evolved in parallel over time. Some good examples of systems that were designed as product lines are NASA's core flight software (CFS)[3] [11] as well as the Goddard Mission Services Evolution Center (GMSEC)[4] [14]. Both these product lines are very successful in the sense that they are reused by many NASA missions. CFS is also an example of a product line that was defined after several similar systems were developed and evolved in parallel and where the need for organized and planned reuse was identified. A product line that was designed a-priori has a need for tools that help managing the variabilities in the product line as well as to ensure that the reusable platform is used in the correct way. A de-facto product line consisting of a set of similar products that evolved in parallel without having a formally defined core set of common features has a need for other tools. Examples of such tools are ones that help identify potential common features so that a product line architecture with variability points can be established allowing new products to be instantiated in a controlled way from the product line architecture.

2 Software Architecture Evolution and Evaluation

2.1 Software Architecture

Software architecture deals with the structure and interactions of a software system. The most basic building blocks of the structure of software architecture are components and the interrelationships among the components. In addition to structure, behaviour is part of software architecture. Constraints, sequences and rules describe how the architectural components communicate with one another. The software architecture of a system may be viewed at different levels for different purposes.

Even at the conceptual or logical level, architectural components can be viewed at several different abstraction levels and vary based on the size of the system. At the highest level, the components are the subsystems, which in the case of a very large system, can be a complex system and can have subsystems of their own. Subsystems are often formed by lower level components, which are, in the case of an object-oriented system, collections of classes. In order for the architectural components to form a system, they must communicate with each other, creating interrelationships or connectors. The division of a system into smaller building blocks is based on the philosophy of "divide and conquer" which lets the architect/designer divide the problem into smaller and less complex pieces.

In software architecture, several mechanisms can be used to support change and hence increase the flexibility and maintainability of the system: design patterns and extension points are some of the prominent examples. These mechanisms specify an abstracted, generic part of system functionality which is expected to remain stable, and provide the possibility to add one or many detailed implementations which satisfy the current requirements and can be replaced when these requirements change. In software

---

[3] https://cfs.gsfc.nasa.gov/.
[4] https://gmsec.gsfc.nasa.gov/.

systems, we observe two principles which led us to the research presented in this paper. Firstly, the technical mechanisms supporting maintainability are frequently the same as the mechanisms used to support variability implementation in software product lines – as in both cases the possibility to change a part of functionality at a predefined location is needed. Secondly, maintainability is a software quality which is relative to *what* is needed to be changed – it is easy to accommodate the expected changes, while for the unexpected ones difficulties might occur as there is no predefined realization mechanism. The design of a maintainable software architecture can only consider and apply change-supporting mechanisms for the changes which can be predicted or expected. Again, this resembles the design of a product line with predefined variation points supporting the differences between product variants that are expected to occur.

In several cases, it has been concluded that specifying an initial maintainable software architecture is not enough because as software systems evolve over time and undergo changes, especially unforeseen ones, these changes can still lead to a degeneration of the systems' architecture. Degeneration may eventually reach a level where a complete redesign of the software system is necessary, which is a task that requires significant effort.

There are several examples of architectural degeneration and decay in the literature, e.g. in 1998, Netscape released their web browser as open-source. Evolving the existing code into the new browser Mozilla was much harder than expected so they re-wrote the code from scratch. An analysis of Mozilla's 2,000,000 lines of code revealed "that either its architecture has decayed significantly in its relatively short lifetime, or it was not carefully architected in the first place" [6].

An analysis of a 100,000,000 SLOC, fifteen year-old telecom software system revealed that the system had decayed over time. The decay did not cause the software to be thrown away as in the Netscape case but caused enough problems to call for action [7].

Even a small 12,000 SLOC Java system quickly degenerated when new programmers made changes without following the architecture guidelines making the system difficult to maintain [8]. These examples all make it clear that architectural degeneration is a significant problem in the software industry as of today.

2.2   Evolving Architectures

Each time software is changed, unless we take great care, there is the opportunity to introduce more errors. The later in its lifecycle that the software is changed, and the more extensive the changes, the more likely it is that there will be a significant impact on the actual structure of the system. *Architectural drift* [9] is, in addition the degeneration and decay, a term used to refer to the loss of consistency between the architecture that was designed at the outset and what it has transformed into.

We use the term "changed" reservedly, since it may refer to a planned evolution over time, or a more haphazard one due to software changes being made in such a way that the architecture (necessarily) deviates from what was planned. If we consider adaptive systems, however, it is very likely that the architecture *must* change over time in order to implement the necessary functionality. If we can understand *a priori* the way that an architecture will change as a result of adaptation, and if we can identify the changes in an architecture over a product line (which is how we view an evolving system, cf. Sect. 1), we will have a better understanding of the adaptation exhibited by the software system.

2.3   The Two Techniques and Their Usage

In this paper we will use two techniques to illustrate how we can analyse variants of a software system. We will apply the techniques to a software called TSAFE, which is thus the system under analysis in this paper.

The first technique is based on the SAVE tool, which is a reverse engineering tool that creates structure diagrams from source code. The SAVE tool can automatically compare the reverse engineered diagrams to a planned architecture to identify differences which might turn out to be architecture violations. The SAVE tool analyses one version of the system's source code at a time.

The second technique is called Variant Analysis (VA). VA analyses several versions (variants) of the source code and compares them in order to detect commonalities and differences. The comparison technique constructs a similarity model, allowing the analyst to compare many code variants at once (as opposed to pair-wise comparison). The commonalities and differences are then visualized using various visualization techniques.

Thus, if one has the need to analyse a software system and has access to the source code one can use these techniques. There are several situations when such an analysis is needed. For example, let us assume that a certain architecture style or design pattern was used in the architecture or design to mitigate certain security vulnerabilities. Thus the analyst must ensure that the mitigation was correctly implemented and does not violate the selected style or the pattern. Another example is when a legacy system must be maintained but the documentation is outdated and critical information about the software architecture must be reverse engineered from the source code. Another example is when a component (e.g. a database) the system uses must be replaced or removed because it is obsolete, then the analyst must understand to what extent the system is dependent on that component. What is common for all of these examples is that typically only one version of the system (the most recent one) needs to be analysed to address these needs and thus the SAVE tool can be used for these types of analyses.

However, there are many other situations where several versions or variants of the system need to be analysed at the same time and thus a variant analysis tool is needed in addition to the SAVE tool. One example is when several variants of the system exist and the analyst needs to understand the commonalities and differences among the variants in order to determine the potential for creating a product line architecture and thereby reducing maintenance costs. The analyst might start by analysing an old version of the system using SAVE in order to understand what the architecture looked like before a large number of variants started to emerge. The analyst might then proceed to use the variant analysis technique to compare several versions to each other in order to understand what the differences are. The analyst might even include the base variant in this analysis in order to also understand how the newer variants relate to the base variant.

The analyst might then proceed to identify the core (i.e. the part of the source code that is common across all variants and seem to be resistant to change) in order to turn it into a reusable component that is part of a defined product line architecture that allows for systematic and planned reuse for future products. Once the core has been identified, the SAVE tool can be used to reverse engineering the actual architecture of the core as part of the documentation effort. This actual architecture now becomes the planned architecture of the core and any future versions of the core can be analysed by the SAVE tool to identify violations of the planned architecture in order to ensure that critical architecture properties are always preserved. In the case that the product line architecture including the core is provided as source code to its users, which is the case for NASA's CFS (discussed above), there is a chance (or risk) that the core is being modified for each project that uses it, and thus variant analysis can be used to determine how the different versions of the core differ from each other and what the differences are. This analysis can also be used to determine if perhaps one (but probably not all) of the modifications of the analysed cores would be beneficial to a wider audience and thus should be harvested and integrated into a new managed version of the core and form part of the product line. In order to determine the effort to harvest and integrate such a new core feature, the analyst might use the SAVE tool to determine its dependencies on the other components of the core as described above.

Finally, since each product in a product line (independently of whether it was planned or emerged over time) consists of source code that is changed to fit a certain purpose, there is a need to check that each product adheres to defined architecture rules, e.g. a certain pattern or style must be used to avoid security vulnerabilities as described above. Variant analysis can be used to detect suspicious inconsistences across all products in the product line and the SAVE tool can be used to detect such violations that require a more detailed and individual analysis that requires checking that the planned architecture is indeed implemented in the actual architecture.

2.4 The SAVE Tool

Fraunhofer's Software Architecture Visualization and Evaluation (SAVE) tool [15] addresses the issues of software comprehension, maintenance and evolution. This allows software architects to navigate, visualize, analyse, compare, evaluate, and improve their software systems.

SAVE analyses, for example, C/C++, Java, Delphi, and Simulink code and identifies violations of interactions between components/modules of the software architecture in the implementation (the actual architecture) as compared the planned (or intended) architecture, thus enabling the identification of architectural drift.

SAVE can also be used to develop a new target architecture by modifying a reverse engineered architecture so that it fits new needs. The analyst can then reason about the impact on current architecture and determine the effort it would take to change the actual system accordingly. SAVE also be used to analyse the product-line potential and deviations of the software in terms of architectural commonalities and differences between different software products.

The tool is tailorable to a project's specific needs, architectural styles, design patterns, general guidelines, and design rationale. It allows the architect to visualize and navigate the architecture of the system in order to understand it as well as to analyse and identify violations on different levels of abstraction.

SAVE identifies architectural violations so that they can be corrected and prevents the architecture from degenerating. It ensures that the architecture is kept flexible despite software change and evolution. The architectural evaluation technology complements and makes reviews more efficient because it provides a high level picture of the software and can be used to identify areas of the software needing more attention.

The technology is best applied on critical long-lived software systems that will evolve over time. SAVE is intended for teams that need to assure that their software will continue to conform to its architectural specifications, and teams that develop and maintain product-line architectures.

The tool has been applied very successfully, for example, to the Common Ground of Johns Hopkins University/Applied Physics Laboratory [16], a shared architecture used in all JHU/APL-supported NASA missions. Deviations between the actual architecture and the planned, architectural deviations and violations were identified. Based on an updated set of architectural goals and design rationale, a new target architecture was defined using a set of components combined into three layers supported by design rules. An analysis of the new target architecture and how it might be impacted by a new requirement demonstrated that the changes were isolated to the middle layer only.

3   Variant Analysis

The Variant Analysis approach [17] and the corresponding tool address the problem of analysing and visualizing similarity of many (possibly large) variants of a software system. This analysis problem is especially relevant when several software system variants were created in the process of cloning or forking, in order to accommodate increasing customization. While system cloning is a frequent phenomenon in the software industry [12], code duplication causes maintenance problems which, after some time, create a need to merge these systems and introduce a systematic reuse approach. In this context, it is crucial to have precise information about the distribution of commonality and variability in the source code of each system variant – for example to identify clusters of similar components, or groups of particularly similar variants. However, this information is often not available because each variant has evolved independently over time. Consequently, VA aims at recovering and visualizing the similarity information using reverse engineering.

Besides the original application scenario described above, the provided technique of multi-comparison and similarity visualization can be used in any other scenario where the similarity information is useful. For example, an organization developing cloned systems might decide not to merge them, but nevertheless still wants to monitor the distribution of similarity in order to manage the evolution of cloned code and, for example, ensure that bug fixes are ported across the relevant variants. Furthermore, the similarity analysis is useful in the "grow-and-prune" approach to product line development [13], where the phases of unconstrained code growth, possibly resulting in cloned features, are interleaved with consolidation phases in which the new code is restructured to a reusable form.

3.1 Set-Based Similarity Concept

Variant Analysis constructs a hierarchical set similarity model to store the information about similarity of analysed software systems. Each analysed system is modelled as a set of elementary comparable elements, for example lines of source code. Whenever some of the defined elements are found to be equivalent (i.e. similar) across two or more systems, the set construction algorithm places these elements in the intersection of the respective sets. Hence, the similarity of any group of analysed systems can be expressed in terms of the relative sizes of resulting element sets and their intersections.

The process of constructing the set similarity model is shortly depicted in the following figures. Let's assume that the analysis goal is to describe the similarity of five variants of a source code file io.c, where the variants are named A, B, C, D and E. The five file variants and their example content are depicted in Fig. 1 which shows that the different io.c files have some commonalities but also differences.

io.c (A)	io.c (B)	io.c (C)	io.c (D)	io.c (E)
1 A	1 W	1 W	1 L	1 Y
2 B	2 B	2 B	2 B	2 B
3 C	3 C	3 C	3 C	3 C
4 D	4 X	4 Z	4 D	4 X
5 E	5 D	5 F	5 E	5 D
6 F	6 E	6 H	6 F	6 E
7 G	7 H	7 I	7 J	7 H
8 H	8 I		8 K	8 I
9 I			9 M	

Fig. 1. The example content of five variants of a source code file io.c. In each line, the line number and its textual content are shown.

In the example, we treat the source code lines as atomic comparable elements. The Longest Common Subsequence algorithm (a.k.a. diff) is used as the equivalence function that defines the similarity of the elements. To illustrate the difficulty of visualizing and understanding the resulting similarity across many variants, Fig. 2 depicts the similarity results provided by the diff algorithm applied to each possible pair of the variant source files. Although the provided result is correct and complete, it is still difficult and time-consuming for a developer to determine e.g. which code lines are identical in all systems, or which of them exist just in one system.

However, the similarity information provided by diff can be used to construct a set similarity model for the example file. For this purpose, we just use the simple principle described above: whenever the lines of code are found to be equivalent (i.e., similar) across two or more systems, the set construction algorithm places these elements in the intersection of the respective sets. This description is sufficient to understand the algorithm nature – its full details are described in [19]. Figure 3 presents the analysed files

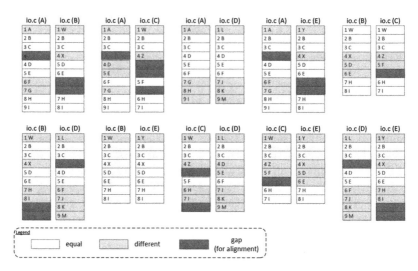

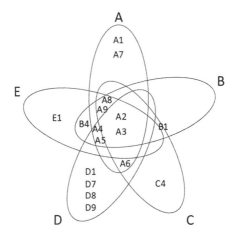

Fig. 2. Diff results for each possible pair of variant files io.c.

as intersecting sets of comparable elements. For a given group of equivalent text lines, just one line number is provided – for example, A2 represents the lines A2, B2, C2, D2, E2, which were all found equivalent by the diff algorithm as shown in Fig. 2.

Fig. 3. The set similarity model constructed for the five variants of io.c.

The set similarity information can be used to provide new, more understandable similarity visualizations. For example, in Fig. 4 the lines of five input file variants are coloured according to their similarity status: green (core) lines are identical in all variants, yellow (unique) lines exist in just one variant, and the remaining blue (shared) lines are identical for 2 to 4 variants. By adding further colours, lines fulfilling any sought condition expressed in the set algebra (e.g. *A AND B AND NOT C*) can be visually highlighted.

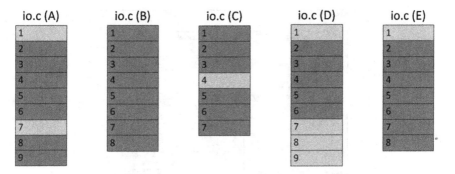

Fig. 4. A set-based similarity visualization for the five variants of io.c.

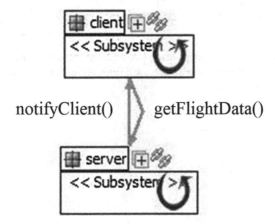

Fig. 5. TSAFE Client-Server structure visualized using SAVE

Fig. 6. Client of variant C before the change illustrated using SAVE

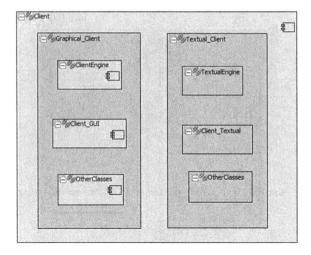

Fig. 7. Preferred solution for C-groups using two separate and parallel packages as part of the client. Expected new classes and new packages are green while existing ones are yellow illustrated using SAVE (Color figure online)

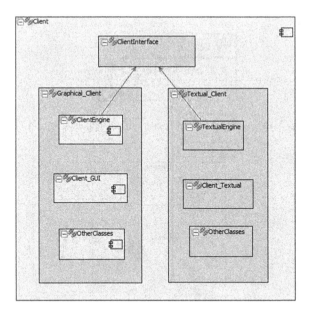

Fig. 8. Preferred solution for variant C through the introduction of an interface class for handling server communication and using a template pattern to connect to the interface class illustrated using SAVE

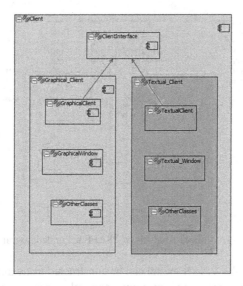

Fig. 9. Preferred solution for D-groups using two separate and parallel packages as part of the client with abstract client template pattern illustrated using SAVE

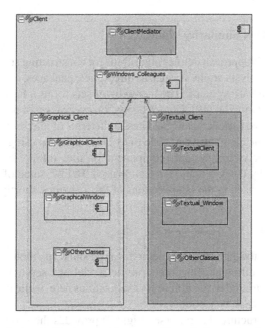

Fig. 10. Preferred solution for D-groups with new mediator design pattern but without the Client Interface showing.

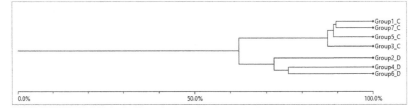

System	Component	Core	Shared	Unique	All Lines	No Query
Group1_C	Code	17 017	3 044	1 040	21 101	0
Group2_D	Code	17 017	3 156	4 596	24 769	0
Group3_C	Code	17 017	2 946	1 642	21 605	0
Group4_D	Code	17 017	3 543	2 526	23 086	0
Group5_C	Code	17 017	3 033	1 295	21 345	0
Group6_D	Code	17 017	3 127	2 893	23 037	0
Group7_C	Code	17 017	2 989	1 156	21 162	0
TSafe2_VA	Code	17 017	6 240	15 148	38 405	0

Fig. 11. Variant Analysis of TSAFE using dendrograms

In a general case, the VA set model can be constructed using any kind of similarity relation, provided that the relation is an equivalence relation (i.e., symmetrical, reflexive and transitive). In the case of non-transitive input, as possible e.g. for diff results, respective input processing steps constructing the equivalence relation are provided in [19].

3.2   Hierarchical Set Similarity Model

The Variant Analysis approach defines algorithms for constructing set similarity models for more complex analysis artefacts, such as directories, packages, components, subsystems and whole software systems. The hierarchy of sets forms a formally defined hierarchical set similarity model [19]. Consequently, on every level of the system hierarchy the similarity of a given artefact can be expressed in terms of intersecting sets composed of atomic comparable elements (e.g. code lines), and analysed using set algebra.

Furthermore, for every system, component or file, the set-based visualization concepts provided by the VA approach can be used. Below, some of the defined visualizations which are used in the later sections of this paper are shortly introduced.

3.3   Visualizations

In order to visualize the data from the hierarchical set similarity model various diagrams are used to present different viewpoints on the model and serve a range of analysis concerns. The background of the different visualizations here, while the example figures are placed in the case study section.

The hierarchy structure diagram (see Fig. 12) provides the summarized similarity information in a navigable UML-inspired view. Each tree element and corresponding child elements are represented by nested rectangles. Furthermore, information about the size (e.g. in LOC), the number of variants sharing an element, as well as the proportional distribution of the core, shared and unique code indicated by colored bars allow recognition of areas of interest according to the analysis goals.

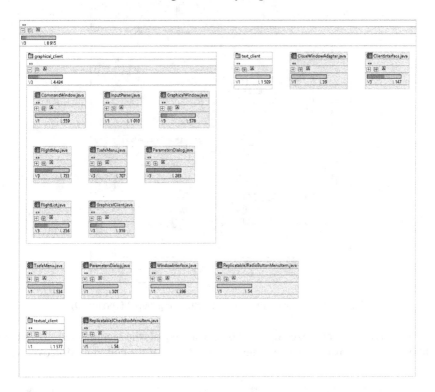

Fig. 12. Hierarchy structure visualization of the three D-versions (Color figure online)

One typical goal is the identification of groups of particularly similar systems. For this purpose we defined a visualization using dendrograms that can be used for similarity clustering of element sets (see Fig. 11). Dendrograms are phylogenetic trees often used in genetic biology for clustering of species. To generate this diagram the set similarity information is used as input. The construction starts with a forest of singleton trees—leafs—one for each system. Then the two most similar ones are merged in one tree with new root. The algorithm iterates over the forest until one tree is left. The length of the path between each two systems is proportional to their similarity. Thus, the depth of each branch intuitively corresponds to the proportion of commonality between leafs. Using this visualization an analyst can easily determine clusters of similar systems and get helpful insights of their relationships. Further phylogenetic tree visualization is available for automated estimation of probable evolution history as discussed in [18].

For the purposes of the case study below we introduce the tree map [20] diagram for similarity analysis. This technique supports a quick identification of large system elements having similar properties. Here we discuss one of the many possible usages of this visualization (more details can be found in [19]). The system elements are represented by nested rectangles according to their hierarchy structure. Each rectangle takes

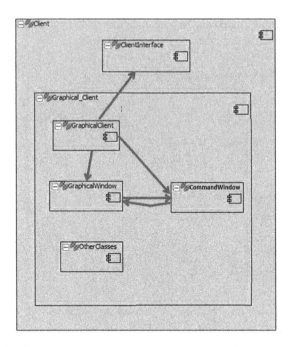

Fig. 13. Focusing on the client structure of group 2 (version D)

an area relative to its code size. Since the parent size equals the accumulated size of their children, they occupy exactly the same space under all of the children. Moreover, each

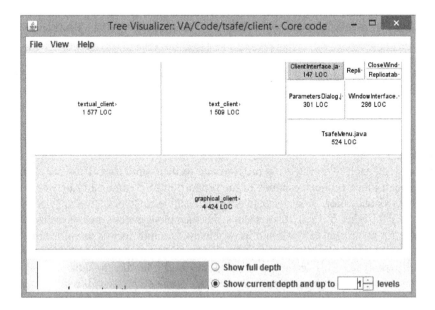

Fig. 14. Tree map of versions 2, 4, and 6 (Color figure online)

displayed rectangle is colored with respect to a metric. In this paper a scale from white to green (gray) is selected to indicate the proportion of core code contained in an element. Due to the hierarchical positioning, the tree map also supports the analyst in indicating if similar elements are located nearby or how they are distributed throughout the system. Figure 14 shows an example of the tree map based similarity visualization. The tree map can be configured to display further metrics, calculations, and variant specific perspectives to reflect specific analysis goals.

4   Case Study

We will now illustrate how we can use these two techniques to analyze variants. The system under study is the TSAFE system, which is described below.

4.1   The System Under Study: The TSAFE Product Line

The Tactical Separation Assisted Flight Environment (TSAFE) concept was defined at NASA Ames Research Center [21] and was proposed as a principal component of a larger Automated Airspace Computing System. The goal of TSAFE is to shift the burden of ensuring aircraft separation from human controllers to computers. The TSAFE software, which turned into a testbed for experimentation [22], is a 20 KLOC Java program that performs two primary functions: conformance monitoring and trajectory synthesis. The reason behind turning TSAFE into a testbed was to provide software researchers with a common and controlled software on which they can perform studies and compare them to each other. TSAFE has now been used in several empirical studies by various software researchers and thus has undergone significant change over time. TSAFE was designed for reuse and thus has the characteristics of a planned product line. At the same time, various versions of TSAFE have evolved in parallel and thus also has the characteristics of a de-facto product line. Thus TSAFE is a good example of many of the problems that can occur when software evolves over time and is good for illustrating the types of tools are needed to deal with those problems. Examples of built-in flexibility that facilitate adding new components are several design patterns that minimize the necessary changes to connect new components of various kinds [5]. Examples of parallel evolving versions is that TSAFE was used in a case study were seven groups of subjects were asked to add new components to TSAFE. Thus this change occurred in parallel without any interaction between the different groups. Below we use SAVE and VA to analyze the change that occurred.

4.2   The Architecture of TSAFE

TSAFE is a single user system running on one PC using one executable. The architecture is based on the client-server architecture style. The client-server style was introduced to separate the server from the client in order to facilitate future multi-user support. The client is responsible for interacting with the user and displaying results. The server is responsible for parsing the incoming radar feed and flight messages, maintaining the database, and processing clients' requests. The client and the server communicate with each other via interface classes. Client-server connections between other classes than these interface classes are not allowed because it would violate the built-in flexibility that allows for an effortless conversion to a true multi-user system using a common server. This client-server connection is thus an important construct that needs to be preserved for future evolution of TSAFE. The high level architecture of TSAFE is provided in Fig. 5. This diagram was generated by the SAVE tool which automatically reverse engineered the source code of the basic version of TSAFE before the seven groups started changing the source code. The fact that SAVE analyzes one version at a time is an important fact since the variant analysis discussed below operates on several versions of a system, not only one. The diagram confirms the fact that TSAFE has two main components: client and server and that they both know of each other, which is indicated by the bi-directional arrow. The diagram has been annotated with the main data items that are exchanged between the two components, namely notifyClient which is sent from the server to the client whenever there is new data to display, and getFlight-Data which is sent from the client to the server in order get the new data.

4.3   Basic TSAFE Variants C and D and the Change Request

Seven groups of students were given the assignment to implement a new a command line user interface in addition to the already existing graphical user interface in the version of TSAFE that was given to them.

TSAFE exists in two basic variants (C and D) that are functionally identical. The look and feel of their GUI is also identical. The high level structures of the two variants are identical in that both variants C and D are based on the client-server architecture as discussed earlier. This structure makes it possible to implement new client modules independently of the server.

The change request instructed the seven groups that the new interface should include a textual output of the flight data as well as a command interpreter with commands for selecting the data to be displayed and commands for setting the parameters for the different computations that occur. The change request also instructed them that the command line interface should be implemented in such a way that the user would have available exactly the same functions and information as the graphical client offers.

In variant C, all Client classes reside in one package. The Client's functions are scattered among these classes. Communication with the server is handled by the ClientEngine class. A high level view of the Client of variant C before the change is provided in Fig. 6. Only the two most prominent classes are shown in the figure. The ClientEngine is responsible for the communication with the server, and handles the processes within the Client. The Client_Gui is responsible for drawing and updating the user interface as well as processing user actions. The other classes are helper classes for the ClientEngine and Client_Gui.

For C-groups, the preferred solution would be to add the new textual client as a new sub component of the client component, in parallel with and independently of the already existing classes of the graphical client, as illustrated in Fig. 7. It should be noted that expected new classes and packages are green while existing ones are yellow. Each client (graphical client as well as textual client) would ideally be enclosed within a package. The class TextualEngine would be responsible for the correct functioning of the textual client and for handling the processes within the textual client. The class Client_textual would be responsible for the user interface in the form of a command line interface, and to initiate the processing of the user's commands once they are interpreted or parsed. The textual window would be part of the class Client_textual, the interpreter would be either in a separate class or within the class Client_textual, e.g. as an inner class together with the code that invokes already existing functions once a valid command has been identified. Therefore, these functions are not typically visible. However, since the structure of variant C is flat and does not have a package called graphical client, this package would have to be added. This also visually distinguishes the two clients from each other and creates a structure within the Client.

In addition, the solution for variant C could be improved by introducing a construct that handles the communication with the server. This can be accomplished by introducing a ClientInterface class and applying a template pattern (explained in more detail below for variant D since it has the structure already) to inherit its functions to the two engine classes as can be seen in Fig. 8. The common parts of the communication with the server would thus be moved from the ClientEngine and the TextualEngine classes to the abstract ClientInterface class. The ClientEngine and TextualEngine classes provide the specific implementations of this interface. Some of the functions of the ClientInterface would only be abstract because the implementations are different depending on whether the user interface is graphical or textual. One example is the public abstract function updateClient(ComputationResults), which is responsible for updates of the client. The ClientEngine and the TextualEngine process the information coming from the server through the interface and update their user interfaces accordingly.

4.4   The Abstract Client Template Pattern

For D-groups, the preferred solution is also to add the new textual client as a new sub component of the client component, in parallel with and independent of, not inside the already existing graphical client that handles the graphical user interface. The new textual client would ideally be enclosed within a new package. The structure of variant D is not flat and already has a package called graphical client so this package does not need to be added. See Fig. 9.

Similar to the C-variant, the classes GraphicalClient and TextualClient are responsible for the correct functioning of its client and to handle the processes within each of them. The classes Graphical_Window and Textual_Window are the user interfaces and handle all user interactions. Functions implemented in the class Textual_Window are the user interface in form of a command line interface, which reads the user commands and the console for displaying information. The parser can be implemented within the class Textual_Window, preferably in a separate class since it belongs to the textual client in the same way as the menu bars and dialog windows belong to the graphical client.

The D variant is also different from variant C in that it has built-in flexibility supporting a parallel implementation of client modules that is supported by the *abstract* *client template pattern.* See Fig. 9. The abstract client template pattern was introduced in order to facilitate for future addition of various client modules.

In addition, variant D has a ClientInterface Class, see Fig. 9. This class contains all functions needed for the communication with the server and facilitates the creation of a new client-module and its connection to the server. The ClientInterface is further connected to the GraphicalClient.

The preferred solution for D-groups would thus be to let the TextualClient class of the new sub component textual_client inherit all functions and attributes from the class ClientInterface using the abstract client template pattern in order to arrive at the preferred solution illustrated in Fig. 10.

Information used by both clients are shared information, and therefore stored within the class ClientMediator. Whenever these settings are changed in one of the clients, the information is passed on to the ClientMediator who gets the latest flight data based on the then current settings and updates the clients.

For a readable display of the flight information, such as latitude, longitude, the conversion functions and parameters provided by a Calculator class in the server could be used. If they are used, they should either be accessed via the client-server interface, thus expanding it with some additional functionality, or by creating (e.g. copying and pasting) such functions within the Client itself.

To implement these functions, in addition to the new client module, we expected no major changes to the server or the client-server interface.

The basic rule was that the two client-modules should not be connected directly to each other. Instead, when parameter settings are changed within one client, a mediator should be made aware of the change and notify the other clients about the new settings. In addition, Server-oriented settings need to be communicated to the server, while client-oriented settings should be kept local in the client.

5   Variant Analysis of TSAFE

We will now illustrate how the different solutions can be analysed using SAVE and VA. The first step in the analysis is to analyse all seven variants together using dendrograms, see Fig. 11. This analysis shows that even though there are two basic variants of TSAFE (C and D), they still have a large common core of 17,017 non-commented non-blank lines of Java code. This commonality is illustrated by the long initial line to the left in the diagram. The diagram also shows that the four groups that implemented the change request using the C-variant are more similar to each other than the three groups that used the D-version, which is expected. In addition, the diagram shows that some groups' solutions (e.g. 1 and 7 as well as 4 and 6) are more similar than other solutions (e.g. 1 and 3 as well as 2 and 4). It should be noted that TSafe2_VA is a hypothetical variant that just adds all lines of code together.

In Fig. 12 the client of the D-versions, i.e. version 2, 4, and 6, are analyzed together using a hierarchy structure visualization diagram. The diagram clearly shows that essentially all classes in the client were changed in order to implement the change request. Only ParametersDialog.java remained unchanged, which we can determine since the bar is green and the number of versions is 3 (V3). All other classes have been changed or are new because either the bar has other colours than green, e.g. cyan and yellow, which indicate change, or the number of versions is 1 (V1), which indicates that the class is new. The tree map in Fig. 14 provides a different perspective of the same changes with the difference that the size of each box, which represents a file, indicates the size of the file, while the colour of a box indicates whether it has been changed or not. White colour indicates that there are many changes in that particular file. Dark green indicates that there has been no changes. The heat map shows all files in the client for all three versions (i.e. 2, 4 and 6). The legend in the heat map provides an overview and confirms that most files were changed. For example, the legend has a long bar to the left in the white area which shows that most files were extensively changed. To the right in the legend, there is a small bar in the green area showing that very few files remained unchanged.

In order to understand how each variant was implemented, we use the SAVE view to analyse group 2's solution in more detail, see Fig. 13. This view tells us that no separate packages for the two client-modules was introduced. One class was added to implement the command line console (CommandWindow) and one class was added to implement the parser (InputParser). Thus, the template pattern was not used. And thus the clients were connected (CommandWindow interacts with GraphicalClient and vice versa. The textual client (here represented by the new classes CommandWindow and InputParser) gets the current stored settings and parameters from the graphical client. An instance of the commandWindow is stored in the GraphicalClient and they use functions in the CommandWindow and the GraphicalClient, for example getSelectedFlightsChanged, to exchange information regarding changed user settings. This shows that the two clients are connected also through this data exchange and thus are not independent of each other as the change request specified. Further analysis shows that without the graphical client, the textual client would not work and the TSAFE system would stop running or even crash because the addressed object does not exist. Thus, the textual client was inserted without having the option to configure the system for running with and without it and thus the desired built-in flexibility was not achieved.

6   Tracing Software Evolution

Our view, as outlined in the introduction, is that an evolving (long-lived or adaptive) system can be viewed as a software product line [4]. We can view particular products in the product line as versions of the software at a given point in time, or as a particular release of the software. If we can identify commonalities between products in this product line, we have identified those components that do not change or evolve. Similarly, identifying differences (however subtle) between products in the product line enables us to identify what parts of the system are changing in successive instances of the system. If we consider various mutations of the product (that is, the product with, perhaps unconstrained, changes), we can determine if these are valid products of the product line and in this way predict or control various changes to the software and the way in which it evolves. The SAVE tool enables us to take visual snapshots of changes of a single variant of the system while VA allows us to study several variants at a time. A potential enhancement to the tool suite would be to allow for mutations and to investigate if these mutations are viable by determining that the mutated product is still conformant to the product line's reference architecture. The ability to achieve the latter is a current feature of the SAVE tool. The SAVE tool can, for example, compare various products from the product line and determine the commonalities and differences among them. This information can be used to determine the "distance" between the various products and how to manage these differences. For example, such analysis can determine that important architecture characteristics are violated in some of the products and that they therefore run the risk of becoming difficult to change. Such analysis can also be used to identify stable components that never seem to change from version to version and that could be turned into a platform that the entire product line would benefit from. The SAVE tool's feature that identifies violations between the planned architecture and the actual can be used in this context to detect violations of important structures supporting built-in flexibility. When such built-in flexibility is violated, then adaptive systems might have difficulty evolving as needed. For example, a plug-in architecture could have been added to allow for adding future components in a flexible way without knowing beforehand the behaviour and functionality of these components. If such an architecture were violated, then the desired flexibility is been lost and the risk is that changes will be significantly more difficult to implement than planned.

7 Conclusion

The complexities of software evolution, which is an unavoidable phase of the software lifecycle, can be significantly reduced by viewing evolving software as a software product line. The view is valid whether we are concerned with software systems that evolve over long periods, or whether we are dealing with constantly adapting software systems.

Such a view requires a software architecture that supports variability management. This includes identifying common components, components that can be added or deleted depending on the current and specific needs, flexible interfaces and constructs that allow for plugging in future components that have not yet been defined (or states of the evolving system that are not yet known). Information for building this product line can be used from previous projects similar to the current system under consideration and/or from previous releases (or states) of the current system.

In this paper, we described how we reverse engineered the actual architecture from the source code of TSAFE. We then showed how we developed new target architectures based on the reverse engineered one and the expected changes derived from the change request and reasoned about the impact. We then described how we can analyse the actual change across seven different implementations at the same time and how we can use that information to visualize where the change actually occurred using different visualization techniques. We then described how we can analyse the implementation of one particular solution and determine if it matches the target architecture or not. To summarize: We described our approach to software evolution management based on the concept of product lines and using two analysis tools: SAVE software architecture analysis, that has previously proven to be highly successful in analysing architecture degradation, and VA code similarity analysis, which we repeatedly used for understanding the similarity of groups of large cloned software systems.. Now, we found both these analysis techniques to be particularly useful for analysing software evolution in our current approach.

Acknowledgements. This work was supported, in part, by a grant from NASA. This work was supported, in part, by Science Foundation Ireland grant 13/RC/2094 and co-funded under the European Regional Development Fund through the Southern & Eastern Regional Operational Programme to Lero - the Irish Software Research Centre (www.lero.ie). Special thanks to Bettina Anders, Jörg Fellmann, and Chris Ackermann who helped conduct the TSAFE case study and analyse the results. Fraunhofer IESE thanks Bo Zhang for discussions on the topics described in this paper.

References

1. Lehman, M.M.: Programs, life cycles, and the laws of software evolution. Proc. IEEE **68**, 1060–1076 (1980)
2. Schneidewind, N.F.: Application of SRE to ultrareliable systems — the space shuttle. DoD SoftwareTech News **8**(1), 19–23 (2004)
3. Sterritt, R., Hinchey, M.: Biologically-inspired concepts for autonomic self-protection in multiagent systems. In: Barley, M., Mouratidis, H., Unruh, A., Spears, D., Scerri, P., Massacci, F. (eds.) SASEMAS 2004–2006. LNCS, vol. 4324, pp. 330–341. Springer, Heidelberg (2009)
4. Pena, J., Hinchey, M.G., Resinas, M., Sterritt, R., Rash, J.L.: Designing and managing evolving systems using a MAS product line approach. Sci. Comput. Programm. **66**(1), 71–86 (2007)
5. Anders, B., Fellmann, J., Lindvall, M., Rus, I.: Experimenting with software architecture flexibility using an implementation of the tactical separation assisted flight environment. In: SEW, pp. 275–284 (2005)
6. Godfrey, M.W., Lee, E.H.S.: Secrets from the monster: extracting Mozilla's software architecture. In: Proceedings of Second Symposium Constructing Software Engineering Tools (CoSET00) (2000)
7. Eick, S.G., Graves, L., Karr, A.F., Marron, J.S.: Does code decay? Assessing the evidence from change management data. IEEE Trans. Softw. Eng. **27**(1), 1–12 (2001)
8. Tvedt, R.T., Costa, P., Lindvall, M.: Does the code match the design? A process for architecture evaluation. In: Proceedings of the International Conference on Software Maintenance (2002)
9. Rosik, J., Le Gear, A., Buckley, J., Babar, M.A., Connolly, D.: Assessing architectural drift in commercial software development: a case study. Softw. Pract. Exp. **41**(1), 63–86 (2011)
10. Hallsteinsen, S., Hinchey, M., Park, S., Schmid, K.: Dynamic software product lines. Computer **41**, 93 (2008)
11. Ganesan, D., Lindvall, M., McComas, D., Bartholomew, M., Slegel, S., Medina, B., Krikhaar, R.L., Verhoef, C., Montgomery, L.P.: An analysis of unit tests of a flight software product line. Sci. Comput. Program. **78**(12), 2360–2380 (2013)
12. Dubinsky, Y., Rubin, J., Berger, T., Duszynski, S., Becker, M., Czarnecki, K.: An exploratory study of cloning in industrial software product lines. In: 17th European Conference on Software Maintenance and Reengineering (CSMR), pp. 25–34 (2013)

13. Mende, T., Beckwermert, F., Koschke, R., and Meier, G.: Supporting the grow-and-prune model in software product lines evolution using clone detection. In: Proceedings of the Euromicro Conference on Software Maintenance and Reengineering, CSMR (2008)

14. Ganesan, D., Lindvall, M., Ruley, L., Wiegand, R., Ly, V., Tsui, T.: Architectural analysis of systems based on the publisher-subscriber style. In: 17th Working Conference on Reverse Engineering (WCRE), pp. 173–182 (2010)

15. Miodonski, T.P., Knodel, J., Lindvall, M., Muthig, D.: Evaluation of Software Architectures with Eclipse, (IESE)-Report 107.04/E, Institute for Empirical Software Engineering, Kaiserslautern, Germany

16. Stratton, W.C., Sibol, D.E., Lindvall, M., Costa, P.: Technology infusion of SAVE into the ground software development process for NASA missions at JHU/APL. In: Proceedings of 2007 IEEE Aerospace Conference, Big Sky, MT, March 2007

17. Duszynski, S., Knodel, J., Becker, M.: Analyzing the source code of multiple software variants for reuse potential. IEEE Computer Society, pp. 303–307 (2011)

18. Tenev, V., Nebel, M., Duszynski, S.: Directed coloured multigraph alignments for variant analysis of software systems. (IESE)-Report 112.11/E, Fraunhofer Institute for Empirical Software Engineering, Kaiserslautern (2011)

19. Duszynski, S.: Analyzing Similarity of Cloned Software Variants Using Hierarchical Set Models. Fraunhofer, Stuttgart (2015)

20. Bederson, B.B., Shneiderman, B., Wattenberg, M.: Ordered and quantum treemaps: making effective use of 2D space to display hierarchies. ACM Trans. Graph. 21(4), 833–854 (2002)

21. Erzberger, H., Paielli, R.A.: Concept for next generation air traffic control system. Air Traffic Control Q. 10(4), 355–378 (2002)

22. Lindvall, M., Rus, I.P., Memon, A.M., Zelkowitz, M.V., Betin-Can, A., Bultan, T., Ackermann, C., Anders, B., Asgari, S., Basili, V.R., Hochstein, L., Forrest Shull, F., Tvedt, R.T., Pech, D., V, D.: Experimenting with software testbeds for evaluating new technologies. Empirical Softw. Eng. Int. J. 12(4), 417–444 (2007)

Compositional Model-Based System Design and Other Foundations for Mastering Change

Stavros Tripakis[1,2]([envelope])

[1] Aalto University, Espoo, Finland
[2] University of California, Berkeley, USA
stavros@eecs.berkeley.edu

Abstract. The topic of this paper is the design of dynamical systems, such as embedded or cyber-physical systems. Is there a science of system design, and if so, what are its elements? We believe that its key elements are three: modeling, analysis, and implementation, and we discuss fundamental research challenges in each category. We then argue that *compositionality* is an essential cross-cutting concern, and one of the foundations for mastering change. Beyond compositionality, we discuss other key problems when dealing with change, namely, multi-view modeling and synthesis.

Keywords: Computer-aided system design · System modeling · Formal verification · Compositionality · Modularity · Synthesis · Multi-view modeling · Learning

1 Systems and Models of Systems

The topic of this paper is system design. It will be useful to briefly discuss *systems* before discussing system design. What is a system? Many definitions exist, but for the purposes of this work, we will define a system as something that has

- a notion of *state*, and
- a notion of *dynamics*, that is, a set of rules that prescribe how the state evolves over time.

The system might also have a notion of *inputs* and *outputs*, which allow to describe how the system interacts with its *environment*. The inputs typically influence the evolution of the state, and as such are the means to *control* a system. The outputs correspond to what is *observable*. Inputs and outputs need not be present in all systems. Some systems are *closed* in the sense that they

---

This work was partially supported by the Academy of Finland and the U.S. National Science Foundation (awards #1329759 and #1139138). Technical details of the works the author has been involved in can be found in the referenced papers, as well as in more pedagogical forms in [Tri15b, Tri16].

B. Steffen (Ed.): Transactions on FoMaC I, LNCS 9960, pp. 113–129, 2016.
DOI: 10.1007/978-3-319-46508-1_7

have no inputs, and are therefore uncontrollable. Some systems have no outputs and are therefore unobservable. Some systems may be completely *black boxes* in the sense that they have neither inputs nor outputs.

Summarizing, in this work we are interested in *dynamical* systems[1]:

$$system = states + dynamics \; (+ \; inputs) \; (+ \; outputs).$$

Our discussion so far does not not really make a distinction between *real* systems and *virtual* systems. A virtual system can be a mathematical model of a system, or a piece of software simulating a real system, etc. The fundamental notions of state, dynamics, inputs and outputs apply to both real and virtual systems. We will often simply use the term system when we refer to both real systems or system models.

As an example, a *finite state machine* (FSM) is a system (in this case, a virtual system, and in particular a mathematical model). An FSM, say of type Mealy, is typically described by a tuple

$$(I, O, S, s_0, \delta, \lambda)$$

where

- I is the set of inputs.
- O is the set of outputs.
- S is the set of states.
- $s_0 \in S$ is the initial state.
- $\delta : S \times I \rightarrow S$ is the *transition function*, describing how the state evolves depending on the input.
- $\lambda : S \times I \rightarrow O$ is the *output function*, describing how the outputs are obtained.

This model contains all the fundamental elements of a system: states, inputs, outputs (captured by the set O and the output function λ) and dynamics (captured by δ and the initial state s_0).

It is worth noting that "hidden" in the dynamics is implicit a notion of *time*. Indeed, the dynamics describes how the state evolves *in time*, therefore, by definition, state and time are interdependent concepts. State is the thing that changes over time. Time on the other hand can be seen as the evolution of state.

Time can be discrete, continuous, etc., depending on the type of dynamics. In an FSM model, time is discrete. The machine evolves in a sequence of discrete steps, moving from state s_0 to s_1, s_2, ..., and so on, depending on the given inputs. In a differential equation model, time is continuous and the state evolves continuously over time. In a distributed system, time may be modeled as a partial order.

The definition of system given above seems reasonable, but it only goes so far. It captures the essence of what a dynamical system is, but it is not very helpful when describing large and complex systems. For instance, how to go

---

[1] One may argue that *static* systems are just a special case of dynamical systems, where the dynamics is trivial: the state never changes.

about defining the state and dynamics of a large distributed software system? or a complex biological system? or a society of interacting agents? when attempting to define the state and dynamics of such complex systems, we must resort to the principle of *compositionality*. Rather than giving a *monolithic* definition of the entire system, we describe on one hand the *components* of the system (i.e., its *subsystems*), and on the other hand how these components *interact*.

Based on this observation, we can refine our definition of system to the following:

$$system = atomic\ system\ or\ composite\ system$$
$$atomic\ system = state + dynamics\ (+\ inputs)\ (+\ outputs)$$
$$composite\ system = set\ of\ subsystems + interaction\ rules$$

As an example, the block diagram below shows two blocks representing two subsystems A and B, each having an input and an output (and possibly internal state, not shown in the figure). The blocks are connected so that the output of A is fed into the input of B:

This connection results in a new composite system. However, in order to define the behavior of the composite system, it is not enough to know the behaviors (states and dynamics) of A and B. We must also know the rules of interaction, or in other words, the composition semantics. Many possibilities exist, including

- *synchronous composition*, where A and B "move simultaneously", as in a synchronous digital circuit, where gates communicate by "wires" which ideally have zero delay;
- *asynchronous composition*, where each subsystem moves at its own pace, and the two communicate via different mechanisms, e.g., a queue, heap, or some other type of shared memory location where A writes to and B (asynchronously) reads from;
- *rendez-vous composition*, where each subsystem moves a-priori independently from the other, except for certain pairs of actions of the two, which must occur simultaneously;
- etc.

Of course, the block diagram itself does not reveal the subtleties of these different types of interaction, in the same way that each block drawing does not reveal the internal dynamics of each subsystem.

To conclude this section, when describing a system, we need to describe each of its subsystems' state and dynamics, and the rules for their composition. The same is true when we build a system. We need to build its subsystems (or reuse existing legacy subsystems) and we also need to build their composition, a process often called *system integration* in industrial circles. System integration has a reputation for being the most difficult problem in system development. Practitioners repeatedly complain about situations where all subsystems work perfectly according to their specifications, yet when assembled together they yield a system which does not work.

2   System Design

We use the term system design to refer to all phases of system development, including initial design, verification, implementation, testing, maintenance and update, and so on. Is there a science of system design and if so, what are its foundations?

In practice, much of system design today is done in an ad-hoc manner, essentially using a *trial-and-error* approach. The system is designed, a prototype is implemented, and that prototype is tested. Errors are found, which could be design errors or implementation errors. These are fixed, and the process is repeated. This approach is problematic in many ways. First, it is costly, especially in the case of design errors. These are very expensive to fix, especially when found late in the process, after a prototype has been built (and sometimes even after the system has been deployed – c.f. car and aircraft recalls). Second, the trial-and-error approach heavily relies on testing to identify errors. Testing can discover errors, but cannot prove their absence. As a result, the trial-and-error approach is not very reliable, and unsuitable for systems which are *safety-critical*. With the advent of embedded or cyber-physical systems [Lee08, RLSS10, KK12], safety-critical systems are in proliferation. From nuclear power plants to automated factories, from airplane to car controllers, from pacemakers to consumer robotics, from smart buildings to the smart power grid, all these applications involve constant interactions with humans, and as such require high degrees of safety and reliability.

A more principled design approach is so-called *model-based design* (e.g., see [NM09]). The model-based design approach (MBD) advocates to first build system *models* rather than system prototypes, and to use these models in order to identify design errors and fix them as early as possible in the design process. Indeed, models are cheaper and faster than prototypes to build, verify, and test. On the other hand, models are only virtual systems, and not the "real thing". Therefore, there is a danger of not being able to bridge the gap between the model and the prototype, when the time comes to eventually build a prototype. This danger is real, as models often make idealistic assumptions about system behavior, which may break down during implementation. For instance, a model may assume perfect synchrony, which is impossible to achieve during implementation, due to clock discrepancies, computation and communication delays, etc.

In order to face this problem, MBD must rely on powerful *automatic implementation* tools. Scheduling and code generation tools belong in this category. They allow to automatically generate executable systems (hardware or software) from models. It is essential that the implementation methods used in these tools are *semantics-preserving*, meaning that the resulting implementation preserves the properties of the model. Otherwise, there is little confidence that the implementation is correct, even if the original model is correct. Ideally, the techniques are "push-button" (i.e., fully automated) and the generated system is equivalent to the original model. Then, assuming that the model is correct, the system is *correct by construction*.

To summarize, the model-based design process includes three key elements:

1. *Modeling*, which addresses the problem of how to express in the best possible way (i.e., easy to describe and understand, economic, mathematically rigorous and unambiguous, etc.) the system that we want to design.
2. *Analysis*, which addresses the problem of how to ensure that what we designed is really what we want (i.e., is free of errors, performance and cost issues, etc.).
3. *Implementation*, which addresses the problem of how to generate, ideally fully automatically, working systems from the design models, in a semantics-preserving manner.

Each of the three elements comes with significant research challenges, some of which are discussed below.

Modeling: A major challenge is coming up with the right modeling languages for capturing different types of systems from a variety of domains: automotive, electronics, energy, health care, biology, etc. Traditionally, languages such as Verilog, VHDL, and SystemC are well-established in the domain of digital circuit design. Languages such as Simulink are widespread in the domains of control, embedded and cyber-physical systems (see also [BLTT12]). Languages such as Promela and LTL are used in formal verification. All these languages are being used in a MBD context, although each class has its own specificities. For example, the concept of *non-determinism* is natural as well as essential in verification languages such as Promela, where the system being verified is typically embedded in an environment which generates (non-deterministically) all possible input sequences. On the other hand, languages such as Simulink are mainly deterministic, since they are primarily targeted at simulation of controllers. As is typical in simulation, the inputs to these controllers are generated by random sequence generators. Modeling the environment has not been a high priority until lately, when it has been realized that this is as important (if not more!) as modeling the system itself. Languages and language extensions such as *e* and *SystemVerilog* aim at filling this gap.

In addition to the above fields, several formal, executable, modeling languages have been developed in the software engineering field, e.g., see [JHS+11,LW14]. There is also a multitude of *domain-specific languages* in a variety of domains, from business and law (e.g., see [GM05,NPB11]), to biology (e.g., see [FH06, BLC+11]).

Analysis: We believe that formal verification is the most important frontier in analysis today. In its basic form, the *model checking* problem is well understood (e.g., see [CGP00,BK08]) and consists in checking (ideally fully automatically) that a given model satisfies a given property (which also needs to be formally specified). Despite several fundamental challenges, both Formal verification has many challenges, including fundamental theoretical, as well as methodological and practical challenges. At the theoretical level, even the most basic problem of checking *reachability* of certain system states becomes undecidable for most systems having a potentially infinite state-space. But even for finite-state systems, state spaces become huge and exploring them exhaustively is often practically infeasible, the so-called *state explosion* problem. In addition, one should not underestimate methodological challenges, including the difficulty of writing formal models and/or formally specifying system properties (e.g., see [BBBB12]). The latter often requires advanced knowledge in logical formalisms, which unfortunately most engineers lack (education here is an issue).

Despite these challenges, as stated in [BH14], the reach and power of verification methods have increased considerably over the past decades, with several important success stories, not just in the traditional domains of hardware and software verification (e.g., see [KGN+09, KAE+10]), but also in what might have seemed "exotic" domains just a few years ago, such as cloud computing [NRZ+15].

Many of the available verification methods and tools focus on discrete systems, however, a large body of research exists also for timed, continuous, and hybrid systems (e.g., see [TD09, KK12, MWM13]).

Apart from verification, many other analysis problems are also significant. Simulation is the workhorse of analysis, and efficient simulation techniques (for instance, which exploit the parallelism of modern hardware) is an interesting avenue for research. Other analysis problems, such as *schedulability analysis*, *worst-case execution time analysis*, *performance analysis*, *reliability analysis*, etc., often belong to lower levels of system design, closer to implementation. It is crucial that such types of analyses be made possible already at the early stages of design, and ideally before the implementation is available. This is of course challenging, as most of these analyses are by definition dependent on the implementation. The way out of this conundrum is *design-space exploration* where the possible implementation options are modeled and analyzed, so that an educated choice can be made. Unfortunately, this is easier said than done, as the complexities of modeling real implementations are often overwhelming. Although a number of empirical solutions exist, primarily in the industry, more research is needed to come up with mathematical approaches, which provide rigorous guarantees on the analysis results (e.g., margin of error in performance analysis).

Implementation: As mentioned above this category includes a number of tools, from scheduling, to code generation and compilation, with the main challenge being bridging the semantic gap between high-level models and low-level implementations. Our experience shows that there is no unique formula for bridging such gaps. For instance, the semantics-preserving implementation of a synchronous model on a distributed asynchronous execution platform requires a FIFO-queue based protocol reminiscent of process networks [TPB+08], whereas the semantics-preserving implementation of the same model on a single computer with multi-tasking requires a very different double-buffer based protocol [CSST08]. And these two solutions are still different from the case where the high-level model is asynchronous (e.g., dataflow) and the low-level implementation is synchronous (e.g., a digital circuit) [TLR+15]. These experiences show that semantics-preserving implementation methods are likely to be quite dependent on the case at hand, both in terms of the type of model we are starting from, as well as the target execution platform.

Before we end this section, we would like to mention one objection often heard about model-based design, namely, that automated methods cannot match human developers. Real systems, critics of MBD might say, have very stringent requirements and optimality constraints. It is impossible to meet those except by careful implementation. This cannot be done at an abstract, modeling level. It needs to be done at the implementation level, and it needs to be done by experienced developers. Although there is some truth to this criticism, it is also reminiscent of arguments against high-level programming languages, and in favor of programming in, say, assembly. Although it may be true that an expert assembly programmer can do a better job than a compiler, it is also true that, first, there are fewer and fewer such experts, and second, a human is much slower than a compiler. Ultimately, as history has shown, it pays off to raise the level of abstraction in design (after all, programming has moved from assembly to FORTRAN, to C, to Java, etc.). Some efficiency may be lost, but the productivity gains outweigh any optimality losses.

3 Compositionality

The size and complexity of real systems is such that monolithic methods, which try to handle an entire system as a whole, do not scale. Because of this, researchers have developed *compositional* methods, which allow to handle systems on a component-by-component basis. Compositionality is a heavily used term with many meanings, but in general, it encompasses the principle of *divide and conquer*. The idea is to make the problem simpler by restricting it to a smaller part of a system, for instance, a component or subsystem.

Compositionality is a cross-cutting concern, affecting all three elements of model-based design:

Modeling: Large models are not built monolithically. They are built by composing simpler models. For instance, graphical languages such as Simulink and Ptolemy [EJL+03] use *block hierarchy* as the main mechanism to structure a model as a tree of submodels, up to basic blocks (the leaves of the tree) which are taken from a predefined library. In this way, although the entire model may be large (e.g., it may contain hundreds or thousands of blocks), at any given level of the hierarchy the user only sees a dozen or so blocks. Textual languages such as Modelica or Promela use similar principles from programming languages, such as classes and modules.

Analysis: Compositionality is key in analysis, in order to avoid problems such as state-explosion. Ideally, one should be able to analyze each subsystem independently, and then somehow combine the results to reason about the properties of the entire system. A plethora of methods aiming at that have been proposed in the verification and formal methods literature. They range from *compositional, or assume-guarantee verification* methods (e.g., see [Pnu85,

CLM89, HQR98, NT10]) to *refinement-based frameworks* and *interface theo-ries* (e.g., see [Dil87, LT89, BS01, AH99, dAH01, TLHL11, PT14, PT16b, DPT16]). Generally speaking, all these methods aim at decomposing a verification task into simpler tasks, using a set of compositionality proof rules. Unfortunately, achieving this decomposition is easier said than done, as it often requires coming up with *abstract models* which capture the essential properties of components or their environment, yet are simpler (smaller) to verify. Devising these abstract models is a manual and often difficult task.

In general, abstraction is a key principle for efficient analysis, and goes hand-in-hand with compositionality. The field of *abstract interpretation*, pioneered in [CC77], offers a general framework for defining and reasoning about abstractions. This framework has found a large domain of applications, especially in program analysis, where several software verification tools employ the framework's basic principles.

Formal methods and verification are not the only fields which need and employ compositional methods. These methods are essential in almost every aspect of system design and analysis, and have been studied in the settings of performance analysis (c.f. the *real-time calculus* [TCN00]), scheduling (c.f. the *compositional real-time scheduling* framework of [SL08]), and many others. They have also been studied for a long time in the context of programming and software engineering in general, see, for instance, [Mey92].

Even in basic system simulation, compositional methods play an important role. Scalability requires that simulation tools be built in a *modular* manner, separating the models, on one hand, from the simulation engines, on the other. Such modular architectures are implemented, for instance, in tools like Simulink and Ptolemy, where the modeling blocks are objects (in the case of Ptolemy, Java objects) which implement a well-defined API. The simulation engines then run the simulation by calling the different methods of this API on the various objects in the model. In this way, when a new modeling block is added to the library, no modification is necessary in the simulation engines. And vice-versa, when a new simulation engine is added, no modification is necessary in the block library. Note that there are more than one simulation engines, in general. For instance, Simulink implements many different numerical integration solvers, among which the user can choose. Ptolemy implements many different concurrency semantics (discrete, continuous, synchronous, dataflow, ...), each having its own simulation engine [TSSL13].

Note that Simulink and Ptolemy use different APIs. Recently, the so-called *functional mockup interface* (FMI) has been proposed as a standard API for model exchange and cosimulation [BOÅ+12]. The question "what is the right API for modular simulation" is an interesting one and currently an active area of research (e.g., see [BBG+13, Tri15a, BGL+15, BGJ+15, CLT+16]).

Implementation: Compositionality is also essential during implementation. For example, consider standard compilers for, say, C or Java. These tools offer so-called *separate compilation*, which exploit the modular structure of the program, to compile it also in a modular manner. In that way, the programmer not only can split the program in multiple files or classes, instead of writing it as a single monolithic piece of code, but he can also compile those files or classes separately. This capability enables many others:

- First, it provides fast, *incremental* compilation. When only part of the program changes, only the part that changed needs to be recompiled.
- Second, it enables software *libraries*. These are software components which are not meant to be used alone, but instead provide a certain functionality to larger programs that use them.
- Third, it enables protection of *intellectual property*, by allowing libraries to hide their internal implementation details, and only allow users to interact with them via a well-defined API (application programming interface).

All the above are quite standard in software engineering, but they are not yet widely available in system engineering. For instance, Simulink employs quite simplistic code generation methods, where either the entire hierarchy of the block diagram is *flattened* (therefore violating the hiding principle), or code generation is monolithic, assuming for instance that all outputs of a block depend on all inputs [LT08]. Modular code generation methods to solve this problem for block diagrams of Simulink type have been developed in [LT08, LST09].

The above are only first steps in compositionality, which still has a long way to go before becoming standard practice. Compositionality is one of the foundations for mastering change, as it enables incremental development. But although compositionality is necessary, it alone is not sufficient. In the following section we touch upon some other important research directions and recent work which we believe is relevant to the topic of mastering change.

4   Beyond Compositionality

Multi-view modeling: Large systems are built by many people organized in teams with different responsibilities. Communication between such teams is often difficult, because of the different backgrounds and concerns of the stakeholders involved. Although each team may follow a model-based design methodology, using state-of-the-art modeling languages and tools, typically the models and results that each team produces will be of a different nature than those of the other teams. For instance, the control engineering team might develop continuous-time block-diagram models in Simulink, whereas the software engineering team develops class diagrams in UML [BLTT12]. The reliability team may build yet another model, say fault trees, in order to evaluate the fault tolerance of the design. Comparing and combining all these models and results in order to reason about the whole system is a difficult task, often resembling "comparing apples with oranges". Inconsistencies between the different models are common, and often due to miscommunication of the assumptions used by the various teams.

To reason about this problem, a formal *multi-view modeling* framework was proposed in [RT14]. This framework is based on the notion of *views* which can be seen as abstractions of a system. The difference with abstract interpretation is that there we often start with a concrete system (e.g., piece of software) and we try to create an abstract model which is easier to reason about. In multi-view modeling, the system typically does not exist yet, as it is being designed. The different views, then, correspond to the different models that each team develops. Each view captures one aspect of the system. Due to miscommunication or other mistakes, the views may contradict each other, i.e., be inconsistent.

Formally, view consistency is defined as follows: a set of views is consistent if (and only if) there *exists* a system which could generate those views. Preliminary results in [RT14] show how consistency can be checked automatically for the case of discrete systems and views, modeled as state machines or transition systems, and where abstractions are *projections* that hide part of the system's state. These results barely scratch the surface, and more research is needed along many directions, among which: studying other types of abstraction than projections (e.g., temporal abstractions that change the time scale); studying heterogeneous views (e.g., combination of discrete and continuous-time views), and developing synthesis methods which not only check consistency but also generate automatically a *witness system*. Such methods are provided in [RT14, PT16a, RST16], but only for discrete systems. Also, these methods do not take into account optimality criteria. Typically, there will be multiple witness systems, and one would like to choose one according to performance, cost, or other concerns.

Synthesis: Beyond analysis such as formal verification, an important current direction of research is system *synthesis*. The main motivation for synthesis is to increase productivity by further raising the level of abstraction in system design. Ideally, we would like designers to state *what* the system should do, and let a synthesis tool discover *how* it should do it. Like automated code generation in MBD, this is consistent with the evolution of programming languages toward higher levels of abstraction, and it is also reminiscent of *declarative programming*.

We can illustrate what synthesis means concretely in the case of controller design, for instance. There, instead of designing the controller (typically in the form of a state machine) "by hand", and then verifying that the controller is correct against some formal specification (e.g., logical formula), the goal of synthesis is to automatically generate a controller which satisfies the specification *by construction*, thus eliminating the manual design, as well as the verification process.

This type of controller synthesis stems primarily from the field of formal methods [PR89] and although it is related to standard code generation and compilation techniques, it appears to be significantly different, at a fundamental level. Specifically, controller synthesis often reduces to a $\forall$-$\exists$ type of logic problem, or *game* between the controller and its environment. The goal of synthesis is to compute a *strategy* for the controller, such that *for any move* of the environment (e.g., for any input), *there exists a move* for the controller (e.g., an output) such that the overall system behavior satisfies a given formal specification. This game theoretic notion is typically missing from traditional compilation and code generation problems, which are only $\exists$ type scheduling or optimization problems.

Although the theory behind such controller synthesis techniques has been known for quite some time now [RW89, PR89, Thi96], it has not become standard practice yet. Partly this is because of fundamental limitations of synthesis methods and tools, which impede scalability. The first limitation is that synthesis algorithms are typically more computationally expensive than verification, which is already a hard problem due to state explosion. The second limitation is methodological in nature, and may be even more important than the first. In standard synthesis methods such as those in [RW89, PR89, Thi96], the input to the synthesis tool is solely the logical specification of the controller requirements. Unfortunately, the full specification of a real-life controller is extremely complex, and difficult to write. Note that specifications for synthesis are typically much more complex than specifications for verification. Indeed, for verification, a full specification is not required. For example, we might only want to check whether the system is deadlock-free, or whether it satisfies a certain safety property. Such incomplete specifications typically result in trivial controllers when doing synthesis. For example, if we try to synthesize a controller which only satisfies a safety property, we might get the trivial controller that does nothing (and is therefore safe).

Because of the above problem, using a state-of-the-art synthesis tool is often as painful as programming the low-level controller itself, the difference being that with the synthesis tool one keeps trying to get the specification right (and in the process also to understand the series of controllers that the tool returns). This motivated several researchers to look for alternatives, and in particular for radically different ways to program systems. One such approach is *programming by example*, where the programmer provides a set of examples and the synthesis tool generalizes those to a complete program. A similar approach is *programming by sketching*, where the programmer provides an incomplete program (e.g., a program with missing conditions or assignment expressions) and the synthesis tool must complete the program by filling the blanks. Examples of these approaches can be found in [Har08, SLRBE05, Gul11, Gul12, RVY14]. Some of the these techniques rely heavily on the *counter-example guided synthesis* principle, which consists in coming up with an initial candidate solution, submitting it to a verification tool to check correctness, and iterating when a counterexample is found, by processing it and modifying the candidate solution accordingly. Recently, this principle has been used to develop a tool for synthesis of distributed protocols, a hard, and generally undecidable problem [PR90, LT00, Tri04]. The tool takes a combined input of example scenarios in the form of *Message Sequence Charts* and a set of formal requirements (e.g., deadlock-freedom, safety, or liveness properties). The scenarios are processed into a set of incomplete automata, and then a search is launched over the space of possible completions, with the aid of a model-checker, and guided by the formal requirements. The tool has been able to synthesize fully automatically simple communication, consensus, and cache coherence protocols [AMR+14, ARS+15].

We believe that synthesis has the potential of being a key mechanism for dealing with change. As systems evolve and requirements change often, re-implementing systems at the low-level becomes a tedious and costly task. Synthesis tools could help to meet the stringent timing and cost constraints, by allowing designers to re-specify the systems at the high level, and re-generate implementations automatically.

Learning in system design: Today, numerous types of sensors and other data collection mechanisms have made available an abundance of data. Machine learning techniques are harvesting the information contained in these data for all sorts of applications, from marketing to personalized medicine. Unfortunately, machine learning and so-called *big data* has so far found little application in system design, despite the fact that automata learning has a long history and is still a very active area of research (e.g., see [Ang92, SB98, CHJS14, HS14, FT14]). Learning is very relevant to mastering change, for the same reason that synthesis is. Learning is typically an adaptive process, and therefore can inherently cope with the evolution of a system over time [BCMS12]. We believe that in the coming years learning will become an important element of system design. Despite the large amount of work on the topic, much remains to be done, even in studying basic problems such as learning state machines (see [GT16]).

5   Conclusions

Dynamical systems are omnipresent today in a variety of cyber-physical system applications that span all areas of our society. Designing such systems is a challenge. As of today we lack a science of design, even though many disciplines are concerned with the study of systems of various kinds. As this paper argues, one might look at the science of system design as having a very concrete goal. Just like computer science might be seen as being the science of building compilers (of all kinds), system design can be seen as being the science of building *system compilers*. These are tools which take as input high-level descriptions of the system we want to build, perform various types of analyses, and ultimately generate real systems, ideally fully automatically with the push of a button. Significant challenges remain in realizing this goal, however, and compositionality is identified as a primary cross-cutting concern, in order to master complexity and scale to systems of real-life proportions.

Real systems are rarely built from scratch. They evolve. New systems are built as newer versions of older systems. The new system reuses many of the components of one or more existing systems. Compositionality frameworks offer some of the answers to coping with this type of change, by allowing for incremental design. But real systems are also often designed by many stakeholders organized in teams with different backgrounds and having different concerns. Some systems are developed by communities of volunteers with loose organization. We identified multi-view modeling as a class of research problems addressing (mis)communication and inconsistencies which may arise in such interactions. In addition, in most cases systems are *open* in the sense that they must interoperate with other (existing or to be developed) systems, about which little is known. This is one of the reasons why system requirements often change.

The assumptions about the environment in which the system is supposed to operate change over time, and therefore the requirements must change as well. In a world of millions of programmers and billions of inter-connected devices, these trends can only intensify. Consequently, the science of system design must encompass variety, change and adaptivity as its primary goals. We believe that synthesis and learning techniques will be key in ensuring this. We hope to see these topics studied in the new, and timely, journal on the *Foundations of Mastering Change* [Ste14].

References

[AH99] Alur, R., Henzinger, T.: Reactive modules. Formal Methods Syst. Des. **15**, 7–48 (1999)

[AMR+14] Alur, R., Martin, M., Raghothaman, M., Stergiou, C., Tripakis, S., Udupa, A.: Synthesizing finite-state protocols from scenarios and requirements. In: Yahav, E. (ed.) HVC 2014. LNCS, vol. 8855, pp. 75–91. Springer, Heidelberg (2014). doi:10.1007/978-3-319-13338-6_7

[Ang92] Angluin, D.: Computational learning theory: survey and selected bibliography. In: 24th Annual ACM Symposium on Theory of Computing, pp. 351–369 (1992)

[ARS+15] Alur, R., Raghothaman, M., Stergiou, C., Tripakis, S., Udupa, A.: Automatic completion of distributed protocols with symmetry. In: 27th International Conference on Computer Aided Verification (CAV), pp. 395–412 (2015)

[BBBB12] Baumann, C., Beckert, B., Blasum, H., Bormer, T.: Lessons learned from microkernel verification - specification is the new bottleneck. In: 7th Conference on Systems Software Verification, SSV 2012, Sydney, Australia, pp. 18–32, 28–30 November 2012

[BBG+13] Broman, D., Brooks, C., Greenberg, L., Lee, E.A., Tripakis, S., Wetter, M., Masin, M.: Determinate composition of FMUs for co-simulation. In: 13th ACM & IEEE International Conference on Embedded Software (EMSOFT 2013) (2013)

[BCMS12] Bertolino, A., Calabrò, A., Merten, M., Steffen, B.: Never-stop learning: continuous validation of learned models for evolving systems through monitoring. ERCIM News **88**, 2012 (2012)

[BGJ+15] Bogomolov, S., Greitschus, M., Jensen, P.G., Larsen, K.G., Mikucionis, M., Strump, T., Tripakis, S.: Co-simulation of hybrid systems with SpaceEx and Uppaal. In: Proceedings of the 11th International Modelica Conference. Linkoping University Electronic Press (2015)

[BGL+15] Broman, D., Greenberg, L., Lee, E.A., Masin, M., Tripakis, S., Wetter, M., Requirements for hybrid cosimulation standards. In: Hybrid Systems: Computation and Control (HSCC 2015) (2015)

[BH14] Beckert, B., Hähnle, R.: Reasoning and verification: state of the art and current trends. IEEE Intell. Syst. **29**(1), 20–29 (2014)

[BK08] Baier, C., Katoen, J.-P.: Principles of Model Checking. MIT Press, Cambridge (2008)

[BLC+11] Bilitchenko, L., Liu, A., Cheung, S., Weeding, E., Xia, B., Leguia, M., Anderson, J.C., Densmore, D.: Eugene - a domain specific language for specifying and constraining synthetic biological parts, devices, and systems. PLoS ONE **6**(4), e18882 (2011)

[BLTT12] Broman, D., Lee, E.A., Tripakis, S., Törngren, M.: Viewpoints, formalisms, languages, and tools for cyber-physical systems. In: 6th International Workshop on Multi-Paradigm Modeling (MPM 2012) (2012)

[BOÅ+12] Blochwitz, T., Otter, M., Åkesson, J., Arnold, M., Clauss, C., Elmqvist, H., Friedrich, M., Junghanns, A., Mauss, J., Neumerkel, D., Olsson, H., Viel, A.: Functional mockup interface 2.0: the standard for tool independent exchange of simulation models. In: 9th International Modelica Conference (2012)

[BS01] Broy, M., Stølen, K.: Specification, Development of Interactive Systems: Focus On Streams, Interfaces and Refinement. Springer, Heidelberg (2001)

[CC77] Cousot, P., Cousot, R.: Abstract interpretation: a unified lattice model for static analysis of programs by construction or approximation of fixpoints. In: 4th ACM Symposium on POPL (1977)

[CGP00] Clarke, E., Grumberg, O., Peled, D.: Model Checking. MIT Press, Cambridge (2000)

[CHJS14] Cassel, S., Howar, F., Jonsson, B., Steffen, B.: Learning extended finite state machines. In: Software Engineering and Formal Methods - SEFM, pp. 250–264 (2014)

[CLM89] Clarke, E.M., Long, D.E., McMillan, K.L.: Compositional model checking. In: Fourth Annual Symposium on Logic in Computer Science (1989)

[CLT+16] Cremona, F., Lohstroh, M., Tripakis, S., Brooks, C., Lee, E.A.: FIDE - an FMI integrated development environment. In: 31st ACM/SIGApp. Symposium on Applied Computing, Embedded Systems Track (SAC) (2016)

[CSST08] Caspi, P., Scaife, N., Sofronis, C., Tripakis, S.: Semantics-preserving multitask implementation of synchronous programs. ACM Trans. Embed. Comput. Syst. (TECS) 7(2), 1–40 (2008)

[dAH01] de Alfaro, L., Henzinger, T.: Interface automata. In: Foundations of Software Engineering (FSE). ACM Press (2001)

[Dil87] Dill, D.L.: Trace theory for automatic hierarchical verification of speed-independent circuits. MIT Press, Cambridge (1987)

[DPT16] Dragomir, I., Preoteasa, V., Tripakis, S.: Compositional semantics and analysis of hierarchical block diagrams. In: Bošnački, D., Wijs, A. (eds.) SPIN 2016. LNCS, vol. 9641, pp. 38–56. Springer, Heidelberg (2016). doi:10.1007/978-3-319-32582-8_3

[EJL+03] Eker, J., Janneck, J., Lee, E., Liu, J., Liu, X., Ludvig, J., Neuendorffer, S., Sachs, S., Xiong, Y.: Taming heterogeneity - the Ptolemy approach. Proc. IEEE 91(1), 127–144 (2003)

[FH06] Fisher, J., Henzinger, T.A.: Executable biology. In: Winter Simulation Conference, pp. 1675–1682 (2006)

[FT14] Fu, J., Topcu, U.: Probably approximately correct MDP learning and control with temporal logic constraints. CoRR, abs/1404.7073 (2014)

[GM05] Governatori, G., Milosevic, Z.: Dealing with contract violations: formalism and domain specific language. In: 2005 Ninth IEEE International EDOC Enterprise Computing Conference, pp. 46–57, September 2005

[GT16] Giantamidis, G., Tripakis, S.: Learning Moore Machines from Input-Output Traces. ArXiv e-prints, May 2016

[Gul11] Gulwani, S.: Automating string processing in spreadsheets using input-output examples. In: Proceedings of the 38th Annual ACM SIGPLAN-SIGACT Symposium on Principles of Programming Languages, POPL 2011, pp. 317–330. ACM, New York (2011)

[Gul12] Gulwani, S.: Synthesis from examples: interaction models and algorithms. In: Proceedings of the 2012 14th International Symposium on Symbolic and Numeric Algorithms for Scientific Computing, SYNASC 2012, pp. 8–14. IEEE Computer Society, Washington (2012)

[Har08] Harel, D.: Can programming be liberated, period? Computer 41(1), 28–37 (2008)

[HQR98] Henzinger, T.A., Qadeer, S., Rajamani, S.K.: You assume, we guarantee: methodology and case studies. In: Hu, A.J., Vardi, M.Y. (eds.) CAV 1998. LNCS, vol. 1427, pp. 440–451. Springer, Heidelberg (1998). doi:10.1007/BFb0028765

[HS14] Howar, F., Steffen, B.: Learning models for verification and testing - special track at ISoLA 2014 track introduction. In: Leveraging Applications of Formal Methods, Verification and Validation. Technologies for Mastering Change, pp. 199–201 (2014)

[JHS+11] Johnsen, E.B., Hähnle, R., Schäfer, J., Schlatte, R., Steffen, M.: ABS: a core language for abstract behavioral specification. In: Aichernig, B.K., Boer, F.S., Bonsangue, M.M. (eds.) FMCO 2010. LNCS, vol. 6957, pp. 142–164. Springer, Heidelberg (2011). doi:10.1007/978-3-642-25271-6_8

[KAE+10] Klein, G., Andronick, J., Elphinstone, K., Heiser, G., Cock, D., Derrin, P., Elkaduwe, D., Engelhardt, K., Kolanski, R., Norrish, M., Sewell, T., Tuch, H., Winwood, S.: seL4: Formal verification of an operating-system kernel. Commun. ACM 53(6), 107–115 (2010)

[KGN+09] Kaivola, R., Ghughal, R., Narasimhan, N., Telfer, A., Whittemore, J., Pandav, S., Slobodová, A., Taylor, C., Frolov, V., Reeber, E., Naik, A.: Replacing testing with formal verification in intel core TM i7 processor execution engine validation. In: Bouajjani, A., Maler, O. (eds.) CAV 2009. LNCS, vol. 5643, pp. 414–429. Springer, Heidelberg (2009). doi:10.1007/978-3-642-02658-4_32

[KK12] Kim, K.-D., Kumar, P.R.: Cyber-physical systems: a perspective at the centennial. Proc. IEEE 100(Special Centennial Issue), 1287–1308 (2012)

[Lee08] Lee, E.A.:Cyber physical systems: design challenges. In: 2008 11th IEEE International Symposium on Object Oriented Real-Time Distributed Computing (ISORC), pp. 363–369, May 2008

[LST09] Lublinerman, R., Szegedy, C., Tripakis, S.: Modular code generation from synchronous block diagrams - modularity vs. code size. In: 36th ACM Symposium on Principles of Programming Languages (POPL 2009), pp. 78–89. ACM (2009)

[LT89] Lynch, N.A., Tuttle, M.R.: An introduction to input/output automata. CWI Q. 2, 219–246 (1989)

[LT00] Lamouchi, H., Thistle, J.: Effective control synthesis for DES under partial observations. In: 39th IEEE Conference on Decision and Control, pp. 22–28 (2000)

[LT08] Lublinerman, R., Tripakis, S.: Modularity vs. reusability: code generation from synchronous block diagrams. In: Design, Automation, and Test in Europe (DATE 2008), pp. 1504–1509. ACM, March 2008

[LW14] Leino, K.R.M., Wüstholz, V.: The dafny integrated development environment. In: 1st Workshop on Formal Integrated Development Environment, F-IDE 2014, Grenoble, France, 6 April 2014, EPTCS, vol. 149, pp. 3–15 (2014)

[Mey92] Meyer, B.: Applying "Design by Contract". Computer 25(10), 40–51 (1992)

[MWM13] Mitra, S., Wongpiromsarn, T., Murray, R.M.: Verifying cyber-physical interactions in safety-critical systems. IEEE Secur. Priv. **11**(4), 28–37 (2013)

[NM09] Nicolescu, G., Mosterman, P.J.: Model-Based Design for Embedded Systems. CRC Press, Boston (2009)

[NPB11] Neskovic, S., Paunovic, O., Babarogic, S.: Using protocols and domain specific languages to achieve compliance of administrative processes with legislation. In: Electronic Government and the Information Systems Perspective, EGOVIS, pp. 284–298 (2011)

[NRZ+15] Newcombe, C., Rath, T., Zhang, F., Munteanu, B., Brooker, M., Deardeuff, M.: How amazon web services uses formal methods. Commun. ACM **58**(4), 66–73 (2015)

[NT10] Namjoshi, K.S., Trefler, R.J.: On the completeness of compositional reasoning methods. ACM Trans. Comput. Logic **11**(3), 16 (2010)

[Pnu85] Pnueli, A.: In transition from global to modular temporal reasoning about programs. In: Apt, K. (ed.) Logics, Models of Concurrent Systems. Subseries F: Computer and System Science, pp. 123–144. Springer, Heidelberg (1985)

[PR89] Pnueli, A., Rosner, R.: On the synthesis of a reactive module. In: ACM Symposium, POPL (1989)

[PR90] Pnueli, A., Rosner, R.: Distributed reactive systems are hard to synthesize. In: Proceedings of the 31th IEEE Symposium on Foundations of Computer Science, pp. 746–757 (1990)

[PT14] Preoteasa, V., Tripakis, S.: Refinement calculus of reactive systems. In: Proceedings of the 14th ACM & IEEE International Conference on Embedded Software (EMSOFT 2014) (2014)

[PT16a] Pittou, M., Tripakis, S.: Multi-view consistency for infinitary regular languages. Infect Dis. Ther. **3**(1), 35–43 (2011). International Conference on Embedded Computer Systems: Observation of strains. Architectures, Modeling and Simulation - SAMOS XVI, 2016

[PT16b] Preoteasa, V., Tripakis, S.: Towards compositional feedback in non-deterministic and non-input-receptive systems. In: 31st Annual ACM/IEEE Symposium on Logic in Computer Science (LICS) (2016)

[RLSS10] Rajkumar, R., Lee, I., Sha, L., Stankovic, J.: Cyber-physical systems: the next computing revolution. In: 2010 47th ACM/IEEE Design Automation Conference (DAC), pp. 731–736, June 2010

[RST16] Reineke, J., Stergiou, C., Tripakis, S.: Basic problems in multi-view modeling (2016). Submitted journal version of [59]

[RT14] Reineke, J., Tripakis, S.: Basic problems in multi-view modeling. In: Tools and Algorithms for the Construction and Analysis of Systems - TACAS (2014)

[RVY14] Raychev, V., Vechev, M.T., Yahav, E.: Code completion with statistical language models. In: ACM SIGPLAN Conference on Programming Language Design and Implementation, PLDI 2014, p. 44 (2014)

[RW89] Ramadge, P., Wonham, W.: The control of discrete event systems. Proc. IEEE **77**(1), 81–98 (1989)

[SB98] Sutton, R.S., Barto, A.G.: Reinforcement Learning: An Introduction. MIT Press, Cambridge (1998)

[SL08] Shin, I., Lee, I.: Compositional real-time scheduling framework. ACM Trans. Embed. Comput. Syst. (TECS) **7**(3), 30 (2008)

[SLRBE05] Solar-Lezama, A., Rabbah, R., Bodík, R., Ebcioğlu, K.: Programming by sketching for bit-streaming programs. SIGPLAN Not. **40**(6), 281–294 (2005)

[Ste14] Steffen, B.: LNCS transaction on the foundations for mastering change: preliminary manifesto. In: Margaria, T., Steffen, B. (eds.) ISoLA 2014. Part I. LNCS, vol. 8802, pp. 514–517. Springer, Heidelberg (2014)

[TCN00] Thiele, L., Chakraborty, S., Naedele, M.: Real-time calculus for scheduling hard real-time systems. In: Circuits and Systems, ISCAS (2000)

[TD09] Tripakis, S., Dang, T.: Modeling, verification and testing using timed and hybrid automata. In: Mosterman, P., Nicolescu, G. (eds.) Model-Based Design for Embedded Systems. CRC Press, Boca Raton (2009)

[Thi96] Thistle, J.G.: Supervisory control of discrete event systems. Math. Comput. Model. **23**(11/12), 25–53 (1996)

[TLHL11] Tripakis, S., Lickly, B., Henzinger, T.A., Lee, E.A.: A theory of synchronous relational interfaces. ACM Trans. Program. Lang. Syst. (TOPLAS) **33**(4), 14 (2011)

[TLR+15] Tripakis, S., Limaye, R., Ravindran, K., Wang, G., Andrade, H., Ghosal, A.: Tokens vs. signals: on conformance between formal models of dataflow and hardware. J. Sig. Process. Syst. **85**(1), 23–43 (2016)

[TPB+08] Tripakis, S., Pinello, C., Benveniste, A., Sangiovanni-Vincentelli, A., Caspi, P., Di Natale, M.: Implementing synchronous models on loosely time-triggered architectures. IEEE Trans. Comput. **57**(10), 1300–1314 (2008)

[Tri04] Tripakis, S.: Undecidable problems of decentralized observation and control on regular languages. Inf. Process. Lett. **90**(1), 21–28 (2004)

[Tri15a] Tripakis, S.: Bridging the semantic gap between heterogeneous modeling formalisms, FMI. Infect Dis. Ther. **3**(1), 35–43 (2011). International Conference on Embedded Computer Systems: Observation of Strains, Architectures, Modeling and Simulation - SAMOS XV, 2015

[Tri15b] Tripakis, S.: Foundations of compositional model-based system design. In: Rawat, D.B., Rodrigues, J., Stojmenovic, I. (eds.) Cyber-Physical Systems: Observation of strains: From Theory to Practice. CRC Press, Boca Raton (2011). Infect Dis Ther. **3**(1), 35–43 (2015)

[Tri16] Tripakis, S.: Compositionality in the science of system design. Proc. IEEE **104**(5), 960–972 (2016)

[TSSL13] Tripakis, S., Stergiou, C., Shaver, C., Lee, E.A.: A modular formal semantics for Ptolemy. Math. Struct. Comput. Sci. **23**, 834–881 (2013)

Proof Repositories for Compositional Verification of Evolving Software Systems
Managing Change When Proving Software Correct

Richard Bubel[1], Ferruccio Damiani[2], Reiner Hähnle[1(✉)],
Einar Broch Johnsen[3], Olaf Owe[3], Ina Schaefer[4], and Ingrid Chieh Yu[3]

[1] Department of Computer Science, Technische Universität Darmstadt,
Darmstadt, Germany
{bubel,haehnle}@cs.tu-darmstadt.de
[2] Department of Computer Science, University of Torino, Turin, Italy
ferruccio.damiani@unito.it
[3] Department of Informatics, University of Oslo, Oslo, Norway
{einarj,olaf,ingridcy}@ifi.uio.no
[4] Institute for Software Engineering, Technische Universität Braunschweig,
Braunschweig, Germany
i.schaefer@tu-braunschweig.de

Abstract. We propose a new and systematic framework for proof reuse in the context of deductive software verification. The framework generalizes abstract contracts into incremental proof repositories. Abstract contracts enable a separation of concerns between called methods and their implementations, facilitating proof reuse. Proof repositories allow the systematic caching of partial proofs that can be adapted to different method implementations. The framework provides flexible support for compositional verification in the context of, e.g., partly developed programs, evolution of programs and contracts, and product variability.

1 Introduction

Deductive software verification [3] made significant advances in recent years, primarily through the development and improvement of verification tools [28] such as Dafny [24], KeY [4], Why [18] or Verifast [21], and through novel techniques and formalisms for *verification-in-the-small*, such as code contracts [17], dynamic frames [22,34], and separation logic [30]. However, similar advances have not been achieved for *verification-in-the-large*. In particular, verification systems typically rely on strong assumptions about how modules compose and

Partly funded by the EU project H2020-644298 HyVar: Scalable Hybrid Variability for Distributed Evolving Software Systems (http://www.hyvar-project.eu), the EU project FP7-610582 Envisage: Engineering Virtualized Services (http://www.envisage-project.eu), the Ateneo/CSP project RunVar, and the ICT COST Actions IC1402 ARVI (http://www.cost-arvi.eu) and IC1201 BETTY (http://www.behavioural-types.eu), and IoTSec (http://cwi.unik.no/wiki/IoTSec:Home).

B. Steffen (Ed.): Transactions on FoMaC I, LNCS 9960, pp. 130–156, 2016.
DOI: 10.1007/978-3-319-46508-1_8

interact. These assumptions come in two flavors. Approaches based on a closed-world assumption require that all code is developed before verification can start, making software verification a *post-hoc* activity. Approaches based on an open-world assumption require that the behavior of the modules complies with a priori fixed contracts, typically up to behavioral subtyping [26]. In both cases, breaking with the chosen assumption has severe consequences: the verification process for the "infected" part of the software needs to restart from scratch, and may in the worst case cascade through the entire program!

Established software development methodologies interleave development and testing activities and they do not enforce behavioral subtyping. Hence, they go against both approaches discussed above and make formal verification prohibitively expensive. Two very common aspects of software development in particular break current formal verification approaches: *program evolution* and *product variability* [32]. In the first, method implementations change frequently; at each change, the code that relies on the modified implementations must be re-verified. In the second, the sheer number of possible implementations for each method call leads to a correspondingly large number of proof obligations for the code depending on these calls or to very weak contracts.

To better support verification-in-the-large and to increase the degree of reuse during the software verification effort, we believe that proof systems used in formal verification need to improve the separation of concerns between the client and server side of behavioral contracts. Recent progress on this issue was made in [9,19] with the concept of *abstract contracts* that permits to separate between when a contract is called and when it is instantiated. In the current paper, we generalize abstract contracts using ideas from [11] to a new and systematic framework for verification proof reuse. In the context of object-oriented software development we address both program evolution and product variability by

1. disentangling the verification of a given piece of code from the implementation of its called methods, and
2. systematically caching partial, abstract proofs that can be instantiated with different method implementations.

Our framework is not restricted to a specific binding strategy for method calls or a specific verification logic. Particular binding strategies can be superimposed to express different ways of composing modules (in the object-oriented setting, classes) such as late binding, feature composition, preprocessing, etc.

Paper organization. In Sect. 2 we introduce the programming and verification model of this paper, as well as our running example. Section 3 presents abstract contracts and Sect. 4 explains the use of proof repositories. Section 5 illustrates how different structuring concepts are expressed in terms of binding strategies. Section 6 presents first evaluation results of our approach using an early prototype. Section 7 discusses related work and Sect. 8 concludes the paper.

2   A Framework for Contract-Based Verification

2.1   The Programming Model

The pivotal idea of our approach is to carefully distinguish between a method call in the code and an actual method invocation. More precisely, when we encounter a method call during the verification of a program, we do not want to make a commitment as to which method implementation is actually invoked. This is similar to the setting of programming languages that allow late binding (such as JAVA), but we do not want to commit to a particular binding strategy: this is *deliberately left open* to allow our approach to be usable for different method binding strategies, including late binding, feature composition, preprocessing, etc. In particular, we want to be able to *revise* a binding to the invocation of a a different method implementation at any time. Consequently, we use a programming model where the binding of method calls to method implementations is recorded explicitly: a method may be bound to no, to one, or to more than one implementation.

We work in a contract-based [27] verification setting (being the most common approach to deductive verification [3]): every method is specified by a contract. That contract may be trivial, but it must always be present. Definitions 1 and 2 below define programs and contracts simultaneously.

Definition 1 (Program, Class, Signature, Method). A *program* consists of a finite set $\mathcal{C}$ of classes and a finite set $\mathcal{B}$ of method call bindings.

A *class definition* $\mathtt{C} = (\mathcal{F}, \mathcal{I})$ in $\mathcal{C}$ has a name $\mathtt{C}$ and finite sets $\mathcal{F}$ of fields and $\mathcal{I}$ of method implementations. For simplicity, assume all fields are public, there are only default constructors, and no static members. Each class defines a type, but class types are unordered.

A *method implementation* consists of a method declaration, i.e., a method signature and method body, plus a contract for this method declaration. The *method signature* contains the method's name and the types of the formal argument and return parameters. Each method implementation has a unique label, by which it can be referred to (prefixing it by the class name $\mathtt{C}$). There can be more than one method implementation for a given method signature. These are distinguished by their labels. *Method bodies* contain standard statements: local variable declarations, assignments, conditionals, loops, method calls, and return statements.

The *method call bindings* $\mathcal{B}$ are a set of pairs, where the first element is the code position of a method call within some method body and the second element is the label corresponding to a method implementation in some class of $\mathcal{C}$.

With this definition the binding of method calls need not be deterministic, nor statically determined. This has the advantage that different method selection schemas (e.g., by inheritance, by features, etc.) can be superimposed on the idea of a proof repository. In a *well-formed program*, the body of each method implementation typechecks w.r.t. all the bindings of the method calls that occur in it—a method call that has no bindings typechecks if all its actual parameters typecheck.

Remark 1. Our approach is agnostic of the target programming language, but to be concrete, we write example programs in a JAVA-like syntax. These are assumed to be well-formed, such that, e.g., used fields are properly defined.

The terminology for method contracts in this paper follows closely that of KeY [4] and JML [23]. We use the following notation to access classes $C \in \mathcal{C}$, method implementations i, fields f, and method declarations m within a program $\mathcal{P} = (\mathcal{C}, \mathcal{B})$: $\mathcal{P}.C$, $\mathcal{P}.C.f$, $\mathcal{P}.C.i$, $\mathcal{P}.C.i.m$, etc. When $\mathcal{P}$ or C are clear from the context, we can omit them.

Definition 2 (Location, Contract). A *program location* is an expression referring to an updatable heap location (variable, formal parameter, field access, array access). A *contract* for a method declaration m consists of:

1. a first-order formula r over program locations called *precondition* or *requires clause*;
2. a first-order formula e over program locations called *postcondition* or *ensures clause*;
3. a set of program locations a (called *assignable clause*) whose value can potentially be changed during execution of m.

The notation for accessing class members is extended to contract constituents: C.i.r is the requires clause of method implementation i in class C, etc.

Contract elements appear in the code before the method declaration they refer to and start with an @, followed by a keyword (requires, ensures, assignable) that identifies each element of the contract. Analogous notation (label) is used to specify the label associated with the method declaration. The JML keyword \old is used to access prestate values. We permit JML's *-notation in assignable clauses to describe unbounded sets of program locations.

Remark 2. There are several ways to implement access to prestate values. For our purposes it is easiest to assume that for each location 1 that occurs in the assignable clause of a contract, there is an implicitly declared variable \old(1) that is set to the value that 1 had at the point when the contract was invoked.

Example 1. Consider a simple class **Bank** through which customers can update the balance on an array **acc** of accounts.

1. Figure 1 shows the class **Bank** with one method implementation labeled with $update_0$. This is a well-formed program, even though the call to deposit() is not bound: Programs are *not necessarily executable*, but *always analyzable* by a verifier.
2. Let us add a class **Account** and its method implementation $deposit_0$ (see Fig. 2). The call to deposit() in update() is still not bound. When to bind and which binding to make depends on the *program composition discipline* which is left open in our approach.

```
1   class Bank {
2     Account[] acc;
3
4   /*@ label      update₀
5     @ requires interest >= 0;
6     @ ensures  (\forall int i; 0 <= i < acc.length;
7                     acc[i].balance >= \old(acc[i].balance));
8     @ assignable acc[*].balance;
9     @*/
10    void update(int interest) {
11      for (int i = 0; i < acc.length; i++) {
12        acc[i].deposit(interest)
13      }
14    }
15  }
```

Fig. 1. The Bank class

3. Now add an explicit binding from the method call deposit(interest) in line 12 to deposit₀. This makes update₀.update() executable.
4. Next add a second implementation of deposit() labeled deposit₁ (see Fig. 3). The binding is not changed, so deposit₁ is not called from anywhere.
5. Finally, add a second binding from the method call deposit(interest) in line 12 to deposit₁. The binding of the call became *non-deterministic*: during execution of update() either deposit₀ or deposit₁ may be invoked.

Example 2. The method implementation Account.deposit₀ in Fig. 2 is specified by a contract whose precondition in the @requires clause says that the deposited amount should be non-negative. The postcondition in the @ensures clause expresses that the balance after the method call is equal to the balance before the method call plus the value of parameter x.

In our programming model, we never delete any method implementation or any binding. Which of the existing implementations and bindings are actually used in a concrete execution is outside the programming model. For example, one could superimpose a class hierarchy and a corresponding dynamic binding

```
1   class Account {
2     int balance = 0;
3
4   /*@ label      deposit₀
5     @ requires x >= 0;
6     @ ensures  balance == \old(balance) + x;
7     @ assignable balance;
8     @*/
9     void deposit(int x) { balance += x }
10  }
```

Fig. 2. The Account class

```
1   class Account {
2     int balance = 0;
3     final int fee = 2;
4
5     ... implementation of deposit₀ ...
6
7   /*@ label     deposit₁
8     @ requires x >= 0;
9     @ ensures  balance >= \old(balance);
10    @ assignable balance;
11    @*/
12    void deposit(int x) {
13      if (x >= fee) {balance += x - fee}  }
14  }
```

Fig. 3. The Account class with a second implementation of deposit()

rule, or one could view a subset of the existing method implementations and bindings as a particular program version evolving in a development process, but this is deliberately left open to render our results general.

Definition 3 (Subprogram, Complete program). Given program $(\mathcal{C}, \mathcal{B})$, a *subprogram* is a well-formed program $(\mathcal{C}', \mathcal{B}')$ such that $\mathcal{B}' \subseteq \mathcal{B}$ and for each class $\texttt{C}' = (\mathcal{F}', \mathcal{I}') \in \mathcal{C}'$ there is a class $\texttt{C} = (\mathcal{F}, \mathcal{I}) \in \mathcal{C}$ with the same name as $\texttt{C}'$, such that $\mathcal{F}' \subseteq \mathcal{F}$ and $\mathcal{I}' \subseteq \mathcal{I}$.

A subprogram $(\mathcal{C}', \mathcal{B}')$ is *complete* if every method call occurring in a method implementation in $\mathcal{C}'$ appears on the left-hand side of at least one binding in $\mathcal{B}'$.

Each program is a subprogram of itself. A complete subprogram is executable, even though the implementation of a method call need not to be uniquely determined and not every method implementation needs to be reachable.

Example 3. The programs resulting from Steps 3, 4, and 5 in Example 1 are complete.

2.2   Contract-Based Verification

Verification is about proving the correctness of programs. We use the notion of contract-based specification of methods as introduced in the previous section. This approach was proposed by Meyer in the context of design-by-contract [27] and subsequently adopted by a number of programming languages and verification tools, including the Eiffel programming language, SPEC# [2] or Microsoft's Code Contracts for the .NET platform.

We define partial correctness in the setting of first-order dynamic logic [4]; we omit total correctness and class invariants as neither adds anything essential to our discussion.

Definition 4. Let $m(\bar{p})$ be a call to method m with parameters $\bar{p}$. A *partial correctness expression* has the form $[m(\bar{p})]\, \Phi$ and means that whenever m is called and terminates, then Φ holds in its final state; the formula Φ is either another correctness expression or it is a first-order formula.

In first-order dynamic logic, correctness expressions are just formulas with modalities. One may also encode correctness expressions as weakest precondition predicates and use first-order logic as a meta language, which is typically done in verification condition generators (VCGs). Either way, we assume that we can build first-order formulas over correctness expressions, so we can state the intended semantics of contracts: Validity of the formula $i.r \rightarrow [i.m(\bar{p})]\, i.e$ expresses the correctness of a method implementation i with respect to the pre- and postcondition of its contract. In addition, we must capture the correctness of $i.m$ with respect to its assignable clause: for the latter, one can assume that there is a formula $A(i.a, i.m)$ whose validity implies that $i.m$ can change at most the value of program locations in $i.a$ (following [16]). Formally, we define:

Definition 5 (Contract satisfaction). A method implementation i of class C *satisfies* its contract if the following formula is valid:

$$C.i.r \rightarrow [m(\bar{x})]\, C.i.e \quad \wedge \quad A(C.i.a, C.i.m) \tag{1}$$

Here, $m(\bar{x})$ is a call to the method declared by i with formal parameters $\bar{x}$, which may be referenced in $C.i.r$.

The presence of contracts makes formal verification of complex programs possible, because each method can be verified separately against its contract and called methods can be approximated by their contracts, see the method contract rule (2) below. The assignable clause of a method limits the program locations on which a method call can have side effects.[1] To keep the treatment simple (and also in line with most implementations of verification systems), we do not allow metavariables to occur in first-order formulas.

To verify a method implementation (such as `update()` in Fig. 1) against its contract in a verification calculus, method calls that may occur in the body (here, `deposit()`) are not inlined, but replaced by their contract using a *method contract rule* to achieve scalability:

$$\text{methodContract} \quad \frac{\Gamma \Rightarrow i.r \qquad \Gamma \Rightarrow \mathcal{U}_{i.a}(i.e \rightarrow \Phi)}{\Gamma \Rightarrow [m(\bar{p})]\Phi} \tag{2}$$

The rule is applied to the conclusion below the horizontal line: given a proof context with a set of formulas Γ, we need to establish the correctness of a program starting with a method call $m(\bar{p})$ with respect to a postcondition Φ. The latter could contain either the continuation of the program or, if $m(\bar{p})$ is the final statement, an ensures clause.

---

[1] We are aware that this basic technique is insufficient to achieve modular verification. Advanced techniques for modular verification, e.g. [1,22,34], would obfuscate the fundamental questions considered in this paper and can be superimposed.

Note that we here assume that a binding of the method call to the method implementation i has been added. We also assume that the underlying verification calculus has associated the formal parameters of m with the actual parameters $\bar{p}$. Rule (2) uses the contract of i to reduce verification of the method call to two subgoals. The first of these (left premise) establishes that the requires clause is fulfilled, i.e., the contract is honored by the callee. This justifies that it is sufficient to prove the second goal (right premise), where the ensures clause may be used to prove the desired postcondition Φ correct. Here, one needs to account for the possible side effects of the call on the values of locations listed in the assignable clause of i's contract. As we cannot know these, the substitution $\mathcal{U}_{i.a}$ is used to set all locations occurring in i.a to fresh Skolem symbols (see [4, Sect. 3.8] for details). Soundness of the method contract rule is formally stated as follows:

Theorem 1. *If method implementation i satisfies its contract, then rule* (2) *is sound.*

Proof. The method contract rule is fairly standard except for the use of the substitution $U_{i.a}$ which encodes the assignable clause of the contract. In [6], a theorem is shown from which the correctness of (2) follows as a special case. □

3   Abstract Method Calls

In the method body of Bank.update_0 in Example 1, there are two possible implementations for the call to deposit(). Clearly, it is inefficient to redo the correctness proof for Bank.update_0 for each of these implementations. For example, the proof of Bank.update_0 might have involved expensive user interaction. In addition, deposit() might be called from many other methods.

Intuitively, the arguments in the proof where Account.deposit_0 is used should be sufficient to justify the proof even when Account.deposit_1 is used. After all, the difference between the proofs occurs only at the first-order level and it should be easy to close the gap with the help of automated first-order reasoning, such as SMT solving.

However, the method contract rule (2) does not permit to detect the similarity between both proof obligations easily, because it works with a fixed binding of method call to method implementation. The proof of Bank.update_0 uses the ensures clause $\text{Account.deposit}_0.e$. When deposit_0 is changed to deposit_1, it is impossible to disentangle the new ensures clause from the steps used to prove Bank.update_0.

We want to achieve a separation of method call and actual contract application, as suggested by the programming model in Sect. 2.1. This can be achieved technically by means of *abstract contracts*, as proposed in [9,19].

The main technical idea is to introduce a level of indirection into a method contract that permits the substitution of the concrete requires, assignable, and ensures clauses to be delayed. We call this an *abstract method contract*. It has the shape shown in Fig. 4 and comprises an abstract section and a definition section.

```
1   /*@
2     @ requires R;
3     @ ensures (∀ l ∈ LS; l == \def(l)) && E;
4     @ assignable LS;
5     @ def R == r;
6     @ def LS == {l₁,...,lₙ};
7     @ def \def(l₁) == e₁, ..., \def(lₙ) == eₙ;
8     @ def E == e;
9     @*/
```

Fig. 4. Shape of an *abstract method contract*

```
1   /*@ label    deposit₀
2     @ requires R;
3     @ ensures (∀ l ∈ LS; l == \def(l)) && E;
4     @ assignable LS;
5     @ def R == x > 0;
6     @ def LS == {balance};
7     @ def \def(balance) == \old(balance) + x;
8     @ def E == true;
9     @*/
10    void deposit(int x) { balance += x }
```

Fig. 5. Abstract method specification for `deposit` from Fig. 2

Its *abstract* section (lines 2–4) consists of the standard requires, ensures, and assignable clauses. But these clauses are now mere placeholders, where R and E are *abstract predicates*, LS is an abstract function that returns a set of assignable locations, and the \def's are abstract functions that specify the precise post value of these locations.[2] The *definition section* of the contract (lines 5–8) provides concrete expressions for each placeholder in the abstract section. Figure 4 merely suggests a convenient notation. The formal definition of an abstract method contract is given in Definition 6 below.

The equational form of the ensures clause is a minor restriction, which enforces that the post value for any assignable location is well-defined after contract application. Field accesses occurring in definitions are expressed using getter methods, e.g., `getBalance()` is used to access the `balance` field. This ensures that their correct value is used at the time when definitions are unfolded.

Example 4. Figure 5 reformulates the contract of `Account.deposit₀` in Fig. 2 as an abstract method contract.

The abstract section of an abstract method contract is completely generic and indeed *the same for each method*. Therefore, an abstract contract is completely specified by its definition section and the signature of the method it relates to. This is reflected in the following definition.

---

[2] Not all locations in LS need to appear in the *def*s. About the ones who do not, nothing is known except what is stated in *E*.

Definition 6 (Abstract method contract). An *abstract method contract* for a method declaration m is a quadruple $(r, e, ls, \textit{defs})$ where

- r, e are logic formulas representing the contract's pre- and postcondition,[3]
- ls is a set of heap locations representing the assignable locations,
- *defs* is a list of pairs $(\textit{defSym}, \xi_{\textit{defSym}})$ where *defSym* are non-rigid (i.e., state dependent) function or predicate symbols used as placeholders in r, e, and definitions ξ. For r, e, and ls, as well as for the defined subset of the $\backslash\text{def}(1_i)$ with $l_i \in ls$, there is a unique function symbol in *defSym*. For simplicity, we use $\backslash\text{def}(1_i)$ as well to refer to that function symbol, as long as no ambiguity arises.

Placeholders must be non-rigid signature symbols to prevent the program logic calculus to perform simplifications over them that are invalid in certain program states.

$$\text{expandDef } \frac{\xi_{\textit{defSym}}}{\textit{defSym}} \tag{3}$$

To ensure completeness of the abstract setup, we add the definitions of the placeholders (i.e., the contents of the definition section of each abstract contract) as a *theory* to the logic, just like other theories, such as arithmetic, arrays, etc. This means that the notion of contract satisfaction (Definition 5) includes symbols with definitions in abstract contracts. Additionally, Rule (3) above substitutes placeholders by their definitions (by a slight abuse of notation, but with obvious meaning for function symbols), is obviously sound. The advantage of this setup is that we can use the standard method contract rule as follows: Applying the method contract for a method invocation at position pc, we instantiate the method contract rule as follows. As precondition i.r we use the placeholder predicate $\text{R}_{\text{i\_pc}}$ for the method implementation i using the program counter pc as a unique marker for the specific method call. This placeholder predicate may depend on the heap, method parameters and depending on the programming language other program locations (e.g., a parameter used to pass the this-reference in Java). The postcondition i.e is of the shape $1 \doteq \backslash\text{def}(1)_{\text{pc}} \wedge \text{E}_{\text{i\_pc}}$ where $\text{E}_{\text{i\_pc}}$ is a placeholder predicate which depends on the same program locations as the precondition placeholder as well as the method result and the prestate of the method.

The anonymization of changed variables uses a placeholder function $\text{LS}_{\text{i\_pc}}$ representing a set of program location (those which may be changed by the method). The update $\mathcal{U}_{\text{i.a}}$ becomes the update $\mathcal{U}_{\text{LS}_{\text{i\_pc}}}$ which is a generic substitution that sets exactly the heap locations in $\text{LS}_{\text{i\_pc}}$ to fresh Skolem symbols. This is expressible provided that quantification over heap locations is permitted in the underlying program logic. Apart from that, the abstract rule is exactly like the old method contract rule, but it ignores the definition section at the time when it is applied.

---

[3] This implies the limitation that no (not even pure) method calls can occur in pre- and postconditions. This could be lifted or worked around in various ways.

$$\text{abstractMethodContract} \ \frac{\varGamma \Rightarrow \texttt{i.r} \quad \varGamma \Rightarrow \mathcal{U}_{\text{LS}_{\text{i\_pc}}}(\texttt{i.e} \rightarrow \varPhi)}{\varGamma \Rightarrow [\texttt{m}(\overline{\texttt{p}})]\varPhi} \tag{4}$$

As we neither changed the satisfaction of contracts nor the method contract rule, Theorem 1 still holds.

Example 5. We illustrate the application of rule (4) with the call to `deposit()` at line 12 of Fig. 1 (pc : 112) during verification of `update`$_0$ in Fig. 1: Applying the contract to the sequent $\varGamma \Rightarrow \{\mathcal{U}\}[\texttt{acc[i].deposit(interest);}]\phi, \varDelta$ splits the proof in two branches:

1. $\varGamma \Rightarrow \{\mathcal{U}\}R_{\text{deposit}_0\_112}, \varDelta$ and
2. $\varGamma \Rightarrow \{\mathcal{U}\}\{\mathcal{U}_{LS_{\text{deposit}_0\_112}}\}(\texttt{balance} \dot{=} \texttt{\textbackslash def(balance)}_{112} \wedge E_{\text{deposit}_0\_112}) \rightarrow []\phi, \varDelta$

Successive applications of rule (3) (`expandDef`) first replace the placeholder by the respective counterpart of the abstract method contract specifications and successively the therein used placeholders such that for instance $R_{\text{deposit}_0\_112}$ is finally expanded to the concrete precondition `interest` > 0.

4   A Proof Repository

The idea of a proof repository is that it faithfully records which method implementations have been proven correct for which possible method call bindings of a given program in the sense of Definition 1. Each program change and each new binding gives rise to new proof obligations, which are then added to the proof repository so that it reflects the changed program. Like for our notion of program, we never delete any information in the proof repository.

For simplicity, with each method implementation we associate a single proof obligation of the form (1) of Definition 5. Assume that we have a program logic that reduces such proof obligations to first-order subgoals. This is possible even for incomplete programs (in the sense of Definition 3) using the abstract contracts introduced in the previous section. Of course, there will in general be unprovable first-order subgoals that contain abstract symbols from the abstract contracts. Constructing such partial proofs might involve considerable work; for example, it is generally necessary to supply loop invariants manually. Therefore, it makes sense to store these partial, abstract proofs in a repository for later reuse.

Definition 7 (Proof repository). A *proof repository* for a well-formed program $(\mathcal{C}, \mathcal{B})$ is a finite set of triples (i, σ, ϕ), where:

- i is the label of a method implementation in a class of $\mathcal{C}$ (to simplify the notation, in the following we use the same metavariable i also to refer to the associated method implementation);
- $\sigma \subseteq \mathcal{B}$ is a set of bindings such that only method call locations inside i occur in its domain (σ can be empty, which is denoted by ϵ);

– ϕ is a first-order formula representing a verification condition; it may contain symbols from abstract contracts that originate from applications of rule (2) to method calls in i.

Intuitively, an element (i, σ, ϕ) of a proof repository S expresses that ϕ is a proof obligation that needs to be established for the correctness of i provided that methods called inside i are bound at most to implementations occurring in σ. Querying a proof repository is done by means of obvious projection functions:

Definition 8 (Repository projection functions). Let S be a proof repository for a well-formed program $(\mathcal{C}, \mathcal{B})$, i a method implementation in a class of $\mathcal{C}$ and $\sigma \subseteq \mathcal{B}$. Let s_j be the j'th component of a triple $s \in S$. Then we define:

– $S \downarrow i = \{s \in S \mid s_1 = i\}$
– $S \Downarrow i, \sigma = \{s \in S \downarrow i \mid s_2 \supseteq \sigma \text{ and } \not\models \sigma(s_3)\}$, and $\models$ is first-order validity.

Let $b \sqsubseteq \sigma$ denote that the left-hand side of the binding b is in the domain of the set of bindings σ.

The set $S \Downarrow i, \sigma$ characterizes those proof obligations that are not valid (and thereby not first-order provable) for a method implementation i with local calls bound by the given set of bindings σ. In the next definition we connect proof repositories with the notion of contract satisfaction in our framework.

Definition 9 (Sound proof repository). *Soundness* of a proof repository S for a well-formed program P is defined inductively:

– The empty proof repository $S = \emptyset$ is sound for the empty program $P = (\emptyset, \emptyset)$.
– Assume S is sound for program $P = (\mathcal{C}, \mathcal{B})$. We distinguish three cases:

Case 0: Extend P to a well-formed program P' by adding a new empty class definition to $\mathcal{C}$ or a new field to a class definition $\mathsf{C} \in \mathcal{C}$. Then S is sound for P'.

Case 1: Extend P to a well-formed program P' by adding a new method implementation i to a class in $\mathcal{C}$.

Then we use the underlying program logic to reduce the satisfaction of i's contract (Definition 5) to a (possibly empty) set Φ of first-order proof obligations. Each of these may or may not be provable. In general they contain abstract symbols originating from abstract contracts. Let $S' = S \cup \{(i, \epsilon, \phi) \mid \phi \in \Phi\}$, then S' is sound for P'.

Case 2: Create a new well-formed program P' by adding a new method binding $b = (\mathrm{pos}, i_b)$ to $\mathcal{B}$.

As P' is well-formed, the method call at pos on the left hand-side of b occurs in some method implementation i in a class of P. As S is sound for P and we never remove anything from S, the elements in $S \downarrow i$ must contain all first-order proof obligations for i. We choose those not yet containing a binding for the left-hand side of b and extend them. Thus, let $S' = S \cup S''$, where

$$S'' = \{(i, \{b\} \cup \mathcal{B}, b(\phi)) \mid (\mathcal{F}, \mathcal{I}) \in \mathcal{C}, i \in \mathcal{I}, (i, \mathcal{B}, \phi) \in S \downarrow i, \ b \not\sqsubseteq \mathcal{B}\}$$

and with $b(\phi)$ we denote replacement of all abstract symbols in ϕ created by the method call at pos with the concrete expressions given by the contract of i_b. Then S' is sound for P'.

The extension of S in Step 2 is a copy-and-substitute operation which does not involve any reproving. Only the addition of new contracts makes it necessary to prove new facts about programs.

Given a sound proof repository for a program, it is possible to query in a simple manner whether a method implementation satisfies its contract:

Theorem 2. *Let S be a sound proof repository for a program $P = (\mathcal{C}, \mathcal{B})$, i a method implementation in a class of $\mathcal{C}$, and $\sigma \subseteq \mathcal{B}$ a set of bindings whose domain are method calls inside i. If $S \Downarrow i, \sigma = \emptyset$ then i satisfies its contract for any possible implementation of its called methods given by σ.*

The correctness of a complete subprogram can be checked by querying the status of each method implementation and bindings of its method calls.

Example 6. We build a sound proof repository S for the program developed in Example 2 step by step. S and P are initially empty.

1. Following Case 0 of Definition 9, we add class `Account` with field `balance` and without any method implementation so far.
2. Following Case 1 of Definition 9, we extend `Account` with method implementation deposit_0. Then we create a proof that deposit_0 satisfies its contract and insert the resulting proof obligations into S. A typical entry is $(\text{deposit}_0, \epsilon, \phi)$, where ϕ is a provable first-order formula without abstract contract symbols (because `deposit()` calls no other methods and the contract is obviously satisfied). This will entail query results such as $S \Downarrow \text{deposit}_0, \epsilon = \emptyset$.
3. Following Case 0 of Definition 9, we add class `Bank` with field `acc`.
4. Again, following Case 1 of Definition 9, we create a partial proof that update_0 satisfies its contract and insert the resulting subgoals into S. A typical entry is: $(\text{update}_0, \epsilon, \phi)$. Now several of the ϕ's will be unprovable and contain abstract symbols from the method call to `deposit()`. The query $S \Downarrow \text{update}_0, \epsilon$ will return these entries, so we know that the contract of update_0 is not satisfied.[4]
5. Now we follow Case 2 of Definition 9 and $b = $ (line 12 in $\text{update}_0, \text{deposit}_0$) to $\mathcal{B}$. Looking for entries in S with the method implementation update_0 in the first component, we find entries of the form $(\text{update}_0, \epsilon, \phi)$. For each of these entries, we add a new entry of the form $(\text{update}_0, \{b\}, b(\phi))$. The resulting first-order subgoals turn out to be provable, because the contract of deposit_0 is sufficient to prove that the contract of update_0 is satisfied. Hence, $S \Downarrow \text{update}_0, \{b\} = \emptyset$.

---

[4] If i is the label of a method implementation that contains at least one method call, then $S \Downarrow i, \epsilon$ will always return a non-empty set. More generally, if i is the label of a method implementation and the domain of $\mathcal{B}$ does not contain all the method calls in i, then $S \Downarrow i, \mathcal{B}$ will always return a non-empty set.

6. We add field `fee` and then method implementation deposit_1 to class `Account`. Similar as in Step 2, new proof obligations are added to S.
7. We add $b' = $ (line 12 in $\text{update}_0, \text{deposit}_1$) to $\mathcal{B}$. Similar as in Step 5, new entries of the form $(\text{update}_0, \{b'\}, b'(\phi))$ are created. As $b' \sqsubseteq \{b\}$, only the entries containing ϵ in the second component are copied. Even these new entries are automatically first-order provable and no new verification effort is necessary.

Remark 3. It would be sound to delete all entries with first-order provable subgoals from the repository, because contract satisfaction queries ask for *unprovable* subgoals. In this case, the proof repository would be unchanged for Steps 2, 5, and 7 of Example 6. This could lead to substantially smaller repositories, but also preclude optimizations based on caching previous results. An obvious compromise would be to replace an entry (i, σ, ϕ) with a first-order provable constraint ϕ with (i, σ, true) to enable caching of first-order provable subgoals. To determine such trade-offs requires further implementation and experimentation, which is planned for future work.

In the evolution of programs, it is typically desirable to work towards correct and complete repositories. However, there could be (older or newer) method implementations that cause problems due to faults in code, contract, or usage. To cope with this in our framework we may remove problematic implementations and bindings, forming a subprogram of the given program. This will not destroy well-formedness nor soundness, and we may regain correctness of the subprogram. In order to obtain completeness, we may then add new implementations (of removed methods and additional ones) and add corresponding bindings, taking care to maintain correctness. This means that our framework supports replacement of methods in this way; allowing a quite flexible program evolution process. Since repositories record information for each implementation and each binding it is easy to form repositories of subprograms, as well as of extended programs.

5 Examples: Integration with Structuring Concepts

5.1 Class Inheritance and Behavioral Subtyping

We show how class inheritance and late binding can be integrated into the programming model presented in Sect. 2.1. With single inheritance one may build treelike class hierarchies, where a class may have several (direct or indirect) subclasses and several (direct and indirect) superclasses, but at most one direct superclass, called the *parent* class. In general a subclass C' will extend an existing parent class C by introducing new fields and new method implementations, possibly including re-implementation of methods (i.e., implementation of methods with a name found in C or a superclass of C). The class inherits all fields and method implementation of its parent class. Inside the subclass C' a method name m refers to the method implementation of C' if any, otherwise that inherited from C. The syntax *super.m* refers to the method m of C (possibly inherited in C).

Objects of the new class C' will contain an instance of all fields declared or inherited. An object variable o declared of class C may at run-time refer to an object of class C or C' or any other subclass of C. Late binding means that the binding of a method call $o.m$ depends on the class of the object that o refers to at run-time. Similarly, a local call m is bound to that of the class of the executing object. For example the call acc[i].deposit(interest) in class Bank may bind to the deposit of class Account or a subclass FeeAccount. At verification time the actual binding of method calls cannot in general be decided, and the binding of a call $o.m$ is treated as non-deterministic, potentially binding to type-correct implementations of any m of the declared class of o (possibly inherited) or any type-correct re-implementation in a subclass. A call is classified as *static* if it contains   , otherwise *late-bound*.

In order to extend the framework of proof repositories, we let (the label of) each call $o.m$ be indexed by the declared class of o, and let each local call m be indexed by the name of the enclosing class, i.e., treating a local call m as *this.m* where *this* refers to the current object. As above we may allow a class to define alternative implementations of the same method m, even though such alternatives are typically controlled by inheritance in object-oriented programs. In this case we must restrict bindings to those that result in type-correct calls considering the type of the actual parameters and that of the result value: A binding of a call $v = o.m(e_1, e_2, ..., e_n)$ to a method implemented in a class C is *type-correct* if C is the declared class of o, or a subclass, and the assignments $x_i = e_i$ (for each i) and $v = w$ are type-correct when x_i has the type of the ith formal parameter and variable w has the type of the declared method result.

The proof repository for a subclass C' with C as parent class is built according to Definition 9, using case 1 for methods implemented or re-implemented in C', resulting in new partial proofs, and case 2 for re-implemented methods, such that for each late-bound call of m occurring in C' or a superclass of C' (i.e., indexed by C' or a superclass of C'), we add a binding associating each (type-correct) re-implemented m with the label of the call. A static call *super.m$_{C'}$* is bound to the (possibly inherited) implementation of m in C (which gives deterministic binding if C has only one type-correct method m).

Thus the framework for proof repositories is well suited for object-oriented inheritance and late binding. Also static binding by means of *super* can be accommodated. Since subclassing implies a kind of subtyping, the notion of type-correct program is specialized to cover (a version of) the standard contra/co-variance for methods signatures, allowing also multiple definitions of methods in a class without any type restrictions. The binding is type-safe since it exploits the type of the actual parameters and return value to select a subset of method definitions yielding well-formed and type-correct programs.

As mentioned it might happen in our framework that a program gives rise to unprovable proof obligations. Even if each class has provable proof obligations when seen in isolation, an unsatisfiable proof obligations may arise for instance when a method defined and used in a class is redefined in a subclass with a conflicting contract specification, and the usage of the method in the superclass

```
1   class Account {
2     int balance = 0;
3
4   /*@ label       deposit₀
5     @ def R   == x >= 0;
6     @ def LS == {balance};
7     @ def \def(balance) == \old(balance) + x;
8     @ def E   == true;
9     @*/
10    void deposit(int x) { ··· }
11
12  /*@ label       transfer₀
13    @ def R   == x >= 0 ∧ x <= balance;
14    @ def LS == {balance};
15    @ def \def(balance) == \old(balance) - x;
16    @ def E   == true;
17    @*/
18    void transfer(Account a, int x) { ··· }
19  }
```

Fig. 6. The Account superclass

depends on the original specification. To resolve the situation one can avoid the call in the superclass or modify the redefined method and its contract, and re-verify the resulting program. But this could give substantial re-verification. In our setting, a resolution can be found by means of a subprogram obtained by removing method definitions, and corresponding bindings, such that the subprogram has a subset of the original bindings and results in provable proof obligations. In this case one can reuse the (corresponding subset of) proof obligations, and re-verification is avoided (apart from applying the verification logic). The subprogram can then be augmented by new versions of problematic methods, and re-verification is limited to these additions.

Consider our example, where class Account in Fig. 6 has one deposit method and one transfer method. We here ignore the standard requires, ensures, and assignable clauses. In Fig. 7 we add a subclass FeeAccount which implements the extension of the bank account deposit with a fee (as in Fig. 3). The subclass adds a new implementation of deposit, which we label with FeeAccount.deposit₀. Given the proof repository S for classes Bank and Account of Example 6, adding the subclass is realized by two steps. First the new implementation gives a partial proof that is added. Second, the implementation FeeAccount.deposit of the subclass results in a new binding for the deposit call in the update method of the Bank class. Thus, a call to deposit in a Bank object may non-deterministically bind to deposit₀ in Account or deposit₀ in FeeAccount. Consider multiple definitions of methods where the subclass FeeAccount implements the extension of the bank account money transfer with a fee. FeeAccount has two implementations of transfer, one labeled transfer₀ with input parameter a of type Account and the other labeled transfer₁ with a of type FeeAccount. In this case a call o.transfer(a) in Bank gives the following possible bindings

```
1   class FeeAccount extends Account {
2     final int fee = 2;
3
4   /*@ label      deposit₀
5     @ def R  == x >= 0;
6     @ def LS == {balance};
7     @ def E  == balance >= \old(balance);
8     @*/
9     void deposit(int x) {  if (x >= fee) {balance += x - fee }
10
11  /*@ label transfer₀}
12  ... contract of transfer₀ ... */
13    void transfer(Account a, int x) { ··· }
14
15  /*@ label      transfer₁
16    @ def R  == x >= 0;
17    @ def LS == {balance};  // or super.assignable
18    @ def E  ==  balance <= \old(balance);
19    @*/
20    void transfer(FeeAccount a, int x) { ··· }
21  }
```

Fig. 7. The FeeAccount class extending the Account class

depending on the typing information: (i) If o evaluates to type Account, we have a deterministic binding to transfer₀ in class Account, (ii) if o evaluates to type FeeAccount and a evaluates to type FeeAccount, the call binds to transfer₁ in FeeAccount using the narrowest type, otherwise (iii) the call binds to transfer₁ in FeeAccount.

At the level of the proof system, the generation of proof obligations corresponds to lazy behavioral subtyping [12,13], since bindings are added to the repository of an implementation only for method calls that occur in the implementation. In particular we do not insist that a redefined method satisfies the original contract of the superclass as in behavioral subtyping [26]. For instance in the example, the contract of deposit₀ in Account is not satisfied by the re-implemented deposit in FeeAccount.

5.2   Delta-Oriented Programming

Delta-oriented programming (DOP) [7,31] is a transformational approach for Software Product Line (SPL) development [32]. It supports developing an SPL by starting from at least one complete product, called the *core product*. To this core product one applies program transformations (the delta modules) that specify changes to implement other products. The alterations inside a delta module act both at the class level, by adding or removing classes, and at the class structure level by modifying the internal structure of existing classes (i.e., changing the super class and adding, removing, or modifying fields, and methods). Modifying a method means either replacing the method body or wrapping the existing body using the original construct. The call original(...) calls a

```
1   /*@
2     @ delta def R == dr;
3     @ delta def LS == [\original(LS) - {l'_1,...,l'_p} +] {l''_1,...,l''_q};
4     @ delta def \def(l'''_1) == de_1, ..., \def(l'''_m) == de_m;
5     @ delta def E == de;
6     @*/
```

Fig. 8. Shape of a *delta abstract method contract* (in line 3, the part enclosed in square brackets is optional, and the symbols "-" and "+" denote set-theoretic difference and union, respectively)

method with the same name as before the modifications, and is bound when the product is generated. This call may only occur in the body of the method provided by a method-modify operation. A method-modify operation that uses the `original` construct adds a new method with a fresh name that is used (instead of `original`) in the body of the modified method in the generated product—the name of the new method is denoted by $m\$\delta$, where m is the name of the modified method and δ is the name of the delta module that contains the method-modify operation.

A delta module may not only change the code of a program, but also its specification. In the setting of this paper, a delta on a method contract may replace the requires or ensures clause or modify it by referring to the previous version of the respective clause using the original construct. These modifications can be expressed by chaining the definition section of an abstract method contract. A *delta abstract method contract* describes how to modify the definition section of an abstract method contract following the delta (the abstract section, which is the same for each method, cannot be modified). It has the shape shown in Fig. 8, where:

- any of the `delta def` clauses can be omitted (meaning that the corresponding def clause in the contract to be modified is unchanged),
- `dr`, `de` may contain occurrences of $\original(R)$, $\original(E)$, resp.
- if $\original(LS) == \{l_1,\ldots,l_n\}$, then
  $\{l'_1,\ldots,l'_p\} \subseteq \{l_1,\ldots,l_n\}$ and $\{l''_1,\ldots,l''_q\} \cap \{l_1,\ldots,l_n\} = \emptyset$,
  $\{l'''_1,\ldots,l'''_m\} \subseteq (\{l_1,\ldots,l_n\} - \{l'_1,\ldots,l'_p\}) \cup \{l''_1,\ldots,l''_q\}$,
  for all $l'''_i \in \{l_1,\ldots,l_n\} - \{l'_1,\ldots,l'_p\}$, the term de_i may contain occurrences of $\original(\def(l_i))$.

We consider the DOP scenario of SPLs of JAVA programs described in [7], where method overloading is not used.[5] Therefore each delta module contains at most one class addition/modification/removal clause for each class name and, inside a class clause, at most one method addition/modification/removal clause for each method name. Whenever a delta module is applied to a (possibly incomplete) program a possibly incomplete program is generated by updating the bindings according to the JAVA binding strategy. We adopt the following convention for the labels of the methods:

---

[5] This is not a restriction since, in JAVA, method overloading is resolved statically.

– The label of each method added or modified by a delta module contains the name of the delta module.
– The label of each method occurring in a product (or intermediate program) contains the ordered sequence of the names of the delta modules that have been applied to generate the product and that effectively contributed to the generation of the code of the method. In particular, if a method m has been added to a product (or intermediate program) $\mathcal{P}$ by a delta module δ and has not been affected by subsequent delta modules used for generating $\mathcal{P}$, then the label of m in $\mathcal{P}$ is the same as in δ.

Example 7. Consider a simple product line, that we call the Bank PL. The Bank PL has two features, Base (mandatory) and Fee (optional), and two products:

– A core product p_1 corresponding to the feature configuration {Base}, which provides the basic functionalities described in steps 1–3 of Example 1.
– Another product p_2, corresponding to the feature configuration {Base, Fee}, which additionally charges each deposit with a fee.

The code base contains:

– The core product, consisting of the class Bank in Fig. 1, the class Account in Fig. 2, and the binding from the method call deposit(interest) in line 12 of Fig. 1 to $deposit_0$.
– The delta module DFee, in Fig. 9, which modifies the class Account to implement the feature Fee and illustrates the concept of a delta abstract method contract.

The program for product p_2 consists of the classes illustrated in Fig. 10 and of the bindings

– from the method call deposit(interest) (line 12, Fig. 1) to $deposit_{DFee}$, and
– from the method call deposit\$DFee(x-fee) (line 27, Fig. 10) to $deposit_0$.

It is obtained by applying the delta module DFee to the core product.

   In order to verify an SPL by exploiting our proof repositories we identify each method name of the form m\$$\delta$ with the name m and we do not replace the occurrences of m in the body of the methods introduced by the method modify operations in the delta modules (i.e., the method renaming introduced, during product generation, for dealing with the **original** construct is ignored). So, the explicit binding management mechanism can be exploited to maximize verification proof reuse across the products of the SPL.

   The *declaration* of deltas will add implementations of methods with potentially changed contracts with partial proofs. In addition to abstract symbols the resulting proof obligations also contain unresolved **original** references. The *application* of deltas to a program and its proof repository in order to generate a program variant results in new bindings, whereby abstract symbols are replaced and original calls are bound. This also includes the original constructs used in

```
1   delta DFee {
2     modifies class Account {
3       adds final int fee = 2;
4
5     /*@ label deposit_DFee
6       @ delta def \def(balance) ==
7       @   (x >= fee) ? \original(\def(\balance)) - fee : \old(balance);
8       @*/
9       modifies void deposit(int x) {
10          if (x >= fee) { original(x - fee) }
11  } } }
```

Fig. 9. The `DFee` delta module providing the functionality for the **Fee** feature (line 7 uses the JAVA syntax for conditional expressions, "... ? ... : ...")

```
1     class Bank {
2       // body of class Bank is the same as in the core product
3     }
4
5     class Account {
6       int balance = 0;
7       final int fee = 2;
8
9     /*@ label     deposit_0
10      @ def R == x > 0;
11      @ def LS == {balance};
12      @ def \def(balance) == \old(getBalance()) + x;
13      @ def E == true;
14      @*/
15      void deposit$DBase(int x) { balance += x }
16
17
18    /*@ label     deposit_DFee
19      @ def R == x > 0;
20      @ def LS == {balance};
21      @ delta def \def(balance) == (x >= \old(getFee())) ?
22      @                   (\old(getBalance()) + x) - fee : \old(getBalance());
23      @ def E == true;
24      @*/
25
26      void deposit(int x) {
27        if (x >= fee) { deposit$DBase(x-fee) }
28      }
29    }
```

Fig. 10. The product with features **Base** and **Fee**

the definition part of the abstract method contracts. Those are bound to the parts of the contracts belonging to the respectively bound methods.

To summarize, for a core product and a set of delta modules changing code and contracts, we construct the following:

– a program $(\mathcal{C}, \mathcal{B})$, that we call the *family program*, such that
   • each class in $\mathcal{C}$ contains all the method implementations that occur in at least one product—there are the method implementations and corresponding contracts of the core product or the method implementations and corresponding contracts that are added or modified by a delta module;
   • the set of method call bindings in $\mathcal{C}$ contains all the bindings in at least one product; and
– a sound proof repository for $(\mathcal{C}, \mathcal{B})$.

Note that, if all the products of the SPL are well-formed programs then the family program $(\mathcal{C}, \mathcal{B})$ is well-formed.

The family program and the associated proof repository can be built incrementally, by iterating over the set of valid feature configurations, as follows.

1. The program (classes and bindings) representing the core product (product p_1, for the Bank PL example) are added.
2. For each other valid feature configuration (product p_2, for the Bank PL example): the methods introduced (either by an add or by a modify operation) by

```
1    class Bank {
2        // body of class Bank is the same as in the core product
3    }
4
5    class Account {
6        int balance = 0;
7        final int fee = 2;
8
9    /*@ label     deposit_0
10     @ def R == x > 0;
11     @ def LS == {balance};
12     @ def \def(balance) == \old(getBalance()) + x;
13     @ def E == true;
14     @*/
15        void deposit(int x) { balance += x }
16
17
18    /*@ label     deposit_{ODFee}
19     @ def R == x > 0;
20     @ def LS == {balance};
21     @ delta def \def(balance) == (x >= \old(getFee()))) ?
22     @                  (\old(getBalance()) + x) - fee : \old(getBalance());
23     @ def E == true;
24     @*/
25
26        void deposit(int x) {
27            if (x >= fee) { original(x-fee) }
28        }
29    }
```

Fig. 11. The family program for the Bank PL

each delta module associated to the configuration are added (if they are not already present)[6] and the associated bindings are added together with the (partial) proofs.

Example 8. The family program for the Bank PL of Example 7 consists of the classes illustrated in Fig. 11 and of the bindings

- from the method call deposit(interest) (line 12, Fig. 1) to $\mathtt{deposit}_0$ (as in product p_1),
- from the method call deposit(interest) (line 12, Fig. 1) to $\mathtt{deposit}_{DFee}$ (as in product p_2), and
- from the method call original(x-fee) (line 27, Fig. 11) to $\mathtt{deposit}_0$ (as in product p_2).

6   Initial Experiments

We used a modified version of the KeY verification system for Java with support for abstract contracts to emulate our proof repository approach. We did the experiment along the lines of the running example and report here our preliminary findings. The proof effort for the experiment outlined below is summarized in Table 1.

Table 1. Proof effort

Account deposit	w/o fee ($\mathtt{deposit}_0$)			with fee ($\mathtt{deposit}_1$)		
	po (abstract)	po (own)	po (bindings)	po (own)	po (bindings)	
po open	4 (of 6)	0	—	0	—	
size	92	9	—	37	—	Σ : 138
Bank update	po (abstract)	po (own)	po ($\mathtt{deposit}_0$)	po ($\mathtt{deposit}_1$)		
po open	21 (of 29)	8	0	0		
size	679	930	1195	998		Σ : 2965

(size is measured in length of proof derivation and an indicator of the required proof effort)

We started to populate the proof repository S by adding class Account including its field balance and added then method deposit(   ) (without fees). This first step created a proof repository with proof obligations that required to verify the correctness of deposit(   ) w.r.t. its own contract. This resulted in six first-order proof obligations with placeholders from its own abstract contract only. In other words, the resulting proof repository contained only entries with empty binding sets, because no method is called from within deposit(   ). Two of the six proof obligations are immediately closeable without expanding the placeholder definitions of the abstract contracts. The remaining four first-order proof obligations are provable by expanding the placeholders, hence, the

---

[6] This can be checked straightforwardly by comparing the labels.

proof repository did not contain any unprovable proof obligations for method `deposit(` `)` (i.e., $S \Downarrow \mathtt{deposit}_0, \epsilon = \emptyset$).

The program was then extended by adding class `Bank` and its method `update()`. Method `update()` invokes `deposit(` `)` (inside the loop) and causes for the first time in our scenario the addition of method bindings into our proof repository. Using abstract contracts 29 proof obligations were generated of which 21 were not first-order provable. Expanding the definitions of the abstract contract of method `update` only eight unprovable first-order proof obligations (PO_1) were left containing the abstract symbols for the method contract of `deposit(` `)`. Interestingly the open proof obligations were all concerned with the verification that the loop invariant is preserved. They were not necessary for proving the initially valid case or use case (loop invariant is used to prove the actual method contract) part of the loop invariant calculus rule.

Adding entries for method binding `deposit(` `)` and instantiating the eight open proof obligations for the specific contracts, all first-order obligations could be closed (i.e., $S \Downarrow \mathtt{update}_0, \{\mathrm{call\ to\ } \mathtt{deposit}_0\} = \emptyset$).

Two variants for the introduction of an account with fees were simulated: The first version was added as a solution where both kinds of accounts could be present in a system at the same time. This solution uses subclassing and makes use of the flexibility of our approach, where behavioral subtyping is not a prerequisite. This version requires only the verification of the method contract for `deposit(` `)` of the new subclass of `Account` and the re-verification of the eight proof obligations PO_1 where the abstract symbols are instantiated with the new method contract ($\mathtt{deposit}_1$). The second variant simulated software evolution, where the method implementation of the original class changes and is extended to support fees. In this scenario it turns out that the verification task is identical with the first one and both give rise to the same proof obligations that need to be re-verified.

Table 1 measures the proof effort in terms of length of the derivation (more precise: number of rule applications). The total effort is the sum of all proof sizes. How does our proposed approach compare with a traditional approach based on behavioral subtyping? In our scenario the traditional approach requires a total proof effort of 4846 for the subclassing scenario (sum of derivation length of the correctness proofs for all methods including those required to ensure that subclasses satisfy the contract of their superclass) and 9292 for the evolution scenario (basically no reuse possible, all proofs had to be redone). In summary, our approach (total effort: $3103 = 138 + 2965$) saves us 36% resp. 66% of verification work. In the current stage, our prototype does not yet include optimizations like identification of identical first-order proof obligations. For instance, in case of the `Bank` class, the proof effort could be reduced further by ca. 200 by identifying that the addition of a new binding to $\mathtt{deposit}_1$ does not require to reprove that (i) the precondition of `deposit` is established (identical first-order proof obligations to the present proof for the precondition of $\mathtt{deposit}_0$), (ii) the loop terminates and that (iii) the assignable clause of `update` is correct.

Please note also that in case of the subclassing scenario, the numbers do not reflect the refactoring effort that is necessary to achieve a code base compatible with Liskov's substitution principle. This means, the introduction of a suitable abstract class and an abstract `deposit(  )` method with a contract strong enough to verify method `update()` of class `Bank`.

A more thorough and general comparison of our approach is future work. It will require more profound changes to the used verification system, which on the specification level is based on JML, and hence, behavioral subtyping by specification inheritance. In addition, a fair comparison should also measure the flexibility of different approaches and their applicability to a variety of structuring paradigms—an area where our proposed solution seems to be promising.

7   Related Work

Proof reuse was studied in [5,29] where proof replay is proposed to reduce the verification effort. The old proof is replayed and when this is no longer possible, a new proof rule is chosen heuristically. The proof reuse focuses only on the proof structure and does not take the specification into account like our work. In [8], it is assumed that one program variant has been fully verified. By analyzing the differences to another program variant, one obtains those proof obligations that remain valid in the new product variant and that need not be reestablished. In [20], evolving formal specifications are maintained by representing the dependencies between formal specifications and proofs in a development graph. The effect of each modification is computed so that only invalidated proofs have to be re-done. In [33], proofs are evolved together with formal specifications. The main limitation is that the composition of proofs is not aligned to the composition of programs as in our framework. The paper [25] studies fine-grained caching of verification conditions that arise during a proof. It is optimized for a highly interactive scenario where each keystroke of the user in an IDE potentially leads to new verification tasks. The labels that identify method implementations in our framework are called "checksums" there. Their approach is specific to call structures of the Boogie language. It uses a simple abstraction mechanism called "assumption variables" that can be seen as conditional requires clauses.

Previous work by the authors explored proof systems with an explicit proof environment (similar to a typing environment) to improve flexibility and reuse for the open world assumption in the context of class inheritance [12,13], traits [10], and (dynamic) software updates [14,15]. One exploits the binding mechanism of a particular code structuring concept to define the proof environment and formalizes the proof environment as a cache for the software verification process. In the context of the proof repositories presented in the current paper, such approaches can still be made use of by mapping them into partial proofs and bindings (details are the subject of future work). This line of work, however, assumes that at least a part of the program beyond the module under analysis is known in order to perform the analysis; e.g., the superclasses, the subtraits, etc. However, even this assumption does not hold in the general case of program evolution and variability, such as DOP. To address this challenge, the authors proposed a proof system which transforms placeholders for assertions for software product lines [11], and explored abstract contracts as a mechanism for verification reuse [9,19]. Our proof repositories generalize and make use of this work while being compatible with such refinements as mentioned above.

8 Conclusion

To increase the applicability of deductive software verification, ongoing efforts on improving verification-in-the-small need to be complemented by better integration in software development processes. The underlying assumptions about module composition and development in our verification systems must be aligned with those of the development processes. For this reason, it is important to investigate more flexible approaches to compositionality in software verification.

This paper has proposed a novel, systematic framework for verification reuse which makes use of abstract method contracts to realize an incremental proof repository aimed for verification-in-the-large. Abstract method contracts provide a separation of concerns between the usage of a method and its (changing) implementations. The proof repository keeps track of the verification effort in terms of abstract proofs which can be reused and completed later. The approach is meaningful for partial programs, so it allows the developer to start the verification effort while the program is being developed. We believe the approach can be combined with many software structuring concepts. To support this claim, we showed how to realize behavioral subtyping for class inheritance as well as delta-oriented variability for software product lines.

References

1. Barnett, M., DeLine, R., Fähndrich, M., Leino, K.R.M., Schulte, W.: Verification of object-oriented programs with invariants. J. Object Technol. **3**(6), 27–56 (2004)
2. Barnett, M., Leino, K.R.M., Schulte, W.: The Spec# programming system: an overview. In: Barthe, G., Burdy, L., Huisman, M., Lanet, J.-L., Muntean, T. (eds.) CASSIS 2004. LNCS, vol. 3362, pp. 49–69. Springer, Heidelberg (2005). doi:10.1007/978-3-540-30569-9_3
3. Beckert, B., Hähnle, R.: Reasoning and verification. IEEE Intell. Syst. **29**(1), 20–29 (2014)
4. Beckert, B., Hähnle, R., Schmitt, P.H. (eds.): Verification of Object-Oriented Software. The KeY Approach. LNCS (LNAI), vol. 4334. Springer, Heidelberg (2007)
5. Beckert, B., Klebanov, V.: Proof reuse for deductive program verification. In: Third IEEE International Conference on Software Engineering and Formal Methods, pp. 77–86. IEEE Computer Society (2004). http://doi.ieeecomputersociety.org/10.1109/SEFM.2004.10013
6. Beckert, B., Schmitt, P.H.: Program verification using change information. In: Proceedings, Software Engineering and Formal Methods (SEFM), Brisbane, Australia, pp. 91–99. IEEE Press (2003)

7. Bettini, L., Damiani, F., Schaefer, I.: Compositional type checking of delta-oriented software product lines. Acta Inform. **50**(2), 77–122 (2013). doi:10.1007/s00236-012-0173-z

8. Bruns, D., Klebanov, V., Schaefer, I.: Verification of software product lines with delta-oriented slicing. In: Beckert, B., Marché, C. (eds.) FoVeOOS 2010. LNCS, vol. 6528, pp. 61–75. Springer, Heidelberg (2011). doi:10.1007/978-3-642-18070-5_5

9. Bubel, R., Hähnle, R., Pelevina, M.: Fully abstract operation contracts. In: Margaria, T., Steffen, B. (eds.) ISoLA 2014. LNCS, vol. 8803, pp. 120–134. Springer, Heidelberg (2014). doi:10.1007/978-3-662-45231-8_9

10. Damiani, F., Dovland, J., Johnsen, E.B., Schaefer, I.: Verifying traits: an incremental proof system for fine-grained reuse. Formal Aspects Comput. **26**(4), 761–793 (2014)

11. Damiani, F., Owe, O., Dovland, J., Schaefer, I., Johnsen, E.B., Yu, I.C.: A transformational proof system for delta-oriented programming. In: Proceedings of the 16th International Software Product Line Conference (SPLC), vol. 2, pp. 53–60. ACM (2012)

12. Dovland, J., Johnsen, E.B., Owe, O., Steffen, M.: Lazy behavioral subtyping. J. Logic Algebraic Program. **79**(7), 578–607 (2010)

13. Dovland, J., Johnsen, E.B., Owe, O., Steffen, M.: Incremental reasoning with lazy behavioral subtyping for multiple inheritance. Sci. Comput. Program. **76**(10), 915–941 (2011)

14. Dovland, J., Johnsen, E.B., Owe, O., Yu, I.C.: A proof system for adaptable class hierarchies. J. Log. Algebraic Methods Program. **84**(1), 37–53 (2015)

15. Dovland, J., Johnsen, E.B., Yu, I.C.: Tracking behavioral constraints during object-oriented software evolution. In: Margaria, T., Steffen, B. (eds.) ISoLA 2012. LNCS, vol. 7609, pp. 253–268. Springer, Heidelberg (2012). doi:10.1007/978-3-642-34026-0_19

16. Engel, C., Roth, A., Schmitt, P.H., Weiß, B.: Verification of modifies clauses in dynamic logic with non-rigid functions. Technical report 2009-9, Department of Computer Science, University of Karlsruhe (2009)

17. Fähndrich, M., Logozzo, F.: Static contract checking with abstract interpretation. In: Beckert, B., Marché, C. (eds.) FoVeOOS 2010. LNCS, vol. 6528, pp. 10–30. Springer, Heidelberg (2011). doi:10.1007/978-3-642-18070-5_2

18. Filliâtre, J.-C., Marché, C.: The Why/Krakatoa/Caduceus platform for deductive program verification. In: Damm, W., Hermanns, H. (eds.) CAV 2007. LNCS, vol. 4590, pp. 173–177. Springer, Heidelberg (2007). doi:10.1007/978-3-540-73368-3_21

19. Hähnle, R., Schaefer, I., Bubel, R.: Reuse in software verification by abstract method calls. In: Bonacina, M.P. (ed.) CADE 2013. LNCS (LNAI), vol. 7898, pp. 300–314. Springer, Heidelberg (2013). doi:10.1007/978-3-642-38574-2_21

20. Hutter, D., Autexier, S.: Formal software development in MAYA. In: Hutter, D., Stephan, W. (eds.) Mechanizing Mathematical Reasoning. LNCS (LNAI), vol. 2605, pp. 407–432. Springer, Heidelberg (2005). doi:10.1007/978-3-540-32254-2_24

21. Jacobs, B., Smans, J., Philippaerts, P., Vogels, F., Penninckx, W., Piessens, F.: VeriFast: a powerful, sound, predictable, fast verifier for C and Java. In: Bobaru, M., Havelund, K., Holzmann, G.J., Joshi, R. (eds.) NFM 2011. LNCS, vol. 6617, pp. 41–55. Springer, Heidelberg (2011). doi:10.1007/978-3-642-20398-5_4

22. Kassios, I.T.: Dynamic frames: support for framing, dependencies and sharing without restrictions. In: Misra, J., Nipkow, T., Sekerinski, E. (eds.) FM 2006. LNCS, vol. 4085, pp. 268–283. Springer, Heidelberg (2006). doi:10.1007/11813040_19

23. Leavens, G.T., Poll, E., Clifton, C., Cheon, Y., Ruby, C., Cok, D., Müller, P., Kiniry, J., Chalin, P., Zimmerman, D.M.: JML reference manual (2009). ftp://ftp.cs.iastate.edu/pub/leavens/JML/jmlrefman.pdf.Draftrevision1.235

24. Leino, K.R.M.: Dafny: an automatic program verifier for functional correctness. In: Clarke, E.M., Voronkov, A. (eds.) LPAR 2010. LNCS(LNAI), vol. 6355, pp. 348–370. Springer, Heidelberg (2010). doi:10.1007/978-3-642-17511-4_20

25. Leino, K.R.M., Wüstholz, V.: Fine-grained caching of verification results. In: Kroening, D., Păsăreanu, C.S. (eds.) CAV 2015. LNCS, vol. 9206, pp. 380–397. Springer, Heidelberg (2015). doi:10.1007/978-3-319-21690-4_22

26. Liskov, B., Wing, J.M.: A behavioral notion of subtyping. ACM Trans. Program. Lang. Syst. **16**(6), 1811–1841 (1994)

27. Meyer, B.: Applying "design by contract". IEEE Comput. **25**(10), 40–51 (1992)

28. Müller, P., et al.: The 1st verified software competition: experience report. In: Butler, M., Schulte, W. (eds.) FM 2011. LNCS, vol. 6664, pp. 154–168. Springer, Heidelberg (2011)

29. Reif, W., Stenzel, K.: Reuse of proofs in software verification. In: Shyamasundar, R.K. (ed.) FSTTCS 1993. LNCS, vol. 761, pp. 284–293. Springer, Heidelberg (1993). doi:10.1007/3-540-57529-4_61

30. Reynolds, J.C.: Separation logic: A logic for shared mutable data structures. In: 17th IEEE Symposium on Logic in Computer Science (LICS 2002), pp. 55–74. IEEE Computer Society (2002)

31. Schaefer, I., Bettini, L., Bono, V., Damiani, F., Tanzarella, N.: Delta-oriented programming of software product lines. In: Bosch, J., Lee, J. (eds.) SPLC 2010. LNCS, vol. 6287, pp. 77–91. Springer, Heidelberg (2010). doi:10.1007/978-3-642-15579-6_6

32. Schaefer, I., Rabiser, R., Clarke, D., Bettini, L., Benavides, D., Botterweck, G., Pathak, A., Trujillo, S., Villela, K.: Software diversity: state of the art and perspectives. Int. J. Softw. Tools Technol. Transf. **14**(5), 477–495 (2012). doi:10.1007/s10009-012-0253-y

33. Schairer, A., Hutter, D.: Proof transformations for evolutionary formal software development. In: Kirchner, H., Ringeissen, C. (eds.) AMAST 2002. LNCS, vol. 2422, pp. 441–456. Springer, Heidelberg (2002). doi:10.1007/3-540-45719-4_30

34. Schmitt, P.H., Ulbrich, M., Weiß, B.: Dynamic frames in java dynamic logic. In: Beckert, B., Marché, C. (eds.) FoVeOOS 2010. LNCS, vol. 6528, pp. 138–152. Springer, Heidelberg (2011). doi:10.1007/978-3-642-18070-5_10

Statistical Model Checking
with Change Detection

Axel Legay and Louis-Marie Traonouez[✉]

Inria Rennes – Bretagne Atlantique, 263 Avenue du Général Leclerc - Bât 12,
Rennes, France
{axel.legay,louis-marie.traonouez}@inria.fr

Abstract. Statistical Model Checking (SMC) is a powerful and widely used approach that consists in estimating the probability for a system to satisfy a temporal property. This is done by monitoring a finite number of executions of the system, and then extrapolating the result by using statistics. The answer is correct up to some confidence that can be parameterized by the user. It is known that SMC mitigates the state-space explosion problem and allows to approximate undecidable queries. The approach has been implemented in several toolsets such as Plasma Lab, and successfully applied in a wide range of diverse areas such as systems biology, robotic, or automotive. In this paper, we add two new modest contributions to the cathedral of results on SMC. The first contribution is an algorithm that can be used to monitor changes in the probability distribution to satisfy a bounded-time property at runtime. Concretely, the algorithm constantly monitors the execution of the deployed system, and raises a flag when it observes that the probability has changed significantly. This is done by extending the applicability of the CUSUM algorithm used in signal processing into the formal validation setting. Our second contribution is to show how the programming interface of Plasma Lab can be exploited in order to make SMC technology directly available in toolsets used by designers. This integration is done by exploiting simulation facilities of design tools. Our approach thus differs from the one adopted by other SMC/formal verification toolsets which assume the existence of formal semantics for the design language, as well as a compiling chain to the rather academic one used by validation tool. The concept results in the integration of Plasma Lab as a library of the Simulink toolset. The contributions are illustrated by using Plasma Lab to verify a Simulink case study modelling a pig shed temperature controller.

Keywords: Statistical model checking · Change detection · CUSUM · Monitoring · Optimisation · MATLAB/Simulink

1 Introduction and Motivations

Complex systems such as cyber-physical systems are large-scale distributed systems, often viewed as networked embedded systems, where a large number of

© Springer International Publishing AG 2016
B. Steffen (Ed.): Transactions on FoMaC I, LNCS 9960, pp. 157–179, 2016.
DOI: 10.1007/978-3-319-46508-1_9

computational components are deployed in a physical environment. Each component collects information and offers services to its environment (e.g., environmental monitoring and control, health-care monitoring and traffic control). This information is processed either at the component, in the network or at a remote location (e.g., the base station), or in any combination of these.

A characteristic of nowadays complex systems is that they have to meet a multitude of quantitative constraints, e.g., timing constraints, power consumption, memory usage, communication bandwidth, QoS, and often under uncertainty of the behavior of the environment. There is thus the need for new mathematical foundations and supporting tools allowing to handle the combination of quantitative aspects concerning, for example, time, stochastic behavior, hybrid behavior including energy consumption. The main difficulties are that the state space of nowadays systems is too large to be analyzed with classical validation technique. Another problem is that combining time with stochastic and quantitative information eventually leads to undecidability [6,21].

In a series of recent works, the formal methods community has studied *Statistical Model Checking techniques* (SMC) [23,30,35,38] as a way to reason on quantitative (potentially undecidable) complex problems. SMC can be seen as a trade-off between testing and formal verification. The core idea of the approach is to conduct some simulations of the system and then use results from the area of statistics in order to estimate the probability to satisfy a given property. Of course, in contrast with an exhaustive approach, a simulation-based solution does not guarantee a correct result. However, it is possible to bound the probability of making an error. Simulation-based methods are known to be far less memory and time intensive than exhaustive ones, and are sometimes the only option. SMC is becoming widely accepted in various research areas such as systems biology [12,26,28] or software engineering [11], in particular for industrial applications [4,5,22,27]. There are several reasons for this success. First, it is very simple to implement, understand and use. Second, it does not require extra modelling or specification effort, but simply an operational model of the system, that can be simulated and checked against state-based properties. SMC can only be apply to fully stochastic models. Nondeterministic models are usually verified by assuming uniform distributions, or exponential distributions for continuous behaviors [16], but there also exists solutions for efficiently sampling the scheduler space of nondeterministic models [13]. Third, it allows to verify properties that cannot be expressed in classical temporal logics, for instance the one presented in [10]. SMC algorithms have been implemented in a series of tools such as Ymer [38], PRISM [29], or UPPAAL [17]. Recently, we have implemented a series of SMC techniques in a flexible and modular toolset called Plasma Lab [8].

In this paper, we propose two new contributions to SMC. As usual with SMC techniques, we focus on requirements that can be represented by bounded temporal properties, i.e., properties that can be decided on a finite sequence of states. Classical SMC algorithms are interested in estimating the probability to satisfy such a property starting from an initial state, which is done by monitoring a finite set of executions from this state. In this paper, we also consider the case where one can only observe the current execution of the system. In this context, we are interested in observing the evolution of the probability to satisfy the property at successive positions of the execution, and detecting positions where it drastically changes from original expectation. In summary, our first contribution is a methodology that can be used to monitor changes in probability distributions to satisfy a bounded property at runtime. Given a possibly infinite sequence of states that represents the continuous execution of the system, the algorithm monitors the property at each position and raises a flag when the proportion of satisfaction has changed significantly. The latter can be used to monitor, e.g., emergent behaviors. To achieve this objective, we adapt CUSUM [3, 33], an algorithm that can be used to detect changes in signal monitoring. Our ambition is not to propose a new version of CUSUM, but rather to show how the algorithm can be used in the monitoring context. This is to our knowledge the first application of CUSUM with SMC.

Our second contribution is to show how the programming interface of Plasma Lab can be exploited in order to make SMC technology directly available in toolsets used by designers. Our approach differs from the one adopted by other SMC/formal verification toolsets which assume the existence of formal semantics for the design language, as well as a compiling chain to the rather academic languages used by validation tool. The concept is illustrated with an integration of Plasma Lab as a library of the Simulink toolset of the MATLAB environment. Concretely, we show that the recently developed Plasma Lab can directly be integrated as a Simulink library, hence offering the first in house tool for the verification of stochastic Simulink models – this tool completes the panoply of validation toolsets already distributed with Simulink. Another advantage of our approach is that any advance on SMC that we will implement within Plasma Lab in the future will directly be available to the Simulink users.

Structure of the Paper. The paper is organized as follows. In Sect. 2, we discuss related work about formal verification of Simulink models. In Sect. 3, we introduce our formal model of systems and define the statistical model checking problems we want to solve. Section 4 discusses solutions to those problems. Section 5 discusses the integration of Plasma Lab within Simulink. Section 6 illustrates our approach on a case-study modelled with Simulink and verified with Plasma Lab. Finally Sect. 7 concludes the paper.

2   Related Work

Simulink includes the *Simulink Design Verifier* to formally verify and validate the models and the generated code. The framework is based on the analysis tools Polyspace [31] and Prover plug-in [34].

All the modelling is done using Simulink : Formal specifications (requirements), operational and structural specifications, and it is possible to annotate the code with assertions. The different analyses exploit the results of the integrated analyzers (Polyspace & Prover Plug-in). To summarize, Polyspace analyses the C-Code of the atomic components and Prover Plug-in verifies the operational specification against the requirements and generate some counter-examples when possible. The Framework can also generate some test cases for different covering mode (Modified Condition/Decision Coverage).

Polyspace is a static analyzer for C/C++ code based on abstract interpretation. Unlike Plasma Lab the analyses are dedicated to some special classes of properties to ensure the C-Code executions are safe for the data handled. But, Polyspace is not able to verify other kind of properties, like liveness properties. It also has apparently no support for models with probabilistic behavior.

Prover Plug-in [34] is a model checker for the verification of embedded systems, integrated circuits, and more generally for systems designed in languages like Verilog, C, Simulink, ..., and also for the UML modelling. A priori, the checker only handles deterministic and sequential systems; it implies neither parallelism, nor probabilities. It is however able to generate counter-examples if the verification of the property fails. Unlike Polyspace, Prover Plug-in is a general model checker like Plasma Lab: it can be used for any kind of properties.

Other formal verification approaches imply translating the Simulink model in the specific language of the model checker. Simulink models can be semantically translated to hybrid automata [1]. However the model checking problem of these models is in general undecidable and intractable for complex systems. More efficient translations can be achieved by restricting the type of blocks that can be used in the Simulink models: in general by removing continuous behaviors in order to obtain a finite state machine. For instance, Honeywell presents in [32] a tool that translates certain Simulink models in the input language of the model checker NuSMV [9]. [2] also presents a tool chain that translates Simulink models in the input language of the LTL model checker DiViNE. This tool chain uses the tool HiLiTe [18], also developed by Honeywell, that can perform semantic analyses of Simulink models. Finally translations exists from Simulink to synchronous languages, like Lustre in the tool SCADE. These translations however are too restrictive to be applied to the avionics proposed by Honeywell for instance [32]. Contrary to these model checking approach, SMC techniques are not restricted by the model, and our Simulink plugin for Plasma Lab is able to handle any type of Simulink and Stateflow diagrams, with both continuous and discrete behaviors.

A first experiment with SMC and Simulink was presented in [39]. Their approach consists in programming one SMC algorithm within the Simulink toolbox. On the contrary, the flexibility of our tool will allow us to incrementally add new algorithms to the toolbox without new programming efforts. The authors used a Bayesian statistical analysis for verifying the Fault-Tolerant Fuel Control System, an example from the basic Simulink examples database. In the paper they consider a version of the model where the failures are triggered following a Poisson distribution. We have used a similar model and reproduced their results with Plasma Lab[1]. However, we do not limit to verification analyses, since we also present in Sect. 6 a case study on which we perform optimization and change detection.

---

[1] https://project.inria.fr/plasma-lab/examples/fault-tolerant-fuel-control-system/.

Finally, our approach is also different from the one in [14] that consists in translating parts of Simulink models into the Uppaal language (which makes it difficult for analyzing counter examples). Therefore Plasma Lab for Simulink offers the first integrated verification tool for Simulink models with stochastic information.

3   Systems and Problems

We denote $\mathbb{R}$ the set of real numbers and $\mathbb{Q}_{\geq 0}$ the set of positive rational numbers. Consider a set of states S and a set of state variables SV. Assume that each state variable $x \in SV$ is assigned to domain $\mathbb{D}_x$, and define the valuation function V, such that $V(s, x) \in \mathbb{D}_x$ is the value of x in state s. Consider also a time domain $T \subseteq \mathbb{R}$. We propose the following definition to capture the behavior of a large class of stochastic systems.

Definition 1 (Stochastic Process [38]). *A stochastic process (S, T) is a family of random variables $\mathcal{X} = \{X_t \mid t \in T\}$, each X_t having range S.*

An *execution* for a stochastic process (S, T) is any sequence of observations $\{x_t \in S \mid t \in T\}$ of the random variables $X_t \in \mathcal{X}$. It can be represented as a sequence $\pi = (s_0, t_0), (s_1, t_1), \ldots, (s_n, t_n)$, such that $s_i \in S$ and $t_i \in T$, with time stamps monotonically increasing, e.g. $t_i < t_{i+1}$. Let $0 \leq i \leq n$, we denote $\pi^i = (s_i, t_i), \ldots, (s_n, t_n)$ the suffix of π starting at position i. Let $\overline{s} \in S$, we denote $Path(\overline{s})$ the set of executions of $\mathcal{X}$ that starts in state $(\overline{s}, 0)$ (also called initial state) and $Path^n(\overline{s})$ the set of executions of length n.

In [38], Youness showed that the executions set of a stochastic process is a measurable space, which defines a probability measure μ over $Path(\overline{s})$. The precise definition of μ depends on the specific probability structure of the stochastic process being studied. We now define the general structure for *stochastic discrete event systems*.

Definition 2 (Stochastic Discrete Event System [38]). *A stochastic discrete event system (SDES) is a stochastic process extended with initial state and variable assignments, i.e., $Sys = \langle S, I, T, SV, V \rangle$, where (S, T) is a stochastic process, $I \subseteq S$ is the set of initial states, SV is a set of state variables and V is the valuation function.*

We denote $Path(Sys)$ the set of executions of Sys that starts from an initial state in I. Properties over the executions of Sys are defined via the so-called Bounded Linear Temporal Logic (BLTL) [7]. BLTL restricts Linear Temporal Logic by bounding the scope of the temporal operators. Syntactically, we have

$$\varphi, \varphi' := \mathsf{true} \mid x \sim v \mid \varphi \wedge \varphi' \mid \neg\varphi \mid X_{\leq t} \mid \varphi \, U_{\leq t} \, \varphi'$$

where φ, φ' are BLTL formulas, $x \in SV$, $v \in D_x$ and $t \in \mathbb{Q}_{\geq 0}$ and $\sim \in \{<, \leq, =, \geq, >\}$. As usual, we define $F_{\leq t}\varphi \equiv \mathsf{true}\, U_{\leq t}\varphi$ and $G_{\leq t}\varphi \equiv \neg F_{\leq t}\neg\varphi$. The semantics of BLTL is defined with respect to an execution $\pi = (s_0, t_0), (s_1, t_1), \ldots, (s_n, t_n)$ of a SDES using the following rules:

- $\pi \models X_{\leq t}\,\varphi$ iff $\exists i$, $i = max\{j \mid t_0 \leq t_j \leq t_0 + t\}$ and $\pi^i \models \varphi$
- $\pi \models \varphi_1\,U_{\leq t}\,\varphi_2$ iff $\exists i$, $t_0 \leq t_i \leq t_0 + t$ and $\pi^i \models \varphi_2$
  and $\forall j,\ 0 \leq j < i,\ \pi^j \models \varphi_1$
- $\pi \models \varphi_1 \wedge \varphi_2$ iff $\pi \models \varphi_1$ and $\pi \models \varphi_2$
- $\pi \models \neg\varphi$ iff $\pi \not\models \varphi$
- $\pi \models x \sim v$ iff $V(s_0, x) \sim v$
- $\pi \models$ true

In the rest of the paper, we consider two problems that are 1. the quantitative (optimization) problem for BLTL, and 2. the detection of changes. The first problem has largely be discussed in SMC papers, and the second problem is a new comer in the SMC area. The motivation to reintroduce the quantitative problem is that it can be used to calibrate the detection algorithm.

3.1   Quantitative and Optimization Problems

Given a SDES $\mathcal{S}ys$ and a BLTL property φ, the existence of a probability measure μ over $Path(\mathcal{S}ys)$ allows to define the probability measure $Pr[\mathcal{S}ys \models \varphi] = \mu\{\pi \in Path(\mathcal{S}ys) \mid \pi \models \varphi\}$. The *quantitative problem* consists in computing the value of $Pr[\mathcal{S}ys \models \varphi]$.

We will also study the *optimization problem*, that is the one of finding an initial state that maximizes/minimizes the value of a given observation. Consider a set $\mathcal{O}$ of observations over $\mathcal{S}ys$. Each observation $o \in \mathcal{O}$ is a function $o : Path^n(\bar{s}) \to \mathbb{D}_o$ that associates to each run of length n and starting at $\bar{s}$ a value in a domain $\mathbb{D}_o$. We denote $(\tilde{o})_n^{\bar{s}}$ the average value of $o(\pi)$ over all the executions $\pi \in Path^n(\bar{s})$. The *optimization problem* for $\mathcal{S}ys$ is to determine an initial state $\bar{s} \in I$ that minimizes or maximizes the value $(\tilde{o})_n^{\bar{s}}$, for all $o \in \mathcal{O}$.

As an example, an observation can simply be the maximal value of a given parameter, like a cost or reward, along an execution. The average observation then becomes the sum of those observations divided by the number of runs. In this context, the optimization could be to find the initial state that minimizes the value of the parameters.

3.2   Change Detection Problem

In this section, we consider a monitoring problem. We want to detect an expected event by looking at the variation of a probability measure over a set of samples of an execution. Therefore, contrary to the previous SMC problems, we consider a single execution on which we checked a BLTL property at regular intervals. On this execution we want to determine the time at which the probability measure of the BLTL property changes sufficiently to characterize an expected event on the system.

More precisely, we consider a (potentially infinite) execution $\pi = (s_0, t_0), (s_1, t_1), \ldots, (s_n, t_n), \ldots$ of a system $\mathcal{S}ys$. We monitor a BLTL property φ from each position (s_i, t_i) of this execution (the monitoring involves a finite sequence of states as BLTL formulas are time bounded) and we compute an ingenious proportion on the numbers of satisfaction and non satisfaction of the property. This proportion is used to detect changes in the probability to satisfy the property at a given point of the execution. Concretely, assuming that this probability is originally $p<k$, we detect a change index in the execution when the probability becomes $p \geq k$.

Example 1. Consider the firefighting services in a city like London. Assume that under normal traffic conditions, the firemen can extinguish a fire within three hours with a probability greater than 0.7. It is expected that this probability decreases when the traffic increases. The challenge is to detect the time t when this change happens.

Formally, we consider a sequence of Bernoulli variables X_i such that $X_i = 1$ iff $\pi^i \models \varphi$. We define that an execution π satisfies a change $\tau = Pr[\pi \models \varphi] \geq k$, iff $Pr[X_i = 1]<k$ for $t_i < t$ and $Pr[X_i = 1] \geq k$ for $t_i \geq t$. Given an execution π, we use $\tau_i!$ to denote the index $i = (s_i, t_i)$ in π at which the execution is subject to the change. We assume an implicit change detection maximal time set by the user. If no change is detected after this time has passed, then we set up the evaluation of $\tau_i!$ to ∞. In case the execution is subject to several changes, we take the first time. Using those notations, one can define Boolean propositions over changes and their respective time. One can also combine changes propositions with BLTL formulas, providing that those propositions are not in the scope of temporal operators. We now introduce extended BLTL change-based relations, an extension of BLTL that incorporates a change detection operator.

Definition 3. *Given an execution π of Sys, an extended BLTL change relation is defined as:*

$$prop := \texttt{let } \tau_1 = change \texttt{ and } \dots \texttt{ and } \tau_n = change \texttt{ in } \delta$$
$$change := Pr[\pi \models \varphi] \star k$$
$$\delta, \delta' := \tau_i! \sim \tau_j! + t \mid \tau_i! \sim t \mid \varphi' \mid \delta \wedge \delta' \mid \neg\delta$$

where $k \in]0,1[$, $t \in \mathbb{Q}_{\geq 0}$, $\star \in \{\leq, \geq\}$, $\sim \in \{<, \leq, =, \geq, >\}$, φ and φ' are BLTL formulae, τ_i and τ_j are change identifiers defined in the prop rule.

This extension allows us, e.g., to express conditions such as "if a change occurs at time t, then the system shall reach a state x in less than 10 units of time". The semantics of extended BLTL change relation easily follows from the one of BLTL and the description of the change operator.

Example 2. We consider again the example of the firefighting services. Let $\varphi = F \leq 3 \ \neg "fire"$ be a BLTL property that we want to evaluate in a change relation, to express the requirement that any fire must be extinguished within 3 h. With an increase of traffic we expect that the probability to satisfy φ decreases. We define a first change relation $\tau_1 = Pr[\pi \models \varphi] \leq 0.4$ to measure the time $\tau_1!$ at which the probability to satisfy φ becomes less than 0.4. We now expect that countermeasures are taken, like choosing a diversion route, in order to improve the services effectiveness. We define a second change relation

$\tau_2 = Pr[\pi \models \varphi] \leq 0.6$ to measure the time $\tau_2!$ at which the probability to satisfy φ becomes greater than 0.6. Finally, we combine these two change relations in an extended BLTL change relation:

$$\text{let } \tau_1 = Pr[\pi \models \varphi] \leq 0.4 \text{ and } \tau_2 = Pr[\pi \models \varphi] \leq 0.4 \text{ in } \tau_2! \leq \tau_1! + 72$$

This expresses the requirement that the two changes must happen in less than 72 h.

4   A Statistical Model Checking Approach

In this section, we detail our statistical model checking algorithmic solutions to the problems described in Sect. 3. SMC solutions to the quantitative verification and optimization problems are well-known and will only briefly be surveyed. SMC solution for extended BLTL change relations is new.

4.1   Quantitative Verification

We first focus on the problem of computing the probability $Pr[\mathcal{S}ys \models \varphi]$ for a SDES $\mathcal{S}ys$ to satisfy a BLTL property φ. With SMC we estimate this probability using a number of statistically independent simulation traces of an executable model. The idea is to monitor the property on each simulation, and to represent the outcome of the ith monitoring with a Bernoulli variable X_i that takes the value 1 if the execution satisfies the property and 0 otherwise. We then use an algorithm from the area of statistics to compute the probability of the Bernoulli variable (which corresponds to the probability for the system to satisfy the property). Those algorithms include Monte Carlo, or importance sampling/splitting [24]. Algorithms for monitoring BLTL properties on a given execution can be found in [20]. In this paper, the quantitative problem will be used to verify classical BLTL properties, and also in the calibration process needed to verify extended BLTL change relations.

Optimization. We now show that a simulation approach can also be used to perform an optimization of the model by varying the model parameters and evaluating the observable quantities to optimize. We consider a SEDS $\mathcal{S}ys$, with a set of initial states I, and a set of observations $\mathcal{O}$ and a bound $n \in \mathbb{N}$.

For each initial state $\overline{s} \in I$ we perform N random simulations π^i from $Path^n(\overline{s})$ and we compute the average value of the observed quantities at the end of the simulations. Therefore, for each observation $o \in \mathcal{O}$ we compute an estimation $\frac{1}{N} \sum_{i=1}^{N} o(\pi_i)$ of the average value $(\overline{o})_n^{\overline{s}}$.

To solve the optimization problem, we must determine the configurations in I that optimize (minimize or maximize) these quantities. When the problem is defined with several observable quantities, we are faced with a multi-objective problem, and the best configurations are then selected by computing the Pareto frontier of the set of observations [15].

4.2   Change Detection with CUSUM

In this section, we consider SMC solutions for verifying extended BLTL properties with changes. We first present an SMC algorithm for change detection, and then briefly discuss the monitoring of extended BLTL. For change detection, we resort to the CUSUM algorithm [3,33], whose principles have already been formalized in other contexts [36]. This algorithm, originally developed in the signal theory world, is used to detect the probability changes during the execution of a stochastic system. The main purpose of the change detection is to detect when some changes in some parameters, not easily observable or measurable, will perturb the measures and the observations done over the system. The principle is to compare the probability p when the system is working normally against the probability p' resulting of the change.

Let Sys be a SDES and $\pi = (s_0, t_0), (s_1, t_1), \ldots$ be an execution of Sys. We consider the change $\tau = Pr[\pi \models \varphi] \geq k$ with φ a BLTL property and $k \in]0, 1[$. Let $X_1, \ldots X_N$ be a finite set of Bernoulli variables such that X_i takes the value 1 iff $\pi^i \models \varphi$. We note $p_n = Pr[Xi = 1 | i <= n]$ the probability of satisfying φ from (s_0, t_0) to the state (s_n, t_n). We will use the CUSUM algorithm to decide between the two following hypothesis:

- H_0 : $\forall\, n,\ 0 \leq n \leq N, p_n < k$, i.e., no change occurs
- H_1 : $\exists\, m,\ 0 \leq m \leq N$ such that the change occurs at time t_m: $\forall n,\ 0 \leq n \leq N$, we have $t_n < t_m \implies p_n < k$ and $t_n \geq t_m \implies p_n \geq k$.

We assume that we know the initial probability $p_{init} < k$ of $Pr[\pi \models \varphi]$ before the change occurs. One solution is to estimate this probability with the Monte Carlo algorithm using an ideal version of the system in which not change occurs. The CUSUM algorithm will use the two probabilities p_{init} and k to decide between the two hypothesis and determine the time of the change, if it occurs.

Like the Sequential Probability Ratio Test (SPRT) [30,37], the CUSUM comparison is based on a likelihood-ratio test: it consists in computing the cumulative sum S_n of the logarithm of the likelihood-ratios s_i over the sequence of samples $X_1, \ldots X_n$ and detecting the change decision as soon as S_n satisfies the stopping rule.

$$S_n = \sum_{i=1}^{n} s_i \qquad\qquad s_i = \begin{cases} \ln \frac{k}{p_{init}}, & \text{if } X_i = 1 \\[2ex] \ln \frac{1-k}{1-p_{init}}, & \text{otherwise} \end{cases}$$

The typical behavior of the cumulative sum S_n is a global decreasing before the change, and a sharp increase after the change. Then the stopping rule's purpose is to detect when the positive drift is sufficiently relevant to detect the change. It consists in saving $m_n = \min_{1 \leq i \leq n} S_i$, the minimal value of CUSUM, and comparing it with the current value. If the distance is sufficiently great, the stopping decision is taken, i.e., an alarm is raised at time $t_a = \min\{t_n : S_n - m_n \geq \lambda\}$, where λ is a sensitivity threshold.

The CUSUM proportion can only be computed during a finite amount of time, which is set by the user. In case there is no detection, we set $t_a = +\infty$.

Note that we presented CUSUM monitoring for the case $p \geq k$, but it could be set up for $p \leq k$ by defining the stopping rule for the maximum value of CUSUM instead.

CUSUM Calibration. It is important to note that the likelihood-ratio test assumes that the considered samples are independent. This assumption may be difficult to ensure over a single execution of a system, but several heuristic solutions exist to guarantee independence. One of them consists in finding a location frequently visited during the execution of the system. Collecting exactly one sample each time such a state is visited, ensures independence between samples. In our context, such a state can be the initial location from which the execution is constantly restarted. However this solution cannot be applied to continuous-time systems. Another solution is to introduce delays between the samples. In that case Monte Carlo SMC analyses can evaluate the correlation between the samples, and help to select appropriate delays.

The CUSUM sensitivity depends on the choice of the threshold λ. A smaller value increases the sensitivity, *i.e.*, the false alarms rate. A false alarm is a change detection at a time when no relevant event actually occurs in the system. Conversely, big values may delay the detection of the changes. The false alarms rate of CUSUM is defined as $E[t_a]$, the expected time of an alarm raised by CUSUM while the system is still running before the change occurs. Ideally, this value must be the biggest as possible $E[t_a] \to +\infty$. The detection delay is defined as the expected time between the actual change of time t and the alarm time t_a raised by CUSUM: $E[t_a - t \mid t < t_a]$. Ideally, this value has to be small as possible. In Sect. 6, we will propose a heuristic that uses the quantitative model checking problem in order to calibrate the algorithm.

The Empirical Way to Choose the Stopping Rule. One of the main difficulties in applying CUSUM is to compute the minimal duration needed to trigger an alarm. Indeed, the algorithm may be subjected to brief local changes that should not impact the final result. Theoretically, the properties of the CUSUM are based on the computation of the Average Run Length function (ARL) [3]. In a very few cases, this function may be computed or approximated using some approximating techniques (Wald or Siegmund) but most of the time, it is too complex to be used and to deduce λ. In this paper we propose a variant of the methodology proposed in [36]. Our approach consists in exploiting Sys_0, that is a version of the system for which the change does not occur. We first compute the probability p_{init} for this system to satisfy the property. We then compute several CUSUM on Sys_0 in order to compute the average frequency of a false alarm. The latter is obtained by observing the mean time between positive drift in the CUSUM as well as its duration in term of samples (observations of the CUSUM ratio). We then compute the minimal sample duration to exceed the change probability k. This value is multiplied by the logarithm of k divided by p_{init} (*i.e.*, the minimal value of a drift).

Monitoring Executions for Change Relation Satisfiability. We now briefly discuss the monitoring of extended BLTL with changes. Let us consider the change relation γ based on $\tau_1, \ldots, \tau_n$ changes. Using the syntax introduced in Sect. 3.2, it is expressed as let τ_1 and $\ldots$ and τ_n in γ, where γ contains Boolean operations over changes and BLTL formulas. We use the following monitoring procedure for each atom:

1. For each change τ_i, we set a CUSUM monitor that splits the monitoring into sub-monitors, one for each random variable, *i.e.*, one to monitor the BLTL formula involved in the change from a given position of the execution. Note that classical tableau-based heuristics allows us to reuse information between monitoring actions.
2. The proposition $\tau_i!$ holds iff $t_i \neq +\infty$. The proposition $\tau_i! \sim t$ holds iff $t_i \sim t$. Similarly, the proposition $\tau_i! \sim \tau_j! + t$ holds only if $t_i \sim t_j + t$ but it is undefined if $t_i = t_j = +\infty$.
3. BLTL formulas can be monitored with classical techniques.

In practice, the tool generates monitors on demand for the given atoms and combines their answers in a Boolean manner.

5 Plasma Lab and Simulink Integration

The results presented in Sect. 4 have been implemented in the Plasma Lab SMC toolbox[2]. In this section, we first recap the main features of the tool, and then show how the architecture of the implementation can be exploited in order to integrate Plasma Lab within Simulink, hence providing an in shell new verification theory for this widely used language. The main contribution in this section with respect to [8] is to show how the architecture can be exploited to perform the integration.

5.1 On Plasma Lab

Plasma Lab is a compact, efficient and flexible platform for statistical model checking of stochastic models. The tool offers a series of SMC algorithms which includes rare events simulation, distributed SMC, non-determinism, or optimization. The main difference between Plasma Lab and other SMC tools is that Plasma Lab proposes an API abstraction of the concepts of stochastic model simulator, property checker (monitoring) and SMC algorithm. In other words, the tool has been designed to be capable of using external simulators, input languages, or SMC algorithms. This not only reduces the effort of integrating new algorithms, but also allows us to create direct plug-in interfaces with industry used specification tools. The latter being done without using extra compilers.

Figure 1 presents Plasma Lab architecture. More specifically, the relations between model simulators, property checkers, and SMC algorithms components.

---

[2] Available at https://project.inria.fr/plasma-lab/.

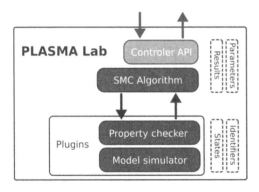

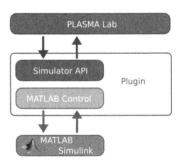

Fig. 1. Plasma Lab architecture

Fig. 2. Interface between Plasma Lab and Simulink

The simulators features include starting a new trace and simulating a model step by step. The checkers decide a property on a trace by accessing to state values. They also control the simulations, with a *state on demand* approach that generates new states only if more states are needed to decide the property. A SMC algorithm component, such as the CUSUM algorithm, is a runnable object. It collect samples obtained from a checker component. Depending on the property language, their checker either returns Boolean or numerical values. The algorithm then notifies progress and sends its results through the Controller API.

In coordination with this architecture, we use a plugin system to load models and properties components. It is then possible to support new model or property languages. Adding a simulator, a checker or an algorithm component is pretty straightforward as they share a similar plugin architecture. Thus, it requires only a few classes and methods to get a new component running. Each plugin contains a factory class used by Plasma Lab to instantiate component objects. These components implement the corresponding interface defining their behavior. Some companion objects are also required (results, states, identifiers) to allow communication between components and the Controller API.

One of the goal of Plasma Lab is also to benefit from a massive distribution of the simulations, which is one of the advantage of the SMC approach. Therefore Plasma Lab API provides generic methods to define distributed algorithms. We have used these functionalities to distribute large number of simulations over a computer grid[3].

5.2 On Integrating Plasma Lab Within Simulink

We now show how to integrate Plasma Lab within Simulink, hence lifting the power of our simulation approaches directly within the tool. We will focus on

---

[3] https://project.inria.fr/plasma-lab/documentation/tutorial/igrida-experimentation/.

those Simulink models with stochastic information, as presented in [39]. But our approach is more flexible because the user will directly use Plasma Lab within the Simulink interface, without third party.

Simulink is a block diagram environment for multi-domain simulation and Model-Based Design approach. It supports the design and simulation at the system level, automatic code generation, and the testing and verification of embedded systems. Simulink provides a graphical editor, a customizable set of block libraries and solvers for modelling and simulation of dynamic systems. It is integrated within MATLAB. The Simulink models we considered have special extensions to randomly behave like failures. By default the Simulink library provides some random generators that are not compatible with statistical model checking: they always generate the same random sequence of values at each execution. To overcome this limitation we use some C-function block calls that generate independent sequences of random draws.

Our objective was to integrate Plasma Lab as a new Simulink library. For doing so, we developed a new simulator plugin whose architecture is showed in Fig. 2. One of the key points of our integration has been to exploit MATLAB Control[4], a library that allows to interact with MATLAB from Java. This library uses a proxy object connected to a MATLAB session. MATLAB invokes, *e.g.* functions `eval`, `feval` ... as well as variables access, that are transmitted and executed on the MATLAB session through the proxy. This allowed us to implement the features of a model component, controlling a Simulink simulation, in MATLAB language. Calls to this implementation are then done in Java from the Plasma Lab plugin.

Regarding the monitoring of properties, we exploit the simulation output of Simulink. More precisely, BLTL properties are checked over the executions of a SDES, *i.e.*, sequences of states and time stamps based on the set of state variables SV. This set must be defined by declaring in Simulink signals as log output. During the simulation these signals are logged in a data structure containing time stamps and are then retrieved as states in Plasma Lab. One important point is that Simulink discretizes the signals trace, its sample frequency being parameterized by each block. In terms of monitoring this means that the sample frequency must be configured to observe any relevant change in the model. In practice, the frequency can be set as a constant value, or, if the model mixes both continuous data flow and state flow, the frequency can be aligned on the transitions, *i.e.*, when a state is newly visited.

6   A Pig Shed Case Study

We now illustrate the change detection contribution of this paper on the model of a temperature controller in a pig shed. This model is inspired by similar studies [15,19,25]. The system under control is a pig shed equipped with a fan and a heater to regulate the air temperature. Air temperature in the shed is subjected to random variations due to the variation of external temperature

---

[4] https://code.google.com/p/matlabcontrol/.

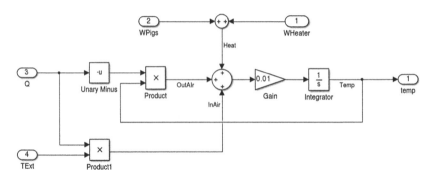

Fig. 3. Simulink model of the differential equation controlling the temperature

and the variation of the number of pigs that produce heat. The objective of the controller is to counter these variations such that the temperature remains within a given comfort zone. To do so, the controller can activate the heater to increase the temperature, and the fan to bring external air and therefore cool the shed. Then the temperature T of the shed is given by the following differential equation:

$$T' = T_{ext} * Q - T * Q + W_{heater} + W_{pigs}$$

where T_{ext} is the external temperature, $Q = Q_{min} + Q_{fan}$ is the air flow created by a minimal flow Q_{min}, and an additional flow Q_{fan} when the fan is activated, W_{heater} is the heat produced by the heater, when activated, and W_{pigs} is the heat produced by the pigs. This equation is modelled by the Simulink subsystem of Fig. 3.

The controller that we study applies a *bang-bang* (also called *on-off*) strategy that is specified by four temperature thresholds, that is (1) when the temperature goes above TFanOn, the fan is turned on, (2) when the temperature returns below TFanOff, the fan is turned off, (3) when the temperature goes below THeaterOn, the heater is turned on, (4) when the temperature returns above THeaterOff, the heater is turned off. This controller is implemented by Stateflow automata given in Fig. 4.

The fan and the heater are subjected to random failures when they are in use. Exponential distributions control the occurrence time of a failure. After a failure a reparation process allows to restart the fan or the heater, but it also takes a random time, exponentially distributed. These failures are modelled by two Stateflow automata, as shown in Fig. 5. In this automaton, rnd is a random number between 0 and 1, and tuse is the duration of use of the fan or heater. The timings tfail and trepair corresponds respectively to the time of next failure, and the repair time, each chosen according to an exponential distribution with parameter lambdaFail and lambdaRepair, respectively. Additionally, the failure rate increases with usage due to wear and tear. This continues until a replacement is performed, which resets the rate.

An overview of the complete Simulink model is shown in Fig. 6.

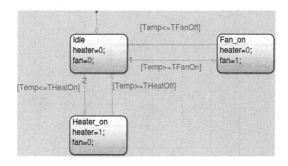

Fig. 4. Temperature controller

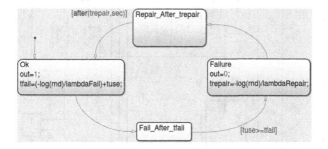

Fig. 5. Failure generator

6.1 Quantitative Verification and Optimization

The controller goal is to maintain the temperature within a comfort zone specified by a minimum and a maximum temperature (resp. $T_{min} = 15\,°C$ and $T_{max} = 25\,°C$). The system contains a predicate Discomfort that is true when the temperature of the system is outside this comfort zone. We first consider the following values for the controller thresholds: TFanOn = $22\,°C$, TFanOff = $20\,°C$, THeaterOn = $18\,°C$ and THeaterOff = $20\,°C$.

We apply statistical model checking to evaluate the efficiency of the controller both in the presence and absence of failures. The first BLTL property that we monitor checks that the system is never in discomfort for an excessive period of time. This is expressed by the following property:

$$\Phi_1 = G_{\leq t_1} F_{\leq t_2} \neg \mathsf{Discomfort}$$

where t_1 is the simulation time, t_2 is the accepted discomfort time. Another safety specification is to check if there exists long periods without discomfort. This is possible with:

$$\Phi_2 = F_{\leq t_1} G_{\leq t_2} \neg \mathsf{Discomfort}$$

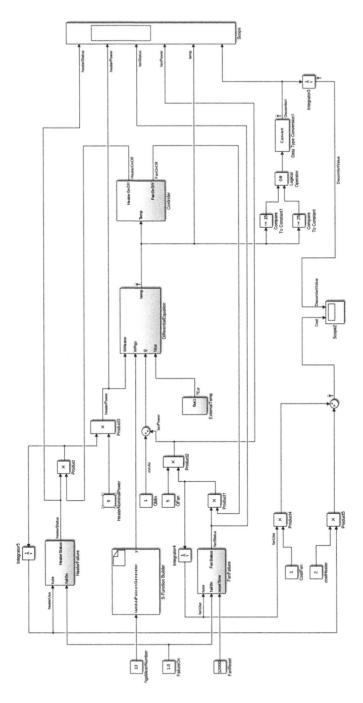

Fig. 6. Pig shed Simulink model

Finally, a third BLTL property checks that each period of discomfort is followed by a period without discomfort:

$$\Phi_3 = G_{\leq t_1}\Big(G_{\leq t_2}\text{Discomfort} \Rightarrow F_{\leq t_3}(G_{\leq t_4}\neg\text{Discomfort})\Big)$$

Here t_1 and t_2 are as previously, while $t_3 \geq t_2$ is the expected time at which the system returns to normal situation, and t_4 is the duration of the period without discomfort.

We use Plasma Lab to estimate the probability to satisfy these properties for different values of the timing constraints, on both models with and without failures. Each property is evaluated over a period of time $t_1 = 12000$ time units (t.u.) with precision $\epsilon = 0.01$ and confidence $\delta = 0.01$. Φ_1 and Φ_2 are evaluated for several values of t_2. Note that for $t_2 = 0$, Φ_1 resumes to checking $G_{\leq t_1}\neg\text{Discomfort}$. Φ_3 is evaluated with $t_2 = 25\,t.u.$ and several values of t_3 and t_4.

The results for properties Φ_1 and Φ_2 are presented in Figs. 7 and 8, respectively. While the probabilities of satisfying Φ_1 show a significant difference between the models with and without failures, the results for Φ_2 are almost identical. This means that discomfort is as frequent in the two models, but it tends to last longer in the presence of failures. The results for Φ_3 are presented in Figs. 9 and 10. It shows again that the model without failures recovers quicker from a discomfort period.

Instead of estimating a probability using SMC techniques, we can compute the average value of two quantities in the model, namely the *discomfort time*, that is the cumulative time when the model is in a discomfort state, and the energy *cost*, computed with the duration of use of the heater and the fan. The cost is 1 per t.u. for the fan and 2 per t.u. for the heater. We aim at minimizing these two values by choosing adequate values of the model parameters.

Using Plasma Lab we can automatically instantiate the model with a range of values for the four temperature thresholds. We specify the ranges $[15, 20]$ for THeaterOn and THeaterOff, and $[20, 25]$ for TFanOn and TFanOff, with an

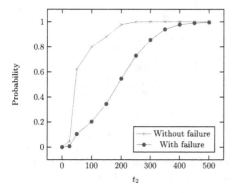

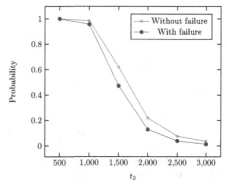

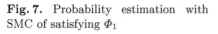

Fig. 7. Probability estimation with SMC of satisfying Φ_1

Fig. 8. Probability estimation with SMC of satisfying Φ_2

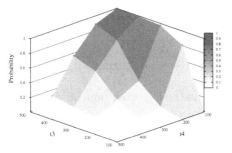

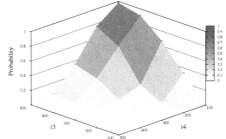

Fig. 9. Probability estimation with SMC of satisfying Φ_3 without failures

Fig. 10. Probability estimation with SMC of satisfying Φ_3 with failures

increment of 1. We additionally specify the following constraints to select a subset of the possible values of the parameters:

$$\mathsf{TFanOff} < \mathsf{TFanOn}$$
$$\mathsf{THeaterOn} < \mathsf{THeaterOff}$$
$$\mathsf{THeaterOn} < \mathsf{TFanOn}$$

Using these constraints Plasma Lab generates a set of 225 possible configurations, for each variant of the models, with and without failures. Each configuration is automatically analyzed with 100 simulations. We then plot the average values of the cost and the discomfort in Figs. 11 and 12. These graphs helps to select the best values of the parameters by looking at the points that lie on the Pareto frontier of the data.

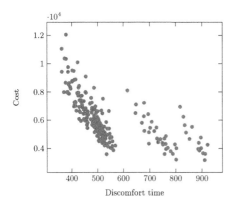

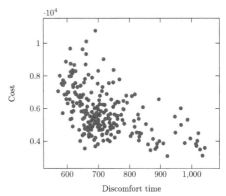

Fig. 11. Optimization of the thresholds parameters without failures

Fig. 12. Optimization of the thresholds parameters with failures

6.2   Change Detection: Detection and Calibration

In our pig shed, the equipment may sometimes fail (heater or fan may break). In such situation, the shed may be too frequently in the discomfort zone, which may lead to the death of several pigs.

As we have seen, the probability of being in the discomfort zone is nominally very low. However, to avoid problems, one should be able to rise a flag as soon as the probability to be in the discomfort zones crosses a given threshold. Our objective is to detect that when such a change happens, there is a maintenance procedure that moves the shed out of the discomfort zone. In our example, this maintenance feature is modelled as a procedure that is regularly applied to the pig shed. Initially, the time between each maintenance is set to a very large value ($500000\,t.u.$). The final objective is to set this time value in order to have an acceptable maintenance delay when the death risk is too heavy for the pigs (emergent behavior). This will be done by detecting changes.

We modelled the property using the change property language we proposed and we used the CUSUM algorithm to check it. We first define τ to be the following change: " the probability to be in the discomfort zone more than $t_1 = 100\,t.u.$ is greater than 0.35". We are now ready to propose a property that expresses that when the change occurs, then the maintenance must be done in less than $t_2 = 1000\,t.u.$ Formally,

$$
\phi_4 = \left|
\begin{array}{l}
\texttt{let} \quad \tau = \; Pr\big[\pi \models G_{\leq t_1}\mathsf{Discomfort}\big] \geq 0.35 \\
\texttt{in} \quad \tau! \implies F_{\leq \tau!+t_2}\mathsf{Reparation}
\end{array}
\right.
$$

In order to perform the analysis, the CUSUM algorithm needs a calibration step. We first require an estimate of p_{init}, the initial probability of being in the discomfort zone before the change occurs, and we determine a minimum delay between the samples that ensures independence between the analyses. We disable failures of the temperature regulation system (fans + heaters) in the shed model and we simulate a $200000\,t.u.$ long trace. We sample the trace with a fixed delay between each sample. For each sample we perform a Monte Carlo analysis of the property $G_{\leq t_1}\mathsf{Discomfort}$ by restarting 600 simulations from the initial state of the sample. For sample delays lower than $100\,t.u.$, the probabilities computed for each sample differ, but they converge to 0 (with a precision 0.05 and a confidence 0.9) for the delays $150\,t.u.$ and $200\,t.u.$ Therefore we will select a sample delay of $200\,t.u.$ and an initial probability of $p_{init} = 0.05$ for the CUSUM analysis.

Next step is to set the stopping sensitivity λ on which depends the false alarm probability and the detection delay. This is done again by observing the model without failures: we simulate 100 executions of the CUSUM and observe 1000 samples during each execution. We compute for each samples the CUSUM cumulative ratio. Since there is no failure, the curve of the cumulative ratio should always decrease. Indeed, it should only increase when failures happen, *i.e.*, when the change happens. In practice, even without failure, the curve may locally increase for a short amount of time, which is due to the uncertainty introduced in the model. The objective is to characterize those local drifts to avoid false alarms.

To do so we analyze the CUSUM simulations and we observed that the mean time between positive drifts is $127.88\,t.u.$ and the mean duration of positive drift is $1.2\,t.u.$. The frequency of positive drifts is thus $1.2/(127.88+1.2)$, which is in the interval $[0, 0.05]$ as predicted by Monte Carlo algorithm. In order to observe a real alarm one needs to push this quotient to 0.35, which is the probability one wants to observe. This amounts to varying the duration of a positive sample, $i.e.$, to replace 1.2 by a higher value in the above quotient. Doing so, we conclude that the probability will become greater than 0.35 when the positive drift is longer that 52 samples. From the definition of CUSUM, we compute that the drift is $\ln\frac{0.35}{0.05}$ for each positive sample. We finally set the stopping rule to $\lambda = 52 * \ln\frac{0.35}{0.05} \approx 101$.

We then launched the CUSUM on the model with failures over an execution of $200000\,t.u.$ that is checked against the property $G_{\leq t_1}$ Discomfort every $200\,t.u.$. Fig. 13 displays the values obtained with Plasma Lab for the CUSUM cumulative ratio and the minimum value reached. From these values Plasma Lab detected that the stopping rule was satisfied after the sample 580, that corresponds to the simulation time $105837\,t.u.$. We reproduced the same experiment several times (20): we determined that the change occurred at $115104\,t.u.$ in average and in earlier at $101847\,t.u.$. We conclude that to satisfy Property ϕ_4 the maintenance operation must be scheduled at $100000\,t.u.$.

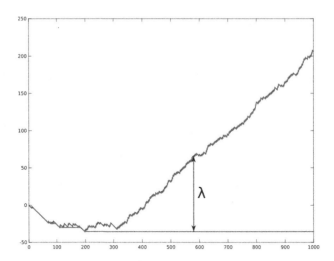

Fig. 13. CUSUM monitoring of $G_{\leq t_1}$Discomfort. CUSUM cumulative ratio (in blue) and minimum value reached (in red). The horizontal axis is the simulation time in samples number and the vertical axis is the value of the CUSUM ratio. The black arrows denote the time of the change when the cumulative ratio exceeds the minimum value by λ. (Color figure online)

7 Conclusion

The paper presents two modest contributions to SMC. The first contribution takes the form of an algorithm used to detect changes on the probability to satisfy a bounded property at runtime. This algorithm based on CUSUM ratio is a non-standard SMC technique that only analyzes a single execution trace. It provides a new application for SMC to perform runtime monitoring. The second contribution illustrates the power of Plasma Lab via a Simulink library integration. This integration constitutes one of the first proof of concept that SMC can indeed be integrated as feature library in a tool largely used in industry.

In future works we would like to continue experimenting the CUSUM algorithm. Our goal will be to perform runtime reconfiguration of energy-aware scheduling systems. On the implementation side, we would like to integrate Plasma Lab with the FMI standard (https://www.fmi-standard.org) in order to verify complex heterogeneous systems. Also a main advantage of SMC techniques is to benefit from a massive distribution of the simulations over computing grids. This is currently not possible with our Plasma Lab Simulink plugin as it would require to launch a new instance of MATLAB on each computing device, which is limited by the number of available licenses and their cost. The solution would be to compile the MATLAB code of the model before it is distributed.

References

1. Agrawal, A., Simon, G., Karsai, G.: Semantic translation of simulink/stateflow models to hybrid automata using graph transformations. Electron. Notes Theoret. Comput. Sci. **109**, 43–56 (2004)
2. Barnat, J., Beran, J., Brim, L., Kratochvíla, T., Ročkai, P.: Tool chain to support automated formal verification of avionics simulink designs. In: Stoelinga, M., Pinger, R. (eds.) FMICS 2012. LNCS, vol. 7437, pp. 78–92. Springer, Heidelberg (2012). doi:10.1007/978-3-642-32469-7_6
3. Basseville, M., Nikiforov, I.V.: Detection of Abrupt Changes: Theory and Application. Prentice-Hall Inc., Englewood Cliffs (1993)
4. Basu, A., Bensalem, S., Bozga, M., Delahaye, B., Legay, A.: Statistical abstraction and model-checking of large heterogeneous systems. Int. J. Softw. Tools Technol. Transf. **14**(1), 53–72 (2012)
5. Basu, A., Bensalem, S., Bozga, M., Delahaye, B., Legay, A., Sifakis, E.: Verification of an AFDX infrastructure using simulations and probabilities. In: Barringer, H., Falcone, Y., Finkbeiner, B., Havelund, K., Lee, I., Pace, G., Roşu, G., Sokolsky, O., Tillmann, N. (eds.) RV 2010. LNCS, vol. 6418, pp. 330–344. Springer, Heidelberg (2010). doi:10.1007/978-3-642-16612-9_25
6. Berendsen, J., Chen, T., Jansen, D.N.: Undecidability of cost-bounded reachability in priced probabilistic timed automata. In: Chen, J., Cooper, S.B. (eds.) TAMC 2009. LNCS, vol. 5532, pp. 128–137. Springer, Heidelberg (2009). doi:10.1007/978-3-642-02017-9_16
7. Biere, A., Heljanko, K., Junttila, T.A., Latvala, T., Schuppan, V.: Linear Encodings of Bounded LTL Model Checking. Log. Methods Comput. Sci. **2**(5) (2006). http://dx.doi.org/10.2168/LMCS-2(5:5)2006

8. Boyer, B., Corre, K., Legay, A., Sedwards, S.: PLASMA-lab: a flexible, distributable statistical model checking library. In: Joshi, K., Siegle, M., Stoelinga, M., D'Argenio, P.R. (eds.) QEST 2013. LNCS, vol. 8054, pp. 160–164. Springer, Heidelberg (2013). doi:10.1007/978-3-642-40196-1_12

9. Cimatti, A., Clarke, E., Giunchiglia, E., Giunchiglia, F., Pistore, M., Roveri, M., Sebastiani, R., Tacchella, A.: NuSMV 2: an opensource tool for symbolic model checking. In: Brinksma, E., Larsen, K.G. (eds.) CAV 2002. LNCS, vol. 2404, pp. 359–364. Springer, Heidelberg (2002). doi:10.1007/3-540-45657-0_29

10. Clarke, E., Donzé, A., Legay, A.: Statistical Model checking of mixed-analog circuits with an application to a third order delta-sigma modulator. In: Chockler, H., Hu, A.J. (eds.) HVC 2008. LNCS, vol. 5394, pp. 149–163. Springer, Heidelberg (2009). doi:10.1007/978-3-642-01702-5_16

11. Clarke, E., Donzé, A., Legay, A.: On simulation-based probabilistic model checking of mixed-analog circuits. Formal Methods Syst. Des. **36**(2), 97–113 (2010)

12. Clarke, E.M., Faeder, J.R., Langmead, C.J., Harris, L.A., Jha, S.K., Legay, A.: Statistical model checking in *BioLab*: applications to the automated analysis of T-cell receptor signaling pathway. In: Heiner, M., Uhrmacher, A.M. (eds.) CMSB 2008. Lecture Notes in Artificial Intelligence (LNAI), vol. 5307, pp. 231–250. Springer, Heidelberg (2008). doi:10.1007/978-3-540-88562-7_18

13. D'Argenio, P., Legay, A., Sedwards, S., Traonouez, L.: Smart sampling for lightweight verification of markov decision processes. Int. J. Softw. Tools Technol. Transf. **17**(4), 469–484 (2015)

14. David, A., Du, D., Larsen, K.G., Legay, A., Mikucionis, M., Poulsen, D.B., Sedwards, S.: Statistical model checking for stochastic hybrid systems. In: Proceedings of the 1st International Workshop on Hybrid Systems and Biology (HSB), EPTCS, vol. 92, pp. 122–136 (2012)

15. David, A., Du, D., Guldstrand Larsen, K., Legay, A., Mikučionis, M.: Optimizing control strategy using statistical model checking. In: Brat, G., Rungta, N., Venet, A. (eds.) NFM 2013. LNCS, vol. 7871, pp. 352–367. Springer, Heidelberg (2013). doi:10.1007/978-3-642-38088-4_24

16. David, A., Larsen, K.G., Legay, A., Mikučionis, M., Poulsen, D.B., Vliet, J., Wang, Z.: Statistical model checking for networks of priced timed automata. In: Fahrenberg, U., Tripakis, S. (eds.) FORMATS 2011. LNCS, vol. 6919, pp. 80–96. Springer, Heidelberg (2011). doi:10.1007/978-3-642-24310-3_7

17. David, A., Larsen, K.G., Legay, A., Mikučionis, M., Wang, Z.: Time for statistical model checking of real-time systems. In: Gopalakrishnan, G., Qadeer, S. (eds.) CAV 2011. LNCS, vol. 6806, pp. 349–355. Springer, Heidelberg (2011). doi:10.1007/978-3-642-22110-1_27

18. Bhatt, D., Madl, G., Oglesby, D., Schloegel, K.: Towards scalable verification of commercial avionics software. In: AIAA Infotech@Aerospace 2010. Infotech@Aerospace Conferences, American Institute of Aeronautics and Astronautics, April 2010

19. Grabiec, B., Traonouez, L.-M., Jard, C., Lime, D., Roux, O.H.: Diagnosis using unfoldings of parametric time petri nets. In: Chatterjee, K., Henzinger, T.A. (eds.) FORMATS 2010. LNCS, vol. 6246, pp. 137–151. Springer, Heidelberg (2010). doi:10.1007/978-3-642-15297-9_12

20. Havelund, K., Roşu, G.: Synthesizing monitors for safety properties. In: Katoen, J.-P., Stevens, P. (eds.) TACAS 2002. LNCS, vol. 2280, pp. 342–356. Springer, Heidelberg (2002). doi:10.1007/3-540-46002-0_24

21. Henzinger, T.A., Kopke, P.W., Puri, A., Varaiya, P.: What's decidable about hybrid automata? J. Comput. Syst. Sci. **57**(1), 94–124 (1998)

22. Höfner, P., McIver, A.: Statistical model checking of wireless mesh routing protocols. In: Brat, G., Rungta, N., Venet, A. (eds.) NFM 2013. LNCS, vol. 7871, pp. 322–336. Springer, Heidelberg (2013). doi:10.1007/978-3-642-38088-4_22

23. Hérault, T., Lassaigne, R., Magniette, F., Peyronnet, S.: Approximate probabilistic model checking. In: Steffen, B., Levi, G. (eds.) VMCAI 2004. LNCS, vol. 2937, pp. 73–84. Springer, Heidelberg (2004). doi:10.1007/978-3-540-24622-0_8

24. Jegourel, C., Legay, A., Sedwards, S.: Importance splitting for statistical model checking rare properties. In: Sharygina, N., Veith, H. (eds.) CAV 2013. LNCS, vol. 8044, pp. 576–591. Springer, Heidelberg (2013). doi:10.1007/978-3-642-39799-8_38

25. Jessen, J.J., Rasmussen, J.I., Larsen, K.G., David, A.: Guided controller synthesis for climate controller using UPPAAL TIGA. In: Raskin, J.-F., Thiagarajan, P.S. (eds.) FORMATS 2007. LNCS, vol. 4763, pp. 227–240. Springer, Heidelberg (2007). doi:10.1007/978-3-540-75454-1_17

26. Jha, S.K., Clarke, E.M., Langmead, C.J., Legay, A., Platzer, A., Zuliani, P.: A bayesian approach to model checking biological systems. In: Degano, P., Gorrieri, R. (eds.) CMSB 2009. LNCS, vol. 5688, pp. 218–234. Springer, Heidelberg (2009). doi:10.1007/978-3-642-03845-7_15

27. Kim, Y., Kim, M., Kim, T.-H.: Statistical model checking for safety critical hybrid systems: an empirical evaluation. In: Biere, A., Nahir, A., Vos, T. (eds.) HVC 2012. LNCS, vol. 7857, pp. 162–177. Springer, Heidelberg (2013). doi:10.1007/978-3-642-39611-3_18

28. Koh, C.H., Palaniappan, S.K., Thiagarajan, P., Wong, L.: Improved statistical model checking methods for pathway analysis. BMC Bioinf. **13**(17), 1–12 (2012)

29. Kwiatkowska, M., Norman, G., Parker, D.: PRISM 4.0: verification of probabilistic real-time systems. In: Gopalakrishnan, G., Qadeer, S. (eds.) CAV 2011. LNCS, vol. 6806, pp. 585–591. Springer, Heidelberg (2011). doi:10.1007/978-3-642-22110-1_47

30. Legay, A., Delahaye, B., Bensalem, S.: Statistical model checking: an overview. In: Barringer, H., Falcone, Y., Finkbeiner, B., Havelund, K., Lee, I., Pace, G., Roşu, G., Sokolsky, O., Tillmann, N. (eds.) RV 2010. LNCS, vol. 6418, pp. 122–135. Springer, Heidelberg (2010). doi:10.1007/978-3-642-16612-9_11

31. Mathworks: polyspace a static analysis tools for C/C++ and Ada, December 2014. http://www.mathworks.fr/products/polyspace/

32. Meenakshi, B., Bhatnagar, A., Roy, S.: Tool for translating simulink models into input language of a model checker. In: Liu, Z., He, J. (eds.) ICFEM 2006. LNCS, vol. 4260, pp. 606–620. Springer, Heidelberg (2006). doi:10.1007/11901433_33

33. Page, E.S.: Continuous inspection schemes. Biometrika **41**(1/2), 100–115 (1954). http://www.jstor.org/stable/2333009

34. Prover: Prover-Plugin, December 2014. http://www.prover.com/products/prover-plugin/

35. Sen, K., Viswanathan, M., Agha, G.: Statistical model checking of black-box probabilistic systems. In: Alur, R., Peled, D.A. (eds.) CAV 2004. LNCS, vol. 3114, pp. 202–215. Springer, Heidelberg (2004). doi:10.1007/978-3-540-27813-9_16

36. Verdier, G., Hilgert, N., Vila, J.: Adaptive threshold computation for CUSUM-type procedures in change detection and isolation problems. Comput. Stat. Data Anal. **52**(9), 4161–4174 (2008)

37. Wald, A.: Sequential tests of statistical hypotheses. Ann. Math. Stat. **16**(2), 117–186 (1945)

38. Younes, H.L.S.: Verification and planning for stochastic processes with asynchronous events. Ph.D. thesis, Carnegie Mellon (2005)

39. Zuliani, P., Platzer, A., Clarke, E.M.: Bayesian statistical model checking with application to Stateflow/Simulink verification. Formal Methods Syst. Des. **43**(2), 338–367 (2013)

Collective Autonomic Systems: Towards Engineering Principles and Their Foundations

Lenz Belzner, Matthias Hölzl, Nora Koch, and Martin Wirsing[✉]

Ludwig-Maximilians-Universität München, Munich, Germany
wirsing@lmu.de

Abstract. Collective autonomic systems (CAS) are adaptive, open-ended, highly parallel, interactive and distributed software systems. They consist of many collaborative entities that manage their own knowledge and processes. CAS present many engineering challenges, such as awareness of the environmental situation, performing suitable and adequate adaptations in response to environmental changes, or preserving adaptations over system updates and modifications. Recent research has proposed initial solutions to some of these challenges, but many of the difficult questions remain unanswered and will open up a rich field of future research.

In an attempt to initiate a discussion about the structure of this emerging research area, we present eight engineering principles that we consider promising candidates for relevant future research, and shortly address their possible foundations. Our discussion is based on a development life cycle (EDLC) for autonomic systems. Going beyond the traditional iterative development process, the EDLC proposes three control loops for system design, runtime adaptation, as well as feedback between design- and runtime. Some of our principles concern the whole development process, while others focus on a particular control loop.

Keywords: Autonomic systems · Awareness · Adaptation · System development life cycle · Control loops · Engineering principles

1 Introduction

Software increasingly models, controls and monitors massively distributed dynamic systems. Systems often operate in highly variable, even unpredictable, open-ended environments. They are based on dynamically forming *ensembles*: sets of parallel, interactive and distributed components able to form groups dynamically and on-demand while pursuing specific goals in changing environments. Each component manages its knowledge and processes (see Fig. 1). Changing requirements, technologies or environmental conditions motivate ensembles that can autonomously adapt without requiring redeployment or interruption of system operation. We call ensembles with these abilities *Collective Autonomic Systems (CAS)*.

This work has been sponsored by the EU project ASCENS IP 257414 (FP7).

B. Steffen (Ed.): Transactions on FoMaC I, LNCS 9960, pp. 180–200, 2016.
DOI: 10.1007/978-3-319-46508-1_10

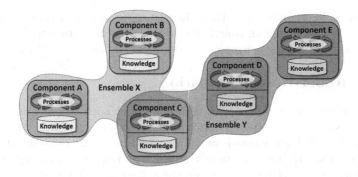

Fig. 1. Two overlapping ensembles [44]

An early vision of autonomic computing was published by Kephart and Chess in 2003 [42]. This work focuses on the self-* properties of autonomic systems, such as self-management, self-optimization and self-protection. The authors discuss a set of scientific challenges, such as learning and optimization theory, and automated statistical modeling.

In 2009 a Dagstuhl seminar group [16] presented the state-of-the-art and research challenges for engineering self-adaptive software systems. Specifically, the roadmap focus on development methods, techniques, and tools that are required to support the systematic development of complex software systems with dynamic self-adaptive behaviour. An updated version of the roadmap was published in 2011 [2].

Recent research has proposed initial solutions to some of these challenges from the engineering point of view, e.g. [66]. There are, however, still many open questions like the interplay of static and dynamic knowledge and the building of societies of systems that require well-founded research in the near future.

In this work we present eight engineering principles that we consider promising candidates for relevant future research, and shortly address their possible foundations. These principles are:

P1 Use probabilistic goal- and utility-based techniques
P2 Characterize the adaptation space and design the awareness mechanism
P3 Exploit interaction
P4 Perform reasoning, learning and planning
P5 Consider the interplay of static and dynamic knowledge
P6 Enable evolutionary feedback
P7 Perform simulation and analysis throughout the system life cycle
P8 Consider societies of systems

We base our discussion on a development life cycle for autonomic systems (EDLC) [32]. In addition to traditional iterative development, the EDLC proposes a control loop for runtime adaptation, as well as feedback between design- and runtime. Some of our principles focus on a particular control loop while others concern the whole system life cycle.

The paper is organized as follows: In Sect. 2 we present a running example and in Sect. 3 we provide an overview of the EDLC. In Sects. 4 to 7 we discuss the proposed engineering principles. Section 8 concludes.

2   The Robot Rescue Scenario

Collective autonomic systems have many potential application areas stressing different aspects of collective adaptation and autonomicity. One domain that places particularly high demands on systems to adapt autonomously to changes in their environment, to continuously adjust task priorities, and even to fulfill requirements that were unknown when the system was deployed is the area of disaster relief and rescue operations.

We will illustrate the principles we propose with the following disaster relief example which is presented in more detail in [30]: An industrial complex has been damaged; workers have been trapped in several buildings and need to be rescued and spills of various chemicals need to be contained and cleaned up. It is expected that some damaged parts of the complex will collapse while the rescue operation is in progress; the rescue team has to take the effects of additional deterioration of the environment into account. In particular, the rescuers should avoid actions that damage the environment in a way that might impair the success of the rescue mission and, if this is beneficial for the progress of the rescue mission, stabilize parts of the environment that are in danger of collapsing.

Having a swarm of autonomous robots capable of performing these kinds of rescue missions would allow humans to stay clear of the dangerous parts of the environment. In some cases it is possible to have remotely controlled robots perform part of the work, but this is often not feasible since buildings, chemicals or radiation may interfere with both wired and wireless remote controls. Therefore, robots that can perform autonomously would be the most suitable solution.

This scenario illustrates many of the complexities of building collective autonomic systems: The robot rescue swarm is a hybrid system; control has to be distributed between the individual agents, it is often unclear which tasks the ensemble of agents should perform and what actions individual agents should take to further progress of the overall system. The environment is continuous, stochastic, only partially observable, and highly dynamic. The presence of multiple adaptive agents complicates many issues, since the effects of actions depend on the adaptations of other agents in addition to the stochastic nature of the environment, and since multiple agents may compete for the same resources, even if they try to cooperate on an overall goal. Since agents may be damaged in the cause of the rescue operation, the system also has to deal with "bad agents".

3   The Development Life Cycle of Collective Autonomic Systems

The development of collective autonomic systems goes beyond addressing the classical phases of the software development life cycle like requirements elicitation, modeling, implementation and deployment. Engineering these complex systems has also to tackle aspects like awareness and self-adaptation, which have to be considered from the beginning of the development process. This has already been recognized by several authors, for example in the MAPE-K architecture [20] or the life cycles proposed by Inverardi and Mori [36] or Brun et al. [11].

Influenced by these approaches, in previous work we proposed the ensemble development life cycle (EDLC) for autonomic systems, which is based on control loops for the design, runtime and evolution [32]. It can graphically be represented as shown in Fig. 2. The left cycle represents the *design* loop and the right one represents the *runtime* loop. Both loops are connected by a third *evolutionary* loop, consisting of system *deployment* to runtime and *feedback* from runtime into system design.

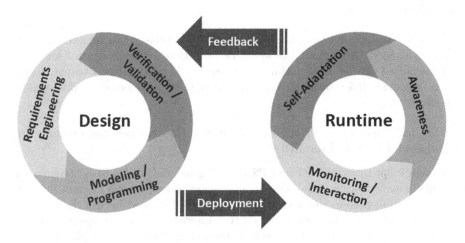

Fig. 2. Ensemble Development Life Cycle (EDLC)

During the design process, work at multiple levels of abstractions and details has to be undertaken simultaneously, providing the basis for the runtime application, which has to be able to monitor the own behaviour and the behaviour of the environment, to reason on these observations, to trigger the learning process, and to adapt to the changes according to the results of the carried out reasoning. System design benefits from the runtime process, too, as feedback can be used to reassess the (adaptation) requirements and the corresponding models.

In summary, we have identified three control loops and propose a software development life cycle for collective autonomic systems based on these three types of control loops: design, runtime and evolution.

Design. The offline phases comprise *requirements engineering, modeling and programming*, and *verification and validation*. Models are usually built on top of the elicited requirements, mainly following an iterative process, in which validation and verification in early phases of the development are highly recommended, in order to mitigate the impact of design errors. A relevant issue is then the use of modeling and implementation techniques for adaptive and awareness features. Our aim is to focus on these distinguishing characteristics of collective autonomic systems along the whole development cycle.

We emphasize the relevance of mathematically founded approaches to validate and verify the properties of the CAS and predict the behaviour of such complex software. This closes the cycle, providing feedback for checking the requirements identified so far or improving the model or code.

Runtime. The online phases comprise *monitoring and interaction, awareness* and *self-adaptation.* They consist of observing the running system and the environment, reasoning on such observations, and using the results of the analysis for adapting the system and computing data that can be used for feedback in the offline activities.

Evolution. Transitions between online and offline phases can be performed as often as needed throughout the system's evolution feedback control loop, i.e. data acquired during the runtime cycle are fed back (*feedback*) to the design cycle to provide information for system redesign, verification and redeployment (*deployment*).

EDLC and Engineering Principles. We outline the relation of our engineering principles for CAS and the EDLC.

- Design loop: Principles P1 and P2 (use of goal- and utility-based techniques, and characterization and design of adaptation and awareness mechanisms) are mainly applicable in the design loop. They are discussed in Sect. 4.
- Runtime loop: Principles P3 and P4 (the interaction between agents, the system and the environment, as well as reasoning, learning, and planning) are typical for the runtime loop. They are discussed in Sect. 5.
- Evolution loop: Principles P5 and P6 (interplay of static and dynamic knowledge, and the evolutionary feedback) support the evolution loop. They are discussed in Sect. 6.
- All loops: Principles P7 and P8 (simulation and analysis throughout the system life cycle, and consideration of societies of systems) are applicable to all phases of the EDLC. They are discussed in Sect. 7.

The Engineering Principles in the Running Example. We briefly illustrate here how the principles apply to our running example.

We start in the design loop with the specification of requirements such as localization and transport of victims using a goal-oriented approach [1, 43]: Goals are identified and subsequently refined. In the robot rescue scenario, initial goals might state the number of victims that the robot swarm should be able to rescue depending on properties of the high-level location graph; later this goal might be detailed in terms of the detailed topography of the underlying map. It is often not possible to guarantee that the system will reach its goals, therefore the designers have to resort to probabilistic characterization. This leads to principle P1: *Use probabilistic goal- and utility-based techniques.*

During the requirements engineering phase, we also need to decide in which environments the system can operate, and what kind of performance we want to achieve in different environments. For example, we need be clear whether the robot swarm is tailored to one particular site or whether it should be able to operate in any site not exceeding a certain size; similarly we need to detail with which kinds of obstacles, damage or environmental danger the swarm can deal, whether it can operate in the presence of other robot rescue swarms or human rescue personnel, etc. In more technical terms, we need to define the adaptation space and the adaptation requirements, as expressed in principle P2: *Characterize the adaptation space and design the awareness mechanism.*

Since in the rescue scenario a large number of robots may act simultaneously, direct communication is often not a feasible strategy. Instead the robots could leave marks in the environment as sources of information for other agents, resulting in stigmergic communication. This interaction with the environment motivates principle P3: *Exploit interaction.*

In the dynamically changing environment in which the robots operate, it is difficult to specify beforehand the precise behavior of the robots. For example, victims will act on their own, continuously creating new situations for robots to cope with. This yields principle P4: *Perform reasoning, learning and planning.*

Nevertheless, complex tasks require modeling before deployment, acquiring runtime information and feeding back this information for further offline improvement of the model. In fact, runtime machine learning can be very useful, but its effectiveness is highly dependent on the quality of the model. However, the quality of the model can only be assessed and improved with the use of runtime data [30]. This is expressed in principle P5: *Consider the interplay of static and dynamic knowledge.*

These models and behaviors learned while operating should be transfered back to the design loop to be used in future iterations. This mutual influence of design and runtime is captured in principle P6: *Enable evolutionary feedback.*

The principles motivated so far yield systems with highly emergent behavior. Thus we propose principle P7: *Perform simulation and analysis throughout the system life cycle.* This supports developers in better understanding the system's dynamics and error conditions. Simulation data can also be used to train adaptive components of the system.

The open-ended environment and possible interaction with other systems leads to principle P8: *Consider societies of systems.* For example, rescue teams of multiple organizations may be deployed to the same disaster site without previous knowledge of each other.

4 Design Loop

Two principles address design-time concerns that support runtime adaptation and evolution: probabilistic goal- and utility-based techniques (P1), and the characterization of the adaptation space and the design of the awareness mechanism (P2).

4.1   Use Probabilistic Goal- and Utility-Based Techniques

Motivation. Collective autonomic systems are typically built to satisfy complex needs that cannot easily be addressed by more static, monolithic systems. Their requirements consist of hard constraints that must not be violated by the system and soft constraints that describe behaviors that should be optimized.

Hard constraints can be expressed as formulas in an appropriate logic that describe properties of the system that should be maintained, avoided or reached (c.f. goal-directed requirements acquisition [22]). A maintain constraint for a robot in the rescue swarm might be to never run out of battery power; an avoid constraint to never injure a rescue worker. Soft constraints are commonly expressed as functions that the system should optimize (see e.g. [23, p. 365]), for example the number of victims rescued by a robot. Most of the time, the soft constraints in CAS describe multicriteria optimization problems. In our scenario, rescuing as many victims as quickly as possible and avoiding damage to itself are competing optimization objectives for individual robots.

Having multiple competing objectives is typical for any requirements specification, since trade-offs between, e.g., possible features, system performance and size, and development time are common for most development tasks. But for traditional systems these trade-offs can be resolved during design time and, while the choices made to resolve them shape the resulting system, they don't have to be considered while the system is operating.

For CAS it is important to be more explicit about the competing requirements for several reasons, such as: 1. A flexible system requires the possibility to weight different criteria according to situation and/or current requirements. This weighting is enabled by explicit distinction of the different optimization criteria. 2. Goals and activities of different agents are intertwined and may lead to emerging phenomena that cannot be derived from properties of the individual agents but only from the system as a whole. Consideration of these kinds of effects by the agents themselves will become increasingly important as systems become more autonomic and adaptive; doing so without an explicit representation of the desired system properties is unlikely to yield favorable results.

We are typically concerned with the behavior of the whole system and not just the software controlling the system, hence most constraints have to take into account physical properties of system components and failure probabilites. Purely goal-based specification can only establish very weak properties. A more likely specification for a CAS would define a required quality of service, e.g., the swarm has to rescue 80 % of the victims with a probability of 95 %.

Therefore, goal and utility-based techniques that explicitly represent the constraints and optimization choices a system faces are more important for CAS than for traditional systems. Given these observations, the first principle we propose is:

Principle P1. Requirements specifications for CAS should be expressed in terms of probabilistic goals and utility functions.

Foundations. Goal-based approaches to requirements analysis, such as KAOS [46], have been widely used in traditional software engineering, and more recently probabilistic variants of these approaches have been proposed [14]. Some goal-based approaches that are concerned with modeling CAS, such as GEM [34], allow modelers to directly express optimization goals in terms of expected utilities.

Most techniques for utility-based modeling and analysis belong to the area of operations research [28]. In particular, expected utility theory [9] and the more general prospect theory [4,40] form the theoretical basis for basing system analysis and design on utility functions. Multicriteria optimization is extensively discussed in [41]. Optimization of probabilistic decisions is often treated in the special context of Markov Decision Processes (MDPs) [56]; stochastic games [49] generalize MDPs and repeated games and are therefore often a more appropriate setting for probabilistic decision problems with multiple agents. Solution techniques for MDPs (and generalizations of MDPs) based on reinforcement learning will be discussed in Sect. 5.2.

Using goal- and utility-based techniques raises the question 1. how system-level goals or utility functions can be decomposed into goals for individual agents, 2. how high-level individual goals or utility functions can be refined into lower-level goals/utilities and eventually individual tasks, and 3. how run-time decision making itself is distributed among the agents in a system. In particular for goal-based techniques there exist a number of multi-agent oriented programming languages and agent-oriented software engineering techniques that address these questions, but most of them are tailored towards deterministic problems and don not address the probabilistic case. The collection [65] contains several relevant summary articles.

4.2   Characterize and Design Adaptation and Awareness

Motivation. The reason for developing Collective Autonomic Systems is often that we need systems that can adjust to many situations, that are resilient to partial failures, and that can easily be changed and enhanced while they are operating. Following [34], we call the range of environments in which a system can operate together with the goals that the system should be able to satisfy in each environment the *adaptation space*. It is important to note that typically the goals and utility functions of a system depend on features of the environment in which it is operating: The more difficult the environment is for the system, the lower the expected utility we can expect it to achieve.

As in [33], we call the parts of the system that are responsible for maintaining information about the environment in which it is operating its *awareness mechanism*. To ensure that the system achieves its desired performance, the awareness mechanism has to provide enough information in each of the possible environments in the adaptation space so that the system can satisfy the goals for that environment.

We often discover new requirements and environmental conditions that influence the capability of a CAS to satisfy its goals in the runtime cycle. When this

happens, we need to be able to determine whether the system can still successfully operate under the newly discovered conditions, and, if this is not the case,
which changes to the system can restore its capabilities most economically. This
is easiest to achieve when the adaptation space is explicitly specified and the
awareness mechanism is designed to recognize the different types of environments and adjust the system's behavior accordingly:

*Principle P2. Characterize the adaptation space and design the system's aware-
ness mechanism.*

Foundations. The notions of adaptation space and awareness mechanism are
introduced in [34] and [33], respectively. The connection between the so-called
"black-box" view of adaptation that is expressed via adaptation spaces and the
"white-box" view of adaptation that is concerned with mechanisms to achieve
adaptation is explored in [12].

Bruni et al. [13] presented a control-data-based conceptual framework for
adaptivity. They provide a formal model for the framework based on a labelled
transition system (LTS). In addition, they provide an analysis of adaptivity
from the control data point of view in different computational paradigms, such
as context-oriented and declarative programming.

Techniques for developing awareness mechanisms are varied and partially
domain dependent. For the robot case study, probabilistic state estimation
and filtering [62] are particularly relevant. Techniques for reasoning, planning
and learning that can be used in a wide variety of awareness mechanisms are
described as part of principle P4 in Sect. 5.2.

5   Runtime Loop

Two principles are mainly rooted in the runtime loop: the exploitation of the
interaction between agents or the system and its environment (P3) and the use
of reasoning, learning and planning techniques at runtime (P4).

5.1   Exploit Interaction

Motivation. Traditionally, the interaction between agents or between a system
and its environment is described in terms of interfaces with protocols that may,
e.g., be expressed as state machines. In CAS these kinds of interactions still exist,
but often agents also have to interact in different ways with the environment or
each other. For example, in the rescue scenario victims may not be able to
communicate actively with the rescue robots, instead the rescuers may have to
analyze their sensor data (i.e., perform a probabilistic state estimation) to detect
the presence of victims and how to rescue them. Similarly, it may not be possible
for rescue robots to directly communicate with all other rescue workers in their
vicinity; they may again have to rely on state estimation to infer their current
activities or intentions. Estimating the internal state of other actors is difficult,

so we may simplify the task of the observer by *signaling* the intent or activities of agents, i.e., by performing the actions in such a way that they are easy to recognize. In the simplest case this might just consist in turning on a colored light whenever performing a certain kind of task. For example, a rescue robot might display a green light when it is searching for victims, a red light while it is picking up a victim and a blue light when it is transporting a victim to the rescue zone. More complex behavioral clues are possible and widely observed in animals.

An example of exploiting the interactions between system and environment is *stigmergy*, the process of indirect coordination via manipulation of the environment. For example, if a robot locates a victim but has currently no capacity to rescue the victim, it might change the environment (e.g. by scratching a mark on the ground) to make it simpler for other agents to locate the victim.

Principle P3. Exploit interactions between agents or between the system and its environment to improve system reliability and performance.

Foundations. Many of the foundations for exploiting interactions, such as speech-act theory, signaling, mechanism design, auctions, negotiations or arguments have been studied extensively in the literature on multi-agent systems, see [60, 65, 67] for overviews. The theory of signaling has been extensively studied in economics and evolutionary biology [19, 61]. Mechanism design is concerned with the development of mechanisms that cause utility-maximizing agents to behave according to a desired utility function [8, 35].

Many bio-inspired or swarm-based approaches to computation exploit interactions to enable groups of agents to perform tasks that are beyond the capabilities of the individual member of the group [7, 68]. Stigmergy can frequently be observed in natural systems [18] and it is an important feature of ant algorithms [25].

5.2 Perform Reasoning, Learning and Planning

Motivation. One approach to cope with complex dynamics and change is to synthesize system knowledge and/or behavior at runtime. This ensures that the system can react flexibly to situations that actually occur and focus its computational effort on concretely encountered problems. Engineering of CAS will require a deep understanding of the requirements and implications of the algorithms and frameworks involved in this process. In general, three different aspects of system synthesis at runtime are *abstraction, learning* and *reasoning*. Abstraction means that a system is able to meaningfully condense or filter perceptions and thus concentrate cognitive effort on relevant portions of low-level data. For example, the visual system of a rescue robot might condense the signal of its video cameras into a short list of relevant objects and their spatial locations.

Based on given abstractions, learning is concerned with the compilation of runtime data to general knowledge about the environment, e.g. in form of causal relationships or probabilistic prediction of dynamics. Learning may be incremental: Already available models may be refined by a learning process accounting for currently available information, like a rescue robot updating its maps based on data gathered while navigating the rescue area.

Reasoning is concerned with the exploitation of available knowledge to generate new knowledge: For example, a formerly unidentified general causal relation is deduced from some already available knowledge. Decision making in general, and planning in particular, are reasoning processes that compile knowledge about valuable system behavior from existing knowledge. Based on this knowledge, concrete system behavior is selected and executed in order to satisfy system goals as much as possible.

Principle P4. Perform reasoning, learning and planning to enable CAS to autonomously cope with change and unexpected events.

Foundations. Efficiency of system synthesis through learning and planning is highly correlating with the representation (i.e. the abstraction) of the problem at hand. Recently, techniques for representation learning have been successfully applied to learning abstractions from low-level data (digit recognition [29], speech synthesis and recognition [24], etc.), yielding systems that closely reach human performance for particular tasks [45]. Representation learning effectively allows to identify meaningful patterns in raw data. Performing this process iteratively yields different levels of abstraction. Final system learning and reasoning can then be based on learned abstractions. As CAS are potentially designed to be deployed to unknown and/or changing environments, the ability of autonomous abstraction from low-level data is expected to be highly valuable.

In the context of CAS, learning is a tool to account for uncertainty in specification. Domains as the exemplary rescue scenario tend to be highly complex and hard to be modeled completely accurate. Allowing a system to learn models about these domains at runtime enables them to potentially recover from misconceptions or errors in the specification made at design time (e.g. via decision forests [21], Gaussian processes [57] or other machine learning techniques [6]). CAS also may be expected to operate in environments where external, uncontrolled entities interact with them, with potentially conflicting or even adversarial interests. In these cases, learning models of these external agents is essential to ensure system stability and robustness (see also principle P8 in Sect. 7.2).

Single agent decision making can be driven by model-based reinforcement learning with open-loop planning, showing promising results in numerous application areas [10, 64]. These techniques particularly suit the highly dynamic and probabilistic environments that CAS are typically designed for. Collective learning and emergent optimization can be achieved with Hierarchical Lenient Multi-Agent Reinforcement Learning [31]. Here, a special emphasis is given to scalability issues in the context of CAS.

While representation learning, supervised machine learning and reasoning each provide powerful tools for their respective problem areas, CAS will require

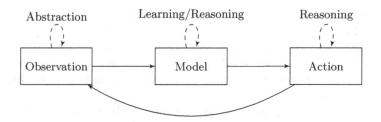

Fig. 3. Interplay of abstraction, learning and reasoning

a deep integration of the aspects involved. Figure 3 illustrates the subtle inter-play of these fields. The subfields of system autonomy are clearly dependent on each other: For example, abstraction influences what is learned, but how does a learned model influence possible changes in abstraction? What ways of com-bining learned models and decision making are there? Answering questions of this kind will be essential for engineering, analyzing and understanding CAS. For recent results combining representation learning and decision making the context of autonomous game players see [17,51]. Further investigation in this direction seems a promising venue for research in the field of CAS.

6   Evolution Loop

Our principles for the evolution loop concern the interplay of static and dynamic knowledge (P5), and a system architecture that enables evolutionary feedback and management of the system's evolution (P6).

6.1   Consider Interplay of Static and Dynamic Knowledge

Motivation. In classical engineering, perceptual abstractions and causal mod-els about system dynamics are usually specified in some particular formalism at design time. We refer to this kind of specification as *static knowledge*. CAS are typically equipped with abilities for gathering and compiling information about their current execution environment. This enables CAS to build percep-tual abstractions and causal models at runtime and to optimize their behavior accordingly (see Sect. 5.2). For engineering CAS this raises the question how to deal with and integrate these different sources of knowledge.

For example, a CAS in the rescue domain could learn about the influence of victims' weights on the success of a transportation task and adjust its behavior accordingly. While dynamic optimization of this kind seems a valuable property, the interplay of static specification and runtime optimization is not obvious. For example, specifying a reward function for providing first aid to an injured victim could lead to robots that cause injuries intentionally to collect the specified reward for subsequently providing first aid.

In order to combine static and dynamic knowledge, we have to ensure compatibility of specified and learned representations. CAS have to incorporate specifications when learning abstractions, and we have to extract useful information from knowledge dynamically synthesized by a system at runtime. This information is fed back to the design cycle, and potentially influences further static knowledge design.

Also, continuous comparison of expectation and observation enables systems to detect discrepancies of system design (e.g. knowledge about the environment) and concrete situation. This may trigger recovery mechanisms by either signaling the discrepancy to system operators, or by activating autonomous recovery mechanisms. For example, a designed environmental model may be autonomously replaced by one learned from observations at runtime in case the latter becomes more accurate. Also, this learned model should be fed back into further iterations of system design and analysis.

Principle P5. Understand, analyze and document the interplay of static and dynamic knowledge over the whole lifecycle of CAS.

Foundations. For concepts and algorithms used to compile knowledge from runtime observations, see Sect. 5.2.

To the best of the authors' knowledge, not much research has yet been dedicated to the relation of specification, and representation and model learning. We argue that researching methods for integrating static and dynamic knowledge is a central challenge for successful development of CAS, in particular the integration of results from representation learning with manual specifications.

6.2   Enable Evolutionary Feedback and Manage Evolution

Motivation. Systems designers are used to the notion that they iteratively adapt and improve systems during the development phase, and that they deploy these improvements as part of a larger system. In this process it is common to move from information-rich analysis and design models to a runtime representation in which many of the concerns that are relevant for the system design are "compiled away," either by manually implementing the design models or by performing model transformations into low-level reprentations.

In the EDLC we assume that the developers cannot exactly predict the environment in which the system is operating and the policies that the system should use. Instead the system dynmically improves the actions it takes in response to various situations and, based on the result of these actions, its model of the environment. It is an important problem in the development of CAS to ensure that the notion of autonomous "improvement" of the system agrees with the goals of the stakeholders, and that learned adaptations can be transferred back to the design cycle so that they can influence future design choices and persist over redeployments of and updates to the system. To this end, larger parts of the design knowledge have to be made explicit and made available to the system at runtime: When manually designing a rescue robot it may not be necessary to provide the robot with the information that further injuring victims is undesirable, since this knowledge is already encoded in the robot's program; when allowing the robot to autonomously adapt its strategy it is imperative that this kind of information is present to inform the robot's choices.

The independent adaptation of the CAS leads to an evolutionary process in which parts of the systems can exploit novel capabilities of other agents in the system to autonomously improve their own performance. For example, a rescue robot might figure out a way to scale walls that allows it to cut down the time it needs to get to the victims. Robots without the wall-scaling capability might then stop rescuing other victims and instead transport medicine to the rescue are to avoid medics running out of medicine.

The resulting evolutionary process may either result in a stable system behavior, or it may result in a system where each robot continuously adjusts its strategy to react to the behavioral changes in other robots. This continuous adaptation may greatly enhance the flexibility and performance of the system, but it may also lead to a system that squanders its resources on permanent adaptation without achieving its goals. But even if the system adapts successfully, its developers now face the challenge that their design loop has to keep up with and exploit the evolutionary process in the system, and that new agents they deploy into the system should manage and improve the evolutionary process, not disrupt it needlessly.

Principle P6. Enable evolutionary feedback and manage the evolutionary process.

Foundations. Evolutionary processes can generate surprisingly complex behavior even when the agents involved in the process follow simple, fixed algorithms. Many algorithms in swarm intelligence [25,68] are based on systems consisting of relatively simple agents that collectively achieve complex behaviors. However, to our knowledge no general, systematic method to derive simple agent rules that result in a desired swarm behavior exists. For many scenarios it seems therefore more tractable to have system designs in which individual agents can perform substantial tasks on their own. Techniques for enabling adaptation of these agents to an evolutionary process are described in the principles in Sects. 4 and 5.

The main tool for understanding and analyzing the system dynamics resulting from continuous adaptation of multiple agents is evolutionary game theory [3,63], and in particular the notions of *evolutionary stable strategy* and *co-evolution*. References [60,65] contain discussions of evolutionary game theory in the context of multi-agent systems.

The foundations mentioned for principle P3 are important to manage the evolutionary process as well. In particular mechanism design [8,35] provides tools to design rules that steer the evolutionary process in the desired direction. In many cases it may be necessary to go beyond utility maximization of individual agents and to institute norms or institutions that regulate parts of the system [38,52,55].

7 Engineering Principles for All Loops

In addition to the engineering principles presented in the previous sections for specific EDLC-loops we present two principles encompassing the whole development process: simulation and analysis throughout the system life cycle (P7), and the consideration of societies of systems (P8).

7.1 Perform Simulation and Analysis

Motivation. Complex requirements documents invariably contain inconsistencies, omissions and errors. In traditional system development these problems often manifest themselves during the design or implementation phases and are resolved before the system is deployed. Since in CAS the requirements also serve as a basis for autonomic adaptation of the system, it is more difficult, and also more important, to ensure that the requirements of the system are complete, correct and actually express the desired properties.

Collective adaptive systems potentially have to operate in large environments with probabilistic dynamics and high branching factors. The system environment typically exposes its own dynamics mostly uncontrolled by the system to be designed. Coordination of numerous components increases the complexity of adaptation mechanisms and their assessment through system engineers. Emergent behavior resulting from the interplay of system and environmental dynamics and from interaction of various system participants has to be tuned to fit a system's original requirements.

Statistical analysis of simulation data enables to quantify system properties. For example, in classical reachability analysis a definite result is possible due to the deterministic nature of systems. In CAS, there will usually be a probabilistic dimension to reachability results, as typically only few of the dynamics of the domain are under direct control of the system. On the other hand, classical verification techniques such as model checking could be used at runtime in order to verify and analyze the actually occurring system configuration. This allows verification without considering all possible adaptations of the CAS.

Principle P7. Perform simulation and analysis throughout the system life cycle. In particular, deploy early to a simulated environment so that feedback from the runtime loop can be used in the design cycle as early as possible.

Foundations. Modern simulation tools allow to access system behavior at various levels of detail by being able to simulate physical dynamics, visual data and audio information with accuracy close to reality [50,53]. Simulation is highly efficient, supported by designated hardware architectures (e.g. graphic processors). High-quality simulation data is especially valuable in situations where algorithms are employed that learn abstractions from low-level data at runtime (e.g. autoencoders [24], principal component analysis [37] or sparse coding [47]).

Simulation provides a way to train and assess systems that employ model or behavior synthesis before actually deploying them (i.e. learning and reasoning systems, see Sect. 5.2). For example, a system that uses some sort of representation learning to compile abstractions from low-level data may use simulated sensory data to start to learn abstractions before being deployed.

Simulation is also the core component of statistical approaches to validation and verification of systems, as e.g. statistical model checking [48,59]. Here, a number of simulated runs of the system is performed and analyzed to provide assertions about system performance with a required statistical confidence. To the best of the authors' knowledge, literature does not provide a generic solution of generating explicit feedback for system design from stochastic simulation data effectively. Identifying relevant parts of simulation data and finding ways to use this information, both at design time and at runtime, are crucial challenges for successfully building and operating CAS.

7.2 Consider Societies of Systems

Motivation. Often multiple ensembles exist that we require to cooperate adaptively, resulting in ensembles that team up to build larger ensembles. While it is possible to define coordinative mechanisms in a centralized manner, it is valuable to provide approaches that allow for emergent control of collaboration to ensure adaptivity and robustness. Various forms of coordination and collaboration can be observed in natural *societies and organizations*: Societal mechanisms of control range from highly centralized (e.g. dictatorial) to extremely distributed (e.g. swarms). Organization forms for managing communication and aggregation of information range from flat to highly hierarchical. Building societies of systems also requires to dynamically define to what extend a member of a society (be it an individual or an ensemble) should weight individual vs. global welfare.

In the robotic rescue example, consider different teams of robots operating in the scene. When an ensemble is built to extinguish a fire in a particular area, the group mainly designed to provide first aid to victims would rather hinder in fulfilling the goal. Also, different ways of organization would be needed for fighting a fire (probably very reactive, with high individual decision impact) and transporting a victim to safety in collaboration (rather centralized, with individuals providing information to a coordinator). Nevertheless it may be the case that some robots have to participate in both tasks.

Conflicting individual goals, openness and the need for collaboration require the ability to deal robustly with potentially adversarial or malfunctioning decision makers. For example, an agent could simply fail without having noticed or it could provide misinformation intentionally. It is valuable for CAS to explicitly maintain a model of reliability of collaborators to base own decisions on this information.

Principle P8. Consider societies of systems and enable CAS to cope adaptively and robustly with the complexity of interaction within and between systems.

Foundations. While it is straightforward to implement social mechanisms adhoc, it is necessary to study their characteristics and implications in order to ensure their support for our design goals. Recent approaches take inspiration from the fields of socio-technical systems [27] and institutional theory [58] to provide formal techniques and languages to capture and express the exact meaning of social institutions and mechanisms [38,55].

Exploiting virtual social institutions to enable adaptive formation and disassembly of coordination collectives yields highly open systems. This openness of CAS disables traditional security solutions. Recent surveys provide an overview of new attacks forms and solution approaches in the changing security landscape of open, autonomous multi-agent systems [5,39]. Research and engineering approaches in the field of CAS have to address the changing security challenges resulting from building societies of systems. Trust- and reputation-based computing provides a principled approach for systems to deal with openness and external decision makers [15,26,54].

8   Conclusions

In this work we presented eight engineering principles that we consider to play a fundamental role in the construction and running of collective autonomous systems (CAS) and that we consider promising areas for future research:

P1 Use probabilistic goal- and utility-based techniques
P2 Characterize the adaptation space and design the awareness mechanism
P3 Exploit interaction
P4 Perform reasoning, learning and planning
P5 Consider the interplay of static and dynamic knowledge
P6 Enable evolutionary feedback
P7 Perform simulation and analysis throughout the system life cycle
P8 Consider societies of systems

The principles are closely related to the ensembles development life cycle (EDLC), which distinguishes a design, a runtime and an evolution loop. Some of our principles concern the whole development process while others are focused on a particular loop (design loop: P1, P2; runtime loop: P3, P4; evolution loop: P5, P6; all loops: P7, P8). We have motivated each principle in the context of CAS and discussed its scientific foundations and challenges.

Our list of principles is far from exhaustive. There are other relevant aspects which could be addressed and analyzed in detail. Some of these address technical properties of CAS, such as safety or security. There are also broader implications of development and deployment of CAS to be considered, for example the ethical and legal concerns raised by systems that autonomously act in environments shared with humans and other autonomous systems. We hope that the principles presented in this paper can serve as guidelines for future research in the area of CAS and foster further discussion and ideas in the field.

References

1. Abeywickrama, D., Bicocchi, N., Zambonelli, F.: SOTA: towards a general model for self-adaptive systems. In: 2012 IEEE 21st International Workshop on Enabling Technologies: Infrastructure for Collaborative Enterprises (WETICE), pp. 48–53, June 2012

2. Lemos, R., et al.: Software engineering for self-adaptive systems: a second research roadmap. In: Lemos, R., Giese, H., Müller, H.A., Shaw, M. (eds.) Software Engineering for Self-Adaptive Systems II. LNCS, vol. 7475, pp. 1–32. Springer, Heidelberg (2013). doi:10.1007/978-3-642-35813-5_1

3. Alexander, J.M.: Evolutionary game theory. In: Zalta, E.N. (ed.) The Stanford Encyclopedia of Philosophy. Stanford Center for the Study of Language and Information, Fall 2009 edn. (2009)

4. Barberis, N.C.: Thirty years of prospect theory in economics: a review and assessment. J. Econ. Perspect. **27**(1), 173–196 (2013). http://www.aeaweb.org/articles. php?doi=10.1257/jep.27.1.173

5. Bijani, S., Robertson, D.: A review of attacks and security approaches in open multi-agent systems. Artif. Intell. Rev. **42**(4), 607–636 (2014)

6. Bishop, C.M.: Pattern Recognition and Machine Learning. Springer, Heidelberg (2006)

7. Bonabeau, E., Dorigo, M., Theraulaz, G.: Swarm Intelligence-From Natural to Artificial Systems. Studies in the Sciences of Complexity. Oxford University Press, Oxford (1999). http://ukcatalogue.oup.com/product/9780195131598.do

8. Borgers, T., Krahmer, D., Strausz, R.: An Introduction to the Theory of Mechanism Design. Oxford University Press, Oxford (2015)

9. Briggs, R.: Normative theories of rational choice: expected utility. In: Zalta, E.N. (ed.) The Stanford Encyclopedia of Philosophy. Stanford Center for the Study of Language and Information, fall 2014 edn. (2014)

10. Browne, C.B., Powley, E., Whitehouse, D., Lucas, S.M., Cowling, P., Rohlfshagen, P., Tavener, S., Perez, D., Samothrakis, S., Colton, S., et al.: A survey of monte carlo tree search methods. IEEE Trans. Comput. Intell. AI Games **4**(1), 1–43 (2012)

11. Brun, Y., et al.: Engineering self-adaptive systems through feedback loops. In: Cheng, B.H.C., Lemos, R., Giese, H., Inverardi, P., Magee, J. (eds.) Software Engineering for Self-Adaptive Systems. LNCS, vol. 5525, pp. 48–70. Springer, Heidelberg (2009). doi:10.1007/978-3-642-02161-9_3

12. Bruni, R., Corradini, A., Gadducci, F., Hölzl, M., Lafuente, A.L., Vandin, A., Wirsing, M.: Reconciling white-box and black-box perspectives on behavioural self-adaptation. In: Wirsing et al. [68]

13. Bruni, R., Corradini, A., Gadducci, F., Lluch Lafuente, A., Vandin, A.: A conceptual framework for adaptation. In: Lara, J., Zisman, A. (eds.) FASE 2012. LNCS, vol. 7212, pp. 240–254. Springer, Heidelberg (2012). doi:10.1007/978-3-642-28872-2_17

14. Cailliau, A., van Lamsweerde, A.: Assessing requirements-related risks through probabilistic goals and obstacles. Requir. Eng. **18**(2), 129–146 (2013). doi:10.1007/s00766-013-0168-5

15. Castelfranchi, C., Tan, Y.H.: Trust and Deception in Virtual Societies. Springer, Heidelberg (2001)

16. Cheng, B.H.C., et al.: Software engineering for self-adaptive systems: a research roadmap. In: Cheng, B.H.C., Lemos, R., Giese, H., Inverardi, P., Magee, J. (eds.) Software Engineering for Self-Adaptive Systems. LNCS, vol. 5525, pp. 1–26. Springer, Heidelberg (2009). doi:10.1007/978-3-642-02161-9_1

17. Clark, C., Storkey, A.: Training deep convolutional neural networks to play go. In: Proceedings of the 32nd International Conference on Machine Learning, pp. 1766–1774 (2015)
18. Special Issue of the Journal for Cognitive Systems Research: Stigmergy 3.0: From Ants to Economics. Elsevier, March 2013
19. Connelly, B.L., Certo, S.T., Ireland, R.D., Reutzel, C.R.: Signaling theory: a review and assessment. J. Manag. 37(1), 39–67 (2011)
20. IBM Corporation: An architectural blueprint for autonomic computing. Technical report, IBM (2005). http://researchr.org/publication/autonomic-architecture-2005
21. Criminisi, A., Shotton, J., Konukoglu, E.: Decision Forests: A Unified Framework for Classification, Regression, Density Estimation Manifold Learning and Semi-supervised Learning. Now, Breda (2012)
22. Dardenne, A., van Lamsweerde, A., Fickas, S.: Goal-directed requirements acquisition. Sci. Comput. Program. 20(1), 3–50 (1993). http://www.sciencedirect.com/science/article/pii/016764239390021G
23. Dechter, R.: Constraint Processing. Morgan Kaufmann, Burlington (2003)
24. Deng, L., Seltzer, M.L., Yu, D., Acero, A., Mohamed, A.r., Hinton, G.E.: Binary coding of speech spectrograms using a deep auto-encoder. In: Interspeech, pp. 1692–1695. Citeseer (2010)
25. Dorigo, M., Bonabeau, E., Theraulaz, G.: Ant algorithms and stigmergy. Future Gener. Comput. Syst. 16(9), 851–871 (2000). http://dl.acm.org/citation.cfm?id=348599.348601
26. Falcone, R., Castelfranchi, C.: Social trust: a cognitive approach. In: Castelfranchi, C., Tan, Y.-H. (eds.) Trust and Deception in Virtual Societies, pp. 55–90. Springer, Netherlands (2001)
27. Geels, F.W.: From sectoral systems of innovation to socio-technical systems: insights about dynamics and change from sociology and institutional theory. Res. Policy 33(67), 897–920 (2004). http://www.sciencedirect.com/science/article/pii/S0048733304000496
28. Hillier, F., Lieberman, G.: Introduction to Operations Research. McGraw-Hill Higher Education, New York (2010). https://books.google.de/books?id=NvE5PgAACAAJ
29. Hinton, G.E., Osindero, S., Teh, Y.W.: A fast learning algorithm for deep belief nets. Neural Comput. 18(7), 1527–1554 (2006)
30. Holzl, M., Gabor, T.: Continuous collaboration for changing environments. In: Steffen, B. (ed.) Transactions on FoMaC I. LNCS, vol. 9960, pp. 201–224. Springer, Heidelberg (2016). doi:10.1007/978-3-319-46508-1_11
31. Hölzl, M., Gabor, T.: Reasoning and learning for awareness and adaptation. In: Wirsing et al. [68]
32. Hölzl, M., Koch, N., Puviani, M., Wirsing, M., Zambonelli, F.: The ensemble development life cycle and best practises for collective autonomic systems. In: Wirsing et al. [68]
33. Hölzl, M., Wirsing, M.: Issues in engineering self-aware and self-expressive ensembles. In: Pitt, J. (ed.) The Computer After Me: Awareness and Self-awareness in Autonomic Systems. Imperial College Press, London (2014)
34. Hölzl, M., Wirsing, M.: Towards a system model for ensembles. In: Agha, G., Danvy, O., Meseguer, J. (eds.) Formal Modeling: Actors, Open Systems, Biological Systems: Essays Dedicated to Carolyn Talcott on the Occasion of her 70th Birthday. LNCS, vol. 7000, pp. 241–261. Springer, Heidelberg (2011). doi:10.1007/978-3-642-24933-4_12

35. Hurwicz, L., Reiter, S.: Designing Economic Mechanisms. Cambridge University Press, New York (2006). https://books.google.de/books?id=Mvn8chTLeFwC
36. Inverardi, P., Mori, M.: A software lifecycle process to support consistent evolutions. In: Lemos, R., Giese, H., Müller, H.A., Shaw, M. (eds.) Software Engineering for Self-Adaptive Systems II. LNCS, vol. 7475, pp. 239–264. Springer, Heidelberg (2013). doi:10.1007/978-3-642-35813-5_10
37. Jolliffe, I.: Principal Component Analysis. Wiley Online Library, New York (2002)
38. Jones, A., Artikis, A., Pitt, J.: The design of intelligent socio-technical systems. Artif. Intell. Rev. **39**(1), 5–20 (2013). doi:10.1007/s10462-012-9387-2
39. Jung, Y., Kim, M., Masoumzadeh, A., Joshi, J.B.: A survey of security issue in multi-agent systems. Artif. Intell. Rev. **37**(3), 239–260 (2012)
40. Kahneman, D., Tversky, A.: Prospect theory: an analysis of decision under risk. Econometrica **47**, 263–291 (1979)
41. Keeney, R., Raiffa, H.: Decisions with Multiple Objectives: Preferences and Value Tradeoffs. Wiley, New York (1976)
42. Kephart, J.O., Chess, D.M.: The vision of autonomic computing. Computer **36**(1), 41–50 (2003). doi:10.1109/MC.2003.1160055
43. Keznikl, J., Bures, T., Plasil, F., Gerostathopoulos, I., Hnetynka, P., Hoch, N.: Design of ensemble-based component systems by invariant refinement. In: Proceedings of the 16th International ACM Sigsoft symposium on Component-based software engineering, CBSE 2013, pp. 91–100. ACM, New York (2013)
44. Koch, N.: ASCENS: autonomic service-component ensembles (brochure), February 2015
45. Krizhevsky, A., Sutskever, I., Hinton, G.E.: Imagenet classification with deep convolutional neural networks. In: Proceedings of Advances in Neural Information Processing Systems, pp. 1097–1105 (2012)
46. van Lamsweerde, A.: Requirements engineering in the year 00: a research perspective. In: Proceedings of the 22nd International Conference on Software Engineering (ICSE 2000), pp. 5–19. ACM (2000)
47. Lee, H., Battle, A., Raina, R., Ng, A.Y.: Efficient sparse coding algorithms. In: Proceedings of Advances in Neural Information Processing Systems, pp. 801–808 (2006)
48. Legay, A., Delahaye, B., Bensalem, S.: Statistical model checking: an overview. In: Barringer, H., Falcone, Y., Finkbeiner, B., Havelund, K., Lee, I., Pace, G., Roşu, G., Sokolsky, O., Tillmann, N. (eds.) RV 2010. LNCS, vol. 6418, pp. 122–135. Springer, Heidelberg (2010). doi:10.1007/978-3-642-16612-9_11
49. Mertens, J.F., Neyman, A.: Stochastic games. Int. J. Game Theor. **10**(2), 53–66 (1981). doi:10.1007/BF01769259
50. Millington, I.: Game Physics Engine Development. Morgan Kaufmann Publishers, Amsterdam (2007)
51. Mnih, V., Kavukcuoglu, K., Silver, D., Graves, A., Antonoglou, I., Wierstra, D., Riedmiller, M.A.: Playing atari with deep reinforcement learning. CoRR abs/1312.5602 (2013). http://arXiv.org/abs/1312.5602
52. Ostrom, E.: Governing the Commons: The Evolution of Institutions for Collective Action. Political Economy of Institutions and Decisions. Cambridge University Press, New York (1990). https://books.google.de/books?id=4xg6oUobMz4C
53. Pharr, M., Humphreys, G.: Physically Based Rendering: From Theory to Implementation. Morgan Kaufmann, Burlington (2004)
54. Pinyol, I., Sabater-Mir, J.: Computational trust and reputation models for open multi-agent systems: a review. Artif. Intell. Rev. **40**(1), 1–25 (2013)

55. Pitt, J., Busquets, D., Bourazeri, A., Petruzzi, P.: Collective intelligence and algorithmic governance of socio-technical systems. In: Miorandi, D., Maltese, V., Rovatsos, M., Nijholt, A., Stewart, J. (eds.) Social Collective Intelligence. Computational Social Sciences, pp. 31–50. Springer International Publishing, Switzerland (2014). doi:10.1007/978-3-319-08681-1_2

56. Puterman, M.L.: Markov Decision Processes: Discrete Stochastic Dynamic Programming, 1st edn. Wiley, New York (1994)

57. Rasmussen, C.E.: Gaussian Processes for Machine Learning. MIT Press, Massachusetts (2006)

58. Scott, W.R.: The adolescence of institutional theory. Adm. Sci. Q. **32**(4), 493–511 (1987)

59. Sen, K., Viswanathan, M., Agha, G.: On statistical model checking of stochastic systems. In: Etessami, K., Rajamani, S.K. (eds.) CAV 2005. LNCS, vol. 3576, pp. 266–280. Springer, Heidelberg (2005). doi:10.1007/11513988_26

60. Shoham, Y., Leyton-Brown, K.: Multiagent Systems: Algorithmic, Game-Theoretic, and Logical Foundations. Cambridge University Press, New York (2008)

61. Spence, M.: Signaling in retrospect and the informational structure of markets. Am. Econ. Rev. **92**(3), 434–459 (2002). http://www.aeaweb.org/articles.php?doi=10.1257/00028280260136200

62. Thrun, S., Burgard, W., Fox, D.: Probabilistic Robotics. MIT Press, Massachusetts (2005)

63. Weibull, J.W.: Evolutionary Game Theory. MIT Press, Cambridge (1995)

64. Weinstein, A., Littman, M.L.: Open-loop planning in large-scale stochastic domains. In: desJardins, M., Littman, M.L. (ed.) Proceedings of the Twenty-Seventh AAAI Conference on Artificial Intelligence, 14–18 July 2013, Bellevue, Washington, USA. AAAI Press (2013). http://www.aaai.org/ocs/index.php/AAAI/AAAI13/paper/view/6341

65. Weiss, G. (ed.): Multiagent Systems, 2nd edn. MIT Press, Massachusetts (2013)

66. Wirsing, M., Hölzl, M., Koch, N., Mayer, P. (eds.): Software Engineering for Collective Autonomic Systems. LNCS, vol. 8998. Springer, Heidelberg (2015)

67. Wooldridge, M.: An Introduction to MultiAgent Systems. Wiley, New York (2009). https://books.google.de/books?id=X3ZQ7yeDn2IC

68. Yang, X.-S. (ed.): Recent Advances in Swarm Intelligence and Evolutionary Computation. SCI, vol. 585. Springer, Heidelberg (2015). doi:10.1007/978-3-319-13826-8

Continuous Collaboration for Changing Environments

Matthias Hölzl[✉] and Thomas Gabor

Ludwig-Maximilians-Universität München, Munich, Germany
hoelzl@pst.ifi.lmu.de

Abstract. Collective autonomic systems (CAS) are distributed collections of agents that collaborate to achieve the system's goals but autonomously adapt their behavior. We present the teacher/student architecture for locally coordinated distributed learning and show that in certain scenarios the performance of a swarm using teacher/student learning can be significantly better than that of agents learning individually. Teacher/student learning serves as foundation for the continuous collaboration (CC) development approach. We introduce CC, relate it to the EDLC, a life cycle model for CAS, and show that CC embodies many of the principles proposed for developing CAS.

Keywords: Autonomic systems · Awareness · Adaptation · Evolutionary systems · Replicator dynamics

1 Introduction

To cope with demanding requirements and open-ended environments, today's software increasingly operates as part of collective autonomic systems (CAS): distributed collections of agents that collaborate to achieve the system's goals but that can autonomously adapt their behavior—either individually or as group.

Some of the expected benefits of CAS are that, by adjusting themselves to the peculiarities of the environment in which they are operating, they can provide the desired functionality in many situations and for different operating conditions, that they are resilient to failures, and that they can exploit new opportunities as they arise. In practice, however, it is difficult to achieve these features. This is to some extent because building software components that are impervious to changes in the situations in which they are deployed or operating is inherently more difficult than building components that are tailored to a particular environment for which many assumptions can be made. But part of the difficulty stems from a mismatch between best practices and architectures for engineering traditional software systems and the properties of agents that are part of a CAS.

Whereas many activities in traditional software engineering processes (whether agile or not) are designed to reduce uncertainty and build components that are tailored to their role in a particular system, for CAS it seems

© Springer International Publishing AG 2016
B. Steffen (Ed.): Transactions on FoMaC I, LNCS 9960, pp. 201–224, 2016.
DOI: 10.1007/978-3-319-46508-1_11

advantageous to design agents that have the potential for a multitude of different behaviors, that can self-organize, and that can autonomously tailor their operations to the demands of the current system configuration and environment. We provide a technical example for such an environment as well as some guidelines which are derived from the work on the *Ensemble Development Life-Cycle* in Sect. 2.

There are even more circumstances CAS are usually expected to cope with that further increase the difficulty of autonomous adaption: As a CAS's respective environments and thus requirements may change while it is operating, there is often no way to guarantee that the evaluation performed during system design is still sound at any given moment in the system's runtime. It is thus necessary for the system to continuously evaluate its performance and its ability to adapt to the environment encountered. As such tasks are typically computationally expensive, some trade-off between the optimality of the solution and the computational effort needed to find it is to be expected. During design time, this trade-off can be handled by experienced software engineers, but at runtime it has to be decided upon automatically. In traditional software engineering there is no connection between these two activities. However, once we have an algorithm at our disposal for runtime use, it seems natural to employ the very same technique during design time as well. Similarly, to come up with good runtime strategies it might be useful to analyze the trade-offs made by the system's designers and encode them in a form that is usable at run time. This idea is one of the central points of the approach we call *continuous collaboration* (CC): Providing a framework that, as far as possible, unifies the tools and processes for design time and runtime decision making, thus allowing for a swift interplay of machine-powered online adaption and human-powered offline development. We base this idea not only on a certain intuition of elegance, the development of CC was strongly guided by results in formal learning theory, knowledge representation, and game theory which are presented in Sect. 3. We apply these theoretical insights in Sect. 4 to define the CC approach. Distributed learning in CC is performed according to the teacher/student pattern which provides a general infrastructure for the combination of learning agents that differ in their applied learning mechanism, scope or locality. Teacher/student learning was first presented in [10]; we recall its essential features in Subsect. 4.1. Since learning theory shows that learning without any kind of prior domain knowledge is futile, we propose to employ Extended Behavior Trees (Subsect. 4.2) as an intuitive way to specify constraints on and circumstances of adaptive behavior.

Building upon these techniques, we fully introduce the continuous collaboration approach, show how it supports ensemble development and present some experimental results in Subsect. 4.3 and Sect. 5. The penultimate Sect. 6 presents related work, Sect. 7 concludes.

2   Motivation

In this section, we illustrate the kind of scenarios toward which CC is tailored. To this end, Subsect. 2.1 describes a concrete example of a complex challenge for distributed, autonomous systems that will be used throughout this work, even though we will limit its total complexity for ease of analysis in Sect. 4. We then continue in Subsect. 2.2 with a short summary of some proposed principles for designing CAS, presented in more detail by Belzner et al. [3]. These principles provide a guideline for the techniques described in the remainder of this paper.

2.1 The "Robot Rescue Force" Example

Disaster relief and rescue operation present a rich source of challenges for systems that can operate in rapidly changing environments. In these scenarios it is often the case that the environment deteriorates in unpredictable ways while the system is operating, and both quick reaction as well as long-term planning play important roles. Furthermore, the very nature of the problem makes it impossible to obtain a precise design-time description of the environment in which the system is operating. We will use the example of a swarm of robots that support rescue operations as running example for CC.

There are many reasons why it would be advantageous to deploy CAS to support rescue missions: The environment of such an operation is often hazardous and non-predictable. Employing robots to perform many of the tasks on a mission would allow humans to stay outside the immediate danger zone, but only if the robots can operate autonomously. There are many different tasks to perform during a rescue operation, therefore a large number of robots might be deployed. To achieve maximum flexibility, each robot should be able to perform many different tasks, e.g. rescue victims, clear blocked paths, clean up spillages of dangerous materials, build walls to insulate radiation sources, etc. Which of these tasks have to be performed depends on the concrete situation encountered in the disaster area and can only be partially be decided in advance, therefore robots have to act collectively and, e.g. dynamically allocate tasks or collaborate on missions that a single robot cannot perform.

Fig. 1. Simulation of the robot rescue scenario

More concretely, we will use the following example: An industrial complex has been damaged; workers have been trapped in several areas of the complex and need to be rescued. In addition, chemicals or radioactive material may have spilled and need to be contained. It is expected that the health of injured victims will decline over time and that some parts of the complex may collapse while the rescue operation is in progress. Therefore, the sequence in which different tasks are performed may greatly impact the performance of the rescue team. The robots have only limited power and need to recharge periodically, otherwise they will break down during rescue missions. Figure 1 shows a screenshot of our simulation environment in which several robots are in the process of rescuing victims.

2.2   Finding an Approach for the Example

Scenarios like the "robot rescue force" example described above have for a long time been beyond the ability of automatic solution finding and, in their full complexity, still continue to be. However, recent advances in making computational power available and powerful learning techniques accessible have managed to put them within reach of software and system developers. It is interesting to note that many approaches developed in recent years can be applied to a wide range of concrete problems as they only operate on rather abstract representations of the problem they are employed to solve.

However, it is this generality that makes it difficult for software developers to identify which techniques work for concrete problem scenarios and how different techniques behave in the face of changing conditions. Trial-and-error of different adaptation techniques is thus still a standard part of system development for adaptive systems and easily testing, e.g., different learning mechanisms in both simulation and during runtime is required for any serious development approach for CAS.

The ASCENS project has developed the *Ensemble Development Life Cycle (EDLC),* a life cycle model for the development of CAS that focuses on the feedback cycles in the development process. Belzner et al. [3] propose a set of principles for engineering CAS based on the EDLC. The proposed principles are:

P1 Use probabilistic goal- and utility-based techniques
P2 Characterize the adaptation space and design the awareness mechanism
P3 Exploit interaction
P4 Perform reasoning, learning and planning
P5 Consider the interplay of static and dynamic knowledge
P6 Enable evolutionary feedback
P7 Perform simulation and analysis throughout the system life cycle
P8 Consider societies of systems

CC is based on the idea that when developing CAS that operate in complex, open-ended environments we should embrace the uncertainty and change inherent in the system's structure and operating conditions, and try to exploit the resulting evolutionary dynamics to achieve adaptation. Applying this concept of handling CAS to the principles above allows us to derive many properties found in our concrete technical implementations in a top-down manner. Our aim is thus to provide a theoretically founded guide for system designers on how to structure CAS. The resulting pattern can be regarded as an instantiation of the EDLC, a detailed discussion of which we defer to Sect. 4.3.

3 Foundations

As mentioned in the previous section, continuous collaboration is based on the teacher/student architecture for locally coordinated distributed learning. In the following sections we motivate some of the design decisions we have made for teacher/student learning based on results from statistical learning, knowledge representation and evolutionary game theory. In particular, we use results from PAC learning to justify why having many students and several teachers may be advantageous, we show using modal logic how knowing that the students share information and strategies can be used to improve the decision making in ways that go beyond the increased learning performance, and we indicate how the selection of teachers by students is influenced by principles from evolutionary game theory.

3.1 PAC Learning

Robots in the rescue force cannot directly access the environment; they have to perform *state estimation* to infer the likely state of the environment based on their observations. Given this estimate, they have to determine the best course of action. Often these two activities cannot be performed without relying on data gained from experience in the actual environment in which the robot is operating. Therefore we can regard them as a learning problem: learn the state of the environment and the best action to perform based on predefined knowledge and previous experience in the environment. To simplify the discussion we will assume that state estimation can be treated as a *statistical learning problem*, e.g. by assuming that we rely on a fixed number of training examples for which the correct decision is known or by restricting the learning to binary decisions. These restrictions could be relaxed without materially affecting the results. We defer the discussion of change in the environment to Sect. 3.4 and focus on the problem of learning correct decisions for a static environment for the moment.

The task we are trying to solve is the following: Assign a label to each element of a set $\mathcal{X}$ after having seen some examples of correctly labeled elements drawn randomly from $\mathcal{X}$. Formally, a general (statistical) learning problem consists of the following components:

- A set $\mathcal{X}$ of elements, called the *domain*. Typically, each $x \in \mathcal{X}$ is a vector of features, $x = (x_1, \ldots, x_n)$ to which we want to assign a label. For a rescue robot the features might be sensor readings or stored data about the environment. If we assume partial observability, each $x \in \mathcal{X}$ corresponds to a set

$\{X^1, \ldots X^j\}$ of environments, namely those in which the observed features are consistent with $(x_1, \ldots, x_n)$.

- A set $\mathcal{Y}$ of *labels* that can be assigned to elements of the domain. For a robot, the labels might denote the algorithm to chose. In the following we restrict ourselves to the label set $\{0, 1\}$ where, e.g. 1 might mean perform a rescue mission, and 0 stay at the home base.
- A set $\mathcal{H}$ of functions $h : \mathcal{X} \to \mathcal{Y}$ called the *hypothesis class*. The output of a learning algorithm is an element h of $\mathcal{H}$, called a *prediction rule* or *classifier*.
- A set Z with σ-algebra $\mathcal{Z}$. The set Z can be thought of as the set of all possible "labeled domain elements" that can be processed the learning algorithm. For supervised learning the set Z is often $\mathcal{X} \times \mathcal{Y}$.
- A finite sequence of *training data* consisting of points from Z, drawn independently, identically distributed (i.i.d) from $\mathcal{D}$. We write $S \sim \mathcal{D}^m$ to indicate that S consists of m samples drawn i.i.d. from $\mathcal{D}$ and generally use z_i to denote the individual samples: $S = (z_1, \ldots, z_m)$.
- A *loss function* $\ell : \mathcal{H} \times Z \to \mathbb{R}_+$ that measures the distance between the label assigned by h and $z \in Z$. If z is a correctly labeled element, ℓ measures how badly $h \in \mathcal{H}$ mis-classifies z. In the following we use the so-called 0 -1 loss ℓ_{0-1} which is defined for $Z = \mathcal{X} \times \mathcal{Y}$:

$$\ell_{0-1}(h, (\boldsymbol{x}, y)) = \begin{cases} 0 & \text{if } h(\boldsymbol{x}) = y \\ 1 & \text{if } h(\boldsymbol{x}) \neq y \end{cases}$$

- A probability distribution $\mathcal{D}$ over $\mathcal{Z}$.

For any $h \in \mathcal{H}$, the expected loss $\ell(h, z)$ when z is drawn from $\mathcal{D}$, i.e. $\mathbb{E}_{z \sim \mathcal{D}}[\ell(h, z)]$, is called the *generalization error*, *risk* or *true error* and written $L_{\mathcal{D}}(h)$. We now define the important concept of probably approximately correct (PAC) learning. Our definition focuses on the sampling complexity of PAC learning and ignores the computational complexity. See [18] for a more detailed discussion.

Definition 1. *A hypothesis class $\mathcal{H}$ is (general, agnostic) PAC learnable with respect to $\mathcal{Z}$ and loss function ℓ, if a function $m_{\mathcal{H}} : (0, 1)^2 \to \mathbb{N}$ and a learning algorithm A exist, such that for every $\epsilon, \delta \in (0, 1)$, for every distribution $\mathcal{D}$ over $\mathcal{Z}$, and for every $m \geq m_{\mathcal{H}}(\epsilon, \delta)$ the following holds: When A is applied to m i.i.d samples drawn from $\mathcal{D}$, A returns $h \in \mathcal{H}$ such that*

$$\mathbb{P}\big(L_{\mathcal{D}}(h) \leq \min_{h' \in \mathcal{H}} L_{\mathcal{D}}(h') + \epsilon\big) \geq 1 - \delta$$

PAC learning is probabilistic since the algorithm A may not find a good solution with probability δ; it is approximately correct since the expected loss of an acceptable solution h may deviate from that of the best possible solution for the given hypothesis class, $\min_{h' \in \mathcal{H}} L_{\mathcal{D}}(h')$, by (at most) ϵ. Usually $m_{\mathcal{H}}$ is assumed to be the minimal function that satisfies the criterion stated in the definition.

3.2   Domain Knowledge and Inductive Bias

The choice of hypothesis class $\mathcal{H}$ determines the *inductive bias* of a PAC learning algorithm: only classifications in $\mathcal{H}$ can be learned, and the minimal generalization error that can be achieved is determined by the element of $\mathcal{H}$ with minimal expected loss, no matter how many training samples are provided. Thus, $\mathcal{H}$ can be seen as the domain knowledge provided by the developers to the learning algorithm: If $\mathcal{H}$ has a rich structure, it contains few preconceived ideas about the domain. If, on the other hand, $\mathcal{H}$ contains only few elements, the learner has little flexibility in choosing a solution.

At first glance it would therefore seem that choosing a large $\mathcal{H}$ maximizes the adaptivity of a system. This is, however, often not the case: If $\mathcal{H}$ is too large (in a sense we will shortly make more precise) it may either not be PAC learnable at all or the system may not find a good solution: Every learning algorithm fails on some learning tasks, even though other learning algorithms succeed on these tasks. This observation is known as "no free lunch theorem" [18]:

Theorem 1 (No Free Lunch). *Let A be any learning algorithm for binary classification, $\ell = \ell_{0\text{-}1}$. Let m be a number with $m < |\mathcal{X}|/2$. Then there exists a distribution $\mathcal{D}$ over $\mathcal{X} \times \{0,1\}$ such that*

- *There exists $f : \mathcal{X} \to \{0,1\}$ with $L_\mathcal{D}(f) = 0$.*
- *With probability $> 1/7$ we have $L_\mathcal{D}(A(S)) \geq 1/8$ for $S \sim \mathcal{D}^m$*

It follows that for an infinite domain $\mathcal{X}$ the set $\mathcal{H}$ consisting of all functions from $\mathcal{X}$ to $\{0,1\}$ is not PAC learnable.

The proof of Theorem 1 takes a subset C of $\mathcal{X}$ of size $2m$, so that S can only sample half the instances in C, and uses this to build a distribution with the properties stated in the theorem. This idea can be extended to obtain a better characterization of the hypothesis classes that can be learned from a given amount of training data. To this end, let $C = \{c_1, \dots, c_n\} \subseteq \mathcal{X}$ and $\mathcal{H}_C = \{h|_C|\ h \in \mathcal{H}\}$ be the set of all functions of $\mathcal{H}$ restricted to C. We say $\mathcal{H}$ *shatters* C if $\mathcal{H}_C$ is the set of all functions from C to $\{0,1\}$.

Definition 2 (VC-Dimension). *The VC-dimension of a hypothesis class $\mathcal{H}$, written $\mathrm{VCdim}(\mathcal{H})$, is the maximal size of a set $C \subseteq \mathcal{X}$ that can be shattered by $\mathcal{H}$.*

The VC-dimension provides a measure for the "complexity of the decision boundary" of a class $\mathcal{H}$ and precisely characterizes PAC learnability: $\mathcal{H}$ is PAC learnable if and only if it has finite VC-dimension. The following theorem characterizes this relationship quantitatively:

Theorem 2. *Let $\mathcal{H}$ be a set of functions from $\mathcal{X}$ to $\{0,1\}$ with $\mathrm{VCdim}(\mathcal{H}) = d < \infty$ and let $\ell = \ell_{0\text{-}1}$. There exist constants C_1 and C_2 such that*

$$C_1 \frac{d + \log(1/\delta)}{\epsilon^2} \leq m_\mathcal{H}(\epsilon, \delta) \leq C_2 \frac{d + \log(1/\delta)}{\epsilon^2}.$$

This theorem states that the number of samples required to learn a probably approximately correct hypothesis to the level of accuracy and certainty determined by $m_{\mathcal{H}}$ is linearly bounded by the VC-dimension of the hypothesis space. Therefore, one important design consideration for adaptive systems is to keep the VC-dimension of the learning mechanisms small enough that they can successfully learn from the available training data. Since the VC-dimension is defined as the largest size of a set that can be shattered by $\mathcal{H}$ this means that in order to exhibit good learning characteristics the learning mechanisms should have relatively few degrees of freedom. This can be seen as a theoretical justification of Belzner et al.'s principle P2: "Characterize the adaptation space and design the awareness mechanism" [3]. In particular, in many domains the problem of learning which actions are appropriate in a given situation is infeasibly large when $\mathcal{H}$ is the space of all low-level actions that the system can perform. If is therefore often necessary to learn which of several higher-level *strategies* is applicable. In this paper we use extended behavior trees (XBTs) for this purpose. The tree structure of XBTs makes it particularly easy for teachers to combine strategies or to update only parts of strategies, but other mechanisms, such as state machines or a general purpose programming language can be used instead.

Theorem 2 influences the teacher/student in two more ways: The first, more obvious conclusion is that in applications in which data has to be gathered from the environment it is often better to build a system that consists of multiple simpler agents that collect data (i.e., students) and aggregate this data, rather than a system that consists of fewer more powerful agents. For the same hypothesis space, obtaining more data allows the learner to decrease the inaccuracy ϵ and/or the uncertainty δ of its predictions, since by definition $m_{\mathcal{H}}$ grows with shrinking ϵ and δ. This can be seen in the experiments in Sect. 5, in which a single robot cannot learn satisfactory behavior whereas a group of robots reaches and maintains near optimal performance after a short while, even though the effort spent on learning is similar in both cases.

A perhaps more surprising influence of the theorem is the use of multiple teachers: If we try to build a single teacher that performs well in many different situations it necessarily has a high VC-dimension, and therefore a large training set, since it needs to shatter at least the set of all situations that require a different response in different environments or situation. If, on the other hand, we provide a number of teachers with different inductive biases, we can design the system in such a way that, in any given environment, some teachers will provide good prediction rules with a limited amount of training data. Other teachers will, obviously, propose bad classifiers since their inductive biases will not match the actual circumstances. If the system designers can ensure that the bad prediction rules do not damage the system when they are enacted, it is possible to use, e.g., an evolutionary strategy as described in Sect. 3.4 to mainly follow the classifiers that match the current environment. In this way, a system designed according to the teacher/student model can learn quickly from data while retaining the flexibility to operate in different situations or environments.

3.3 Distributed and Common Knowledge

Before discussing the selection of "good" teachers in the next section, we address one more aspect that influences the design of the teacher/student model: Since students update their knowledge and strategies during exchanges with their teachers, they know that other students have the same[1] knowledge and strategies. This common knowledge allows teachers to propose behaviors that would not be feasible for agents operating on their own.

In the context of a collective adaptive system, we have multiple agents $\alpha_1, \ldots, \alpha_n$. We write $\mathcal{X}_i$ for the domain of α_i. As mentioned in Sect. 3.1 each $x_i \in \mathcal{X}_i$ corresponds to a set of environments (or *worlds*) $X_i = \{X_i^1, \ldots X_i^{j_i}\}$ that α_i considers possible given the features in x_i. We say α_i *knows* a proposition ϕ given x_i and write $K_i\phi$, if ϕ holds in all worlds the agent considers possible, i.e. if $X_i^j \models \phi$ for all worlds X_i^j corresponding to x_i. This definition of K_i is consistent with the usual definition of knowledge using modal logic [7].

Given a group G of agents, we define three operators:

- D_G means "it is distributed knowledge in group G,"
- E_G means "everyone in group G knows," and
- C_G means "it is common knowledge in group G."

The distributed knowledge of a group of agents G consists of all formulas ϕ that hold in the *intersection* of the sets X_i for all α_i in G, i.e. formulas that can be derived by combining the knowledge of all agents in G. D_G often allows a more precise characterization of the possible worlds than the individual knowledge: Suppose there are three possible locations of victims and write v_i for the proposition "there is a victim in location i." If robot α_1 has determined $(v_1 \lor v_2) \land \neg v_3$ using a long-range infrared camera that cannot distinguish between locations 1 and 2, and robot α_2 has determined $\neg v_1$, then we can infer $v_2 \land \neg v_1 \land \neg v_3$ using the distributed knowledge of the group $G = \{\alpha_1, \alpha_2\}$, e.g. we can locate the victim exactly using D_G when neither robot in G can. Therefore, by sharing data between a group of learners G we can achieve a double benefit:

- Learner α_i can use D_G instead of X_i to remove impossible worlds from $\mathcal{X}$, therefore achieving better coverage of the remaining alternatives for a hypothesis class of a given VC-dimension.
- Each learner has a larger set of training examples, thereby increasing the VC-dimension that it can learn.

The operator C_G for common knowledge describes a fixed point of E_G: if $C_G\phi$ holds, then everyone in group G knows ϕ, i.e. $E_G\phi$ holds, everyone in G knows that everyone in G knows ϕ, i.e. $E_G E_G\phi$ holds, and so on. Knowing $C_G\phi$ is sometimes advantageous for cooperation: Let ϕ be the statement "Rescuing victim v is the most important task, α_1 and α_2 can cooperate to rescue v but

---

[1] Taking into account the different times at which students exchange information with teachers, the knowledge and strategies the students share are typically similar, not identical. This does not change the gist of the following discussion.

neither can rescue v on its own." Simply knowing ϕ is not enough for α_1 to locate v and wait for α_2 to arrive in order to perform the joint rescue mission: if α_2 does not know ϕ, then α_2 will not initiate the common rescue operation and α_1 will wait in vain for it to arrive. Therefore $K_2\phi$ has to hold, and α_1 has to know this, i.e. $K_1K_2\phi$ has to hold as well. Similar reasoning for α_2 shows that $K_2K_1\phi$ has to hold for it to start the rescue mission, and therefore α_1 has to know $K_1K_2K_1\phi$. It is easy to see that these formulas have to hold for every level of knowledge. Therefore, the required property is $C_{\{\alpha_1,\alpha_2\}}\phi$, i.e. ϕ has to be common knowledge between α_1 and α_2. If agents exchange not only their knowledge but also the fact that the shared information is common knowledge, they increase their potential for collaboration. In the teacher/student model it is easy to incorporate this knowledge in the exchange between teachers and students.

3.4   Selecting Prediction Rules and Changing Environments

It is well known that an environment in which other agents are operating presents much more difficult problems for learning and adaptation than a purely stochastic environment. For example, while many reinforcement learning techniques converge to an optimal solution for stochastic environments, these guarantees are no longer valid when they operate in settings in which multiple agents are learning simultaneously. This has been verified experimentally: Q-learning is one of the foundational algorithms for reinforcement learning and provably converges to the optimal solution in the single-agent case [21]. Claus and Boutilier [5] show that this is no longer true in multiagent-learning scenarios, even when the agents cooperate. Wiegand [27] shows that cooperative evolutionary algorithms may not just converge to but even be attracted by suboptimal solutions, even though their convergence to an optimal solution is guaranteed in the single-agent case (given sufficient exploration).

Recently, evolutionary game theory (EGT) has been proposed as a theoretical foundation for multi-agent learning. In contrast to classical game theory, EGT is concerned with the process in which the behavioral strategies used by individuals in a population change over time in response to the strategies used by other members of the population, and whether the mix of strategies converges to an equilibrium. One particularly important concept from EGT for our purposes is the *replicator dynamics* which we now introduce for the simple case of a homogeneous population of agents that can each chose between n actions. We assume that time is discrete, $t \in \mathbb{N}$. Let a_{ij} be the reward for joint action (i,j), $\boldsymbol{A} = (a_{ij})_{i,j\in[1,n]}$, let $p_i(t)$ the percentage of agents choosing action i at time t (or, equivalently, the probability that an agent chooses action i at time t), and let $\boldsymbol{p}(t) = (p_1(t), \ldots, p_n(t))$. If agents prefer actions with better reward, we obtain the equation for *general discrete time replicator dynamics* as

$$\frac{\Delta p_i(t)}{p_i(t)} = \frac{\sum_{j=1}^{n} a_{ij}p_j(t) - \boldsymbol{p}(t)\boldsymbol{A}\boldsymbol{p}(t)}{\boldsymbol{p}(t)\boldsymbol{A}\boldsymbol{p}(t)}$$

This equation states that the rate of change that we observe for a particular action is the difference between the expected payoff of this action $\sum_{j=1}^{n} a_{ij}p_j(t)$ and the expected payoff for all actions $\boldsymbol{p}(t)\boldsymbol{Ap}(t)$. This principle underlies biological processes that are mainly based on selection (as opposed to mutation) [20]. In teacher/student learning, each student selects its teacher for the next episode based on the previous performance of the teacher's students, as well as potentially other criteria, such as whether the teacher provides a role that is currently underrepresented in the mix of agent behaviors. By selecting the parameters on which this choice is based as well as the weighting of the result, developers set up an evolutionary game whose replicator dynamics determine the behavior of the system and its reaction to changes.

One particularly interesting concept related to a system's evolutionary dynamics is the notion of *evolutionary stable state*. An evolutionary stable state (ESS) $E(t) = (p_1^E(t), \ldots, p_n^E(t))$ is a solution of the replicator equation that describes states of a system in which small disturbances do not cause the system to leave E. ESS can be used to identify situations or environments in which the system settles into a fixed strategy. For teacher/student systems it is often desirable to reach an ESS for unchanging environments; the disturbance to leave this state can be used to estimate how sensitive the reaction of the system to changes in the environment is.

4   Continuous Collaboration

In this section, we apply the theoretical insight gained in Sect. 3 to the development of CAS in order to derive the continuous collaboration approach from the principles introduced in Sect. 2. We start by introducing the teacher/student pattern for distributed learning systems in Subsect. 4.1 and then formally introduce Extended Behavior Trees (XBTs) in Subsect. 4.2. Finally, we can conclude in Subsect. 4.3 by discussing the CC approach itself and how it relates to the Ensemble Development Life-Cycle (EDLC).

4.1   Teacher/Student Learning

Employing learning techniques is a crucial prerequisite for the development of adaptive systems. However, the analysis performed in the previous section shows that learning behaviors for a collective system is a complex challenge. The general idea behind the concepts presented in the following sections is to alleviate some of the difficulty of designing collective systems by exploiting the structural properties of a CAS. Therefore, in teacher/student learning and continuous collaboration, learning takes place in a distributed manner inside the CAS; the structure of the learning system mimics the distributed structure of the CAS and can be adjusted to directly represent features of the solution, e.g. the spatial locality of many learning tasks. In addition, CC tries to employ competition between agents with the same function based on self-regulating feedback loops

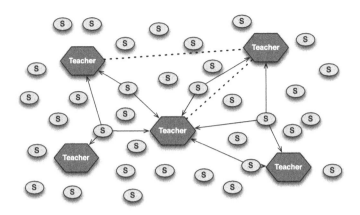

Fig. 2. Illustration of a CAS with a teacher/student architecture

whenever possible, so that errors, misunderstandings or incomplete knowledge in the design of the system are compensated.

For this purpose, we define two roles called *teacher* and *student* to be enacted by the agents of the CAS. Since we regard it as one of the central objectives of the CAS to find (i.e. learn) a plan of action leading to a suitable behavior of the CAS with respect to some external objective or fitness, teachers are agents mainly concerned with the generation and distribution of potentially suitable plans while the students' main purpose is to actually enact the behavior taught to them and thus provide the desired functionality of the CAS. Figure 2 depicts a schematic representation of a group of teachers and students. In a pure teacher/student architecture, as depicted in Fig. 2, students only communicate with teachers (as represented by the continuous arrows) while teachers may also communicate with one another (as represented by the dotted lines). Hybrid or multi-layer forms of teacher/student learning, in which agents simultaneously play the roles of teachers and students are also possible.

The basic idea behind teacher/student learning is that teachers dispose of plans they want to spread among the students of the CAS. Students choose their teachers, receive their plans and execute them. The choice of teachers by students is an important component of the architecture since it provides a dampening mechanism for the system's "plan distribution" control loop.

In more detail, each teacher of the CAS

– spreads its plans by teaching students within the reach of its communications facilities,
– improves its plans by incorporating experience gathered from the students, simulation or other external learning techniques, or communication with other teachers (altruistic or competitive).

Likewise, each student

– chooses a teacher to learn from based on the results promised by the teacher and the *trust* the student has gained in the teacher over time,

– executes the plans received from the teacher and uses the results and experiences gained to send a report to the teacher and to update the trust value accordingly.

As mentioned above, the trust value that a student assigns to a teacher may depend on many factors: the historical reliability of a teacher, the organization to which a teacher belongs, whether the teacher has previously provided plans containing actions that were dangerous to the student, etc.

Thus, in a typical implementation of the "robot rescue scenario," we will have multiple teachers accompanying a group of students capable of performing the rescue operation. These teachers may be more powerful stationary computers located at key points such as the home base. Some teachers may offer various plans of action for the whole rescue operation while other teachers may specialize in plans for specific subtasks. This allows for hierarchical learning approaches to be embedded inside the teacher/student architecture. However, students may also combine various plans from different teachers using, e.g. the technique described in Sect. 4.2. Applications for enabling these properties have been found, e.g. in long-term and short-term motion planning [6].

As a concrete example, we may have one teacher spreading a simple plan that instructs robots to look for a victim and attempt to carry it back to the home base. Another teacher may offer a more sophisticated plan according to which students check for the victim's weight first and call for help if it exceeds their individual lifting strength. Which of these plans is more successful depends on the environment in which the robots are operating: If the proportion of heavy victims is low, checking the weight of a victim is expensive and trying to lift a heavy victim does not have a negative impact on the robot, the plan of the first teacher may be more appropriate and thus be used by most robots. If, however, there are many heavy victims or if trying to lift a heavy victim is expensive for a robot, students following the plan of the first teacher will often gain low rewards for their mission because they failed to carry a heavier victim, while students acting according to the second teacher's plan will have a higher success rate. This will cause the students of the first teacher to lower their trust value for that teacher while students of the second teacher will gain more trust in that teacher. Over time, students in that environment will be more likely to listen to the second teacher, making its plans more prevalent in the CAS.

This example illustrates how a competition between teachers arises: Teachers with worse plans face the risk of losing the students' trust and become almost ignored by the CAS. The systems thus exhibits the behavior discussed in Sect. 3.4. Moreover, as teachers can communicate between one another, they can provide a basis for shared knowledge between all agents of the ensemble, as is deemed necessary in Sect. 3.3.

The teacher/student architecture supports many of the principles from [3]: It enables evolutionary feedback (P6) while exploiting interaction (P3), since the mix of strategies used by the CAS results is determined by a dynamic process based on the interaction between teachers and students. Because of the open-ended nature of the exchange between teachers and students it also supports societies of systems (P8) in which teachers and students with new capabilities can be dynamically introduced into the system and in which teachers with new capabilities can introduce previously unavailable strategies into a system.

4.2   Extended Behavior Trees (XBTs)

As mentioned in Sect. 3 we use extended behavior trees (XBT), an extension of behavior trees (BTs), to specify the behavioral strategies that provide the inductive bias for efficiently learning how to act. BTs are a technique for describing agent behaviors as a hierarchical tree structure. A BT is a tree containing *actions* that are executed by an agent as leaf nodes, and *choice nodes* or *sequence nodes* as internal nodes. Choice nodes allow the choice between different courses of action whereas sequence nodes allow sequential execution of actions. Each BT is periodically activated by the control loop of its containing system (we say it is *ticked*) and returns a result indicating that its execution was either successful, that execution failed, or that it is still running and needs more time to continue. A choice node succeeds when any of its child nodes succeeds and fails when all of its child nodes have failed. A sequence node fails whenever one of its children fails and succeeds when all its children succeed. Both choice and sequence nodes return a status "running" whenever one of their children does.

BTs have originally been introduced as a mechanism for allowing designers to control the behavior of non-player characters in computer games, and many variants of BTs exist. Most of them extend the basic node types with nodes such as *decorators*, internal nodes having a single child and modifying the execution behavior of that child, e.g. by "negating" the result (from succeeded to failed and vice versa); all these extension (as well as the XBT extension proposed later) retain the tree structure of the BT. This tree structure is one of the main advantages BTs have over formalisms such as state machines when used inside learning mechanisms: Since behaviors are always represented by leaves of a subtree it is easy to identify, access or modify a behavior and it is straightforward to determine the conditions that have to be satisfied for a behavior to apply.

Figure 3 shows an BT for a simple rescue robot. The topmost node is a choice between four alternatives: The leftmost subtree checks whether the robot is in

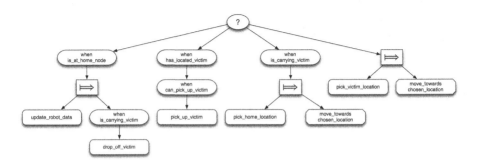

Fig. 3. BT for a rescue robot

one of its home locations. In that case, it executes its child node, a sequence node that first updates the robot's data and then drops off the victim. If this alternative fails, either because the robot is not in a home location or because it is not carrying a victim, the choice node proceeds to the second subtree, checks whether there is a victim in the current location and picks up the victim if possible. If this branch of the tree also fails and the robot is carrying a victim, it picks a home location and moves toward this location, otherwise it picks a new location where it expects to find a victim to rescue and moves toward that location.

Returning a result status of "running" is similar to yielding in a coroutine: execution of the currently running branch of the BT is suspended and control returns to the control loop; when the BT is ticked again, it will resume execution starting with the suspended node. The possibility to fail and continue with the next choice leads to a convenient handling of situations where the outcomes of actions are not certain. In the next section we will show how robots using the BT in Fig. 3 can cooperate to adapt to changes in the environment using teacher/student learning.

Despite their simplicity, BTs allow surprisingly complex behaviors to be specified, but they suffer from a number of well-known limitations, for example: (1) Every action performed by the BT is immediately executed so that possibilities for off-line planning are limited. (2) It is difficult to implement state-based behaviors using BTs, since the child nodes of each node have to be specified in the tree which leads to clumsy specifications if different states require different behaviors.

To address these issues we have proposed *Extended Behavior Trees (XBTs)* in [10]. XBTs extend behavior trees in several ways, among them:

- The nodes return an indicator about the reward they obtained to their parent in addition to the execution status.
- A state object is threaded through the activations of the nodes. All operations on the environment have to be mediated by the state, e.g. by being implemented as methods of the state object. States can be *virtualized* so that operations on the state simulate the expected behavior but do not change the real environment.
- There is a node type *external choice node* that is similar to choice nodes but calls a function to generate its child nodes whenever it is ticked and not already running.

These extensions of behavior trees allow the specification of, e.g. state-based behaviors, nodes that learn using reinforcement-learning techniques and nodes that perform offline-planning.

Figure 4 shows the movement XBT for a robot that autonomously learns the navigation decisions for unknown terrain. This navigation system uses a node (RL(Q)) that performs reinforcement learning using a so-called Q-function. Nodes that perform HTN-Planning can be integrated into the XBT in a similar manner.

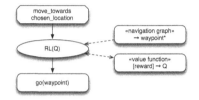

Fig. 4. Reinforcement-learning XBT node

While traditional behavior trees are sufficient for performing teacher/student learning, XBTs with integrated learning- and planning-based techniques simplify the application of several principles is [3] to a teacher/student system: Firstly, planning nodes perform goal-based reasoning, and reinforcement-learning nodes are based on utility maximization, therefore XBTs enable principle P1: Use probabilistic goal- and utility-based techniques on a per-agent basis. An important feature of integrating these techniques into XBTs is that the overall structure of each agent's behavior can be specified in the XBT and utility-based optimization can be applied to individual decisions inside the tree. This ameliorates one problem with utility-based specifications, namely that it is often difficult to find a utility function that corresponds to a complex task [26]. Obviously, the use of planning and learning inside an XBT is also an instance of principle P4: Perform reasoning, learning and planning.

Another interesting property of XBTs is that they are abstract enough to describe behaviors in the design loop, but low-level enough that they can be directly executed at runtime. In addition, the results of runtime HTN-planning and reinforcement learning can easily be fed back into the development loop: The result of HTN-planning can be expressed as an XBT, and the result of a reinforcement-learning node is a choice node with importance-weighted branches. Both items can directly be used and refined in further development iterations, thereby supporting P6: Enable evolutionary feedback.

4.3 Life-Cycle Integration in Continuous Collaboration

The teacher/student architecture defines a lightweight, extensible structure of the learning mechanisms inside the CAS that provides locally coordinated distributed learning at runtime. It also defines precise limits as to how adaptation may occur in the system.

However, the development of a CAS provides other feedback loops besides the runtime-learning loop, as can be seen from the ensemble development life-cycle (EDLC, see Fig. 5) proposed by the ASCENS project [11]. Besides the traditional design-time loop and the runtime loop addressed by teacher/student learning, the EDLC also features a so-called *evolutionary loop* that provides feedback between the design-time and runtime loops. To support the evolutionary loop it seems sensible to exploit the knowledge gained via online adaptation performed by the CAS to aid the development team.

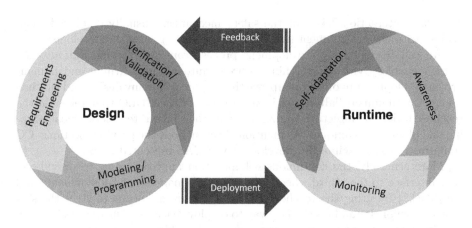

Fig. 5. The ensemble development life cycle (EDLC)

To evaluate the feedback from the runtime cycle, developers are often more concerned with the success of specific plans enacted by the CAS than with the success of specific agents. This is well supported by the teacher/student architecture, since the aggregation of agent success with the plans responsible for the student's behavior is already performed by the teachers. More specifically, the feedback provided by students to their teachers about their missions, as well as the trust values assigned to a teacher by its student body provide a rough but easy-to-analyze estimate of the success of the teacher's set of plans. If necessary, teachers can also perform a more sophisticated analysis of their students' experiences in the environment and thus provide better feedback to the design cycle regarding the system's more intricate dynamic behavior at runtime.

Looking at the second arrow of the evolutionary cycle, the teacher/student structure simplifies the deployment of a CAS or updates of it: Novel behaviors can be introduced into the CAS by deploying additional teachers. Initially, the programs proposed by these teachers will only be executed by a small number of students. However, if the teachers are successful, their solutions will spread and be adopted by more and more students in the CAS. Students executing XBTs provide a rich execution platform to which a teacher can either assign a large degree of autonomous decision making (by employing learning or planning nodes in the XBT passed to the student), or that the teacher can advise to execute a precisely specified task. Thus, there is no need to stop a system currently in operation, since new or modified behaviors can be introduced by adding or modifying teachers, and there is also no need to interfere with the distributed parts of the system's program since the students executing XBTs provide a flexible deployment target. This technique of deploying and modifying a system can be viewed as an instance of *guided self-organization* [2], as it allows developers to steer the system's behavior without executing external control but only by interaction with the system in the same way other system components would do. Another advantage of restricting the deployment of new features to these "standard interactions" is that the safety mechanisms usually employed when dealing with the environment also apply when dealing with the developer.

We call the resulting development process *continuous collaboration (CC)* since it enables dynamic switching between autonomous learning and human-driven development in order to improve the system over many design and runtime cycles. Continuous collaboration is an instance of the EDLC that relies on the teacher/student architecture and XBTs, with their integrated hierarchical learning and planning techniques. As mentioned throughout the previous sections, CC conforms to the principles for development of CAS presented in [3].

More generally, the continuous collaboration approach aims to provide an easy interface to the "third wheel" of the EDLC (made up of "deployment" and "feedback") by using the teacher/student structure as means to steer the system's behavior. It can be seen as a way to employ teachers as mediators between the development and runtime cycle, supported by high-level programming and modeling languages such as XBTs as a common vocabulary, in order to simplify the development of a CAS in which both machine learning and traditional software development techniques coexist.

5   Experiments

To demonstrate some of the issues discussed in the previous sections we give a short overview of some experimental results. The setting of these experiments is similar to the one presented in [9]. In the experiments a swarm of robots has to rescue victims in an environment that is represented as a graph with 100 nodes connected by (initially) 1004 randomly generated edges. Robots can perform the following actions:

1. navigate an edge to a neighboring node
2. pick up a victim (if no victim is present at the node this is a no-op but the robot incurs a penalty for performing the action), or
3. drop off a victim.

Edges have a weight that determines the cost for traversing that edge; when a robot drops off a victim at a designated home node it receives a reward. All robots use the XBT in Fig. 3 with state-dependent navigation.

Each experiment is divided into 100 episodes. At the start of the first episode all robots are located at the home node. They start executing their XBTs, therefore they obtain navigation instructions from a teacher and then start exploring the graph and rescuing victims. When a robot returns to the home node it provides a log of its actions and the obtained rewards to the teacher from which it obtained its plan; it can then request a new plan from the same or another teacher. In each episode each robot performs 250 ticks of its XBT. After each episode, each teacher can update its internal model of the world; the end of the episode has no effect on the robots (i.e., they stay where they are and start the next episode in the state in which they finished the previous one).

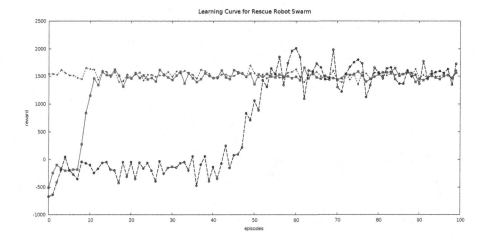

Fig. 6. Performance of the rescue robots over time, static case

To demonstrate the behavior for swarms with a single teacher we present the results of three experiments, each performed for three robot swarms.

Figure 6 shows the performance of three swarms in an unchanging environment. The swarm represented by blue dotted curve (starting at the top left corner of the diagram) contains 10 robots and a teacher with perfect information about the environment following an optimal policy, i.e., in the average case this represents the best possible performance in this environment. This teacher does not take into account information provided by the students and does not suggest exploratory moves to its students. The red, solid curve is another swarm with 10 robots. This swarm has a teacher that starts with erroneous information about the edges in the graph but learns from the experience provided by its students using a dynamic programming algorithm. We therefore call this teacher the DP-teacher. The black, dashed curve represents a single robot using the same initial graph and the same learning algorithm as the DP swarm, but this robot learns individually. To simplify the comparison with the other swarms, the y-coordinate of this curve is scaled by a factor of 10.

The imprecise initial model of the DP-teacher is reflected by the very poor performance of the swarm during the first episodes. Since the results reported by the students are significantly different from its estimates, the DP-teacher suggests the maximum exploration rate to its students, which causes the students to essentially perform random walks. However, as can be seen from Fig. 6, after only 8 episodes, the swarm of the DP-teacher rapidly approaches the optimal performance for this environment. The behavior of the single robot is similar, but since it can use data from only one robot it converges much more slowly to the optimal solution.

This first experiment shows that teacher/student learning can converge to the optimal solution in a static environment, and it also demonstrates the claim from Sect. 3.3 that a swarm that shares knowledge can learn more efficiently than

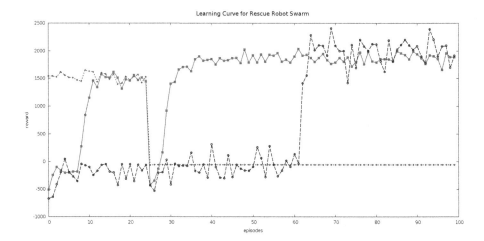

Fig. 7. Performance of the rescue robots over time, "catastrophic" change

individual learners: The teacher has more training data since it can exploit the results collected by multiple students; in addition the students do not explore regions of the map that other students have already explored.[2]

The more realistic and interesting case is the behavior of the system in dynamic environments. We simulate two different scenarios:

Figure 7 shows the same experiment as Fig. 6, but after 25 episodes a "catastrophic event" happens in the environment and the structure of the graph is changed significantly: 25 % of the existing edges are destroyed, 5 % of the previously unconnected nodes are connected, and the weights of the remaining edges are modified. As expected, the previously optimal teacher fares very badly in this situation since its map no longer reflects the reality of the new environment and it does not try to adjust the plans it teaches to its students to the new environment. The performance of the DP-teacher drops rapidly for a short period, but after about 5 episodes its performance recovers and it retains near-optimal performance thereafter. The single robot is still in the exploration phase and the immediate impact of the change in the environment is not directly visible in Fig. 7. However, convergence to the optimal solution happens later in

---

[2] The careful reader may observe that the single robot takes only approximately 6 times as long as the swarm to reach its maximal performance, not more than 10 times as might be expected. This is an artifact of our learning schedule which learns only at the end of each episode, so that the single agent performs many more iterations of the DP algorithm before it reaches its maximum performance than the DP-learner and thus better exploits the data it has available. This means that the single agent can focus a larger percentage of its exploration on promising parts of the graph, thereby negating the advantages that the swarm has over a single learner. However, a swarm of 10 single learners would use 10 times the computational resources of a swarm with a DP-learner, which would justify running the DP-learner 10 times as frequently with corresponding improvements to the swarm's performance.

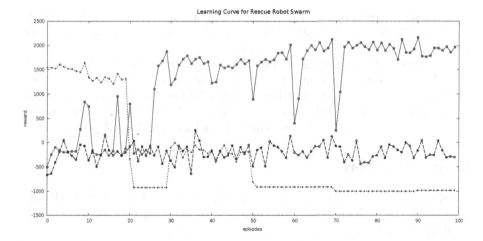

Fig. 8. Performance of the rescue robots over time, gradual change

this scenario than in the one without change in the environment, suggesting that the "catastrophe" also had an impact on the single learner.

The third experiment simulates an environment that degrades not in one catastrophic event but periodically; the results for this experiment are shown in Fig. 8: 15 % of the existing edges are destroyed, 2.5 % of the unconnected nodes are connected and the weight of the existing edges is modified every 10 episodes. As expected, the performance of the blue (non-learning) teacher decreases significantly as the graph starts to deviate from its map.[3] The performance of the DP-teacher decreases, sometimes significantly, at the beginning of each episode, but it recovers quickly and remains near the optimal result level most of the time. The single-agent learner demonstrates the phenomenon mentioned in Sect. 3.2: Its learning rate is too low to keep up with the environment. The ability of the teacher to update its information about the environment is lower than the rate of change, therefore the teacher never achieves a performance that deviates significantly from that of a random walk. Note that having multiple single-agent learners in the environment would not improve this situation: none of these learners would succeed in learning the structure of the environment quickly enough to keep up with changes.

If several teachers are teaching simultaneously, any memoryless evolutionary dynamics will keep the performance of the swarm between the values achieved by the best and the worst teacher, since the students incur no cost for switching between teachers. In the simple scenario used for the experiments in this section, the reward obtained by the swarm can be kept near the performance of the best teacher if every agent selects a teacher in proportion to the performance

---

[3] Between episodes 30 and 50 the random modifications result in a graph in which some of the routes computed by the non-learning teachers are viable, therefore the performance is slightly better than in the other episodes in which the graph is damaged.

differential between the teacher's last performance and the average last performance of all teachers. A detailed discussion of the replicator dynamics of this scenario is beyond the scope of this paper.

In summary, the principles presented in Sect. 3 can be shown experimentally to lead to a system architecture that can adapt to different kind of changes in its environment. By integrating the data gathered by multiple students the system can learn much more quickly than a single learner and operate in environments in which a swarm of single learners could not achieve the desired performance.

6   Related Work

Continuous collaboration is modeled on the structure of the EDLC [11] and tries to adhere to the practices introduced in [3]. Other papers focusing on the challenges of developing autonomic systems are [4,13].

Many languages for modeling and implementing behaviors exist, but none of them seems to be a perfect fit for the requirements of CAS: UML activity and state diagrams [16] are commonly used to describe the behavior of embedded systems, but they are not particularly well-suited for specifying goal-directed behaviors or integrating learning or planning mechanisms into a system. Programming languages extended with constructs for incorporating learning or planning, such as ALisp [1], are very flexible and expressive but it is often difficult to understand how planning, learning and adaptation integrate with the preprogrammed behavior, and the resulting programs are difficult to understand for non-programmers.

Behavior trees have been implemented in a number of game engines [15] and are increasingly used for applications in robotics and avionics [14,17].

Embodied evolution is defined in [25]. A more in-depth discussion as to why this approach is reasonable for scenarios like the "robot rescue force" is given in [12], including special characteristics of "embodied evolution" and possible pitfalls.

Many mechanisms for learning and adaptation have been proposed. In Sect. 3 we rely on the basics of statistical learning theory; this theory is discussed in more detail in [23,24]. XBTs can contain include planning and reinforcement learning nodes; [8] introduces automated planning techniques, [28] presents the state-of-the-art for reinforcement learning techniques. The books [19,26] contain further references to many techniques for multi-agent learning, planning and communication.

7   Conclusion and Future Work

We have motivated our teacher/student approach to learning by referring to results from statistical learning theory and evolutionary game theory. Together with XBTs for behavioral specification, teacher/student learning forms the basis for the continuous collaboration approach to CAS development. Experimental results show that the system achieves competitive performance even in static scenarios and excels in situation where frequent adaptation is necessary.

There are many interesting directions for future work. On the theoretical level, the connections to statistical learning theory, knowledge representation and evolutionary game theory that we have used to motivate the approach in Sect. 3 could be strengthened so that they can serve as formal foundations. Similarly, there are strong connections between CC and techniques such as distributed reinforcement learning, online planning and artificial evolution.

We have restricted the experiments in this paper to one a simple subproblem of the "robot rescue force" scenario that ignores many of the difficulties present in the interaction with a physical environment as well as problems such as allocation of scarce resources that arise when many agents are interacting. As next step we have implemented the more detailed simulation shown in Fig. 1. Using this more detailed simulation environment we plan to investigate how CC can be applied to the full robot rescue scenario, and in particular how the techniques presented in this paper can extend existing algorithms from probabilistic robotics, such as Simultaneous Localization and Mapping (SLAM) [22].

From a software engineering point of view, approaches like teacher/student learning, XBTs and continuous collaboration that are mostly focused on system architecture, behavioral specification and the feedback loops of the development process raise the question with which requirements, analysis and design methodologies they are compatible and how the ongoing integration of run time data and knowledge into the system influences the rest of the development process. Another important aspect is how verification and validation can be combined with continuous collaboration, and how constraints on the system's behavior can be guaranteed.

References

1. Andre, D.: Programmable reinforcement learning agents. Ph.D. thesis, University of California at Berkeley (2003)
2. Ay, N., Der, R., Prokopenko, M.: Guided self-organization: perception-action loops of embodied systems. Theory Biosci. **131**(3), 125–127 (2012)
3. Belzner, L., Hölzl, M., Koch, N., Wirsing, M.: Collective autonomic systems: towards engineering principles and their foundations, July 2016
4. Cheng, B., et al.: Software engineering for self-adaptive systems: a research roadmap. In: Cheng, B., de Lemos, R., Giese, H., Inverardi, P., Magee, J. (eds.) Software Engineering for Self-Adaptive Systems. LNCS, vol. 5525, pp. 1–26. Springer, Heidelberg (2009). doi:10.1007/978-3-642-02161-9_1
5. Claus, C., Boutilier, C.: The dynamics of reinforcement learning in cooperative multiagent systems. In: Proceedings of the 15th National/Tenth Conference on AI/Innovative Applications of AI, AAAI 1998/IAAI 1998, pp. 746–752. AAAI (1998)
6. Colombo, A., Fontanelli, D., Legay, A., Palopoli, L., Sedwards, S.: Efficient customisable dynamic motion planning for assistive robots in complex human environments. J. Ambient Intell. Smart Environ. **7**(5), 617–634 (2015)
7. Fagin, R., Moses, Y., Vardi, M., Halpern, J.: Reasoning About Knowledge. MIT Press, Cambridge (2003)

8. Ghallab, M., Nau, D.S., Traverso, P.: Automated Planning - Theory and Practice. Elsevier, Amsterdam (2004)
9. Hölzl, M., Gabor, T.: Continuous collaboration: a case study on the development of an adaptive cyber-physical system. In: Proceedings of the 1st International Workshop on Software Engineering for Smart Cyber-Physical Systems (SEsCPS). IEEE (2015)
10. Hölzl, M., Gabor, T.: Reasoning and learning for awareness and adaptation. In: Wirsing et al. [29]
11. Hölzl, M., Koch, N., Puviani, M., Wirsing, M., Zambonelli, F.: The ensemble development life cycle and best practices for collective autonomic systems. In: Wirsing et al. [29]
12. Karafotias, G., Haasdijk, E., Eiben, A.E.: An algorithm for distributed on-line, on-board evolutionary robotics. In: Proceedings of the 13th Annual Conference on Genetic and Evolutionary Computation, GECCO 2011, pp. 171–178. ACM, New York (2011)
13. Kephart, J.O., Chess, D.M.: The vision of autonomic computing. Computer **36**(1), 41–50 (2003)
14. Marzinotto, A., Colledanchise, M., Smith, C., Ögren, P.: Towards a unified behavior trees framework for robot control. In: 2014 IEEE International Conference on Robotics and Automation, ICRA 2014, Hong Kong, pp. 5420–5427. IEEE (2014)
15. Millington, I., Funge, J.: Artificial Intelligence for Games, 2nd edn. Morgan Kaufmann, San Francisco (2009)
16. Object Management Group: UML Specifications. http://www.omg.org/spec/. Accessed 26 Feb 2015
17. Ogren, P.: Increasing modularity of UAV control systems using computer game behavior trees. In: AIAA Guidance, Navigation and Control Conference, Minneapolis, Minnesota, pp. 13–16 (2012)
18. Shalev-Shwartz, S., Ben-David, S.: Understanding Machine Learning: From Theory to Algorithms. Cambridge University Press, New York (2014)
19. Shoham, Y., Leyton-Brown, K.: Multiagent Systems: Algorithmic, Game-Theoretic, and Logical Foundations. Cambridge University Press, New York (2008)
20. Sigmund, K.: A survey of replicator equations. In: Casti, J.L., Karlqvist, A. (eds.) Complexity, Language, and Life: Mathematical Approaches. Biomathematics, vol. 16, pp. 88–104. Springer, Heidelberg (1986)
21. Sutton, R.S., Barto, A.G.: Reinforcement Learning. MIT Press, Cambridge (1998)
22. Thrun, S., Burgard, W., Fox, D.: Probabilistic Robotics. MIT Press, Cambridge (2005)
23. Vapnik, V.: The Nature of Statistical Learning Theory. Information Science and Statistics. Springer, New York (2013)
24. Vapnik, V.N.: Statistical Learning Theory. Wiley-Interscience, New York (1998)
25. Watson, R.A., Ficici, S.G., Pollack, J.B.: Embodied evolution: distributing an evolutionary algorithm in a population of robots. Robot. Auton. Syst. **39**(1), 1–18 (2002)
26. Weiss, G. (ed.): Multiagent Systems, 2nd edn. MIT Press, Cambridge (2013)
27. Wiegand, R.P.: An analysis of cooperative coevolutionary algorithms. Ph.D. thesis, George Mason University (2003)
28. Wiering, M., van Otterlo, M.: Reinforcement Learning: State-of-the-Art. Adaptation, Learning, and Optimization, vol. 12. Springer, Heidelberg (2012)
29. Wirsing, M., Hölzl, M., Koch, N., Mayer, P. (eds.): Software Engineering for Collective Autonomic Systems: Results of the ASCENS Project. LNCS, vol. 8998. Springer, Heidelberg (2015)

Issues on Software Quality Models for Mastering Change

Michael Felderer[✉]

University of Innsbruck, Innsbruck, Austria
michael.felderer@uibk.ac.at

Abstract. A promising cornerstone to master change and to continuously control software quality in the context of todays dynamically evolving complex software systems are software quality models. These models provide an abstract and analyzable view of software artifacts with the objective to describe, assess and/or predict quality. Although software quality models have a high potential to improve effectiveness and efficiency of quality assurance to cope with software change, their acceptance and spread in the software industry is still rather low, as there are several unresolved issues that have to be addressed by upcoming research. This article discusses and exemplifies unresolved key issues on descriptive, generating and predictive software quality models with regard to the (1) creation and maintenance of models, (2) support for extra-functional aspects, (3) traceability between quality models and unstructured artifacts, (4) integration of software analytics and runtime information, (5) balance between quality and risk, (6) process integration, as well as (7) justification by empirical evidence, and relates these issues to challenges of mastering change in terms of the manifesto of the LNCS Transactions on Foundations for Mastering Change.

Keywords: Model-based software engineering · Software quality models · Software quality engineering · Software product quality · Software quality · Software evolution

1 Introduction

Quality of software and software-based systems, i.e., the degree to which it satisfies the stated and implied needs of its various stakeholders, is playing an increasingly important role for the success of products [1]. As requirements to products inevitably change over time, for instance, new or adapted functionalities, technologies or regulations have to be taken into account, also software has to change or its quality decays. As software also becomes more complex and interconnected, mastering software quality for changing software products is challenging, and proactive measures are needed to counter quality decay during software evolution. A promising cornerstone to continuously control quality in this dynamic and evolving context are *software quality models* which provide an abstract and analyzable view of software artifacts with the objective to describe,

© Springer International Publishing AG 2016
B. Steffen (Ed.): Transactions on FoMaC I, LNCS 9960, pp. 225–241, 2016.
DOI: 10.1007/978-3-319-46508-1_12

assess and/or predict quality [2,3]. Quality models in this broad sense comprise all types of models supporting analytical software quality assurance and can be descriptive, generating, or predictive software quality models.

Descriptive software quality models define quality factors and optionally also metrics to assess them. Examples for descriptive software quality models are hierarchical software product quality models like ISO/IEC 25010 [4] or Quamoco [5] defining a hierarchy of quality characteristics and metrics to assess them. *Generating software quality models* are used to derive software quality assurance artifacts. Examples for generating software quality models are test models defined in languages like the UML Testing Profile [6] or Telling TestStories [7] which allow the generation of software quality artifacts like test cases. Finally, *predictive software quality models* use statistical models to predict outcomes like number of defects [8] or reliability [9].

Our view on software quality models comprises and integrates modeling concepts from software quality engineering [3,10], model-driven software engineering [11,12], as well as from software analytics [13,14]. However, note that our focus is on models supporting analytical quality assurance and not on constructive quality assurance. From model-driven software engineering, we therefore consider models supporting model-based testing [15], but not models solely used to generate production code. Furthermore, note that a software quality model can be at the same time descriptive, generating and predictive. In general, combinations of different types of software quality models are called *multi-purpose software quality models*.

Quality models have a high potential to improve effectiveness and efficiency of quality assurance to cope with software change, as they support decisions, automation, adaptation and re-use. Nevertheless, their acceptance and spread in the software industry is still rather low, as there are several open issues to be addressed by actual and upcoming research. Especially, the following issues with regard to software quality models for mastering change, which have so far only partially been addressed, require suitable solutions:

– Creation and maintenance of models
– Traceability between quality models and unstructured artifacts
– Support for extra-functional aspects
– Integration of software analytics and runtime information
– Balance between quality and risk
– Process integration
– Justification by empirical evidence

In Sect. 3 of this article, we discuss each of these issues, provide an overview of the available literature based on current literature reviews and present promising approaches addressing the issues. As a basis for this endeavor, in Sect. 2 we provide background on software quality models. Finally, in Sect. 4 we conclude this article and relate it to the vision raised in the manifesto of the LNCS Transactions on Foundations for Mastering Change (FoMaC) [16]. This article significantly extends a preliminary collection of current issues on software quality models for mastering change [17] and also differs by providing a detailed overview of descriptive, generating, and predictive software quality models.

2   Software Quality Models

Software quality models provide an abstract and analyzable view of software artifacts with the objective to describe, assess and/or predict quality [2,3]. Regarding its purpose, we distinguish between descriptive, generating, and predictive software quality models. Differing from other classifications using the term software quality models [3], we also take generating software quality models into account, which generate software quality artifacts to describe, assess or predict software quality. In the following sections, these three model types are discussed in more detail.

2.1   Descriptive Software Quality Models

Descriptive software quality models define quality factors and optionally also metrics to assess them. These models are used to describe software quality requirements and serve as a basis for software design and implementation. They provide direct recommendations on system implementation and maintenance, and means to measure the degree of compliance. Following the Factor-Criteria-Metrics approach of McCall et al. [18], most descriptive software quality models like ISO/IEC 25010 [4] or Quamoco [5] are hierarchical. The main modeling concept is to provide a taxonomy that breaks the concept of software product quality into smaller, hopefully more manageable parts. The idea is that the decomposition reaches a level on which one can measure the parts and use that to evaluate the software product's quality [3].

The most prominent hierarchical descriptive software quality model is ISO/IEC 25010 [4] released in 2011. Its hierarchical structure divides quality into characteristics, which can consist of subcharacteristics and, in turn, of sub-subcharachteristics. All these quality factors might be measurable by metrics. If a direct measurement is not possible, we use measurable quality properties that cover the quality factor. ISO/IEC 25010 contains a product quality model and a quality in use model.

The product quality model comprises eight characteristics each with subcharacteristics comprehensively describing the quality of a software product. The product quality model of ISO/IEC 25010 is shown in Fig. 1. Its quality characteristics are functional suitability, reliability, performance efficiency, usability, maintainability, security, compatibility, and portability. The product quality model of ISO/IEC 25010 explicitly considers maintainability with its subcharacteristics modularity, reusability, analysability, modifiability, as well as testability. The description of the quality model structure explicitly mentions the connection to measures. Hence, it is considered important to assess quality by being able to quantify quality and its characteristics. The details of this are not part of the quality model. However, specifications like the CISQ Specifications for

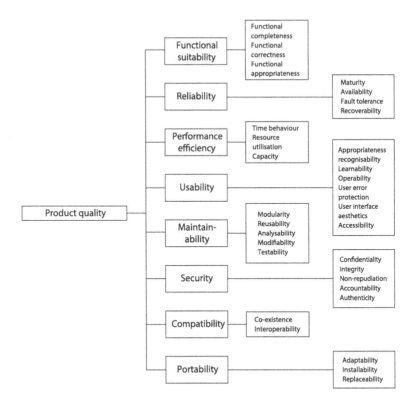

Fig. 1. Product quality model of ISO/IEC 25010 [4]

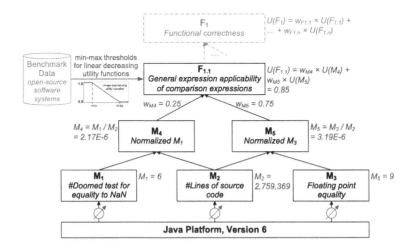

Fig. 2. Quamoco measurement example [5]

Automated Quality Characteristic Measures [19] provide concrete metrics for quality characteristics including maintainability which is especially important to master change. Metrics are often measured by static analysis tools [3], which monitor and control metrics over time. Figure 2 shows an example measurement in the descriptive software quality model Quamoco [5].

The quality in use model of ISO/IEC 25010 looks at characteristics of the interactions of different stakeholders like the primary user with the product. The characteristics of the quality in use model are satisfaction, effectiveness, freedom from risk, efficiency, as well as context coverage.

2.2 Generating Software Quality Models

Generating software quality models are used to derive software quality assurance artifacts. A prominent example of such an artifact type are test cases derived from models in model-based testing. Pretschner and Phillips [20] distinguish four scenarios with regard to code and test case generation from models, i.e., (1) a common model is used for both code and test case generation, (2) automatic model extraction from a system specification or from code and subsequent test case generation, (3) manually building the model for test case generation, and (4) two reduntant and distinct models, one for code generation and one for test case generation. Deriving software quality assurance artifacts in this broad sense comprises, for instance, also verifying the correctness of formal specification. For the prominent artifact type test cases, test models are the type of generating software quality model applied to derive them. The derivation of test cases from test models is called model-based testing (MBT). In model-based testing, manually selected algorithms automatically and systematically generate test cases from a set of models of the system under test or its environment [15]. Advantages of model-based testing are that it allows (1) early and explicit specification, modeling, and review of system behavior, (2) better documentation and transparency of test cases, (3) the ability to automatically generate useful tests and measure and optimize test coverage, and (4) higher test quality through model-based quality analysis. In addition, model-based testing is highly beneficial for mastering change, mainly for two main reasons. First, it improves the evaluation and selection of regression test suites. Second, it facilitates test case maintenance [21] for changed requirements and designs. Today, many model-based testing approaches are available [22], which can be classified according to the taxonomy for model-based testing of Utting et al. [23] shown in Fig. 3.

In this taxonomy, three general activities are defined, which together constitute model-based testing: model specification, test generation, and test execution. Each of the activities is determined by parameters. Model specification is determined by scope, characteristics, and paradigm. Test generation is determined by test selection criteria and technology. Finally, test execution can be performed online or offline. In [24], the taxonomy has been further refined to model-based security testing by adding filter criteria (i.e., model of system security, security model of the environment, and explicit test selection criteria) as

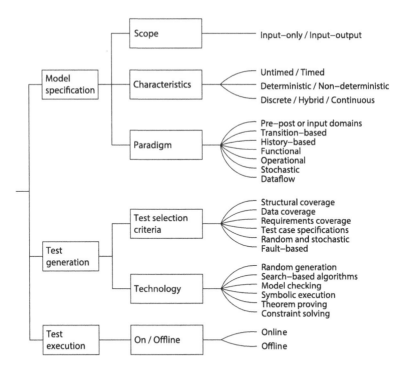

Fig. 3. Overview of the MBT Taxonomy of Utting et al. [23]

well as evidence criteria (i.e., maturity of evaluated system, evidence measures, and evidence level).

Languages for model-based testing, which take model specification, test generation as well as test execution aspects as defined in the taxonomy of Fig. 3 into account are often based on meta models, which define modeling language concepts as well as their constraints and relationships. Model transformations are then often used to generate test cases. Prominent test modeling languages with an underlying meta model are the UML Testing Profile [6] and Telling TestStories [7]. Both languages rely on test case specifications as a test selection criterion and have successfully been applied for regression testing taking test maintenance aspects into account [25,26]. Figure 4 shows an example test case modelled with the UML Testing Profile.

2.3 Predictive Software Quality Models

Predictive software quality models have — amongst others — been applied to predict the number of defects of a system or specific modules, mean time between failures, repair times and maintenance efforts [3]. As these models have to take uncertainty into account they are typically statistical models. A prominent example for such models are reliability growth models [9], which observe failure behavior of a software, for instance, during system testing, and predict

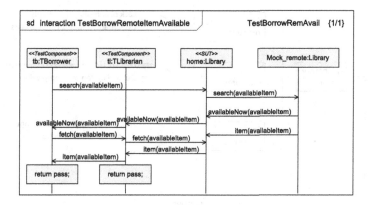

Fig. 4. Example test case in the UML Testing Profile [6]

how this behavior will change over time. Similar models are the maintainability index [27], a predictive model based on regression from code metrics.

Predictive software quality models require a decision on a suitable statistical model and underlying metrics that adequately represents the actual data. It is therefore essential to compare the performance of different predictive models, for instance, in terms of confusion matrices or via the receiver operating characteristics. For defect prediction models, a systematic comparison of model types as well as their underlying metrics and performance assessment is provided by Arisholm et al. [28]. Figure 5 provides an overview of the resulting types of predictive models for defect prediction taken into account in the study by Arisholm et al. [28].

The taxonomy takes explanatory variables, the classifier type, and the evaluation criteria into account. Explanatory variables are input variables for classification and categorized into code measures like cyclomatic complexity, delta measures like delta of cyclomatic complexity, as well as process measures like the number of fault corrections. The classifier is of type logistic regression, neural network, decision tree, coverage rule, or support vector machine. Finally, the evaluation is performed via a confusion matrix (and measures like recall and precision related to it), the receiver operating characteristic or cost-effectiveness.

As an example for a predictive model, Fig. 6 shows a simple Bayesian network for value estimation. There are two arrows pointing from the customer-related factors (parent nodes) towards the Overall Value factor (child node). Every arrow in a Bayesian network represents a cause and effect relationship between the factor that is the arrows origin (parent node) and the one that is the arrows destination (child node), respectively. This means is that any type of impact relating to the value factors Customer Retention and Customer Satisfaction will have an effect upon Overall Value. Further, every node in a Bayesian network has an associated table that quantifies probabilistically numerous decision making scenarios based its causes modeled in the parent nodes.

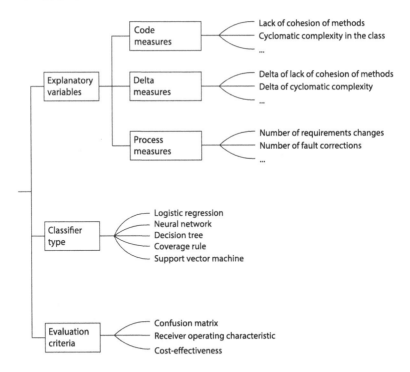

Fig. 5. Types of defect prediction models based on Arisholm et al. [28]

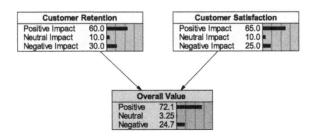

Fig. 6. Bayesian network for value estimation

Predictive models are often defined on top of descriptive models which define the quality characteristics and metrics the prediction is based on. For instance, the constructive quality model of Kitchenham [29] combines a descriptive and a predictive software quality model.

3   Discussion of Current Issues

In this section, we discuss the following current issues on software quality models mentioned before: creation and maintenance of models (Sect. 3.1), traceability

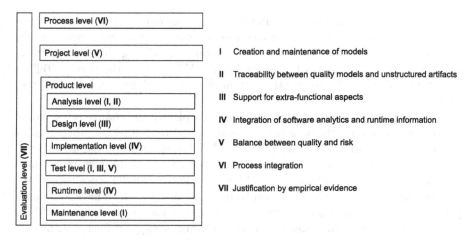

Fig. 7. Assignment of software product, project, process and evaluation levels to current issues on software quality models addressed in this article

between quality models and unstructured artifacts (Sect. 3.2), support for extra-functional aspects (Sect. 3.3), integration of software analytics and runtime information (Sect. 3.4), balance between quality and risk (Sect. 3.5), process integration (Sect. 3.6), and justification by empirical evidence (Sect. 3.7). Figure 7 links the issues to the product, project, process and evaluation level of software development. Starting from the *product level* (which comprises the phases of software product development, i.e., analysis, design, implementation, test, runtime and maintenance levels), over the *project* and *process level*, to the *evaluation level* (which addresses all other levels), the issues are assigned to the levels they primarily address.

All issues highlighted in this section are relevant for each of the three types of software quality models as well as their integration to multi-purpose software quality models. For each issue discussed in the following sections, we provide a short explanation and an overview of the available literature for specific aspects of each issue based on published current reviews as well as a discussion of selected promising approaches already addressing it.

3.1   Creation and Maintenance of Models

One main obstacle to dissemination of model-based approaches in general, is the overhead to initially create and to continuously maintain models. To lower this barrier, support to either automatize model creation and maintenance or to clearly simplify these tasks is required. Former can, for instance, be supported by machine learning technologies and formal methods. A promising approach in this direction is Active Continuous Quality Control [30], where incremental active automata learning technology is applied to infer evolving behavioral automata. Latter, can be supported by modern modeling workbenches for domain specific languages [31] which provide powerful model engineering support to simplify manual model creation and maintenance. Domain specific languages are specialized to specific domains. In the domain of software quality assurance, domain specific languages are commonly used as generating modeling languages for testing like in the graphical UML Testing Profile (UTP) [6] or the textual Telling TestStories [7] which have recently been applied for modeling and deriving test artifacts.

To maintain models in context of growing complexity and change rates, model repositories have recently been investigated. Model repositories enable collaborative modeling and let team members check out, commit, and update software models [32]. Di Rocco et al. [32] provide an overview of the 14 most representative model repository technologies and their challenges. Model repositories have to overcome several technical and non-technical challenges which have so far only partially been solved. Technical challenges are the management of different kinds of modeling artifacts, advanced querying mechanisms, support for modeling as a service, extension mechanisms, as well as federation of model repositories. Non-technical challenges are incentives to share modeling artifacts, licensing related to shared artifacts, as well as guidelines to manage the sharing of artifacts and to control their quality.

3.2 Traceability Between Quality Models and Unstructured Artifacts

In an industrial setting, software quality models never capture relevant quality information completely, but have to be aligned with material (usually documents) of an unstructured nature (usually text) like requirements specifications or test reports to gain full traceability. Traceability is the ability to follow the life of software artifacts [33] and therefore essential for mastering change in software and its environment. Especially traceability between requirements and other development artifacts can support impact analysis, lower testing and maintenance costs, and increase test coverage and thereby quality in the final product [34]. Essential to benefit from these advantages, but also challenging [34] is tracing between requirements and test cases, which can be performed via software quality models, for instance in the context of model-based testing. A promising approach to detect and maintain links between requirements and test (models) is information retrieval [35]. Information retrieval approaches are generally based on chunks of natural language text and usually do not rely on any structural properties of the input. In a nutshell, information retrieval returns a set of matching documents from a set of documents (called a corpus) for a given query. Borg et al. [36] provide a systematic map of 79 selected publications on information retrieval approaches to software traceability. Most of the approaches focus on traces between requirements, or between requirements and source code. But approaches linking requirements and test models are rare and require further investigation to continuously check their quality.

3.3   Support for Extra-Functional Aspects

Extra-functional aspects like security (which may today also trigger safety issues), performance, or sustainability [37] require specific modeling approaches to cope with change. So far, this problem has not adequately been tackled for all types of quality models. For instance, further research on model-based (regression) testing of extra-functional aspects is required [38].

For security regression testing, i.e., re-testing of security properties to ensure that changes made to software do not harm its security properties, Felderer and Fourneret [39] provide a mapping study of available approaches. The authors extract 17 security regression testing approaches including nine model-based approaches and eight code-based. Model-based regression testing analyses changes at the level of formal representation of a software or its environment, for instance, represented as diagrams in the Unified Modeling Language (UML). Models for security regression testing are generating software quality models used for test case generation. As model-based approaches to regression testing have several advantages (for instance, they allow the early design and analysis of tests, automatic re-generation of test cases as well as the suitable management of complexity, scale and change of systems), more approaches are required to cope with changes in security properties. Most available approaches address security mechanisms (e.g., [40]) or security requirements (e.g., [25]), but suitable model-based security regression testing approaches for vulnerabilities are still rare.

3.4   Integration of Software Analytics and Runtime Information

Software quality models are often applied in a static manner taking historical and recent data into account, but do not efficiently and effectively benefit from runtime data which is essential to cope with dynamic aspects of ever-changing software and its environment. For this purpose, runtime data requires analytical support provided by software analytics, i.e., the use of analysis, software data, and systematic reasoning for managers and software engineers with the aim of empowering stakeholders of software development to make better decisions [13]. It is an area of explosive growth and especially for software quality purposes analytics is promising to evaluate the current quality status, to predict future statuses, and to continuously monitor quality. Analytics normally combines some degree of automation with human involvement. The integration of analytics with available software quality models, so mainly descriptive and predictive ones, could foster this combination and lead to new visualization and interpretation of software engineering data to control quality of evolving software.

For generating models, Szvetits and Zdun [41] performed a systematic literature review of models at runtime. The authors identified different objectives (i.e., adaptation, abstraction, consistency, conformance, error handling, monitoring, simulation, prediction, platform independence, and policy checking/enforcement), techniques (i.e., introspection, model conformance, model comparison, model transformation, and model execution), and architectures (i.e., monolithic, local dataflow, middleware, and repository architectures) for runtime processing of models. The authors point out that monitoring, adaptation and synchronization mechanisms are already quite mature, but that especially support for testing systems using models at runtime are needed. The reason for this is that the vast amount of models combined with different architectures and techniques lead to a high number of test cases which have to be executed to reduce the possibility of runtime errors in such highly dynamic environments.

3.5 Balance Between Quality and Risk

The quality of software or software-based system is the degree to which the system satisfies the stated and implied needs of its various stakeholders, and thus provides value [4]. In contrast to quality, risk is the degree to which a product does not satisfy the stated and implied needs of its various stakeholders and thus represents potential damages and losses [42]. The concept of risk supports decisions on good enough quality for software release or changes and relates quality investments to budget and time. It is therefore important to also consider the concept or risk in software quality models and to use these models to perform quality assurance and to reduce risk.

Especially for software testing, which always been one of the most widely practiced techniques of software quality assurance in industry [39,43,44], risk-based approaches are available and have recently gained considerable interest in research [45–47]. Erdogan et al. [48] provide a systematic literature review on the combined use of risk analysis and testing. The authors distinguish between test-based risk analysis (i.e., risk analysis that makes use of testing to identify potential risks or validate risk analysis results) and risk-based testing (i.e., testing that makes use of risk analysis). Overall, Erdogan et al. systematically collected 24 approaches (i.e., two test-based risk analysis approaches and 22 risk-based testing approaches). The collection comprises risk-based testing approaches based mainly on descriptive software quality models (e.g., Felderer et al. [49]) and generating software quality models (e.g., Stallbaum et al. [50]). Although many predictive software quality models for defects [8] are available, predictive models to risk-based testing are still rare and require further investigation [51]. For instance, Adorf et al. [52] provide a promising approach adopting the Bayes risk criterion to select test cases.

3.6 Process Integration

Software quality models can work as a project- or company-wide quality knowledge base. This requires integration into the overall development process taking the relationship to artifacts, activities and the involved roles into account.

A key aspect of process integration is automation, which comprises automated generation of artifacts and continuous efficient execution of automated and semi-automated activities to support roles within software quality management. Automation is a cornerstone of the continuous quality management of evolutionary and adaptive IT systems. Models play a major role within automation because they can help represent systems at different levels of abstraction, and scale serving as a basis for automation. In this way, models enable business-oriented systems representation, the management of varying service technologies, or specification across system and platform boundaries at a uniform level of abstraction [53]. Especially, generating software quality models producing executable artifacts like test cases have attained an attractive level of productivity in recent years [22]. But, especially for semi-automated decision support with regard to software quality models further support is needed.

For instance, with regard to release decisions, Svahnberg et al. [54] provide a systematic literature review on strategic release planning models, i.e., models to select an optimum set of features or requirements to deliver in a release within given constraints. The authors collected 28 strategic release planning models, only two of them take quality aspects into account [55,56]. Recently, quality-driven release planning has successfully been applied in industry [57], and there is a high demand for more approaches integrating (predictive) software quality models into release planning and software development in general.

3.7 Justification by Empirical Evidence

For industrial application, evidence following the strict guidelines of empirical software engineering [58] has to be provided to show in which context specific model-based quality assurance approaches actually provide support to master change, and what the practical limitations of these approaches are. Empirical (research) studies are important in order to get objective and quantifiable information on the impact of changes. The observation of human behavior and their interactions with technology in the real world (industry) cannot sufficiently be investigated by an analytical research paradigm [59]. Therefore, the importance of empirical studies in software engineering and their contribution to knowledge is continuously growing, but still underrepresented in computer science research [60,61]. Empirical studies can also be part of a knowledge exchange and improvement endeavor jointly between academia and industry [58]. From software engineering, research on industrially relevant problems is expected [58]. Thus, it is preferably conducted jointly by academia and industry to enable transfer of knowledge in both directions and to improve industrial software development and quality engineering based on concrete empirical evidence. As for the whole field of software engineering in general, also empirical studies on model-based quality assurance and especially also on software quality models are still rare. An exemplary empirical investigation for hierarchical quality models is provided in [5], for generating test models in [62], and for predictive models in [63]. Especially for effectiveness (i.e., the capability of producing a desired result) and efficiency (i.e., the capability to produce the intended outcome, relative to the amount of resources used) of software quality models in context of modern dynamic and evolving software-based systems, further empirical studies are needed.

4   Conclusion

Software quality models which provide an abstract and analyzable view of software artifacts with the objective to describe, assess and/or predict quality are a promising cornerstone to continuously control quality in the dynamic and evolving context of modern software-based system. In this article, we addressed the following current issues on descriptive, generating and predictive software quality models for mastering change: creation and maintenance of models, traceability between quality models and unstructured artifacts, support for extra-functional aspects, integration of software analytics and runtime information, balance between quality and risk, process integration, and justification by empirical evidence.

Suitable solutions to the issues mentioned before will heavily improve model-based quality assurance of software and contribute to mastering change in terms of the manifesto of the LNCS Transactions on Foundations for Mastering Change (FoMaC) [16]. FoMaC is concerned with mastering change during the whole system lifecycle at various conceptual levels, in particular during meta modeling, modeling and design, implementation, runtime, as well as maintenance, evolution and migration. Solutions to the issues raised in this article support mastering change in all these areas. For instance, the creation and maintenance of software quality models as well as their traceability to textual requirements address change aspects during meta modeling, modeling and design, but also during implementation; support for extra-functional aspects and analytics as well as balance between quality and risk promote change aspects at runtime as well as during maintenance, evolution and migration. Process integration addresses automation at all levels. Finally, the justification by empirical evidence is a cross-cutting issue to evaluate technology transfer in any of these areas.

References

1. Breu, R., Kuntzmann-Combelles, A., Felderer, M.: New perspectives on software quality. IEEE Softw. **31**(1), 32–38 (2014)
2. Breu, R., Agreiter, B., Farwick, M., Felderer, M., Hafner, M., Innerhofer-Oberperfler, F.: Living models-ten principles for change-driven software engineering. Int. J. Softw. Inform. **5**(1–2), 267–290 (2011)
3. Wagner, S.: Software Product Quality Control. Springer, New York (2014)
4. ISO/IEC 25010: 2011 Systems and software engineering - Systems and software Quality Requirements and Evaluation (SQuaRE) - System and software quality models (2011)
5. Wagner, S., Goeb, A., Heinemann, L., Kläs, M., Lampasona, C., Lochmann, K., Mayr, A., Plösch, R., Seidl, A., Streit, J., et al.: Operationalised product quality models and assessment: The Quamoco approach. Inf. Softw. Technol. **62**, 101–123 (2015)
6. Baker, P., Dai, Z.R., Grabowski, J., Haugen, Ø., Schieferdecker, I., Williams, C.: Model-Driven Testing. Springer, New York (2008)
7. Felderer, M., Chimiak-Opoka, J., Zech, P., Haisjackl, C., Fiedler, F., Breu, R.: Model validation in a tool-based methodology for system testing of service-oriented systems. Int. J. Adv. Softw. **4**(1–2), 129–143 (2011)

8. Catal, C.: Software fault prediction: a literature review and current trends. Expert Syst. Appl. **38**(4), 4626–4636 (2011)
9. Goel, A.L.: Software reliability models: assumptions, limitations, and applicability. IEEE Trans. Softw. Eng. **12**, 1411–1423 (1985)
10. Kan, S.H.: Metrics and Models in Software Quality Engineering. Addison-Wesley Longman Publishing Co., Inc., Reading (2002)
11. Völter, M., Stahl, T., Bettin, J., Haase, A., Helsen, S.: Model-Driven Software Development: Technology, Engineering, Management. Wiley, New York (2013)
12. Steffen, B., Margaria, T., Nagel, R., Jörges, S., Kubczak, C.: Model-driven development with the jABC. In: Bin, E., Ziv, A., Ur, S. (eds.) HVC 2006. LNCS, vol. 4383, pp. 92–108. Springer, Heidelberg (2007). doi:10.1007/978-3-540-70889-6_7
13. Menzies, T., Zimmermann, T.: Software analytics: so what? IEEE Softw. **30**(4), 31–37 (2013)
14. Bird, C., Menzies, T., Zimmermann, T.: The Art and Science of Analyzing Software Data. Elsevier, Amsterdam (2015)
15. Schieferdecker, I.: Model-based testing. IEEE Softw. **29**(1), 14–18 (2012)
16. Steffen, B.: LNCS transactions on foundations for mastering change: preliminary manifesto. In: Margaria, T., Steffen, B. (eds.) ISoLA 2014, Part I. LNCS, vol. 8802, pp. 514–517. Springer, Heidelberg (2014)
17. Felderer, M.: Current issues on model-based software quality assurance for mastering change. In: ISoLA 2014, Part I. LNCS, vol. 8802 pp. 521–523. Springer, Heidelberg (2014)
18. McCall, J.,P.K., R., G.F., W.: Factors in software quality. Technical report, NTIS, vols. 1, 2 and 3 (1997)
19. CISQ: CISQ Specifications for Automated Quality Characteristic Measures. Technical report, Consortium for IT Software Quality (2012). http://it-cisq.org/wp-content/uploads/2012/09/CISQ-Specification-for-Automated-Quality-Characteristic-Measures.pdf. Accessed 12 June 2015
20. Pretschner, A., Philipps, J.: 10 methodological issues in model-based testing. In: Broy, M., Jonsson, B., Katoen, J.-P., Leucker, M., Pretschner, A. (eds.) Model-Based Testing of Reactive Systems. LNCS, vol. 3472, pp. 281–291. Springer, Heidelberg (2005). doi:10.1007/11498490_13
21. Garousi, V., Felderer, M.: Developing, verifying, and maintaining high-quality automated test scripts. IEEE Softw. **33**(3), 68–75 (2016)
22. Dias-Neto, A.C., Travassos, G.H.: A picture from the model-based testing area: concepts, techniques, and challenges. Adv. Comput. **80**, 45–120 (2010)
23. Utting, M., Pretschner, A., Legeard, B.: A taxonomy of model-based testing approaches. Softw. Test. Verif. Reliab. **22**(2), 297–312 (2012)
24. Felderer, M., Zech, P., Breu, R., Büchler, M., Pretschner, A.: Model-based security testing: a taxonomy and systematic classification. Softw. Test. Verif. Reliab. **26**(2), 119–148 (2016)
25. Felderer, M., Agreiter, B., Breu, R.: Evolution of security requirements tests for service–centric systems. In: Erlingsson, Ú., Wieringa, R., Zannone, N. (eds.) ESSoS 2011. LNCS, vol. 6542, pp. 181–194. Springer, Heidelberg (2011). doi:10.1007/978-3-642-19125-1_14
26. Zech, P., Felderer, M., Kalb, P., Breu, R.: A generic platform for model-based regression testing. In: Margaria, T., Steffen, B. (eds.) ISoLA 2012. LNCS, vol. 7609, pp. 112–126. Springer, Heidelberg (2012). doi:10.1007/978-3-642-34026-0_9
27. Coleman, D., Lowther, B., Oman, P.: The application of software maintainability models in industrial software systems. J. Syst. Softw. **29**(1), 3–16 (1995)

28. Arisholm, E., Briand, L.C., Johannessen, E.B.: A systematic and comprehensive investigation of methods to build and evaluate fault prediction models. J. Syst. Softw. **83**(1), 2–17 (2010)
29. Kitchenham, B.: Towards a constructive quality model. Part 1: software quality modeling, measurement and prediction. Softw. Eng. J. **2**(4), 105–113 (1987)
30. Windmüller, S., Neubauer, J., Steffen, B., Howar, F., Bauer, O.: Active continuous quality control. In: Proceedings of the 16th International ACM Sigsoft Symposium on Component-Based Software Engineering, pp. 111–120. ACM (2013)
31. Völter, M., Benz, S., Dietrich, C., Engelmann, B., Helander, M., Kats, L.C., Visser, E., Wachsmuth, G.: DSL Engineering - Designing, Implementing and Using Domain-Specific Languages (2013). http://dslbook.org
32. Di Rocco, J., Di Ruscio, D., Iovino, L., Pierantonio, A.: Collaborative repositories in model-driven engineering [software technology]. IEEE Softw. **3**, 28–34 (2015)
33. Lago, P., Muccini, H., Van Vliet, H.: A scoped approach to traceability management. J. Syst. Softw. **82**(1), 168–182 (2009)
34. Bjarnason, E., Runeson, P., Borg, M., Unterkalmsteiner, M., Engström, E., Regnell, B., Sabaliauskaite, G., Loconsole, A., Gorschek, T., Feldt, R.: Challenges and practices in aligning requirements with verification and validation: a case study of six companies. Empirical Softw. Eng. **19**(6), 1809–1855 (2014)
35. Baeza-Yates, R., Ribeiro-Neto, B., et al.: Modern Information Retrieval, vol. 463. ACM Press, New York (1999)
36. Borg, M., Runeson, P., Ardö, A.: Recovering from a decade: a systematic mapping of information retrieval approaches to software traceability. Empirical Softw. Eng. **19**(6), 1565–1616 (2014)
37. Penzenstadler, B., Raturi, A., Richardson, D., Tomlinson, B.: Safety, security, now sustainability: the non-functional requirement for the 21st century (2014)
38. Häser, F., Felderer, M., Breu, R.: Software paradigms, assessment types and non-functional requirements in model-based integration testing: a systematic literature review. In: Proceedings of the 18th International Conference on Evaluation and Assessment in Software Engineering. ACM (2014). Article no 29
39. Felderer, M., Fourneret, E.: A systematic classification of security regression testing approaches. Int. J. Softw. Tools Technol. Transfer **17**(3), 305–319 (2015)
40. Hwang, J., Xie, T., El Kateb, D., Mouelhi, T., Le Traon, Y.: Selection of regression system tests for security policy evolution. In: Proceedings of the 27th IEEE/ACM International Conference on Automated Software Engineering, ASE 2012, pp. 266–269. ACM (2012)
41. Szvetits, M., Zdun, U.: Systematic literature review of the objectives, techniques, kinds, and architectures of models at runtime. Softw. Syst. Model. **15**, 1–39 (2013)
42. Wieczorek, M., Vos, D., Bons, H.: Systems and Software Quality. Springer, New York (2014)
43. Felderer, M., Ramler, R.: Integrating risk-based testing in industrial test processes. Softw. Qual. J. **22**(3), 543–575 (2014)
44. Felderer, M., Ramler, R.: A multiple case study on risk-based testing in industry. Int. J. Softw. Tools Technol. Transfer **16**(5), 609–625 (2014)
45. Felderer, M., Schieferdecker, I.: A taxonomy of risk-based testing. STTT **16**(5), 559–568 (2014)
46. Felderer, M., Wendland, M.-F., Schieferdecker, I.: Risk-based testing. In: Margaria, T., Steffen, B. (eds.) ISoLA 2014. LNCS, vol. 8803, pp. 274–276. Springer, Heidelberg (2014). doi:10.1007/978-3-662-45231-8_19
47. Neubauer, J., Windmüller, S., Steffen, B.: Risk-based testing via active continuous quality control. Int. J. Softw. Tools Technol. Transfer **16**(5), 569–591 (2014)

48. Erdogan, G., Li, Y., Runde, R.K., Seehusen, F., Stølen, K.: Approaches for the combined use of risk analysis and testing: a systematic literature review. Int. J. Softw. Tools Technol. Transfer **16**(5), 627–642 (2014)
49. Felderer, M., Haisjackl, C., Breu, R., Motz, J.: Integrating manual and automatic risk assessment for risk-based testing. In: Biffl, S., Winkler, D., Bergsmann, J. (eds.) SWQD 2012. LNBIP, vol. 94, pp. 159–180. Springer, Heidelberg (2012). doi:10.1007/978-3-642-27213-4_11
50. Stallbaum, H., Metzger, A., Pohl, K.: An automated technique for risk-based test case generation and prioritization. In: Proceedings of the 3rd International Workshop on Automation of Software Test, pp. 67–70. ACM (2008)
51. Ramler, R., Felderer, M.: Requirements for integrating defect prediction and risk-based testing. In: Euromicro SEAA 2016. IEEE (2016)
52. Adorf, H.M., Felderer, M., Varendorff, M., Breu, R.: A Bayesian prediction model for risk-based test selection. In: Euromicro SEAA 2015. IEEE (2015)
53. Margaria, T., Steffen, B.: Service engineering: linking business and it. Computer **39**(10), 45–55 (2006)
54. Svahnberg, M., Gorschek, T., Feldt, R., Torkar, R., Saleem, S.B., Shafique, M.U.: A systematic review on strategic release planning models. Inf. Softw. Technol. **52**(3), 237–248 (2010)
55. Ruhe, G., Eberlein, A., Pfahl, D.: Trade-off analysis for requirements selection. Int. J. Softw. Eng. Knowl. Eng. **13**(04), 345–366 (2003)
56. Regnell, B., Svensson, R.B., Olsson, T.: Supporting roadmapping of quality requirements. IEEE Softw. **25**(2), 42–47 (2008)
57. Felderer, M., Beer, A., Ho, J., Ruhe, G.: Industrial evaluation of the impact of quality-driven release planning. In: Proceedings of the 8th ACM/IEEE International Symposium on Empirical Software Engineering and Measurement. ACM (2014). Article no. 62
58. Wohlin, C., Runeson, P., Höst, M., Ohlsson, M.C., Regnell, B., Wesslén, A.: Experimentation in Software Engineering. Springer, New York (2012)
59. Runeson, P., Höst, M.: Guidelines for conducting and reporting case study research in software engineering. Empirical Softw. Eng. **14**(2), 131–164 (2009)
60. Ramesh, V., Glass, R.L., Vessey, I.: Research in computer science: an empirical study. J. Syst. Softw. **70**(1), 165–176 (2004)
61. Sjøberg, D.I., Hannay, J.E., Hansen, O., Kampenes, V.B., Karahasanovic, A., Liborg, N.K., Rekdal, A.C.: A survey of controlled experiments in software engineering. IEEE Trans. Softw. Eng. **31**(9), 733–753 (2005)
62. Pretschner, A., Prenninger, W., Wagner, S., Kühnel, C., Baumgartner, M., Sostawa, B., Zölch, R., Stauner, T.: One evaluation of model-based testing and its automation. In: Proceedings of the 27th International Conference on Software Engineering, pp. 392–401. ACM (2005)
63. D'Ambros, M., Lanza, M., Robbes, R.: Evaluating defect prediction approaches: a benchmark and an extensive comparison. Empirical Softw. Eng. **17**(4–5), 531–577 (2012)

Traceability Types for Mastering Change in Collaborative Software Quality Management

Boban Celebic, Ruth Breu, and Michael Felderer[✉]

Institute of Computer Science, University of Innsbruck, Innsbruck, Austria
{boban.celebic,ruth.breu,michael.felderer}@uibk.ac.at

Abstract. Software is constantly evolving and to successfully comprehend and manage this evolutionary change is a challenging task which requires traceability support. In this paper we propose a novel approach to traceability as a cornerstone for successful impact analysis and change management, in the context of collaborative software quality management. We first motivate the crucial role of traceability within lifecycle management of the new generation of distributed fragmented software services. Based on the model-based collaborative software quality management framework of Living Models, we then categorize software quality management services and identify novel types of traceability. This is followed by an overview and classification of sample software quality management services from literature, enabled by the interrelation with the identified types of traceability. From this classification we derive the need for further research on traceability in collaborative software quality management.

Keywords: Collaborative software quality management · Traceability · Software change management · Software evolution

1 Introduction

In modern IT systems distributed across organizational and system boundaries the grand challenge for software quality management becomes the coordination of people, methods, processes and tools [5]. Current quality management processes and methods are not yet capable to scale up to the novel arising scenarios like cars and aircrafts communicating to each other, health records exchanged on national level or energy traded all over continents, for several reasons.

First, an integrated view of the full service life cycle from business alignment, service design to deployment and runtime monitoring is of utmost importance. This becomes immediately obvious for the quality attribute of security. Security requirements are mostly negative requirements and security vulnerabilities may originate from all parts of the service lifecycle including, for instance, organizational flaws, design failures or deficiencies in runtime configuration. The necessary integration of different processes and data, for example from IT management and software development, is hardly supported in current practice and theory.

© Springer International Publishing AG 2016
B. Steffen (Ed.): Transactions on FoMaC I, LNCS 9960, pp. 242–256, 2016.
DOI: 10.1007/978-3-319-46508-1_13

Second, the new generation of software services is of inherent evolutionary character. Novel technologies make flexible composition of services technically feasible. However, current quality management methods and tools do not support change and evolution at a level of effectiveness which is required by the complexity of the novel application scenarios.

Finally, new business models require new kinds of quality management processes. As an example, Sneed [44] has recently pointed out the new role of testing for systems incorporating cloud services.

To successfully comprehend and manage continuous software change, stakeholders must first identify what will be affected by any proposed change - forecast and analyze its potential impacts. This implies the necessity to record and maintain the traces among artifacts to guarantee traceability. *Traceability*, as a general term in software engineering, is the ability to describe and follow the life of software artifacts [50]. This is a generalization of the requirements traceability definition of Gotel and Finkelstein [21] to arbitrary artifacts. In a model-based context, the artifacts of interest are models, conforming to one or more meta models. Traceability in this context is predominantly concerned with typed relationships (often called *trace links* or *traces*) between models and model elements - i.e., traceability needs to relate elements in a source model to the corresponding elements in a target model (in a transformation chain) and vice versa (which further implies that trace information ought to be generated as a result of model transformations). For example, trace links help with tracking which part of the code satisfies which requirements, monitoring the (implementation, test) status of requirements, or measuring coverage of artifacts by test cases. Unfortunately, impact analysis and traceability are not easy tasks, due to the complexity and size of software systems nowadays, their ever-changing artifacts with complex interdependencies, short development cycles, and numerous stakeholders involved in the process. Moreover, the information amount increases significantly over time, as the services evolve. As a result, keeping trace links synchronized is a cumbersome, time-consuming, expensive and error-prone task, often resulting in undesired confusion concerning the software product's current status.

In this paper we argue that a novel approach to traceability (as a cornerstone for successful impact analysis and, thus, software change and quality management) is a prerequisite to overcome the aforementioned challenges. This novel approach presupposes identification of novel trace types, particularly those specific to concrete environments (so to achieve the full potential and benefits of traceability use in such environments).

The paper is structured as follows. Section 2 provides an overview of the state-of-the-art. Section 3 sketches Living Models, a conceptual framework for collaborative software quality management, and identifies as well as categorizes relevant types of collaborative software quality management services. Section 4 presents the associated new types of traceability. Section 5 provides examples of beneficial use of traceability in all service categories. Finally, Sect. 6 concludes this paper.

2   State-of-the-Art

Before discussing the existing classifications of traceability, we must first justify the need for such classifications. In short, classification of traceability into types leads to: better understanding of the traceability links, their meaning and semantics [37]; better management and evaluation of trace links [37]; ability to perform automatic operations with traces [33]; and better visual representation of trace links, as a result of the possibility to customize the visualization to a specific type of traceability link.

Classification of software traceability has been addressed earlier on several occasions [45]. These classifications were based on several criteria: the types of the related artifacts, the activities connected to the relation (e.g., evolution, verification, impact analysis), the elements and properties of trace links (different tasks may require access to a specific set of links, based on their properties [29]), and others.

Besides the well-known concepts of *pre-* and *post- requirement specification*, *forward* and *backward*, *horizontal* and *vertical*, *functional* and *non-functional* traceability [50], some other, *model-specific* classifications have been proposed. The simplest taxonomy is the one with *manual* (trace link established manually in the trace model) and *automatic* (created by a tool) trace types [36]. According to *transformation traceability*, traces are produced as a result of (automatic) model transformations and indicate how source elements are related to target elements and vice versa. Galvao et al. [18] classify the traceability approaches in model-based and model-driven engineering into three categories: *requirements-driven approaches* use requirements models as abstractions to guide their traceability methods; *modeling approaches* are interested in how meta models, models and conceptual frameworks are involved in the tracing process; *transformation approaches* make use of model transformation mechanisms for generating trace information. Another taxonomy is on *post-model-specification* (i.e., traceability of models to and from various artifacts produced by their use) and *pre-model-specification* traceability [39]. A similar taxonomy is given in [50]: *pre-model-*, *intra-model-*, and *post-model-* traceability - *"denoting traceability between early artifacts and the first model, traceability between the gradually refined models, and traceability between the final model and the non-model artifacts generated or derived from it, respectively"*.

Further traceability classifications in model-based software engineering have been developed so to emphasize different attributes or characteristics of traceability [37]. More precisely, two directions for classifications can be identified in the literature: classifications that focus on *explicit* trace links (captured directly in models by using a suitable concrete syntax) and *implicit* trace links (trace information is generated as a result of an application of model management operation(s)) [37].

Problems with Existing Traceability Classifications. Unfortunately, all of the proposed classifications are difficult to evaluate and compare because there is no common level of abstraction and usually no unambiguous or formal definition of the different categories, and, additionally, the categories themselves cannot be separated clearly [50]. The classifications vary from more or less abstract, conceptual classifications to concrete ones (i.e., traceability meta models). It can be stated that the definition and the basic classifications of model-related traceability are still not agreed upon.

Furthermore, some of the more obvious open issues in model-based traceability can easily be identified by analyzing the referenced traceability classifications and types: lack of automation to cope with traceability in the early development stages in model-based approaches should be addressed, as well as mechanisms for the evolution of trace links; better trace meta models for enhancing model-based traceability should be developed; more efficient management of fine grained trace links is needed.

3   Collaborative Software Quality Management

In this section, we outline the model-based collaborative software quality management framework Living Models and related quality management services, which together provide the context for identifying novel traceability types. For a more detailed presentation of Living Models, we refer to [2].

3.1   The Living Models Framework

The scope of Living Models is not only software engineering but includes also IT management and systems operation. Accordingly, the stakeholders we envisage range from IT and security managers to system analysts, developers, testers to platform responsibles and network administrators.

In a Living Models environment all kind of information is conceptualized in a model-aware way. We distinguish functional data (like data about business processes, services, components or physical infrastructure elements [30,31]) and non-functional data (like a security requirement, a test case or a bug attached to a component [16]). We assume that each non-functional data instance is attached to a functional data instance. Our minimum requirement to model awareness is that all data instances adhere to a global meta model. The global meta model may vary in the degree of rigor, e.g., comprising both a partial meta model representing the abstract syntax of a programming language and a partial meta model capturing informally described requirements and their interdependencies. In [2] we have presented a reference meta model integrating the enterprise architecture and the software engineering domain (Fig. 1).

Living Models suggests stakeholder-centric model-based work environments. These environments support the tasks of the stakeholders involved and use models to provide concepts and information at an appropriate abstraction level. An example for a stakeholder-centric model-based work environment is a model-based testing tool supporting the tester to design, execute and evaluate tests [17],

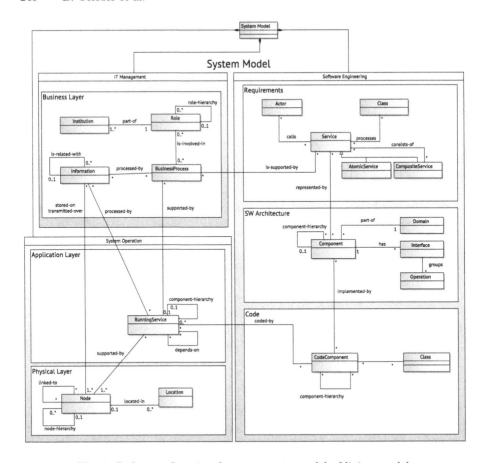

Fig. 1. Reference functional system meta model of living models

whereas IT architects may use a UML tool for modeling and analyzing a system's components.

Third, Living Models comprise close coupling of models and the runtime as a prerequisite that stakeholders can take proper decisions. The minimum requirement for this coupling is a process defining the responsibilities, the points of time when the synchronization between model and runtime takes place and the automated and manual tasks within the synchronization. Examples for such synchronization processes are model-based software development (i.e., generating runtime artifacts out of models) [32,47] or semi-automated workflow-controlled model maintenance [13].

A fourth major principle is concerned with the collaboration of stakeholders. Living Models proposes a change-driven interaction between stakeholders. This comprises *change events* (e.g., a modified model element or a time event), *change propagation* to linked elements and *change handling* encompassing coordinated

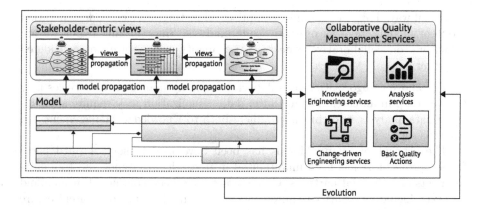

Fig. 2. Core concepts of living models

manual and automated actions. As a reference model we employ state machines attached with model elements to control the change-driven workflows (Fig. 2).

3.2 Collaborative Quality Management Services

The Living Models paradigm incorporates the following categories of executable software quality management services:

- **Knowledge Engineering Services** provide each stakeholder with information at the appropriate level of abstraction, way of presentation and degree of quality (e.g., preciseness, actuality). The information may potentially originate from all data resources in the software life cycle, comprising, for example, software portfolio management, business process modeling, requirements engineering, test reports, code, bug tracking, and many more. Examples of Knowledge Engineering services are services for information aggregation, visualization and maintenance, for example sophisticated views for Enterprise Architecture Models or code bases [25] and semi-automated maintenance services for Enterprise Architecture Models [11].
- **Analysis Services** apply assistive analysis techniques at model instance and meta model level and on runtime data to enhance model quality and to control processes. Examples for analysis services comprise analysis of code level information (service code, tests, bugs) [1], model consistency checks [9,27] or risk models [15,35,46] controlling test processes.
- **Change-Driven Engineering Services** coordinate quality relevant actions of stakeholders in dynamic contexts. These services track and propagate changes and coordinate change handling. Services of this kind can be found in many tools, e.g., in form of tickets in requirements and defect management tools.
- **Basic Quality Actions** refer to any quality related action performed on a homogeneous data base or in a given tool, either in a (semi-)automated or

manual way. This, for example, comprises all testing services, code generation out of models, reviews or static code analysis. Since in this paper we are focusing on collaborative aspects, basic quality actions are not considered further.

The above categorization of collaborative quality management services may not be sharp in all cases. For instance, data visualization may require sophisticated data analysis, and thus may adhere both to Knowledge Management and Analysis services.

The concept of Living Models has been developed in several third party funded projects. It has been materialized in research prototypes and tool environments of industrial partners. Case studies have been conducted in manifold contexts, including security requirements engineering [3], enterprise architecture management [11] and system testing [14].

4   Traceability Categories

Traceability between artifacts is the core concept to provide the services listed before in the context of the model-based collaborative software quality management framework of Living Models. Having also in mind the aforementioned benefits of traceability classifications, and the services of Living Models, we identified the following traceability categories.

Design Time Traceability. Design time traceability denotes traceability at the level of design time and management artifacts. This includes both the well-known notions of horizontal and vertical traceability in literature, as defined, for example, in [22,49]. Horizontal traceability concerns the interconnection of data at the same level of abstraction (e.g., recording dependencies between requirements), whereas vertical traceability concerns the interconnection of data across levels of abstraction (e.g., linking requirements with software architecture artifacts or linking application level model elements with infrastructure model elements in an Enterprise Architecture Model).

Deployment Traceability. Deployment traceability is the traceability between design time artifacts and information collected at runtime (e.g., deployed system components, runtime events, key performance indicators like service duration). An example for deployment traceability is the attachment of workflow models with the maximum number of running instances.

Evolution Traceability. Evolution traceability is the traceability of information across versions, like versions of component implementations or models. Evolution traceability may vary in its granularity and kind of representation. For instance, model history may be documented on model element level (documenting the history of each model element) or on model type level (documenting the history of the whole model), and may be stored as change operation or as sequence of model versions [2].

Stakeholder Action Traceability. Stakeholder action traceability means the association of events or actions with the stakeholders involved. Stakeholder action traceability has many facets since the tracking may vary in the kind of information that is tracked and in the way how stakeholders are represented (e.g., as institutions, roles or persons). Accordingly, stakeholder traceability might be unwanted or even legally prohibited due to privacy reasons.

5   Traceability Supporting Collaborative Software Quality Management Services

In this section we interrelate the categorized kinds of software quality management services with the categorized kinds of traceability (Fig. 3). We do this by referring to *approaches from literature* which consider applications of traceability within the domain of software quality management services. The following categorization may not be sharp in all cases, due to the previously mentioned non-sharp categorization of Collaborative Software Quality Management Services. Some of the examples may fall into several service and/or traceability types but are representative for the category where they are listed.

Fig. 3. Collaborative quality management services and traceability types

5.1   Traceability Support for Knowledge Engineering Services

Design Time Traceability. Mohan and Ramesh [34] discuss the key role played by a traceability-based knowledge management system in documenting design decisions associated with various configurations of basic building blocks on which service family architectures are based on and in tracing variability. A framework for managing traceability knowledge for the design and development of e-service families, based on the REMAP (Representation and Maintenance of Process Knowledge) environment [41], is presented. Using the case study, they illustrate the importance of using such a knowledge management system for the design and development of service families. Furthermore, in [38] traceability across design artifacts in software project, i.e., from product specification to interface requirements specification, software requirement specification and system components, is addressed.

Deployment Traceability. Conklin and Begeman [7] describe an application-specific hypertext system designed to facilitate capturing of early design deliberations. As consequence, traceability relations may lead to the reuse of system components when these components are related to requirements of existing systems that are similar to requirements of new systems.

Evolution Traceability. Goknil et al. [20] present a tool built to support reasoning about requirements relations, as well as consistency checking of relations and for inferring new relations. This tool supports better understanding of dependencies between requirements, tracking model history and changes (either at model element or type level).

Stakeholder Action Traceability. Li and Maalej [26] present a comparative study of common traceability visualization techniques, including an experiment and interviews with 24 participants. This study supports the finding that traceability, in general, helps users in describing and tracking the relationships between software artifacts, while different visualization techniques (matrices, graphs, hyperlinks, lists) visualize these relationships and help users to access and understand them.

5.2 Traceability Support for Analysis Services

Design Time Traceability. Felderer et al. [15] and Stallbaum et al. [46] apply risk models based on traceable design artifacts for testing purposes.

Deployment Traceability. Gander et al. [19] present a pluggable framework for multi-level security monitoring of workflows, which links event information and modeling specification in order to perform compliance detection and anomaly detection. In [51] authors propose a traceability based knowledge management approach to support adaptation of workflows capability in Workflow Management Systems. They present a framework for representing traceability knowledge to capture the context in which workflows are specified and evolved. They also discuss the functionalities of a knowledge management system that can support dynamic reconfiguration of workflows in the context of changing business processes as well as for maintaining their integrity.

Evolution Traceability. Hata et al. [23] present a fine-grained version control system for Java called Historage. This system targets Java software and conducts fine-grained prediction of bugs with well-known historical metrics (fine-grained module histories). Maletic et al. [28] present an XML based approach to support the evolution of model-to-model traceability links is presented. This approach allows for versioning and differencing of specific elements of the models versus just lines or whole files.

Stakeholder Action Traceability. Zimmermann et al. [52] apply data mining of version histories in order to guide programmers along related changes.

5.3   Traceability Support for Change-Driven Engineering Services

Design Time Traceability. Felderer et al. [14] present a model-driven system testing methodology for service-centric systems called Telling TestStories, its tool implementation and the underlying model validation mechanism. This methodology is based on tightly integrated but separated platform-independent requirements, system and test models. Telling TestStories is capable of test-driven development on the model level and provides full traceability between all system and testing artifacts. Change propagation between the system, test and requirements artifacts is used for regression test derivation. In [48] authors discuss facilitating change management in geographically distributed software engineering by effective discovery and establishment of dependency links using domain models which provide a common reference point. The proposed method advocates the use of domain models throughout the whole development life-cycle and is apt to facilitate multi-site software engineering.

Deployment Traceability. The authors of [4, 12, 24] deal with synchronization of Enterprise Architecture Models with the runtime environment. The first paper investigates a specific Enterprise Service Bus (ESB) considered as the nervous system of an enterprise interconnecting business applications and processes as an information source. A vendor-specific ESB data model is reverse-engineered and transformation rules for three representative EA information models are derived. These transformation rules are further employed to perform automated model transformations making the first step towards an automated EA documentation. In the second paper the authors propose network scanning for automatic data collection and uses an existing software tool for generating EA models based on the IT infrastructure of enterprises. The third paper presents (semi-)automated processes for maintaining enterprise architecture models by gathering information from both human input and technical interfaces and discusses implementation issues for realizing the processes in practice. This work aims toward the direction of minimizing manual work for EAM by automation and increasing EA data quality attributes such as consistency and actuality.

Table 1. Examples of traceability supporting Collaborative Software Quality Management Services

	Knowledge management	Data analysis	Change-driven engineering
Design time traceability	Framework for managing traceability knowledge for the design and development of e-service families [34] based on the REMAP (Representation and Maintenance of Process Knowledge) environment [41] Traceability across design artifacts in software project, i.e., from product specification to interface requirements specification, software requirement specification and system components [38]	Risk models based on design artifacts are used for testing purposes [15, 46] Identify components and objects which satisfies a requirement [10] Test procedures, if traceable to requirements or designs, can be modified when errors are discovered [40] Rigorous system testing by supporting vertical traceability; Rigorous vertical software system testing In IDE [42] System testing by relating requirements with test models and indicating routes for demonstrating product compliance [45]	Change propagation between the system, test and requirements artifacts is used for regression test derivation [14] Propagation of changes during redesign [8] Facilitating change management in geographically distributed software engineering by effective discovery and establishment of dependency links using domain models [48]
Deployment traceability	Traceability may lead to the reuse of system components when these components are related to requirements of existing systems [45]	Multi-level security monitoring of workflows [19] Dynamic reconfiguration of workflows in the context of changing business processes as well as for maintaining their integrity [51]	Synchronisation of Enterprise Architecture Models with the runtime environment [4, 12, 24]
Evolution traceability	Tracking model history and changes (either at model element or type level) [20]	Prediction of bugs based on fine-grained module histories [23] An XML based approach to support the evolution of model-to-model traceability links [28]	Event-Based Traceability for Managing Evolutionary Change [6]
Stakeholder action traceability	Visualization of traceability [26]	Data mining of version histories in order to guide programmers along related changes [52]	Change-driven collaborative security requirements management [43] - maintenance and evaluation of security requirements in multi-user environments through state-based workflows

Evolution Traceability. Cleland-Huang et al. [6] propose a new method of event-based traceability for managing evolutionary change, which is applicable even in a heterogeneous and globally distributed development environment. Traceable artifacts are no longer tightly coupled but are linked through an event service, which creates an environment in which change is handled more efficiently, and artifacts and their related links are maintained in a restorable state. The method also supports enhanced project management for the process of updating and maintaining the system artifacts.

Stakeholder Action Traceability. Sillaber and Breu [43] elaborate on change-driven collaborative security requirements management, maintenance and evaluation of security requirements in multi-user environments through state-based workflows.

Summarizing, we can state that there are many existing approaches in research that focus on *design time* traceability, as visible in Table 1. For the use of *deployment, evolution* and *stakeholder action* traceability much less research has been conducted. However, in each category recent research could be identified [12,23,26].

6 Conclusion

In this paper we first presented novel categories of software quality management services, i.e., knowledge engineering, analysis, and change-driven engineering, and types of traceability, i.e., design-time, deployment, evolution, and stakeholder action traceability, derived from the conceptual framework of Living Models for collaborative software quality management. These trace types empower the software quality management services of Living Models. Through interrelating the traceability and quality management services we demonstrated not only the bandwidth of software quality management services exploiting traceability but also the need for further research in this area.

In our future work we will further develop our classification of trace types, for example by identifying trace types for supporting IT management, systems operation and software engineering. In addition, we will invest efforts in developing and integrating powerful interactive visual solutions, based on premises from this paper, to support the exploration of trace links belonging to the newly identified trace categories.

Acknowledgements. This work was partially funded by the research project QE LaB - Living Models for Open Systems (www.qe-lab.at).

References

1. Binkley, D.: Source code analysis: a road map. In: Future of Software Engineering, 2007. FOSE 2007, pp. 104–119. IEEE (2007)
2. Breu, R., Agreiter, B., Farwick, M., Felderer, M., Hafner, M., Innerhofer-Oberperfler, F.: Living models - ten principles for change-driven software engineering. Int. J. Softw. Informatics 5(1–2), 267–290 (2011)
3. Breu, R., Hafner, M., Innerhofer-Oberperfler, F., Wozak, F.: Model-driven security engineering of service oriented systems. In: Kaschek, R., Kop, C., Steinberger, C., Fliedl, G. (eds.) UNISCON 2008. LNBIP, vol. 5, pp. 59–71. Springer, Heidelberg (2008). doi:10.1007/978-3-540-78942-0_8
4. Buschle, M., Grunow, S., Matthes, F., Ekstedt, M., Hauder, M., Roth, S.: Automating enterprise architecture documentation using an enterprise service bus. In: 18th Americas Conference on Information Systems, AMCIS 2012 (2012)
5. Capgemini: World quality report 2011/12 (2011)
6. Cleland-Huang, J., Chang, C.K., Christensen, M.: Event-based traceability for managing evolutionary change. IEEE Trans. Softw. Eng. 29(9), 796–810 (2003)
7. Conklin, J., Begeman, M.L.: gIBIS: a hypertext tool for exploratory policy discussion. ACM Trans. Inf. Syst. (TOIS) 6(4), 303–331 (1988)

8. Dömges, R., Pohl, K.: Adapting traceability environments to project-specific needs. Commun. ACM **41**(12), 54–62 (1998)
9. Egyed, A.: Instant consistency checking for the UML. In: Proceedings of the 28th International Conference on Software Engineering, pp. 381–390. ACM (2006)
10. Egyed, A., Grünbacher, P.: Supporting software understanding with automated requirements traceability. Int. J. Softw. Eng. Knowl. Eng. **15**(05), 783–810 (2005)
11. Farwick, M., Schweda, C., Breu, R., Voges, K., Hanschke, I.: On enterprise architecture change events. In: Aier, S., Ekstedt, M., Matthes, F., Proper, E., Sanz, J.L. (eds.) TEAR and PRET 2012. LNBIP, vol. 131, pp. 129–145. Springer, Heidelberg (2012). doi:10.1007/978-3-642-34163-2_8
12. Farwick, M., Agreiter, B., Breu, R., Ryll, S., Voges, K., Hanschke, I.: Automation processes for enterprise architecture management. In: 2011 15th IEEE International Enterprise Distributed Object Computing Conference Workshops (EDOCW), pp. 340–349. IEEE (2011)
13. Farwick, M., Pasquazzo, W., Breu, R., Schweda, C.M., Voges, K., Hanschke, I.: A meta-model for automated enterprise architecture model maintenance. In: EDOC, pp. 1–10 (2012)
14. Felderer, M., Chimiak-Opoka, J., Zech, P., Haisjackl, C., Fiedler, F., Breu, R.: Model validation in a tool-based methodology for system testing of service-oriented systems. Int. J. Adv. Softw. **4**(1 and 2), 129–143 (2011)
15. Felderer, M., Haisjackl, C., Breu, R., Motz, J.: Integrating manual and automatic risk assessment for risk-based testing. In: Biffl, S., Winkler, D., Bergsmann, J. (eds.) SWQD 2012. LNBIP, vol. 94, pp. 159–180. Springer, Heidelberg (2012). doi:10.1007/978-3-642-27213-4_11
16. Felderer, M., Agreiter, B., Breu, R.: Evolution of security requirements tests for service–centric systems. In: Erlingsson, Ú., Wieringa, R., Zannone, N. (eds.) ESSoS 2011. LNCS, vol. 6542, pp. 181–194. Springer, Heidelberg (2011). doi:10.1007/978-3-642-19125-1_14
17. Felderer, M., Zech, P., Fiedler, F., Breu, R.: A tool-based methodology for system testing of service-oriented systems. In: 2010 Second International Conference on Advances in System Testing and Validation Lifecycle (VALID), pp. 108–113. IEEE (2010)
18. Galvao, I., Goknil, A.: Survey of traceability approaches in model-driven engineering. In: 11th IEEE International Enterprise Distributed Object Computing Conference, 2007. EDOC 2007, p. 313. IEEE (2007)
19. Gander, M., Katt, B., Felderer, M., Breu, R.: Towards a model- and learning-based framework for security anomaly detection. In: Beckert, B., Damiani, F., Boer, F.S., Bonsangue, M.M. (eds.) FMCO 2011. LNCS, vol. 7542, pp. 150–168. Springer, Heidelberg (2013). doi:10.1007/978-3-642-35887-6_8
20. Goknil, A., Kurtev, I., van den Berg, K., Veldhuis, J.W.: Semantics of trace relations in requirements models for consistency checking and inferencing. Softw. Syst. Model. **10**(1), 31–54 (2011)
21. Gotel, O., Finkelstein, C.: An analysis of the requirements traceability problem. In: Proceedings of the First International Conference on Requirements Engineering, 1994, pp. 94–101. IEEE (1994)
22. Gotel, O., Finkelstein, A.: Contribution structures [requirements artifacts]. In: Proceedings of the Second IEEE International Symposium on Requirements Engineering, 1995, pp. 100–107. IEEE (1995)
23. Hata, H., Mizuno, O., Kikuno, T.: Bug prediction based on fine-grained module histories. In: 2012 34th International Conference on Software Engineering (ICSE), pp. 200–210. IEEE (2012)

24. Holm, H., Buschle, M., Lagerström, R., Ekstedt, M.: Automatic data collection for enterprise architecture models. Softw. Syst. Model. **13**, 825–841 (2012)
25. Lanza, M., Marinescu, R.: Object-Oriented Metrics in Practice: Using Software Metrics to Characterize, Evaluate, and Improve the Design of Object-oriented Systems. Springer, Heidelberg (2006). doi:10.1007/3-540-39538-5
26. Li, Y., Maalej, W.: Which traceability visualization is suitable in this context? A comparative study. In: Regnell, B., Damian, D. (eds.) REFSQ 2012. LNCS, vol. 7195, pp. 194–210. Springer, Heidelberg (2012). doi:10.1007/978-3-642-28714-5_17
27. Lucas, F., Molina, F., Toval, A.: A systematic review of UML model consistency management. Inf. Softw. Technol. **51**(12), 1631–1645 (2009)
28. Maletic, J.I., Collard, M.L., Simoes, B.: An XML based approach to support the evolution of model-to-model traceability links. In: Automated Software Engineering: Proceedings of the 3rd International Workshop on Traceability in Emerging Forms of Software Engineering, vol. 8, pp. 67–72 (2005)
29. Marcus, A., Xie, X., Poshyvanyk, D.: When and how to visualize traceability links? In: Proceedings of the 3rd International Workshop on Traceability in Emerging Forms of Software Engineering, pp. 56–61. ACM (2005)
30. Margaria, T., Steffen, B.: Service engineering: linking business and it. Computer **39**(10), 45–55 (2006)
31. Margaria, T., Steffen, B.: Business process modelling in the jABC: the one-thing-approach. In: Handbook of Research on Business Process Modeling, pp. 1–26 (2009)
32. Margaria, T., Steffen, B.: Continuous model-driven engineering. Computer **42**(10), 106–109 (2009)
33. Maté, A., Trujillo, J.: A trace metamodel proposal based on the model driven architecture framework for the traceability of user requirements in data warehouses. In: Mouratidis, H., Rolland, C. (eds.) CAiSE 2011. LNCS, vol. 6741, pp. 123–137. Springer, Heidelberg (2011). doi:10.1007/978-3-642-21640-4_11
34. Mohan, K., Ramesh, B.: Managing variability with traceability in product and service families. In: Proceedings of the 35th Annual Hawaii International Conference on System Sciences, 2002. HICSS, pp. 1309–1317. IEEE (2002)
35. Neubauer, J., Windmüller, S., Steffen, B.: Risk-based testing via active continuous quality control. Int. J. Softw. Tools Technol. Transf. **16**(5), 569–591 (2014)
36. Olsen, G.K., Oldevik, J.: Scenarios of traceability in model to text transformations. In: Akehurst, D.H., Vogel, R., Paige, R.F. (eds.) ECMDA-FA 2007. LNCS, vol. 4530, pp. 144–156. Springer, Heidelberg (2007). doi:10.1007/978-3-540-72901-3_11
37. Paige, R.F., Olsen, G.K., Kolovos, D.S., Zschaler, S., Power, C.: Building model-driven engineering traceability classifications (2008)
38. Ramesh, B., Powers, T., Stubbs, C., Edwards, M.: Implementing requirements traceability: a case study. In: Proceedings of the Second IEEE International Symposium on Requirements Engineering, pp. 89–95. IEEE (1995)
39. Ramesh, B.: Representing and reasoning with traceability in model life cycle management. Ann. Oper. Res. **75**, 123–145 (1997)
40. Ramesh, B., Jarke, M.: Toward reference models for requirements traceability. IEEE Trans. Softw. Eng. **27**(1), 58–93 (2001)
41. Ramesh, B., Tiwana, A.: Supporting collaborative process knowledge management in new product development teams. Dec. Support Syst. **27**(1), 213–235 (1999)
42. Seo, K.I., Choi, E.M.: Rigorous vertical software system testing in ide. In: 5th ACIS International Conference on Software Engineering Research, Management & Applications, 2007. SERA 2007, pp. 847–854. IEEE (2007)

43. Sillaber, C., Breu, R.: Managing legal compliance through security requirements across service provider chains: a case study on the german federal data protection act. In: GI-Jahrestagung, pp. 1306–1317 (2012)
44. Sneed, H.M.: Testing web services in the cloud. In: Winkler, D., Biffl, S., Bergsmann, J. (eds.) SWQD 2013. LNBIP, vol. 133, pp. 70–88. Springer, Heidelberg (2013). doi:10.1007/978-3-642-35702-2_6
45. Spanoudakis, G., Zisman, A.: Software traceability a roadmap. Handb. Softw. Eng. Knowl. Eng. **3**, 395–428 (2005)
46. Stallbaum, H., Metzger, A., Pohl, K.: An automated technique for risk-based test case generation and prioritization. In: Proceedings of the 3rd International Workshop on Automation of Software Test, pp. 67–70. ACM (2008)
47. Steffen, B., Margaria, T., Nagel, R., Jörges, S., Kubczak, C.: Model-driven development with the jABC. In: Bin, E., Ziv, A., Ur, S. (eds.) HVC 2006. LNCS, vol. 4383, pp. 92–108. Springer, Heidelberg (2007). doi:10.1007/978-3-540-70889-6_7
48. Strasunskas, D., Hakkarainen, S.E.: Domain model-driven software engineering: a method for discovery of dependency links. Inf. Softw. Technol. **54**, 1239–1249 (2012)
49. Von Knethen, A., Paech, B.: A survey on tracing approaches in practice and research. Frauenhofer Institut Experimentelles Software Engineering, IESE-Report No 95 (2002)
50. Winkler, S., Pilgrim, J.: A survey of traceability in requirements engineering and model-driven development. Softw. Syst. Model. (SoSyM) **9**(4), 529–565 (2010)
51. Xu, P., Ramesh, B.: Supporting workflow management systems with traceability. In: Proceedings of the 35th Annual Hawaii International Conference on System Sciences, pp. 1519–1528. IEEE (2002)
52. Zimmermann, T., Weibgerber, P., Diehl, S., Zeller, A.: Mining version histories to guide software changes. In: Proceedings of 26th International Conference on Software Engineering, 2004. ICSE 2004, pp. 563–572. IEEE (2004)

Author Index